AMERICAN PHILANTHROPY

American

THE CHICAGO HISTORY OF AMERICAN CIVILIZATION

Daniel J. Boorstin, EDITOR

Philanthropy

By Robert H. Bremner

 THE UNIVERSITY OF CHICAGO PRESS

CHICAGO AND LONDON

The University of Chicago Press, Chicago 60637
The University of Chicago Press, Ltd., London

© 1960 by The University of Chicago

All rights reserved. Published 1960
Midway reprint 1982
Printed in the United States of America
ISBN: 0-226-07328-9
LCN: 60-7246

Editor's Preface

We have long thought of ourselves immodestly as a nation of philanthropists. But in our generation American private philanthropy has dwarfed all our earlier good works, and the United States government has become a philanthropist on an unprecedented scale. Having cast ourselves in the role of a philanthropic nation—only to be blamed all over the world for the shortsightedness and selfishness of our good works—we should now try to discover precisely what our tradition has been.

Americans today need to understand the meaning of philanthropy and to see what is distinctive about our ways of doing good. Faithful Christians have often remarked that one of God's purposes in creating poverty was to make charity possible. In the United States, as Mr. Bremner shows in this volume, the emphasis has generally been quite different. One of God's purposes in creating American wealth, it is said, must have been to make philanthropy possible. Without great wealth, how could there be great philanthropy?

In this pioneering volume, Mr. Bremner gives us some much-needed help in defining our philanthropic tradition. He is neither a sentimentalist, a cynic, nor a muckraker. He is a ruthless and sympathetic historian. He does not suggest that Americans are by nature any more selfless or altruistic than other peoples. He does show how the peculiarly American situation has given a special character to our efforts to do good by private means. He shows both the opportunities offered by our great wealth, and the temptations to disingenuousness (accentuated recently, for example, by our tax laws). He shows how the dogmas of individualism and of equal opportunity, and the chance to rise in the world, have made the spirit of philanthropy sometimes seem at odds with the spirit of democracy.

Mr. Bremner does not deny that Americans, like other men, have often wanted simply to help their fellow men. But he shows how the facts of our history—our colonial origins, the American Revolution, the institution of slavery and the efforts to abolish it, the rise of an American Standard of Living, and the accumulation of industrial wealth—have provided temptations to misuse philanthropic slogans for personal, political, or economic ends, just as they have provided opportunities for the unalloyed philanthropic spirit.

By putting a familiar, but largely unexamined, American institution into the main stream of our civilization, Mr. Bremner admirably serves the purposes of the "Chicago History of American Civilization," which aims to make each aspect of our culture a window to all our history. The series contains two kinds of books: a *chronological* group, which provides a coherent narrative of American history from its beginning to the present day, and a *topical* group, which deals with the history of varied and significant aspects of American life. This

Editor's Preface

book is one of the topical group. Titles already published in the series are listed at the end of this book.

DANIEL J. BOORSTIN

Table of Contents

Illustrations

Introduction

It's a serious, stern, responsible deed,
To help an unfortunate soul in his need.
And your one reward, when you quiet his plaint,
Is to feel like an opulent, careworn saint.
CLARENCE DAY

Ever since the seventeenth century, when Cotton Mather announced that Boston's helpfulness and readiness to every good work were well and favorably known in Heaven, Americans have regarded themselves as an unusually philanthropic people. In the twentieth century, celebration of American philanthropy has reached such heights that one can scarcely read a newspaper or magazine without being reminded, in editorials or advertisements, that the United States is the country with a heart, that giving is the great American game, and that philanthropy ranks as one of the leading industries of the age. Americans seem never to tire of saying, or of hearing, that they are generous to a fault—the most compassionate, open-handed people the world has ever known. The philanthropic streak in the national character is taken so much for granted that it is sometimes deemed more a genial failing than an asset or virtue.

As this tendency suggests, the word philanthropy and the ideas it carries with it arouse mixed emotions in American breasts. Many Americans have been concerned lest their countrymen's generosity be abused. But on a deeper level there is something about philanthropy that seems to go against the democratic grain. We may be willing to help others, but we are not humble enough to appreciate the efforts of those who would bend down to help us. "Don't try to uplift me," we say. "I can lift myself." We expect rich men to be generous with their wealth, and criticize them when they are not; but when they make benefaction, we question their motives, deplore the methods by which they obtained their abundance, and wonder whether their gifts will not do more harm than good.

Criticism of philanthropy and distrust of philanthropists are of course not peculiar to the United States, but there has been no lack of either in this country. Our literature abounds in portraits of foolish or hypocritical philanthropists. Newspaper and magazine editors decry the activities of "do gooders" and "bleeding hearts"; conservatives denounce "sentimental humanitarianism"; and radicals sneer at the "palliatives" offered by "mere philanthropic reform." The prejudice against philanthropy is felt even by its practitioners. Many of our most active and generous benefactors resent being called philanthropists and deny that their works have a philanthropic purpose. Until quite recently theoretical writings on the subject of philanthropy seem to have consisted mainly, and sometimes exclusively, in condemnations of "unwise giving."

Whether we approve or disapprove of philanthropy, the fact remains that it has been one of the principal methods of social advance. And we do not need to exaggerate the extent of our

Introduction

generosity to recognize that voluntary benevolence has played a large role and performed important functions in American society. Here, as elsewhere, philanthropy has covered a wider field than charity; the problems of the poor have not been philanthropy's only or even primary concern. The aim of philanthropy in its broadest sense is improvement in the quality of human life. Whatever motives animate individual philanthropists, the purpose of philanthropy itself is to promote the welfare, happiness, and culture of mankind.

We are all indebted to philanthropic reformers who have called attention to and agitated for abatement of the barbarities inflicted by society on its weaker members. We are all, in some degree, beneficiaries of philanthropy whenever we attend church, go to college, visit museums or concert halls, draw books from libraries, obtain treatment at hospitals, or spend leisure hours in parks. Most of us use, or may have occasion to use, institutions and services now tax-supported, which originated as philanthropic enterprises. We continue to rely on philanthropy for the support of scientific research, for experimentation in the field of social relations, and for diffusion of knowledge in all branches of learning.

The record of American philanthropy is so impressive that it would require several lengthy volumes to list its achievements. In a book as brief as this one, some of those achievements can only be alluded to, and many important benefactors and benefactions must be omitted. The author extends his apologies to readers who may look in vain in the following pages for mention of favorite philanthropists; many of the author's favorites have been left out too. The book is not an encyclopedia of good works but a narrative of some of the major trends in American philanthropy, broadly defined, set

American Philanthropy

against the background of the main developments in American social history. The study is a survey of voluntary activity in the fields of charity, religion, education, humanitarian reform, social service, war relief, and foreign aid. It deals with representative donors, whether of money or service, with promoters of moral and social reform, and with the various institutions and associations Americans have founded to conduct their philanthropic business. The author hopes that the book will advance the growing interest in philanthropy as a subject of research and that the story told in the following pages will offer occasional insights into the character of American civilization.

I

Doing Good in the New World

If any man ask, Why it is so necessary to do good?
I must say, it sounds not like the question of a good
man.

COTTON MATHER

The earliest American philanthropists, as far as European records go, were those gentle Indians of the Bahama Islands who greeted Columbus at his first landfall in the New World. In view of the cruelty and exploitation these natives were to suffer at the hands of white men there is something ominous in Columbus' report that they were "ingenuous and free" with all they had, gave away anything that was asked of them, and bestowed each gift "with as much love as if their hearts went with it."

From other Indians pioneer white settlers obtained a wealth of practical assistance in the difficult task of adjusting to life in an alien land. The names of most of these benefactors are forgotten, but one at least is familiar to every schoolboy. Squanto, who had once been kidnapped by an Englishman and carried off to be sold into slavery, escaped from bondage and returned to New England. There, during the starving time at Plymouth in the winter of 1620–21, Squanto proved "a special instrument sent of God" for the good of the enfeebled, bewildered Pilgrims. He taught them, in the words of William Bradford, "how to set their corn, where to take fish, and to procure other commodities, and was also their pilot to bring them to unknown places for their profit, and never left them till he died." Sad to relate, Squanto used his connections with the Pilgrims to extort gifts for himself from other Indians, and so his hands, like those of some other eminent philanthropists, were not entirely clean. On his deathbed he asked the governor "to pray for him that he might go to the Englishman's God in Heaven, and bequeathed sundry of his things to sundry of his English friends as remembrances of his love. . . ."

Philanthropy is philanthropy wherever and by whomever practiced. When we speak of American philanthropy, however, we usually have in mind an imported product rather than an indigenous growth. Our systems and principles of benevolence, both public and private, originated in Europe before the colonization of America began. They were brought to this country by Europeans, and their subsequent development was influenced by European experience and theory. For many years our philanthropic institutions sought and received support from abroad; and until quite recently those institutions were copies of European models. All we can lay claim to on the score of uniqueness is that philanthropy *in* America took such firm root and grew so prodigiously that it early assumed a stature and significance all its own.

To understand why this happened we must remember, first,

Doing Good in the New World

that the age of colonization coincided with one of the great periods of European philanthropy. The seventeenth century saw the launching of heroic missionary enterprises, a revival of interest in charitable works, the development in England of a system of tax-supported poor relief, and the organization of a host of associations for specialized philanthropic purposes. America inspired some of these undertakings and benefited directly or indirectly from nearly all of them, for the discovery of the New World affected the conscience as well as the cupidity of the Old. Almost every effort at colonization had, or claimed to have, a philanthropic motivation: there were natives to be converted to Christianity, poor men to be provided with land and work, and a wilderness to be supplied with the institutions of civilization. It is not too much to say that many Europeans regarded the American continent mainly as a vastly expanded field for the exercise of benevolence.

The real founders of American philanthropy, however, were men and women who crossed the Atlantic to establish communities that would be *better* than, instead of like or different from, the ones they had known at home. The Puritan leader, John Winthrop (1588–1649) forthrightly stated their purpose in the lay sermon, "A Model of Christian Charity," which he preached on the ship "Arbella" to "the great company of religious people" voyaging from old to New England in the year 1630. Winthrop used "Charity" as a synonym for love rather than in the modern sense of aid to the poor; and the "Model" he proposed was not a new scheme of benevolence but a code of conduct for a company of Christians who had entered into a covenant with God. The Puritans' God permitted no breach of contract but demanded strict performance of each article in the covenant. Therefore, as Winthrop said, "in this duty of love we must love brotherly without dissimulation, we must love one another with a pure heart fervently, we must bear one another's burdens, we must not look only on our own things but also on the things of our brethren. Neither must we think that the Lord will bear with such failings at our hands as He doth from those among whom we have lived. . . ."

Like later philanthropists, Winthrop justified disparities in wealth and condition as divinely ordained. He had no wish to tamper with God's design, and he did not hesitate to distinguish between "the great ones," "high and eminent in power and dignity," and "the poor and inferior sort" of men. Winthrop looked upon such distinctions as necessary for the good and preservation of society. He was convinced however, that no man was made richer or more honorable than his neighbor for his own sake, but only "for the glory of his creator and the common good of the creature man." The poor must not rise up against their superiors; neither should the rich and mighty be allowed to eat up the poor. Differences in condition existed, not to separate and alienate men from one another, but to make them have more need of each other, and to bind them closer together "in the bond of brotherly affection." And those differences, important and essential though Winthrop believed them to be, seemed less significant to him than "our community as members of the same body." "We must be knit together in this work as one man," he said. "We must delight in each other, make others' conditions our own, rejoice together, mourn together, labor and suffer together. . . ." The common objective—"to improve our lives to do more service to the Lord"—must never be lost sight of, and "the care of the public" must take precedence over all private interests.

Doing Good in the New World

Winthrop's vision of a community united and exalted by religious dedication was not to be realized even in Puritan New England. The mean and despised were not content to remain in the state to which God had assigned them; the powerful showed little disposition to forego opportunities to profit at the expense of the weak; and neither rich nor poor was willing to remain for long under the rule of divinely commissioned magistrates. Competition, individualism, and self-interest proved too strong to be suppressed, and what Roger Williams, in a letter to Winthrop's son, called "the common trinity of the world— Profit, Preferment, Pleasure"—soon made their appearance. Even so, Winthrop's ideal was never entirely forsaken. The forces of disunity, although they could not be held down, did not quite prevail; and, not only in the colonial period, but in later eras as well, Americans continued to feel under a special obligation to bring the duty of neighborly and brotherly love, everywhere professed, into "familiar and constant practice."

Half a century after Winthrop and the Puritans started to build their city upon a hill in New England, William Penn (1644–1718) began his holy experiment in Pennsylvania. Although Penn founded the colony as a refuge for Quakers and members of other persecuted sects, the idea of withdrawing from or renouncing the world had no place in his plans. "True Godliness," he said, "don't turn men out of the World, but enables them to live better in it, and excites their Endeavors to Mend it." To Penn and the Quakers there was no conflict between efforts to live better in the world and endeavors to improve it. The two were inseparably bound together, and the one was the means of achieving the other. Living better in the world meant following the rule of moderation or, more specifically, observing diligence (the middle path between drudgery and idleness) and frugality (as opposed to the extremes of miserliness and extravagance) in one's daily affairs. Mending the world was to be accomplished by employing the rewards of diligence and frugality for benevolent and humanitarian purposes—not casually and incidentally, but wholeheartedly—as the major business of life.

A good deal of the hostility the Quakers encountered arose from the fact that they regarded the conduct of daily life as much, if not more, a part of religious observance than formal worship. But the Quaker outlook, radical in its belief in separation of church and state and in its insistence upon the individual's right of freedom of conscience, was conservative in its attitude toward social organization. Penn, no less than Winthrop, deemed class distinctions an essential part of the divine order. God has not placed men "on the level," he said, but has arranged them in descending orders of subordination and dependency; due respect for these God-ordained differences required "Obedience to Superiors, Love to Equals, . . . *Help* and *Countenance* to Inferiors."

Assumptions of social superiority and inferiority, however, were typical of seventeenth-century thought rather than peculiar to the Quakers. Penn himself emphasized the responsibilities rather than the privileges that went with rank. He took the doctrine of stewardship both seriously and literally, believing that men were indebted to God not only for their wealth but for their very being, and accountable to Him for the way they spent their lives as well as their fortunes. His concept of stewardship was free of the condescension with which it is so often associated because, in his case, the doctrine of stewardship was joined to an equally serious and literal

Doing Good in the New World

belief in the brotherhood of man. Penn was, after all, one of "The People called Friends," and, like other Quakers, he rejected the Calvinistic notion of the Elect. Whatever the differences in material conditions among men, all men were children of God, carriers of His seed, and spiritually equal in His sight.

Penn anticipated Benjamin Franklin in admiration for industry, thrift, and the other economic virtues that are now attributed to the middle class. Practical man that he was, Penn certainly had an appreciation for the value of money, but he believed that God gave men wealth to use rather than to love or hoard. Of all the vices, avarice struck him as worst. The spectacle of men, already comfortably fixed, who scrambled by day and plotted by night to increase their wealth moved him to scorn. "They are running up and down," he commented, "as if it were to save the life of a condemned innocent." Their conduct, personally disgraceful, was socially ruinous; for the reason the poor had too little was that the rich, already possessing too much, were striving to pile up even more.

Next to avarice Penn abhorred waste, display, and the pursuit of pleasure. Here again Penn's puritanical attitude expressed his social conscience: if all the money wasted on luxury and extravagance were put to public use, the wants of the poor would be well satisfied. To be sure, mortal man required diversion; but (or so Penn said), "The best recreation is to do good." There will be time enough for making merry "when the pale faces are more commiserated, the pinched bellies relieved and naked backs clothed, when the famished poor, the distressed widow, and the helpless orphan . . . are provided for."

11

American Philanthropy

Penn's writings, personal influence, and deeds left an indelible influence on Quakerdom and, through his followers, on nearly all subsequent humanitarian movements. Penn was, however, an Englishman. He visited America only twice, at widely separated intervals, and his total stay in this country amounted to no longer than four years. It is not Penn, therefore, but a native Yankee, the grandson of two of the founders of Massachusetts, who must be considered the chief exponent of do-goodism in colonial America.

Cotton Mather (1663–1728), unfortunately better remembered today for his part in the witchcraft trials than for his benevolent activities, is one of the commanding figures in the history of American philanthropy. The son of a president of Harvard, and himself one of the founders of Yale, Mather was the most prolific and conspicuously learned writer of the colonial period. Of the approximately four hundred and fifty works he is known to have published, one of the least pretentious, *Bonifacius*, or, as it is usually known, *Essays To Do Good* (1710), enjoyed the greatest and longest popularity. In it Mather proposed that men and women, acting either as individuals or as members of voluntary associations, should engage in "a perpetual endeavor to do good in the world." Such advice, coming from a son of the Puritans, was hardly novel. It was the method Mather outlined rather than the objective that was new. And it was this individualistic, voluntary method —taken not from the Quakers, whom Mather disliked, but from the German Pietists, especially August Hermann Francke of Halle—that was destined to characterize American philanthropy for many years to come.

In the passage quoted at the head of this chapter, Mather disposed in summary fashion of one of the persistent objections

Doing Good in the New World

to the gospel and practice of doing good. It is interesting, however, to consider why Mather himself thought it so necessary to do good. He regarded the performance of good works as an obligation owed to God rather than as a means of salvation; yet, as a constant expounder of the doctrine of stewardship, he had no doubt that God would punish the unfaithful steward. Moreover, as he was frank enough to admit and bold enough to proclaim, doing good was a reward in itself. To help the unfortunate was an honor, a privilege, "an incomparable pleasure." Not content to let the case rest here, Mather cited an entire catalogue of worldly advantages including long life and business success he thought would surely accrue to the benevolent. Besides, as Mather took pains to point out, doing good was sound policy, a mild but effective instrument of social control. Pious example, moral leadership, voluntary effort, and private charity were the means by which competing and conflicting interests in society might be brought into harmony.

To Mather charity emphatically did begin at home; for he believed that each man must start his career of doing good by correcting whatever was amiss in his own heart and life. Yet for all the emphasis on personal reform, Mather's was a social gospel. Keep a list of the needy in your neighborhood, he urged his readers; be on the lookout for persons who may require help, and seize each opportunity to be useful with "rapturous assiduity." Always bear in mind that "charity to the *souls* of men" is the highest form of benevolence. Send preachers, Bibles, and other books of piety to heathens at home and abroad; support the church, and keep a watchful eye on the spiritual health of the community. Very often, he said, the poor need "admonitions of piety" quite as much as

13

alms. "Cannot you contrive to mingle a spiritual charity with your temporal bounty?"

Mather's own charitable gifts were sufficient to make him a one-man relief and aid society. But Mather's real contribution to the practice of philanthropy lay in his recognition of the need for enlisting the support of others in benevolent enterprises. He was a tireless promoter of associations for distributing tracts, supporting missions, relieving needy clergymen, and building churches in poor communities. At the same time, in sermons and private conversations, he called the attention of the rich to the needs, physical as well as spiritual, of the poor. From personal experience he learned that the recompense of the charitable was multiplication of occasions to be serviceable. "Those who devote themselves to good devices," he drily observed, "usually find a wonderful increase of their opportunities." In a beautiful simile he likened a good deed to "a stone falling into a pool—one circle and service will produce another, till they extend—who can tell how far?"

Despite, or as Mather would have said, because of his sincere concern for the poor, he advocated extreme care in the bestowal of alms. "Let us try to do good with as much application of mind as wicked men employ in doing evil," was his motto. Giving wisely was therefore an even greater obligation than giving generously; and withholding alms from the undeserving as needful and essentially benevolent as bestowing them on the deserving. In a famous and widely approved sermon delivered in 1698 Mather told the good people of Boston: "Instead of exhorting you to augment your charity, I will rather utter an exhortation . . . that you may not *abuse* your charity by misapplying it." He was disturbed by the

Doing Good in the New World

increase of idleness and fearful that an excess of benevolence might nourish and confirm the idle in their evil ways. "The poor that can't work are objects for your liberality," he said. "But the poor that *can* work and *won't*, the best liberality to them is to *make* them." The thing to do was to cure them of their idleness: "Find 'em work; set 'em to work; keep 'em to work. Then, as much of your bounty to them as you please."

The most famous tribute to the *Essays To Do Good* came from an unlikely source. In youth—actually boyhood—Benjamin Franklin (1706–90) had been an enemy of the Mathers, and the pseudonym adopted in his earliest published work, Silence Dogood, was an unkind thrust at Cotton Mather. In old age, however, Franklin advised Samuel Mather, Cotton's son, that the *Essays* had influenced his conduct throughout life. "I have always set a greater value on the character of a *doer of good*, than on any other kind of reputation," he wrote, "and if I have been . . . a useful citizen, the public owes the advantage of it to that book."

Franklin did not acknowledge and possibly was not aware of the influence Quakerism exerted on his character and career. Nevertheless there was much in his approach to life that bore witness to his prolonged association with the Friends. He did not learn the virtues of discretion, moderation, and attention to his business from his first master, his brother James; in these, as in so many other arts, Franklin was self-taught. Yet he presumably derived something, if only concern for reputability, from the example of solid Quaker businessmen for whom he worked as a young man and whose patronage he solicited when he entered business for himself. At any rate it was a happy circumstance that Franklin, with his Puritan back-

15

ground and avowed indebtedness to Mather, should have carried out his highly successful experiments in useful living in the city founded by William Penn.

In addition to numerous similarities, there was a significant difference between Franklin's views and those of Penn and Mather. Penn demanded that money, instead of being hoarded or spent on impious luxuries, should be used for comforting the poor. Mather dreamed of a city in which each house would have an alms-box bearing the message "*Think* on the Poor." Franklin, however, conceived of a society in which there would be no poor and little need for relief or charity. He sprang from a different class and addressed himself to a different audience than Penn or Mather. Far from forgetting his humble origin, he traded on it throughout life. In the successive volumes of *Poor Richard's Almanack* Franklin spoke to "leather-aproned" folk as a man of their own sort. As he preached it, the gospel of industry, frugality, and sobriety was worldly wisdom rather than spiritual discipline. Contrary to what is sometimes assumed, Franklin did not advise his readers to seek riches or tell them how to gain wealth. If he had really wanted to do so, with his knowledge of the world, he could have offered more practical suggestions than maxims of self-help. It was the road to independence, not the "Way to Wealth" that Franklin pointed out. "Be *industrious* and *free;* be *frugal* and *free*," he counseled—free among other things of dependency upon the uncertain charity of the world.

In conducting his own affairs Franklin observed the maxims of the *Almanack*, if not to the letter, closely enough to become financially independent at a relatively early age. At forty-two he sold his printing house and devoted most of the rest of his life to serving the public. Long before quitting business, however, he had begun to practice what he so often preached to others: "Leisure is Time for doing something useful." It goes without saying that Franklin used his leisure to advance his own knowledge and reputation; but he employed it as earnestly for social as for self-improvement. Although the fact is well known, it is worth recalling that instead of patenting and seeking profit from his inventions, Franklin willingly gave the products of his ingenuity to the world. He introduced a secular spirit into the do-good gospel and shifted the emphasis from pious works and personal charity to efforts to further the general welfare. To Franklin, God was "the Great Benefactor." His religion consisted in the belief that men should show their gratitude to God "by the only means in their power, promoting the happiness of his other children."

Franklin was above all a man of the eighteenth century and it is not wise to insist too strongly on the modernity of his approach to social problems. In much that he did or suggested, however, it is possible to recognize principles that later came to be recognized as characteristic both of enlightened public policy and of constructive philanthropy. Preventing poverty always impressed him as a more sensible course than relieving it. In calling for repeal of the poor laws on the ground that public provision for the needy had an even greater tendency than almsgiving to pauperize the poor, Franklin went beyond Mather, who had warned of the abuses of private charity, and foreshadowed the scientific philanthropists and reformers of the nineteenth century. "I am for doing good to the poor," he wrote "but I differ in opinion about the means. I think the best way of doing good to the poor is, not making them easy *in* poverty, but leading or driving them out of it." In practice Franklin relied on leading rather than driving, on persuasion and encouragement rather than coercion. Unlike some later advocates of individualism, however, Franklin was not content merely to exhort the poor to become self-supporting. He was ever mindful of the need for widening opportunities for self-help, and throughout life he strove, as he put it, "to promote the happiness of mankind" by working for the establishment of conditions in which men would be able to take care of themselves.

Franklin's philanthropic activities, although varied, followed a consistent pattern. Starting in 1727 with the Junto, a club for the mutual improvement of its members, and the library (1731) which was the Junto's first offshoot, Franklin proceeded to organize or assist in organizing a host of civic projects. He founded a volunteer fire company, developed schemes for paving, cleaning, and lighting the streets of Philadelphia, and sponsored a plan for policing the city. His political talents were never better displayed than in his ability to unite public and private support behind municipal improvements. He played a leading part in the establishment of both the Pennsylvania Hospital (1751) and the academy which became the University of Pennsylvania. Funds provided in his will made possible the founding, more than a century after his death, of a technical institute in Boston. His interest in "improving the common Stock of Knowledge" led to the formation in 1743 of the American Philosophical Society, the first and for many years the foremost American institution for promoting research in the natural and social sciences.

Franklin demonstrated that the sovereign remedy of self-help, so often prescribed for individuals, could be applied with equally beneficial results to society. He did not invent the principle of improving social conditions through voluntary associations, but more than any American before him he showed the availability, usefulness, and appropriateness of that method to American conditions. The voluntary method, as Franklin's success with it suggested, and as later events were to prove, was precisely suited to the inclinations of his countrymen.

II

Religious and Revolutionary
Humanitarianism

The Humane Mania: . . . Persons afflicted with
this madness, feel for every species of distress, and
seem to pour forth tears upon some occasions, from
every pore of their bodies. . . . Gracious heaven!
if ever I should be visited with this species of madness, . . . my constant prayer to the divine fountain of justice and pity—shall be, that *I may never
be cured of it.*

BENJAMIN RUSH

In the third and fourth decades of the eighteenth century a
series of religious revivals collectively known as the Great
Awakening, swept over the American colonies. The revival
fervor reached its peak around 1742 and thereafter quickly
subsided, perishing, as Jonathan Edwards' biographer has
written, in its own noise. Brief though its sway, the Great
Awakening effected what may with some slight exaggeration
be called an American Reformation, for by strengthening in-

Religious and Revolutionary Humanitarianism

dividual religiosity it encouraged a spirit of religious independence and thus weakened the authority of the churches. George Whitefield (1714–70), Jonathan Edwards (1703–58), and other preachers of the revival made religion an intensely personal concern. Their emphasis on an inner experience of spiritual rebirth revealed possibilities of a whole religious existence outside the established forms of worship. The number of churches, sects, and church members increased as a result of the Awakening, but never again would the hold of the meeting house on individual consciences be secure, and never again would organized religion provide the only outlet for men's strivings for a better life. While religious and sectarian charities continued to flourish, a vast new interest in secular and humanitarian philanthropies developed both within and without the churches.

Among the most important results of the Great Awakening were the fostering of humane attitudes and the popularization of philanthropy at all levels of society, but especially among the poorer classes. The Awakening was a mass movement. It derived its strength from, and made its greatest impact on, humble men and women, many of whom belonged to no church and were therefore beyond the reach of religious appeals for charity. The revival gave them an opportunity to indulge in sentiments usually regarded as above their proper station in life and to partake more fully in the pleasures of piety and benevolence. Of all the conversions wrought by the Great Awakening certainly the most remarkable was the transformation of do-goodism from a predominantly upper- and middle-class activity—half responsibility, half recreation—into a broadly shared, genuinely popular avocation.

The man chiefly responsible for this achievement was George

American Philanthropy

Whitefield a young English evangelist who had not yet turned twenty-five when, in the autumn of 1739, he began the most famous preaching tour in American history. On this, the second of the seven visits Whitefield was to make to the colonies, he spent fourteen months (in his own words) "ranging and hunting the American woods after poor sinners." Whitefield found the quarry eager to be caught, for the fame of his eloquence had preceded him across the Atlantic and earlier revivals in the middle colonies and New England had prepared the way for his message of the awful need and wondrous possibilities of a new birth in Christ. The Awakening was already in progress when Whitefield arrived. He linked isolated, local revivals into an intercolonial movement, and turned the torrents of religious excitement unloosed by these revivals in the direction of practical benevolence.

It was not only the suffering of the damned but the misery of the poor that Whitefield preached. Other exhorters equaled or excelled him in ability to terrorize audiences with threats of hell-fire, but none approached him in ability to move the hearts and purses of listeners. He appealed to conscience and altruism as well as to fear, pleaded as earnestly for money as for souls, and made the collection plate hardly less important than the mourners' bench. With his superb voice, extraordinary histrionic talent, and instinctive feeling for human interests he could stir vast throngs to frenzies of pity and remorse. Responding generously, even extravagantly, to Whitefield's cry for alms became more than a demonstration of piety: it was a welcome and almost essential means of relieving emotional tension.

The principal object of the donations Whitefield collected was an orphanage, modeled after Francke's celebrated institution in Halle, which he founded in the impoverished colony of Georgia in 1740. This project, although appealing, was not well thought out and proved to be a costly undertaking. Whitefield raised money for the orphanage in England as well as in America; he purchased and operated a slave-manned plantation in South Carolina to obtain additional revenue for its support; and agitated for removal of the prohibition of slavery in the Georgia charter. For thirty years Whitefield devoted as much care to the management of the institution as the circumstances of his career permitted. In the closing years of his life he tried vainly to turn the orphanage into a college. Whitefield, however, was a better fund-raiser than administrator; and despite the energy and expense he lavished on the orphan home it never fulfilled his expectations.

The indifferent success of Whitefield's pet charity did not dampen his enthusiasm for benevolence. Throughout his mature life he made it his practice to improve his acquaintance with the rich for the benefit of the poor. Like Cotton Mather, whom Whitefield resembled in this respect, if in no other, he was ever ready to find support for good causes. He took up collections for poor debtors, raised money for victims of disaster, and secured books and financial assistance for hard-pressed colonial colleges. Harvard, Dartmouth, Princeton, and the University of Pennsylvania all benefited from his assistance. If no single institution can be regarded as his monument, the reason is partly that he helped so many.

The thirty-odd years between the Great Awakening and the Revolution brought a succession of emergencies that placed severe strains on American philanthropy. During much of the period the colonies were officially, if not always actively, at war with the French and Indians. The problem of poor relief, serious even before 1740, was made still more acute by the military struggle. Disabled soldiers, displaced Acadians, and refugees from the frontier swelled the numbers of the orphaned, widowed, aged, ill, and improvident for whom care had to be provided. The ranks of the distressed were further increased by two serious depressions, an influx of needy immigrants, recurring epidemics of smallpox, dysentery, and other diseases, and destructive fires in Charleston, South Carolina, and Boston. Despite the humanitarian sentiments spread by the Awakening, colonial society was poorly equipped to deal with these accumulated misfortunes. Private fortunes were too few and wealth neither widely enough distributed nor sufficiently fluid to permit large-scale or sustained private giving. Public relief under the poor laws was ordinarily available only to persons having legal settlement in a given community. In Massachusetts and some other colonies provincial legislatures reimbursed towns for the care of refugees and certain other needy wanderers who could not meet residence requirements for local relief. In time of depression or disaster, however, communities were hard put to care for their own poor.

In these circumstances welfare necessarily became a joint public-private partnership. Services that could not otherwise have been provided could be, and were, established through the willingness of public bodies and private citizens each to assist and supplement the philanthropic activities of the other. This co-operative approach was an expedient, but in view of the antagonism later thought to exist between governmental and voluntary efforts in the field of welfare, it stands out as one of the noteworthy aspects of colonial philanthropy. The line between public and private responsibility was not sharply

Religious and Revolutionary Humanitarianism

drawn. In seasons of distress overseers of the poor frequently called on the churches for special collections of alms, and throughout the colonial period giving or bequeathing property to public authorities for charitable purposes remained a favorite form of philanthropy. Friendly societies organized along national, occupational, or religious lines relieved public officials of the necessity for caring for some of the poor by supplying mutual aid to members and dispensing charity to certain categories of beneficiaries. New institutions, notably the Pennsylvania Hospital and the Philadelphia Bettering House, jointly financed by taxation and private contributions, offered unsurpassed facilities for treating and sheltering the poor. Gifts from overseas, added to funds raised by colonial churches and assemblies, made possible the founding of new colleges, better support for those already in existence, and an expansion of missionary and educational work among the Indians.

The sponsors of these undertakings appealed to common sense and self-interest as well as to compassion. Certainly this was true of the friendly societies, which, in addition to performing charitable and convivial services, gave members a sense of economic security. Dr. Thomas Bond (1712–84), the principal founder of the Pennsylvania Hospital, presented the project as "a means of increasing the Number of People, and preserving many useful Members to the Public from Ruin and Distress." The Philadelphia Bettering House and similar houses of industry in other cities asked and received support on the grounds that they not only relieved but employed the destitute, promoted industry and frugality among the poor, and thereby reduced the number of beggars and paupers. Eleazar Wheelock's (1711–79) success in obtaining money for his Indian school (later Dartmouth College) stemmed partly from his argument that the spread of Christianity and civilization among the tribesmen would provide "a far better Defense than all our expensive Fortresses."

Such rationalizations, although useful in giving humane motives a practical justification, are not sufficient to explain the vigor of colonial philanthropy. More revealing than these public pronouncements is the private observation of John Smith, a Philadelphia Quaker, who wrote in his diary in 1747 that he had not yet turned any beggar away empty handed, since "a fellow feeling of the Infirmities and wants of our Brethren—as all mankind are—is a duty, and not sufficiently practiced without Administering Relief when in our power." How seriously Americans took that duty became clear in 1760 when individuals, churches, town meetings, and legislatures throughout the colonies raised impressive sums for the relief of Boston's fire sufferers. Fourteen years later the closing of Boston's harbor in punishment for the Boston Tea Party threatened that city with economic ruin and produced the greatest relief crisis in the colonial period. Once again, but even more generously than before, other towns and colonies dispatched money, clothing, food, and livestock to Boston as if to prove that Americans, although not yet united politically, were already knit together by bonds of sympathy and affection.

Anthony Benezet (1713–84) was one of the men who drafted an appeal to Pennsylvania and New Jersey Quakers asking contributions for the relief of "the necessitous of every religious denomination" in Boston and other afflicted areas of New England. It was not the first time that the French-born Benezet, always frail in health and almost as poor as those he helped, had lent his assistance to such tasks. At the start of the French and Indian War he had organized relief for frontier

Religious and Revolutionary Humanitarianism

settlers driven from their homes by Indian raids; and for more than a decade after 1756 he had been the self-appointed guardian of the Acadians in Philadelphia, obtaining grants for these French-Catholic war victims from a grudging legislature and begging gifts for them from his fellow Quakers. Benezet had come to Pennsylvania in 1731 and was by profession a schoolmaster. By 1775 he had instructed a fair portion of the youth of Philadelphia—rich and poor, boys and girls, black and white. Meanwhile, through unflagging efforts as almoner and pamphleteer, he had extended his pedagogy to the entire community. Justice, and charity in the old sense of love, were the lessons Benezet taught. Because his conscience was alert to wrong as well as misfortune, and because he not only labored to ameliorate suffering, but courageously exposed and fought injustice, he deserves to rank as one of America's first humanitarian reformers.

The most famous picture of Benezet is Benjamin Rush's recollection of him as he appeared in old age: "His face was grave, placid, and full of benignity. In one hand he carried a subscription paper and a petition; in the other he carried a small pamphlet on the unlawfulness of the African Slave-trade, and a letter directed to the King of Prussia, upon the unlawfulness of war." "He is small, old and ugly," said a French officer during the American Revolution, "but his countenance wears the stamp of a peaceful soul and the repose of a good conscience." That benign countenance masked a ready wit and sharp tongue. Benezet laughed tolerantly when he heard that an aged Acadian, long a beneficiary of his charity, had concluded that such kindness as Benezet had shown over so many years could not possibly be disinterested, and that the author of it must have some design to profit at the expense of the

27

Acadians. For the ungenerous, however, especially those of his own sect, Benezet had nothing but scorn. He told his friend John Smith that he was weary of begging vainly of men who could afford to give a thousand pounds "without having one tear the less dropt on that account by their Heirs." It was no excuse for these men to say that they were insufficiently acquainted with the misery of the poor: they did not wait for full details before acting when they heard rumors that some extraordinary bargain might easily be attained. "The appellation of *Steward* is what we often take upon ourselves," he observed, "but indeed, in the mouth of many it is but a cant, unmeaning expression."

Benezet accompanied his services to war sufferers with an attack on war itself. Men of letters have exposed the follies of prejudice and intolerance, he observed in 1780; "Will they not endeavor too, to disgust men with the horrors of war, and to make them live together like friends and brethren?" Benezet, at least, was willing to make the endeavor and he pressed the campaign most strenuously when it was least politic to do so, that is, in the midst of war. He wrote the letter to Frederick the Great, to which Rush alluded, in 1776. Inclosed with the letter was his pamphlet, "Thoughts on the Nature of War," first printed in 1766 and reissued in the year of Independence. Benezet also sent the pamphlet to Henry Laurens, president of the Continental Congress. Two years later he prepared another antiwar tract and presented copies to members of Congress, governors of states, and influential persons on both sides of the Atlantic. "If people had never seen War kindled in countries and between neighboring Nations, they could hardly believe that man would be so inattentive to the dictates of Reason, the tender feelings of humanity, and the Gospel . . . as deliberately to engage in battles for the destruction of each other," he told his readers. We should pray, he said, "not for the destruction of our enemies, who are still our Brethren, . . . ; but for an agreement with them."

Benezet devoted much of his voluminous correspondence and some of his most trenchant pamphlets to improving relations between Indians and whites. He was not alone in this work, but unlike some of his contemporaries, who were interested mainly in baptizing the Indians and making them allies in war and trade, Benezet's concern was to obtain consideration for Indians as fellow beings, and to secure recognition for them of rights to which they—in his opinion—were as much entitled as any other people. He publicized every instance that came to his attention of the friendly disposition of Indian chiefs or tribesmen. "Is it not notorious that they are generally kinder to us than we are to them?" he asked in the last of his many pamphlets. The difference between us and them, he said, "is chiefly owing to our different ways of life, and different ideas of what is necessary and desirable." The advantage we have over them is one of education "which puts it in our power to gloss over our own conduct, however evil; and to see theirs, however defensible, in the most odious point of light."

Of all the crusades in which Benezet engaged, the most fruitful was his long struggle in behalf of the Negro. Benezet, in common with his friend John Woolman (1720–72), was troubled by the effect of slaveholding on the religion and morals of slaveowners; and, like Woolman, he was particularly distressed at the countenancing of slavery by his own sect. In 1776, after more than twenty years of effort, he succeeded in bringing Philadelphia Friends to agree to censure and disown members of the Society who refused to give up their slaves. But Benezet was animated more by love for the Negro as a brother creature than by hatred for slaveholders. In his first important defense of Negro rights, written in 1754, he argued that if we sincerely desire to live by the golden rule, "we shall never think of bereaving our fellow-creatures of that valuable blessing liberty, nor endure to grow rich by their bondage." "Let us make their case our own," he continued, "and consider what we should think, and how we should feel, were we in their circumstances."

Through experience gained as a teacher of both Negro and white children Benezet had come to believe that there was as great a variety of talent in the one race as in the other and that the notion of Negro inferiority in intellectual capacity was "a vulgar prejudice." Combatting racial prejudice and showing that white superiority was based on illegal force and unjust laws became his major mission in life. In pamphlet after pamphlet he returned to the theme of Negro equality. Thus, on the eve of the Revolution— "at a time," as Benezet said, "when the general rights and liberties of mankind" were ardently proclaimed—he raised the question that still haunts Americans: How can "those who distinguish themselves as the advocates of liberty" deny equality and justice to others on the grounds of race?

Benezet showered his letters and pamphlets on those he thought would benefit from them as liberally as a rich man might have scattered alms. Two thousand copies of *A Caution and Warning to Great Britain and Her Colonies* (1767) went to the Society of Friends in London for distribution to members of Parliament and officers of the crown. An expanded version of this attack on the slave trade appeared in 1771 under the title *Some Historical Account of Guinea.* This book, also widely distributed, made a strong impression on John Wesley, who borrowed from it in his own *Thoughts on Slavery* (1774). Thomas Clarkson, the chief English foe of the slave trade, called Benezet's work "influential, beyond any other book ever before published, in disseminating a proper knowledge and detestation of this trade."

During the 1770's Benezet enlisted the support of the young physician Benjamin Rush in the fight against the slave trade, and he encouraged the antislavery views of his old friend and neighbor, Benjamin Franklin. Benezet lived long enough to lobby for the passage of Pennsylvania's gradual emancipation act of 1780, the first abolition law passed by any American state. After Benezet's death in 1784 Rush and Franklin reconstituted an association Benezet had founded to assist free Negroes into the Pennsylvania Society for Promoting the Abolition of Slavery. Franklin's last public act was to forward a petition of the Abolition Society to the First Congress urging that body to go to the very limit of its powers to discourage the traffic in human beings; and his last publication, as witty as anything he ever wrote, was a parody of the proslavery arguments advanced against the petition.

Benjamin Rush (1746–1813) was a generation younger than Benezet and Franklin—which means that he belonged to that remarkable group of Americans, born around the time of the Great Awakening, who came to maturity, and in a sense were reborn, during the American Revolution. Rush was a physician, teacher, soldier, statesman, writer, and, in all his callings, a reformer. The breadth of his interests was matched only by the intensity of his feelings. He approached every issue not only as though his own life were at stake but as if the fate of the world hung in balance. As a boy of fifteen he found and stated his life-mission: "to spend and be spent for the Good of Mankind is what I chiefly aim at."

Rush's ancestors included Quakers, Episcopalians, and Baptists but he grew up in an atmosphere of revivalistic Presbyterianism. His pastor, whom he eulogized in his earliest known publication, was the great revivalist, Gilbert Tennent. He studied under an uncle, Samuel Finley, who was a leader of the "New Light" wing of Presbyterianism, and he received his B.A. at the Presbyterian stronghold of Princeton. Rush met Whitefield as a boy and renewed his acquaintance with him while studying medicine in London during the late 1760's. For the rest of his life Rush treasured "the original, pious and eloquent sayings" of Whitefield and felt that he had been particularly fortunate to have known him.

In later years Rush rejected the Calvinistic doctrines in which he had been trained, but he never shed his youthful religiosity. He had a puritanical attitude toward idleness, deplored the use of tobacco and distilled liquors on grounds of morals as well as health, advocated adoption of the Bible as a schoolbook, and was acutely disturbed by the sin of Sabbath-breaking. "The clergy and their faithful followers of every denomination are *too good to do good*" he complained on one occasion. "It is possible we may not live to witness the approaching regeneration of our world," he wrote a friend, "but the more active we are in bringing it about, the more fitted we shall be for that world where justice and benevolence eternally prevail." Rush was given to visions, which he called dreams, and in one of them he envisaged Philadelphia spared from justly deserved destruction on several occasions by the intervention of the Angel of Mercy who, in each emergency, was able to point out some philanthropy sufficient to appease God's wrath.

In choosing a career Rush wavered between the ministry and medicine. Although he chose medicine, we may wonder whether religion did not really win out in the end. At almost any time in his life he might have said what he actually did say in a letter written while a medical apprentice: "Though now I pursue the study of physic, I am far from giving it any pre-eminence to Divinity." The Bible passage which he took most to heart and quoted most often— "The son of Man is not come to *destroy* men's lives but to *save* them"—gave ^c religious justification to the practice of medicine. Rush was a great physician and quite naturally believed that the principles of what he called "the healing art" could be applied to society. But his medical opinions, far from affecting his religious views, were themselves influenced by religion. There was something theological in Rush's belief in the unity of disease, something evangelical in his teaching and preaching of the one sure cure for all ailments, and a family resemblance between the drastic remedies he employed in effecting cures and the violent methods used by the revival preachers to obtain conversions.

For Rush, as for others of his generation, the American Revolution was the central experience of life. "This great event has everywhere shaken the human mind to its centre" he wrote in 1788. A quarter of a century after Independence he said "I still believe the American Revolution to be big with important consequences to the world, and that the labor of no individual, however feeble his contributions to it were, could have been spared." Rush, not yet thirty when the war began, had already gained some notoriety as a reformer through his tracts on temperance and the slave trade. In 1775 he encouraged

33

another pamphleteer, Thomas Paine, to write an appeal for American independence. Rush read drafts of the work as Paine composed it and suggested *Common Sense* as the title. He was a member of the Continental Congress, a signer of the Declaration of Independence, and, for about a year, surgeon-general and physician-general of Washington's army. In the latter posts Rush's zeal for improving medical services embroiled him in disputes with brother officers, and his criticism of superiors, including Washington, forced his resignation early in 1778.

The Revolution intensified the sense of mission that already possessed Rush. Termination of his military career, instead of disgusting him with the struggle, strengthened his ardor for the cause of liberty. Possibly because his participation in the war was so brief and unsatisfying, he continued to wage the Revolution on other fronts long after Independence had been won. The war is over, he was fond of saying, but the Revolution has just begun. The more important and the more difficult task of bringing "the principles, morals, and manners of our citizens" into harmony with republican institutions remained to be accomplished.

In the decade after 1783 Rush addressed himself to this task with energy and conviction seldom matched by any American reformer. "The world seems to be on the eve of a great change for the better," he exulted in 1787, and he rejoiced in the privilege of speeding the better day. In the midst of a growing medical practice he continued his political activities, took on new teaching duties, founded the Philadelphia Dispensary, the first free medical clinic in the United States, and began the study of mental disease and the experiments in humane treatment of the insane that were to be among his greatest services to the medical profession. Meanwhile he renewed his attack on slavery and strong drink; he wrote against tobacco and in favor of the sugar maple tree, cultivation of which he believed would free the world from dependence upon slave-produced West Indian cane sugar. He agitated for moderation of the criminal laws, opposed capital punishment and all public punishments, and sought to convert prisons into agencies of repentance and reform. A teacher himself, Rush tried to excite public interest in education in every form, at all levels, and for both sexes. He advocated establishment of free public schools, gave enthusiastic support to movements for broadening opportunities for higher education, and proposed reforms in school curriculum, teaching methods, and discipline. In one of his letters he referred to "a new pamphlet written by that turbulent spirit Dr. Rush, who I hope will never be quiet while there is ignorance, slavery, or misery in Pennsylvania." A correspondent, half-admiring, half-despairing of Rush's efforts likened him to Mr. Great Heart in *Pilgrim's Progress*.

Rush professed little respect for "the cold blood of common sense" but he frequently appealed to this sentiment in his pleas for reform. Noting the moderate expense involved in treating large numbers of needy patients at the Philadelphia Dispensary, he declared that the principles of mechanics had been applied to morals, "for in what other way would so great a weight of evil have been removed by so small a force?" He defined capital punishment as the punishment of murder by murder and called it an act of legal revenge which did no practical good and much demonstrable harm. In arguing for milder discipline in the classroom Rush pointed out that schoolmasters were the only despots still tolerated in free countries. He defended public expenditure for education as true economy, since, in his opinion, diffusion of education could result only in promoting order, prosperity, and morality and thus in lessening of taxes. We can never suppress vice and immorality by enacting laws against them, he asserted, but we can prevent them from becoming serious problems by making adequate provision for the instruction of the manners and morals of young people.

Varied though Rush's crusades were, and whimsical as some of his arguments seem, they were parts of a consistent and nobly conceived design. In the years of hope and promise that followed the Revolution, Rush directed his anger not at individuals but at the relics of barbarism in human institutions. The doctrines of universal salvation which he embraced in the 1780's bound him, as he said, to the whole human race. "I was animated constantly by a belief that I was acting for the benefit of the whole world, and for future ages," he recalled years later. He thought that Independence offered Americans a God-given opportunity, if not obligation, to root out old errors and vices and to erect a society whose humanity, civilization, and Christianity would be a beacon to the world. Rush was sanguine of the outcome for, as he wrote John Howard the English prison reformer in 1789, "we are at present in a *forming* state. We have as yet but few habits of any kind, and *good* ones may be acquired and fixed by a good example and proper instruction as easily as *bad* ones. . . ."

Ironically enough, it was a local emergency and the needs of Rush's own time which called forth his greatest efforts, brought him most fame, and involved him in the bitterest and longest controversies of his career. The emergency was an epidemic of yellow fever—the worst calamity of its kind in American history—which almost decimated the population of

Religious and Revolutionary Humanitarianism

Philadelphia between August and November of 1793. In the epidemic Rush lost his sister, three of his apprentices, many of his friends, and more of his patients than he liked to admit. He himself suffered three attacks of the fever, but as long as his strength permitted he treated all who asked for his help. During one week in September he estimated that he called on and prescribed for between 100 and 120 patients a day, while his apprentices visited from 20 to 25 more. For many weeks he carried on consultations even while taking his meals; and after his own illness confined him to his home, he reported, "In my parlor, on my couch, and even in my bed I prescribe for 50 to 100 people, chiefly the poor, every day."

It was characteristic of Rush that, in the very depth of disaster, he could say, "Never was the healing art so truly delightful to me." It was also characteristic of him to deal with the epidemic in the manner of a reformer. He maintained, in the first place, that the fever was generated locally by filth and that it could be prevented by improved sanitary practices. This view involved him in protracted disputes with those who deemed his opinion a slur on the good name of Philadelphia and who insisted that yellow fever was an imported pestilence to be stopped by stricter quarantine. Even sharper controversies arose, however, over Rush's remedy for the disease. He did not claim to have discovered, but he practiced and publicized what he called "the successful mode of treating" yellow fever. The treatment consisted of extremely strong purges followed by copious bloodletting. In private letters and public pronouncements Rush boasted of "the triumphs of mercury, jalap, and blood letting." He stoutly maintained that if administered early enough the remedy was a sure cure for yellow fever. Rush's remedy, which we now know was ineffective, was widely condemned as well as devoutly praised in his own day. There can be no doubt, however, that Rush's faith in his cure and the confidence he inspired in others were factors in quieting the panic that accompanied the early stages of the epidemic. While the doctors were disagreeing and the sick dying, with or without benefit of "the successful mode" of treatment, many residents of Philadelphia fled the city. Among those who stayed behind were the mayor, Matthew Clarkson, and a small group of public spirited citizens. These men organized themselves into a voluntary committee to carry on the normal business of the city and to provide the extraordinary services made necessary by the epidemic. To the best of their abilities and resources, and in a heriocally matter-of-fact spirit, they combatted the panic, tended the sick, buried the dead, and cared for the poor, the unemployed, the abandoned, and orphaned.

Perhaps the least likely candidate for heroism in this valiant band of volunteers was the squint-eyed, close-mouthed businessman, Stephen Girard. At the time of the epidemic Girard was forty-three years old, a self-made man whose gospel was work, laissez faire, and *caveat emptor*. Born in France, in 1750 (d. 1831), Girard had left home as a boy, and, after a dozen years of seafaring, had settled in Philadelphia at the start of the Revolution. For a decade or more before 1793 he had been engaged in trading ventures with the French West Indies. It was a lucrative business, but sometimes dubious and always risky. In the summer of 1793 Girard's affairs were more unsettled than usual owing to the slave uprising in Santo Domingo, and for a while he was more disturbed by disorders in the West Indies than by yellow fever in Philadelphia. "It seems as if the misfortunes at Cap Français will be fatal to me,"

The Pennsylvania Hospital in 1800. Engraving by William Birch. (From R. M. Palmer, *Reproduction of Birch's Celebrated Views of Philadelphia*, Philadelphia, 1908.)

Stephen Girard. (From E. A. Duyckinck, *National Portrait Gallery of Eminent Americans*, New York: Johnson, Fry & Co., 1862.)

he wrote to a business associate early in September, adding that
the so-called plague in Philadelphia was "only a malignant fever
which, by the pernicious treatment of our doctors, has sent
many of our citizens to another world." He had easily thrown
off a slight case of the fever, and he resented the interruption
of business caused by the panic. "It is to be hoped," he wrote,
"that the month of September will bring all the inhabitants
back to their homes, and that business will resume its usual
trend."

Before the month was half-gone, however, Girard notified his
correspondent that fear, fright, and disease had reduced the city
to a deplorable condition. "I shall accordingly be very busy for
a few days," he advised, "and if I have the misfortune to be
overcome by the fatigues of my labor I shall have the satisfaction of having performed a duty which we owe to one
another." The few days stretched into two months. The duty,
voluntarily assumed, was the arduous and unpleasant one of
administering the pesthouse established in an old mansion on
Bush Hill. With the help of another volunteer, Peter Helm, and
a French doctor, Jean Devèze (emphatically not a follower of
Rush), Girard made the makeshift hospital into a model institution. The managers of Bush Hill could claim no miraculous
cures. Most of their patients came to them in advanced stages
of the disease, and about half of them died. But Girard's businesslike management, combined with the tender care he and
his staff rendered to the sick and dying, turned Bush Hill from
a place of horror into a haven of mercy.

Neither before nor after the epidemic were Rush and Girard
on friendly terms. To Rush, Girard's character seemed as
singular as his prosperity was extraordinary. He believed and
repeated rumors of Girard's niggardliness toward impecunious

relatives and of his despotic treatment of employees. *"Men will be Gods!"* he exclaimed in his commonplace book after recording instances of Girard's arrogance. For his part, Girard never tired of denouncing American doctors as charlatans, "ignorant jackasses," and "executioners of the human race." From Girard's point of view almost the worst crime committed by the doctors was the harm they did to commerce by frightening the population out of town when yellow fever returned in 1794, 1797, and 1798. He railed at preventive measures such as quarantine which interfered with trade, and declared that the only way of dealing with the fever was to take care of the sick, especially the sick poor. In his opinion it was fear that made people ill and the doctors rather than the disease that killed. After the epidemic of 1798 he wrote Jean Devèze that, of all the patients he had tended, "I do not suppose I cured one; nevertheless, you will agree with me that in my capacity as Physician of Philadelphia I have been very moderate and, that no one of my confreres has killed less than I."

Girard would be remembered as one of America's greatest philanthropists even if his work at Bush Hill were entirely forgotten. He provided financial assistance to the United States government during and after the War of 1812, when his generous subscriptions made possible the floating of a war loan and the establishment of the Second Bank of the United States. Girard's chief fame, however, came after his death in 1831 and as a result of the provisions of his will. Never before had an American bequeathed such a large estate to charitable and public purposes. A childless widower, at odds with his relatives, Girard made bequests to the city of Philadelphia for improvement of certain streets, to the state of Pennsylvania for development of canals, to the Masonic order to create a loan

Religious and Revolutionary Humanitarianism

fund (and to cancel a debt owed to Girard), to the Pennsylvania Hospital, and to a number of philanthropic institutions and organizations in Philadelphia. The bulk of his estate he set aside (shades of Whitefield!) for founding a boarding school for poor, white, male orphan children. Girard's munificence set a high standard for later millionaires, some of whom, impressed by his example, persisted in establishing or endowing orphan homes many years after the need for such institutions was less pressing than it had been in Girard's day.

It is probable that Girard's interest in orphans dated back at least to the yellow-fever days. Certainly his palliative approach to philanthropy was as clearly revealed in the emergency of 1793 as was Rush's reformistic bent. Then, no less than in his later, more celebrated philanthropic bequests, Girard responded to specific needs rather than to general causes. Unlike Rush and other humanitarian reformers who came before and after him, Girard felt under no obligation to cure or prevent social disorders or to try to remold society by any means other than economic self-interest. Yet within the limits of a somewhat misanthropic philosophy, Girard, in times of emergency, was capable of acts of public usefulness and private kindness.

Rush and Girard are fair representatives of the two types of philanthropists the United States has produced. Their disparate interests and objectives point the directions American philanthropy was to follow through most of the nineteenth century.

III

Benevolence in the Young Republic

> In the United States hardly anybody talks of the
> beauty of virtue, but they maintain that virtue is
> useful and prove it every day.
>
> ALEXIS DE TOCQUEVILLE

Alexis de Tocqueville was twenty-five years old in the spring
of 1831 when he began a nine-months' journey through the
United States. The supposed purpose of the trip was to gather
material for a report on American prison systems. From the
outset, however, Tocqueville had a broader and bolder work in
mind. He was interested not only in prisons but, as he said, in
"all the mechanism of that vast American society which everyone talks of and nobody knows." In *Democracy in America*
(1835) Tocqueville had a good deal to say about the ways in
which Americans performed and justified acts of helpfulness to
one another, and on the effect of substantial equality of condition in producing mild and humane customs. The young
aristocrat was particularly impressed by the uncertain status

of the rich in a democratic society. The rich seemed to spring up daily from the multitude and almost as often to relapse into it again. Hence, Tocqueville said, there was no "race" of rich men in America. The rich did not form a distinct class, but were connected to the rest of the people by a thousand secret ties.

The strongest of those ties, or so it seems today, was the widespread acceptance of a common set of moral values and economic principles. These values and principles were better suited to the interests of the middle and lower classes than to the development of an aristocracy, for they justified the acquisition of wealth but condemned the display, enjoyment, waste, or hoarding of it. Few Americans seriously questioned the right of any man to get rich by personal effort, but a great many voiced endless concern about the uses to which wealth was put once it had been won. Democracy imposed or sought to impose, the same rules of conduct on the rich as on other members of society. In practice the rich often flouted convention, but the pervasive influence of custom and belief tended to hold them to middle-class standards of thrift, sobriety, and responsibility.

In view of the popular prejudice against ostentatious enjoyment of riches, the luxury of doing good was almost the only extravagance the American rich of the first half of the nineteenth century could indulge in with good consciences. Even the bequeathing of large estates to one's children was frowned on. A fortune left to children is a misfortune, declared Horace Mann, since it takes away the stimulus to effort, the restraints from indulgence, "the muscles out of the limbs, the brain out of the head, and virtue out of the heart." Mann, it must be admitted, had no fortune to bequeath; but his views were shared (although not rigidly adhered to) by the rich merchant and industrialist Amos Lawrence (1786–1852). Lawrence hailed his brother Abbott's gift of $50,000 to Harvard in 1847 in these words: "It enriches your descendants in a way that mere money never can do, and is a better investment than any you have ever made."

In an age of criticism and conscience, when vast fortunes were still a novelty, the methods by which wealth was acquired were scrutinized almost as carefully as the ways in which it was used. "They cheats one another and they calls that business," John Jacob Astor was reported to have said of the commercial classes of New York City. Emerson, who hoped and expected that the amelioration of society would come from the concessions of the rich rather than from the grasping of the poor, was discomfited by the discovery that the ways of trade were "selfish to the borders of theft, and supple to the borders, if not beyond the borders, of fraud." A Lowell physician, Dr. Joseph Curtis, advised the American Medical Association in 1849 that there was not a prison or reformatory in New England in which the hours of labor were as long, the time for meals as short, or ventilation as neglected as in the textile mills owned by Boston philanthropists. Thoreau, who remarked that philanthropy was the only virtue sufficiently appreciated by mankind, was not alone in thinking that "he who bestows the largest amount of time and money on the needy may be doing the most by his mode of life to produce the misery he strives in vain to relieve." Thus early Americans began to voice the suspicion that philanthropy was a device used by the rich to atone for their way of acquiring wealth.

Reasonable though the atonement theory of philanthropic motivation seems in the abstract, the diaries and private correspondence of pre–Civil War philanthropists betray no hints of feelings of guilt. On the contrary, these men seem to have been blandly confident that their prosperity came from God. Before retiring from business Amos Lawrence sometimes berated himself for "over-engagedness" in secular affairs; and Peter Chardon Brooks, an insurance broker and money lender who had amassed a million dollars by 1817, admitted that a self-made man was apt to value his money too highly and hug it too close. The major concern of such men, however, seems to have been to discharge the obligations of stewardship faithfully, so that, at the appointed hour, they might hear the joyful sound of "Well Done!" from the lips of their Divine Master. They gave out of a feeling of religious duty, because they frankly enjoyed giving, because some appeal touched their hearts, and because, as they frequently said, they thought giving for certain purposes was a good investment.

If proof of the complex motives of philanthropy were needed, it would be supplied by the variety of objects donors chose to support. Boston boasted—alas, in the literal sense— "such a number and combination of charities as has never before been found in any city of its size," and in almost every American community well-to-do citizens contributed to the founding and support of churches, hospitals, and orphanages. A breadline in New York, a cemetery in Morristown, New Jersey, a home for fallen but repentant women in Philadelphia, and a fund to assist young brides to set up housekeeping in the vicinity of Northampton, Massachusetts, all impressed their donors as proper objects of benevolence. Some of the most important gifts went to states or cities for public purposes: Girard left money for internal improvements in Philadelphia and Pennsylvania; Theodore Lyman won some sort of im-

45

mortality by supplementing legislative appropriations for the Massachusetts state reformatory; and Thomas H. Perkins and Cyrus Butler, great men in their day, would be forgotten today save for their contributions toward the establishment of asylums for the blind and insane.

It is easy to laugh at the highly specialized and seemingly trivial purposes of many philanthropic activities. Yet who can deny, for example, that old people often suffer from failing eyesight? And who but Elias Boudinot, first president of the American Bible Society, was thoughtful enough to leave money in his will for purchasing spectacles for the aged poor? Amos Lawrence, having disengaged himself from business, rode out on fine days to distribute the tracts of the American Temperance Society and the Sunday School Union; on bad days he busied himself in selecting clothes, books, and other useful articles from storerooms in his house, bundled them into packages, and sent them off to needy students, professors, and clergymen. John Jacob Astor, not renowned for charitable giving, made an exception in favor of the Association for the Relief of Respectable Aged and Indigent Females. On the other hand, George Cheyne Shattuck, Boston's leading physician and a generous patron of education, passed up an opportunity to contribute to an old ladies' home; he preferred to give his money for such ends as the building of an observatory at his alma mater, Dartmouth. It was a halcyon day for philanthropists when a man could say, as the very rich and very generous William Appleton did in 1853, "I part with money in various ways of charity but much like to do it in my own way and not to be dictated to or even asked but in a general way, to give with others."

But giving with others was already a well-established feature

Benevolence in the Young Republic

of American philanthropy. The principle of voluntary association accorded so well with American political and economic theories that as early as 1820 the larger cities had an embarrassment of benevolent organizations. For the rest of the century, and even to our own day, one of the major problems of charity reformers would be to discover ways to co-ordinate the activities and fund drives of these competing agencies. In 1829 the economist and publisher, Mathew Carey, attempted—without much success—to interest Philadelphians in a single subscription campaign for the thirty-three benevolent societies then operating in the city. During the first half of the nineteenth century, societies for moral reform of individual sinners, and for the redemption and regeneration of a sinful world, multiplied even more rapidly than relief and aid organizations. As improvements in transportation and communication made it easier for people to join together, local societies merged into regional and then into national associations. William Ellery Channing, who disliked the substitution of the group for the individual conscience, remarked in 1829 that there was scarcely an object, good or bad, for whose advancement an association had not been formed.

The 1830's, an era of religious, political, and economic ferment, was the age of the "Benevolent Empire," a coalition of separate but closely related interdenominational religious societies. These various organizations collected and dispersed funds for distributing Bibles and religious tracts, for promoting foreign and home missions, for advancing the cause of temperance, Sabbath observance, and the Sunday-school movement; they supplied financial assistance to poor youths who wished to become clergymen and labored mightily to uplift the morals of seamen. Their combined membership ran into the hundreds of thousands and contributions to them amounted to several million dollars a year. Each of the societies held rousing national conventions and had officers, life-members, and, of course, rich angels. Elias Boudinot, Stephen Van Rensselaer, David Olyphant, Arthur and Lewis Tappan, and other philanthropists—usually although not always Federalist-Whig in their political leanings—took one or more of the societies to their bosoms, made generous contributions to their treasuries, and exerted a dominant influence on their policies and programs. In the hard times following the panic of 1837 many contributors had to curtail their gifts to the moral reform societies. The associations were further harassed by sectarian jealousies, by mounting sectional tensions, and by demands that they either denounce or defend the institution of slavery. The mission and tract societies adopted a policy of silence on the slavery issue, partly because it was politic to do so, and partly because (or so they maintained) their concern was with personal, not social, reform.

The American Colonization Society was founded (in 1817) about the same time as the moral reform societies and derived its support from approximately the same classes. Its work, which was the transporting of free Negroes to Africa, received the blessings of statesmen, the indorsement of state legislatures, and indirect assistance from the federal government. During the 1820's the Society raised enough money in the North and South to purchase land and found a struggling colony in Liberia. The Society managed to send a few hundred emigrants to the colony each year—a total of 11,000 by 1860 —but its operations proved a disappointment both to southerners, who seem to have expected it to rid the slave states of free Negroes, and to northerners who had hoped that the

Benevolence in the Young Republic

Society would promote the manumission of slaves. After 1832, when William Lloyd Garrison denounced colonization as a scheme to strengthen slavery, the Society lost the support of the Tappans and other militant antislavery men. Its endeavors yielded such slight returns that critics labeled it "an American humane farce." Yet simply because it was *not* an antislavery organization it continued to receive contributions from conservative philanthropists such as James Beekman of New York and Robert Winthrop and Nathan Appleton of Boston. Appleton, a founder of the Massachusetts textile industry, and sensitively aware of the property rights of slaveowners, said in 1847 that he did not regard colonization as either an attack on or a solution to slavery. He supported the Colonization Society because he thought it was engaged in an experiment to ascertain whether the African race was fit for self-government and civilization.

At least some slaveowners were, or had been, prepared to go considerably farther than Appleton. The large number of free Negroes in Maryland and Virginia testified that hundreds of slaves had obtained freedom with the consent of their masters. After the 1830's legal restrictions made manumission more difficult to practice, but even so John McDonogh, a Louisiana planter and land speculator who conceived many ambitious philanthropies, allowed his slaves to use the proceeds of their labor over a fifteen-year period to buy their liberty. McDonogh sent his freed Negroes to Liberia, but John Randolph, in one of his several wills, conferred freedom on his four hundred slaves, valued at about a half-million dollars, and provided for their colonization in other parts of the United States. After a long legal battle the court carried out the terms of the will.

American Philanthropy

Few of the very rich were identified with the abolition movement before the mid-fifties. Among the exceptions were Arthur Tappan (1786–1865) and his brother Lewis (1788–1873). The Tappans, who attributed the success of their New York silk-importing business to moral supervision of their clerks and a strictly cash, one-price system of merchandising, came close to being caricatures of blue-nosed reformers. They worried about the "unchurched poor," the desecration of the Sabbath, and the use of wine in communion services. They founded a society to establish asylums for reformed prostitutes and, when that failed, organized a Society for Promoting the Observance of the Seventh Commandment. That the Tappans were pious busybodies cannot be denied, but they were also dedicated to the gospel of stewardship. They spent their wealth generously on religious and educational philanthropies, and when their championship of unpopular causes exposed them to the wrath of street mobs and the pressure of the business community, they faced their foes with uncommon courage. It was Arthur Tappan who secured William Lloyd Garrison's release from a Baltimore jail in 1830 by paying the fine and court costs imposed on him for libeling the owner of a vessel engaged in the domestic slave trade. As an alternative to colonization they proposed schemes for educating free Negroes for citizenship in the United States. They were among the organizers of the American Anti-Slavery Society in 1833, and active workers in the Society until it split in 1840. Thereafter, although somewhat reduced in influence because of Arthur's bankruptcy, they gave their support to the anti-Garrisonian political wing of the abolition movement.

Education, which loomed so large in the thought of the Tappans, also occupied a major share of the attention of other

Benevolence in the Young Republic

philanthropists. At the start of the century the provision of free schools for poor children was a favorite form of charity; but with the expansion and reform of the public school system philanthropists became active in endowing private academies for the children of the rich. The field of higher education, neglected by the federal government and very poorly supported by the states, gave philanthropists their greatest opportunity for service. A nation growing rapidly in population and wealth possibly needed more colleges than the twenty-odd in existence at the start of the century. As events proved, however, the nation did not require and could not support nearly all of the five hundred or more colleges that were founded between 1800 and 1860.

It would be logical to assume that supposedly practical Americans would have given first priority to the establishment of schools for engineers and technicians. In practice, however, they seem to have believed that the crying need was for institutions to train more clergymen and devout laymen. By 1830 twenty theological seminaries had been founded, with Andover, the seat of "sound, orthodox, Calvinistic principles of divinity" receiving particularly generous benefactions. Meanwhile, churches of all denominations organized a host of small colleges, many of which called themselves universities. Of all the new institutions, Amherst, founded by Congregationalists in 1821, seems to have been the pet of the philanthropists, largely because of its reputation as a feeder of ministerial students to the seminaries.

Promoters of colleges in the western states appealed to the East for financial assistance in much the same way that the colonial colleges had sought help from England. In their campaigns for funds they often claimed that the indoctrination of young westerners in sound moral principles was the best defense against the twin evils of religious indifference and political radicalism. The Tappans, who contributed to the founding of both Oberlin and Kenyon, thought that the solution to the financial problems of poor colleges and college students lay in attaching farms and workshops to classrooms. To this end they organized in 1831 a Society for Promoting Manual Training in Literary Institutions. The manual labor idea, although it furthered the founding of small schools, did not solve the needs of the larger and better established western colleges. After the depression of 1837 a number of these institutions, finding that frequent and competing solicitations increased the resistance of eastern philanthropists, formed the Society for Promotion of Collegiate and Theological Education in the West and, for a number of years, conducted a united fund drive.

The great increase in the number of colleges made it difficult for older institutions to attract and retain philanthropic support. Even Harvard, Unitarian since 1805, suffered from the competition of younger but more religiously orthodox colleges. Bostonians had contributed slightly more than a quarter of a million dollars to Harvard between 1800 and 1830; in the next fifteen years, while raising $330,000 for Amherst, they gave but $84,000 to Harvard. Beginning in the late 1840's, however, and increasingly in the 1850's, Harvard began to receive the gifts of Abbott Lawrence, Samuel Appleton, and other industrialists. Numerous institutions were favored by the families or individuals whose names they bore or adopted, but in at least one instance, Rutgers, college authorities made the mistake of renaming the institution in honor of a prospective benefactor who failed to make the expected princely donation.

Benevolence in the Young Republic

On the other hand, a public lecture by Mark Hopkins, the president of Williams College, made such a favorable impression on Amos Lawrence that the philanthropist made a large unsolicited gift to the college and followed his initial donation with several more.

The federal government was the recipient of another unsolicited and quite unprecedented gift in the form of James Smithson's bequest of approximately $500,000. Smithson, a British chemist who died in 1829, left his fortune to a nephew with the proviso that if the latter died without issue (as he obligingly did) the entire estate should pass "to the United States of America to found at Washington, under the name of the Smithsonian Institution, an establishment for the increase and diffusion of knowledge among men." Upon the death of the nephew in 1835 Congress debated the constitutionality and propriety of accepting the gift, John C. Calhoun opposing and John Quincy Adams favoring acceptance. As President, Adams had been unsuccessful in his efforts to expand the activities of the federal government in education and research; now, however, he was not to be denied, and in 1836 Congress voted to accept the bequest. Not until ten years later, after further controversy and debate, and after the loss of the original gift through unwise investment (Congress appropriated $500,000 to cover the loss) did "the establishment" at last come into being. Adams again played an important role in securing approval of the act that set up the Institution, but it remained for Joseph Henry, the brilliant physicist who served as director of the Smithsonian from its founding in 1846 until his death more than thirty years later, to establish research and publication as the means by which the Institution was to carry out its mission of increasing and diffusing knowledge among men.

53

American Philanthropy

While Congress was still debating what to do with the Smithson gift, another institute for disseminating knowledge opened in Boston. The donor, John Lowell, retired from business after the death of his wife and two young daughters and spent the rest of his brief life in restless travel through Europe and the Middle East. Shortly before his death in 1836 he put his will into final shape, directing that a sum of $250,000 be used to found the Lowell Institute. Lowell stipulated that the endowment, instead of being spent on buildings, should be used to sponsor public lectures to instruct the people of Boston in science, literature, history, and religion. Although imparting more knowledge to serious-minded Bostonians might seem like carrying coals to Newcastle, the Institute opened in 1840 with a series of lectures on geology by Benjamin Silliman. Through a policy of generous remuneration the Institute was able to bring to its platforms some of the foremost men of letters and science of both the old and new worlds.

Beginning in the 1840's, as the founding of Lowell Institute and the Smithsonian Institution suggest, scientific research and intellectual inquiry—as opposed to moral instruction and reform—began to figure more prominently as objects of American philanthropy. Louis Agassiz, who came to the United States to lecture at Lowell Institute, remained to become professor of zoology and geology at Harvard. There his work was supported by the gifts of Abbott Lawrence, Francis Gray, and other Boston capitalists as well as by grants from the Massachusetts legislature. Agassiz's insatiable requirements for funds for his museum of comparative zoology gave philanthropists an object lesson in the cost of scientific research. At about the same time, by founding Cooper Union in New York City, Peter Cooper (1791–1883) continued the Franklin tradition of advancing science and art "in their application to the varied and useful purposes of life." George Peabody (1795–1869), the American-born banker who lived in London after 1837, made it possible for his countrymen to display their industries and inventions at the Crystal Palace Exhibition of 1851 and through his gift of the Peabody Institute enriched Baltimore's cultural life with an art gallery, lecture hall, and conservatory of music. Peabody's and Henry Grinnell's under-writing of the expenses of polar expeditions during the 1850's popularized geographical exploration as an object of philanthropic support. Similarly, the bequest of John Jacob Astor, which established the Astor Library in New York, and the gifts of Joshua Bates for the founding of the Boston Public Library in 1852, presaged what was to become one of the standard forms of philanthropy in the second half of the nineteenth century.

Promoters of two patriotic undertakings met difficulty in raising money for objects that would, offhand, seem to have had popular appeal. The Bunker Hill Monument Association of Boston ran out of money and into debt three years after laying the cornerstone of the monument in 1825. Construction had to be suspended for almost a decade. The obelisk was not completed until the 1840's, after Amos Lawrence and Judah Touro of New Orleans had each contributed $10,000 and a "Ladies Fair" had raised $30,000 for the project. Meanwhile, the Washington National Monument Society, founded in 1833, sought subscriptions for a memorial to George Washington in the national capital. More than fifty years passed before the beautiful shaft was finished, for although the Society had collected enough money to begin construction in 1848, funds were exhausted by 1855, and for many years thereafter efforts to obtain additional support from private citizens or the federal government yielded disappointing returns. Partisan feelings and, in the case of the Washington Monument, religious considerations were partly responsible for the indifference and even hostility to these undertakings. But more important was the fact that the sense of national patriotism was still comparatively weak in pre–Civil War America, despite Fourth of July orations and the vogue of eulogistic biographies and histories.

In contrast to the lagging support accorded patriotic monuments, Americans gave enthusiastically and liberally for foreign relief. In the 1820's volunteer committees arranged balls, fairs, auctions, debating contests, and theatrical benefits to raise money for the cause of Greek independence. The committees employed nearly all the devices of modern charity drives to levy contributions for Greek relief from merchants, shippers, laborers, and school children, and brought a number of Greek war orphans to this country for adoption. In the autumn of 1832, when the starving people of Cape Verde Islands rowed out to a ship hoping to buy food, they were astonished to learn that the vessel had been sent from the United States for the express purpose of relieving their necessities. Individuals and churches in New England, Philadelphia, and New York had heard of their need and had raised thousands of dollars for their assistance. Boston gentlemen sent a relief ship to the Madeira Islands in 1843 and were rewarded when appreciative islanders sent the ship back laden with casks of choice old Madeira. The Irish famine of 1846–47, the worst calamity of the entire period, called forth the largest and most widely shared response from the American people. New York's merchant prince, A. T. Stewart, and other Irish-Americans showed sympathy in abundance, but generosity cut across national and religious lines. To carry the contributions of Massachusetts alone required two sloops of war, four merchant ships, and two steamers. It was both fitting and ironic that the Boston bluebloods, Josiah Quincy and Robert Winthrop, the latter an Episcopalian descendant of Puritan John Winthrop, should have taken leading parts in organizing relief efforts for the distressed people of Catholic Ireland.

American readiness to assist the unfortunate in foreign lands seemed to bear out Tocqueville's view that democracy, by destroying barriers of class and privilege, fostered a general feeling of compassion for all members of the human race. But in the 1830's and 40's thoughtful Americans were less concerned about the consequences of democracy than about the work that remained to be done for its realization. There was need, said William Ellery Channing in 1841, for "vigorous efforts, springing from love, sustained by faith" for diffusing knowledge, self-respect, self-control, morality and religion through all classes of the population. At the time these were the areas in which philanthropy was most interested and best fitted to serve.

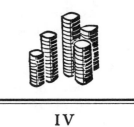

IV

Saints and Scolds

What is it we heartily wish of each other? Is it to
be pleased and flattered? No, but to be convicted
and exposed, to be shamed out of our nonsense of
all kinds. . . .

RALPH WALDO EMERSON

With some exceptions, like the Tappans, contributions to
moral reform and gifts to the unfortunate involved few
sacrifices by donors. Not even the Tappans insisted that the
rich should give away all they possessed, and Amos Lawrence
once reflected that the more he gave the more he seemed to
have. Some men, like Girard, gave up their money only after
death; others, like Lawrence, gave liberally of their income
during life but made no significant charitable bequests. "I have
given in my lifetime what I felt it was my duty to give," Edward Delavan, the angel of the temperance movement, said in
his will. "I think my family is entitled to what is left of my
estate." Generally speaking, philanthropists made their contri-

butions out of surplus wealth and stopped giving whenever they thought it prudent to do so.

To some guardians of conscience neither the ends nor the means of conventional giving warranted the name of philanthropy. Emerson, in "Self-Reliance" (1841), warned the "foolish philanthropist" not to come to his door begging for "your miscellaneous popular charities; the education at colleges of fools; the building of meeting-houses to the vain end to which many now stand; alms to sots, and the thousandfold Relief Societies." Thoreau scorned "a charity which dispenses the crumbs that fall from its overloaded tables, which are left after its feasts!" He wondered at the boasts of men who gave one-tenth of their income to charity while keeping nine-tenths for themselves; and he asked whether such a distribution was to be explained by the generosity of the givers or by "the remissness of the officers of justice."

There were a number of philanthropists in the pre–Civil War period, however, who were as little impressed by the common run of charities as Emerson, who were as alert as Thoreau to inhumane social practices, and who offered more than passive resistance to injustice. These reformer-philanthropists conducted a general inquest into the abuses of their time and were more than willing to point out better ways of doing things. Not all the causes they championed were unpopular, but they did have to contend with complacency, and, at times, sentimentality. Mainly it was inertia—passive good will combined with prejudice against change and reform—rather than active opposition that they encountered. The vehemence of their agitation shocked persons of milder temperaments and easier consciences. Their peculiarities, prejudices, and blind spots are all too apparent, as are the inadequacies of some of the remedies they proposed. They were neither revolutionaries nor visionaries, and perhaps were not much more sensitive to wrong than ordinary men and women; but they had a much stronger than ordinary sense of personal responsibility for ending or mitigating wrongs. They became excited about issues in which their own interests were not involved, and they had the energy and daring to carry their feelings into action.

The miscellaneous popular charities whose numbers increased during the hard times of 1816–21, and in each succeeding depression, were among the principal targets of the reformers. The trouble with such agencies, in the opinion of Joseph Tuckerman (1778–1840) of Boston and John Griscom (1774–1840) of New York, two of the most influential of the charity reformers, was that while relieving the sentiments of the comfortable classes, they did more harm than good to the poor. The American charity reformers, like their British and Continental counterparts with whom they were in frequent communication, were obsessed by a fear of pauperism. They wanted to help the poor but were so fearful of pauperizing them that the only commodity they dared offer was advice. That they gave liberally: hints on household management, admonitions on waste, intemperance, and idleness, and sermons on the virtues of self-help.

Individualistic and moralistic in outlook though the charity reformers were, they were not as naïve as they sometimes seem. Tuckerman, Griscom, and their associates put in motion schemes for the spread of savings banks, life insurance, and benefit societies among the poor; and in the course of their attack on pauperism they lent support to a host of reform movements. The material as well as the moral state of the poor

Amos Lawrence. (From Freeman Hunt, *Lives of American Merchants*, New York: Derby & Jackson, 1858.)

"Please Sir, May I Have a Bed." Newsboys' Lodging House of Children's Aid Society of New York, 1854. (From Charles Loring Brace, *The Dangerous Classes of New York*, New York: Wynkoop & Hallenbeck, 1872.)

Saints and Scolds

engaged the attention of Robert M. Hartley (1796–1881), who founded the New York Association for Improving the Condition of the Poor in 1843 and managed it for the next three decades. Under Hartley's leadership the A.I.C.P. devoted part of its energies to "incidental labors" for social betterment, particularly in the fields of housing, sanitation, and child welfare.

Although suspicious of unwise private charity, the reformers were even more critical of public poor relief. Tuckerman urged repeal of existing poor laws and abolition of all public assistance except that furnished in closely supervised institutions. England attempted a revision of her poor laws along these lines in 1834, but public opinion in the United States (where the votes of the poor counted more at the polls) would not accept such a drastic step. Nevertheless during the 1820's legislatures in several states ordered investigations of prevailing methods of poor relief. The reports of the investigating committees confirmed the reformers' charges that some of the poor were maintained in their own homes at the taxpayers' expense; others, however, were either farmed out to contractors at a stipulated price or "sold" to the person who bid the lowest sum for keeping them. Since the bidders themselves were often desperately poor, the money paid them for keeping paupers constituted a kind of relief— "a species of economy" (said the New York report) "much boasted of by some of our town officers." With rare unanimity the reports indorsed the almshouse or poor farm—utilized by the more populous communities for a century or more—as the most humane and economical method of caring for paupers. A well-regulated institution, such as the one at Poughkeepsie, New York, employed its inmates at picking oakum, washing, spinning, cooking, and farm work, and fed and clothed each at an annual cost of twenty-five dollars. "Our house of industry," reported the gratified managers, "affords an opportunity to economize, and to support our paupers at least 50 per cent less than formerly."

The reformers were more successful in inducing communities to build almshouses than in policing them once they had been established. The poorhouses founded in the 1820's and 30's soon become catchalls for victims of every variety of misery, misfortune, and misconduct. The old and the young, the vagrant and the abandoned, the feeble-minded, insane, and disabled, were all herded together in buildings that were poorly constructed, foully maintained, and wretchedly furnished. "Common domestic animals are usually more humanely provided for than the paupers in some of these institutions" was the verdict of one investigatory commission at mid-century. In New York in the 1850's a committee of the State Senate found evidence of such "filth, nakedness, licentiousness, . . . and . . . gross neglect of the most ordinary comforts and decenies of life" that it forbore to publish its findings in detail lest the report disgrace the State.

The children in prison rather than those in pauper asylums first aroused the sympathy of nineteenth-century reformers. John Griscom, representing the New York Society for the Prevention of Pauperism, and Thomas Eddy, who had been active in prison reform movements since the 1790's, worked for five years after 1819 to get youthful offenders out of jails and into reformatories. Through their efforts the New York House of Refuge, the first reformatory for juvenile delinquents in the United States, was founded in 1825. Shortly afterward, Philadelphia, traditionally the center of American prison reform activities, built a similar House of Refuge; and Boston, under the prodding of Mayor Josiah Quincy, soon established a House of Reformation which, in the opinion of informed students might have served as a model for all correctional institutions. The success of the Boston House of Reformation led Theodore Lyman in the 1840's to make gifts totaling almost $75,000 for the establishment of the first state juvenile reformatory at Westborough, Massachusetts.

While other humanitarians were demanding special institutions for wayward youth, Charles Loring Brace (1826–90), a twenty-seven-year-old city missionary in the Five Points district of New York, developed a comprehensive program for combatting delinquency at its source. The New York Children's Aid Society, organized by Brace in 1853, provided religious meetings, workshops, industrial schools, and lodging houses for the poorest and most neglected children of the metropolis. Brace, who regarded these undisciplined and often homeless youngsters as menaces to society, described the Children's Aid Society as "a moral and physical disinfectant." He was particularly interested in the possibility of "draining" New York of destitute children. Beginning in 1854 the Children's Aid Society annually sent hundreds of boys and girls to foster homes in the West. The success of the emigration scheme rested in part on the demand for unpaid farm labor. To Brace this circumstance did not lessen the charity of those who gave poor children homes in return for work. Brace, like Cotton Mather, believed the best charity that could be offered the idle was an opportunity to work, and he was convinced that boys and girls were better off in Christian homes, especially farm homes, than in any institution.

Brace's informal placement methods set off a long controversy. Roman Catholics complained that Catholic children were being sent to Protestant homes; westerners protested that the Children's Aid Society was filling western jails and reformatories with petty criminals; and welfare workers objected that the Society did not carefully scrutinize the homes in which it placed children. Brace investigated the charges, modified his methods, and persisted in his labors for almost forty years. His work did much to popularize foster-home care for dependent children as opposed to institutionalization, and his preventive "child-saving" approach, adopted at a time when so much emphasis was placed on correctional or reformatory methods, exercised a wholesome influence on later development in child welfare.

The founding of juvenile reformatories was part of the larger movement for prison reform. In the United States this movement went back at least to 1776 when a Society for Alleviating the Miseries of Public Prisons had been organized in Philadelphia. By the 1820's, after half a century of experience in substitution of confinement for corporal punishment, two rival systems of prison discipline had emerged: the Pennsylvania or "separate" plan used at the great and costly Eastern State Penitentiary at Cherry Hill; and the Auburn, or "congregate" system developed in New York State. In the former, inmates lived, worked, ate, and slept in solitary cells; under the Auburn plan prisoners were locked up alone at night, but worked and ate together during the day, theoretically in absolute silence and subject to harsh punishment for breaking rules against communicating with one another.

Each of the methods had staunch advocates. The Pennsylvania system appealed to humanitarians because of the supposed penitential benefits of solitary confinement, while the

Saints and Scolds

Auburn plan found support among persons impressed by its demonstrated economy. Auburn won the indorsement of the influential Boston Prison Discipline Society, which, under the leadership of Louis Dwight, a former agent of the Tract and Bible Societies, issued propaganda for adoption of the congregate system throughout the nation. On the other hand Samuel Gridley Howe, Horace Mann, Charles Sumner, and many other reformers remained partisans of the Pennsylvania system. The dispute produced a spate of pamphlets, the most valuable of which was Dorothea Dix's *Remarks on Prisons and Prison Discipline* (1845), and Nathaniel Hawthorne made a visionary prison reformer the villain of *The Blithedale Romance* (1852). In the heat of the controversy legislatures and prison administrators initiated reforms in the construction and management of penitentiaries which for a brief period made American prisons rank among the most progressive in the world.

In the long run it proved impossible to maintain interest in prison reform at the high level necessary to effect lasting improvement. Other issues intervened, and reformers soon found prison discipline a less interesting subject of debate and speculation than projects for preventing crime. Before interest had cooled, however, a New York Quaker, Isaac Hopper (1771–1852), had begun his work of helping discharged prisoners find homes and jobs. Meanwhile in Boston a shoemaker named John Augustus (1785–1859) voluntarily assumed and performed the duties of probation officer. Over a period of almost twenty years Augustus devoted the earnings of his shop and applied the contributions of well-wishers to bailing and rehabilitating drunkards and persons convicted of petty crimes. Necessarily selective in the bestowal of assistance, since his resources were limited, he nevertheless helped many unfortunates who were "undeserving" by conventional standards. Augustus was "extraordinarily given to help the helpless and love the unlovely," said the radical preacher, Theodore Parker. "Ministers preach benevolence and beneficence—he *went* and *did* it."

Three more famous philanthropists, among the most justly celebrated America has produced, also *went* and *did* acts of extraordinary usefulness to classes previously neglected and often deemed beyond help. The Reverend Thomas Hopkins Gallaudet (1787–1851), Dr. Samuel Gridley Howe (1801–76), and Dorothea Dix (1802–87) were not specially qualified by training for the service which won their fame. They abandoned their intended careers in order to help deaf mutes and the blind, and to rescue the insane from cages in jails and almshouses. Gallaudet, a graduate of Andover Theological Seminary, demonstrated to the nation that deaf mutes could be educated. He founded the first American school for the deaf, gained support for this work from private donors, state legislatures, and even Congress, and lived to see state schools for the deaf widely established. Howe's special field was instruction of the blind, and his most celebrated feat was teaching Laura Bridgman—blind, deaf, and mute—the use of language and a variety of manual skills. But before Howe became a teacher of the blind in the 1830's, he had fought in the Greek War of Independence and administered relief to Greek civilians; and long after he won renown as head of Perkins Institution, he plunged into other causes, and embarked on new crusades to educate the feeble-minded and teach the mute to speak. Howe was a latter-day Benjamin Rush in the multiplicity of his interests, in his love of liberty, aptitude for controversy, and unquenchable optimism. Even oysters, he said, were capable of improvement!

As for Dorothea Dix, her career offers one of the best examples the nineteenth century affords of sustained and constructive agitation for humanitarian reform. She was not a pioneer in the field of better treatment of the insane. Much had already been accomplished when she began her work. Several reputable hospitals for the mentally ill had been founded by incorporated bodies; John McLean and other donors had given money for improving and expanding facilities for the insane, and a number of states had opened publicly supported asylums. Nearly all of these institutions made at least nominal provision for caring for the dependent insane at low cost. So much progress seemed to have been made in the years just before Miss Dix's investigations that there was danger, not that her proposals would seem outlandish, but that further action and expenditure for the insane might seem superfluous. Dorothea Dix's task was the difficult one of puncturing complacency, indicating omissions, specifying mistakes and abuses, and stirring the public conscience to greater exertions.

Like another great agitator, Anthony Benezet, Miss Dix was a teacher by profession. Largely self-taught, she had conducted a successful school for daughters of Boston's leading families and had tutored the children of her friend and pastor, William Ellery Channing. In the winter of 1841, somewhat at loose ends following a long illness, she agreed to teach a Sunday-school class for women prisoners in the East Cambridge jail. Here she found insane women locked in unheated cells. Anyone might have done what she then did. She petitioned the court for warmer quarters for these women. But Dorothea Dix was not content to stop there. She made it her business to find out how the insane were cared for in the rest of Massachusetts. After two years she was ready to report her findings in a *Memorial to the Legislature of Massachusetts* (1843), a document which proved that Victorian decorum was not inconsistent with the presentation of sordid social truths.

"I proceed, gentlemen," Miss Dix began, "briefly to call your attention to the *present* state of insane persons confined within the Commonwealth, in *cages, closets, cellars, stalls, pens; chained, naked, beaten with rods*, and *lashed* into obedience." Armed with facts, figures, names, places, and dates, she cited instance after instance of the mistreatment or neglect of the mentally ill. Poor-law officials, as she pointed out, found it cheaper to "lodge" the pauper insane in jails and almshouses than to send them to asylums. In any case, the number of dependent insane and idiotic persons was at least twice as large as the total capacity of the three asylums in the state. Fortunately she had friends as well as facts at her disposal. Horace Mann lent his assistance, and Samuel Gridley Howe was chairman of the legislative committee to which the *Memorial* was referred. Howe's committee indorsed both the findings and conclusions of her investigation and secured passage of a bill enlarging the Worcester Asylum to provide more space for poor patients.

Massachusetts was the first phase of a forty-year campaign that took Miss Dix throughout the United States, into Canada, Scotland, England, Italy, and Turkey, and spread her influence as far as Japan. It would be incorrect to imply that she single-handedly worked a revolution in the care of the insane. Yet it is true that her "sad, patient, deliberate" investigations resulted in the founding of many new state hospitals and at least a temporary improvement in the treatment of the mentally ill. Wherever she went her methods were essentially the same: inquiry and research to determine the facts about the number and condition of the insane; efforts to arouse public opinion through articles in the press and memorials to the legislature; and cultivation of powerful figures in and out of public office. She professed a lady-like repugnance of politics, but she had a real talent for political maneuver. She knew when to sprinkle her humanitarian pleas with the salt of economy and often concluded her appeals by observing that "it is cheaper to take charge of the insane in a curative institution than to support them elsewhere for life." She was adept at discovering the most influential men in legislatures and in bringing them into her camp. The men she feared most were not those who openly opposed her but those who said they sympathized with her aims, wept over her reports, and then found compelling, noble reasons for steeling their hearts against compassion.

Such a man was President Franklin Pierce, at whose hands Miss Dix suffered one of her few major defeats. In 1848 she sent a *Memorial* to Congress in which she estimated that not more than one-twelfth of the insane population of the country could be accommodated in existing hospitals and asylums. As a means of dealing with the problem she proposed federal assistance in financing care of the insane through land grants to the states. Grants of this sort had frequently been made for education and internal improvements, and, on two occasions, for schools for the deaf. In 1854, after six years of lobbying by Miss Dix, both houses of Congress passed her bill. It apportioned 12,225,000 acres of public land among the states for the support of insane asylums and institutions for the deaf.

American Philanthropy

President Pierce, professing regret for having to do so, vetoed the bill. He acknowledged that the duty of providing for those who suffered from want and disease of body or mind was "among the highest and holiest" of human obligations, but he said he feared the effect of Miss Dix's bill would be "prejudicial rather than beneficial to the noble offices of charity," since it would dry up the normal springs of benevolence. "If Congress have the power to make provision for the indigent insane . . . ," he warned, "it has the same power to provide for the indigent who are not insane; and thus to transfer to the Federal Government the charge of all poor in all the states." For his part, continued Pierce, "I cannot find any authority in the Constitution for making the Federal Government the great almoner of public charity throughout the United States."

Of course Miss Dix and her supporters were not asking the federal government to play such a role, or to assume exclusive responsibility for all the poor in all the states. They wanted only to have a portion of the public lands granted to the states to enable them to fulfill their obligations better than they were then able. But to Pierce principle was more important than policy, and his principle, as a critic has remarked, was that no power that might be abused should be used. Yet Pierce sensed the implications of the Dix bill accurately. Had it become law, not only the care of the insane but all public welfare programs might have developed quite differently. As it was the United States had to wait another eighty years before the federal government began to assist and strengthen state programs for certain categories of needy persons.

To Horace Mann (1796–1859) and some other friends of Miss Dix, Howe, and Gallaudet, the improvement of common

schools for normal children seemed an even more urgent matter than the establishment of institutions for the afflicted. No
nineteenth-century reform movement had a broader base than
the crusade for good schools, and none was expected to yield
greater benefits. The educational reformers maintained that
raising the general level of culture through more and better
schools was the only sure way of accomplishing a thorough-
going reform of society. A nation which made education
freely available to all would not neglect its unfortunate members; it would not have to bear the burdens of pauperism,
crime, immorality, and intemperance; and it would be prepared
to meet social crises with wisdom and humanity.

The task of the reformers, however, was not to praise education, which nearly everybody did, but to obtain adequate
financial support for it. They did not ask free schools for the
poor, since both private philanthropists and public authorities
were ready to provide that. They wanted free, public, entirely
tax-supported education for all children—rich, poor, and mid-
dling—without any stigma of charity attached to it. The story
of their struggle to win this objective lies outside the realm of
the history of philanthropy, and yet it involves the difficult
problem of the relationship of philanthropy to reform. Theoretically, philanthropy pioneers, proves the value of a service,
then allows the community or the state to assume responsibility
for the task, and moves on to some new field. In practice, as
in the public school controversy when societies operating
charity schools presented one of the numerous obstacles to
the establishment of tax-supported educational systems, philanthropy may become a vested interest and display no eagerness
to surrender its prerogatives. Fortunately there are philan-

thropists and philanthropists, and no one would deny that title to Horace Mann, the lawyer, politician, bureaucrat, college president, and reformer.

Mann had been a poor boy who studiously observed the maxims of self-help in his own career, and he preached those maxims with less humor and even more zeal than Benjamin Franklin. It was characteristic of him to find Richard Henry Dana's *Two Years before the Mast* deficient in statistics, wanting in moral lessons, and too full of descriptions. But Mann's earnestness and seriousness were well suited to his time and purpose, and he revealed in all his works a dedication to great ends. He was a figure of some prominence in Massachusetts politics when, in 1837, he accepted the relatively minor post of secretary of the State Board of Education. His long tenure in this office gave him an opportunity to canvass every shortcoming in the existing school system and to promote improvements in instruction, discipline, curriculum, textbooks, and the training of teachers. His *Annual Reports*, each as carefully prepared as a legal brief and as hortatory as a sermon, aroused interest and controversy not only in Massachusetts but in nearly every other state.

Like Howe and other humanitarian reformers of his day Mann found in phrenology an apparent scientific justification for his belief in the improvability and infinite educability of the human race. He had unbounded faith in the practical uses of education, particularly in overcoming poverty. But it was the common welfare rather than individual success that excited him, and it was the religious doctrine of stewardship much more than scientific rationalism that guided his thought. He believed that property owners were indebted to the social intelligence of preceding generations for their wealth and that they were therefore obligated to use it to transmit the common body of knowledge to future generations through schools. He was disappointed that rich men contributed little beyond their taxes to public education. When Abbott Lawrence, in making a gift of $50,000 to Harvard, said, "Elementary education appears to be well provided for in Massachusetts," Mann replied that salaries for women teachers in the public schools averaged $68.40 for the entire school term and that the average number of books in school libraries was twenty-five. In his last *Annual Report* he took a hard look at Massachusetts' latest wonder, the reform school at Westborough. "One tenth part of its cost," said Mann, "would have done more in the way of prevention than its whole amount can accomplish in the way of reclaiming."

In 1848, convinced that a man or child must be free before he could be educated, Mann gave up his official post and re-entered politics on an antislavery platform. During the 1850's, in response to the Fugitive Slave Law, the Kansas-Nebraska Act, and the struggle for Kansas, other reformers also put the cause of the Negro above their earlier interests. Miss Dix was an exception to the general rule because she, in order not to jeopardize her usefulness to the insane, refused to become involved in the sectional controversy. But Howe, as impetuous in full-bearded middle-age as in his Byronic youth, flung himself wholeheartedly into the abolition movement. Charles Sumner, the foremost peace orator of the 1840's, was anything but pacifistic in his utterances about slavery and slaveholders in the 1850's, and Gerrit Smith, a generous contributor to the peace movement, had concluded by the late 1850's that there was no possibility of ending slavery by peaceful means. Smith gave financial assistance to John Brown and was so deeply implicated in Brown's plans for direct action against slavery that he became temporarily insane after the debacle at Harpers Ferry. Theodore Parker and a few other clergymen, not content to denounce slavery from the pulpit, enrolled in Vigilance Committees which raised funds to speed fugitives to Canada or pay for the legal defense of Negroes held under the Fugitive Slave law. Prominent lawyers offered their services free of charge or at nominal costs as counsel to fugitives, and philanthropists who had once given money to colonize Negroes in Africa now contributed funds to send white settlers to Kansas. Amos Lawrence's son discharged his obligation of stewardship by paying for rifles shipped to the free-soil settlers.

If philanthropy means spending time and effort and risking personal safety to aid the down trodden, the ranks of pre–Civil War philanthropists must be broadened to include the men and women who violated federal laws to shelter fugitives, as well as those who raided the South to rescue or abduct slaves. Levi Coffin, reputed head of the Underground Railway, is said to have assisted about one hundred fugitives a year over a period of more than thirty years. The intrepid Harriet Tubman, herself a fugitive, repeatedly returned to the South to lead her fellows to freedom. Some who engaged in this dangerous work paid a heavy price. John Brown sacrificed not only his own life but those of two of his sons. Reverend Charles Torrey, who resigned from a Providence pulpit to work for abolition, died in a southern jail for his efforts. Calvin Fairbanks spent more than seventeen years in prison in Kentucky as punishment for abducting slaves and, according to his own account, received something like 35,000 lashes at the hands of his jailers. One Rush R. Sloane of Sandusky, Ohio paid a fine of $3,000 for assisting fugitives to Canada, while

Saints and Scolds

Thomas Garrett of Wilmington, Delaware, convicted of numerous breaches of the Fugitive Slave law, surrendered all his property in payment of fines totaling $8,000. This doughty old Quaker, undeterred by his punishment, continued to give aid and comfort to refugees until 1861. "The war came a little too soon for my business," he said. "I wanted to help off three thousand slaves. I had only got up to 2,700."

The Civil War came too soon for all the philanthropists. None of their work was finished and parts of it were hardly begun when the fighting started, bringing new opportunities for service.

V

Civil War Philanthropies

Long, too long America,
Traveling roads all even and peaceful you learn'd
    from joys and prosperity only,
But now, ah now, to learn from crises of an-
    guish . . .
And now to conceive and show to the world what
    your children en-masse really are, . . .

right
WALT WHITMAN

The first need of the Civil War was for men to fight it; the next
was for civilians to support and succor the armies; and the
third was for marshaling material and spiritual resources into
an overpowering will to victory. In April, 1861, neither the
North nor the South anticipated a struggle of the magnitude
and duration that in fact took place. Both parties looked, as
Lincoln said in his Second Inaugural Address, "for an easier
triumph, and a result less fundamental and astounding."
Throughout the war, patriots on each side, from Lincoln and
Davis down, complained of laxity, indifference, self-seeking,
and internal opposition that weakened war efforts. Yet from

Civil War Philanthropies

the very beginning the war roused the charitable energies and impulses of the American people, and of American women in particular, as they had never been aroused before. Charitable enterprises were of great importance, not only in providing needed supplies and services to the troops, but in building up civilian morale and the will to win.

"The uprising of the women of the land" (as the Reverend Henry W. Bellows, chairman of the United States Sanitary Commission called the phenomenon) began on the day Lincoln summoned 75,000 militia to meet the challenge of Fort Sumter. Women in several New England cities, soon followed by others from New York to Iowa and California, organized to aid soldiers and their families. Before the war ended something like 15,000 soldiers' aid societies had been founded and almost every Northern home had been canvassed for funds and supplies. One of the first women to volunteer for more onerous duties, and almost the last to leave the field, was Dorothea Dix. Although nearing sixty, she presented herself at the War Department in the first week of the war and shortly thereafter accepted the post of Superintendent of Female Nurses. Miss Dix's specifications for female nurses—and she was not one to relax her standards—were mature years, good health, and plainness in person and dress. "No bows, no curls, no jewelry, and no hoop-skirts," she decreed.

With or without Miss Dix's approval, for her authority was challenged by the Medical Bureau of the Army, an estimated thirty-two hundred women served as nurses with Union forces. Among them were six hundred Roman Catholic nuns, frowned upon by Miss Dix, but highly esteemed by the troops and hospital surgeons. More to the superintendent's liking were the three Woolsey sisters, daughters of the president of

77

Yale, and Katharine Prescott Wormeley, whose father was a British admiral. Illness cut short Louisa May Alcott's career as a nurse, but she served long enough to gather material for *Hospital Sketches* (1863), her first successful book. Most of the regular female nurses served in hospitals behind the lines, but "Mother" Mary Ann Bickerdyke, once a student at Oberlin and an herb-doctor at the start of the war, worked with such devotion and efficiency in battle zones that she became one of the authentic heroes of the war. Harriet Tubman, following Massachusetts troops to the South, mingled hospital chores with scouting and spying behind enemy lines. After every important battle free-lance "reliefers" and nurses hastened to the field. The most celebrated and ubiquitous of these independent operators was Clara Barton (1821–1912). A former teacher and Patent Office clerk, Miss Barton displayed her genius for obtaining relief supplies and getting them promptly to places of need long before she succeeded in organizing the American Red Cross. The prestige she gained through her war work helped in the later undertaking.

In zeal for war relief the women of the Confederacy equaled their sisters in the North. They organized hundreds of aid associations and during the first year of the war assumed almost complete responsibility for clothing southern troops. Soldiers on their way to or from the front found hospitality, entertainment, and medical service in Wayside Inns maintained by volunteers. Nursing appealed as strongly to southern as to northern women. They took battle casualties into their homes, and after Gettysburg some of them were permitted to go to the battlefield to tend their wounded. In 1862 the "petticoat gunboat" fever struck the Confederacy; in state after state women took collections at prayer meetings and Sunday schools, and held fairs, bazaars, raffles, and concerts to raise money to build gunboats. In the South, as in the North, there were drives for gifts to widows and orphans of war heroes. Southern sympathies and pocketbooks seem to have been particularly susceptible to appeals for the relief of families of men killed either in defense of the flag of the Confederacy or in pulling down the emblem of the Union.

Measured by money expended, the largest charitable efforts, North and South, were devoted to relieving families of service men. Oft-repeated warnings of the dangers of unwise giving were forgotten for the moment as community and state-wide relief organizations solicited contributions from farmers, merchants, railroad companies, factory owners, and workers, and showered gifts on the needy. Local, county, and state aid in the form of enlistment bounties and direct relief to dependent families seems to have been even more bountiful. Wartime generosity brought increased public debt and higher taxes, factors which had considerable bearing on the revival of hostility to public poor relief in the postwar years.

Religious charities flourished on both sides of the battle lines. "Both read the same Bible, and pray to the same God; and each invokes His aid against the other," mused Lincoln in 1864. The Bible Society of the Confederacy, with some assistance from the American Bible Society, labored to collect Bibles and testaments for distribution to southern soldiers; and the Evangelical Tract Society of Petersburg, Virginia published a religious paper and kept rebel troops well supplied with tracts against swearing, drinking, and gambling. In the North, the work of the Christian Commission was generously supported by the evangelical churches, the Young Men's Christian Associations, the American Tract Society, and business firms such as the Baldwin Locomotive Company, which gave 10 per cent of annual earnings during the war years. The Christian Commission waged an aggressive campaign to furnish Union soldiers with material and spiritual comforts. It sent boxes of food, clothing, and religious literature to troops and employed a large staff of delegates, mainly clergymen on leave from their congregations, to distribute supplies, preach sermons, and conduct prayer meetings in army camps and to preform such helpful services as they could for the sick and wounded.

It remained for another organization, broader in scope and more scientific in intent than any of those so far mentioned, to demonstrate the real usefulness of philanthropy in wartime. The United States Sanitary Commission, which despite its official-sounding name was privately financed and directed, was organized in June, 1861, by a group of humanitarians and reformers led by Henry W. Bellows, a Unitarian clergyman of New York City, and Dr. Elisha Harris, a well-known sanitary reformer. These men, and others like them throughout the nation, were impressed by the achievements of the British Sanitary Commission in the Crimean War and were determined to make use of the medical and sanitary knowledge acquired at such tragic cost in that conflict. Their aim, in large part realized, was to unite local relief societies into a national organization that would do much more than supplement the work of official agencies: it would use its money, influence, and knowledge to improve conditions in military camps and hospitals so as to prevent needless suffering and loss of life through disease.

In short, the tasks of the Sanitary Commission were to organize and direct the activities of thousands of women's societies and to bring the force of informed opinion to bear on the administration and military leaders. To accomplish these difficult and delicate assignments the Commission, a purely voluntary association, had to rely on persuasion and moral pressure. It would have been strange indeed if such an audacious undertaking had won universal acceptance. As it was Lincoln viewed the inception of the Commission without enthusiasm and wondered whether it might not become "a fifth wheel to the coach." The Medical Bureau, indifferent to the Commission at the start, was later often hostile. Secretary of War Stanton impeded rather than advanced its operations. And religious groups affiliated with the Christian Commission condemned the Sanitary Commission as godless. On the other hand Sanitary agents won the respect of field commanders and received enthusiastic backing from Catholics, Jews, and Protestants of liberal or advanced views. Working in or for the Sanitary Commission were veterans of prewar humanitarian crusades: Samuel Gridley Howe, for example, and able women such as Louisa Lee Schuyler, whose administrative talents later advanced many postwar reform movements. The Commission was unusually fortunate in having as its first secretary general the energetic Frederick Law Olmsted. Already famous in 1861 (and still remembered) for his books on the Old South, Olmsted brought to the Sanitary Commission the vision and foresight that he afterward applied to the planning and construction of some of América's greatest public parks.

From first to last the Sanitary Commission carried on inspections of camps and hospitals to uncover and help correct defects in sanitary arrangements, drainage, water supply, ventilation, and diet. It helped secure a needed reorganization of the Medical Bureau, promoted improvements in hospital design, and developed better and more humane methods of transporting the wounded. Through its local branches it collected food, clothing, bandages, and other supplies; stored them in supply depots; and distributed them through its agents in hospitals, on battlefields and in emergency shelters. The Commission provided lodges and feeding stations for soldiers in the major cities, established hospitals for convalescents, and maintained offices to assist distressed soldiers obtain back pay and bounties or pensions due them. It maintained a hospital directory—later adopted by the Army—which enabled relatives and other interested persons to locate the wounded and missing, collected and tabulated vital statistics on military personnel, and prepared and distributed thousands of medical monographs to surgeons in the armed forces. The greatest service rendered by the Sanitary Commission was to save lives; without it the number of deaths from disease in the Union forces—high as it was— would have been much larger. It influenced later developments in hospital administration, nursing service, and medical and surgical practice. That the Commission was a precedent for the American Red Cross goes without saying; of more immediate importance was the fact that it gave to thousands of civilians a sense of purpose and participation in the struggle for the Union.

Contributing to or raising funds for the Sanitary Commission was one practical means of obtaining that sense of participation. Numerous charitable campaigns and the Greek and Irish relief drives had already demonstrated the formidable talent of American women for fund-raising. All earlier efforts were dwarfed, however, by the giant Sanitary Fairs that the women of northern cities staged in 1863 and 1864. Through admission fees, sales or auctions of gifts, and encouragement to conspicuous giving, these carnivals of benevolence netted about half the total cash contributions to the Sanitary Commission. Fair managers received and profitably disposed of such diverse items as pianos, threshing machines, watches, jewelry, a famous trotting horse, an album containing the autographs of all the Presidents of the United States, and a cardboard representation of the American eagle "feathered" with hair cut from the heads of the President and members of the cabinet. In addition to his autograph and hair Lincoln donated a copy of his Gettysburg address and the original draft of the Emancipation Proclamation. Cornelius Vanderbilt and A. T. Stewart, determined not to be outdone by the other, each gave the New York Fair $100,000. Everywhere the fairs yielded quantities of goods of all kinds—a mixed blessing as far as the Commission was concerned, since the sudden increase in supplies created storage and transportation problems.

In spite of large sums collected at the fairs, financial questions gave the commissioners many anxious hours. Generally speaking, the branches and local societies, quick and generous in contributions of supplies, were slow and reluctant to recognize the need for money to handle and distribute supplies efficiently. The twenty-one commissioners worked without compensation except travel expenses, but the Commission at times had as many as five hundred agents, inspectors, doctors, cooks, and teamsters on its payroll. Inspections and preventive activities, which the Commission regarded as its particular contribution and which were costly to perform, lacked the emotional appeal of relief work. Other agencies competed for public sympathy and financial support, and at least two, the Christian Commission and the Western Sanitary Commission (an independent organization which conducted large-scale relief operations west of the Mississippi) were serious rivals. Bellows and Olmsted, stressing the constructive and scientific aspects of their Commission's program, looked to insurance companies for assistance; they found a valuable ally in Thomas Starr King, a popular and influential San Francisco preacher who was able to channel the lion's share of the Far West's exuberant contributions to the United States Sanitary Commission. Pope Pius IX's gift of $500 for suffering soldiers found its way, after a roundabout journey, into the treasury of the Commission. English and European branches raised some money abroad, and a rich American dentist who lived in Paris paid for the Commission's prize-winning exhibit at the Paris World's Fair of 1867. Contributions to the Sanitary Commission and its branches amounted to an estimated $25,000,000, a sum considerably larger than that raised by any of its rivals. Money gifts made up about $7,000,000 of the total, and the remainder represented the value of supplies and services furnished the Commission.

While the Sanitary and Christian Commissions organized assistance for fighting men, other groups, including many prewar abolitionists, sought means to help the Negro, for the "fundamental and astounding" result of the war, apparent long before victory had been won, was the ending of slavery. From the beginning of the war fugitive slaves had made their way to Fortress Monroe and other Union-held positions in the South, and as northern armies occupied portions of the Confederacy the number of refugee, abandoned, and captured slaves in or on Union hands rapidly increased. The status of these Negroes was at first uncertain, but step by step in 1862 actions of both the Congress and the President conferred immediate freedom on some and made it clear that emancipation awaited all. Early in 1862 societies were organized in Boston, New York, and Philadelphia to send money, clothing, books, teachers, missionaries, and plantation supervisors to distitute Negroes in the Sea Islands. In the next three years these original societies swelled into regional and national freedmen's aid associations which undertook to relieve the physical and spiritual wants of Negroes in conquered parts of the South and to train them for citizenship.

The relief and other assistance provided by these associations were desperately needed. Military officers and treasury agents had dealt with the freedmen as best they could, occasionally in an enlightened manner. But investigations conducted in 1863 by Robert Dale Owen, Samuel Gridley Howe, and James McKaye of the Freedmen's Inquiry Commission and James Yeatman of the Western Sanitary Commission revealed shocking conditions in the "contraband" camps and on plantations taken over by the government and leased to private individuals. McKaye estimated that neglect and disease had killed one-fourth of the Negroes herded in the contraband camps. Yeatman warned that unless the conditions of the freedmen were drastically bettered "one-half are doomed to die in the process of freeing the rest." The freedmen's aid associations redoubled their efforts and were able to report substantial progress in religious uplift and education. To their credit, however, they realized that the job was too big for private philanthropy. In December, 1863, a joint committee representing the freedmen's aid societies of Boston, New York, Philadelphia, and Cincinnati urged Lincoln to recommend establishment of "a regularly constituted government bureau, with all the machinery and civil powers of the government behind it," to supervise and care for freedmen. Voluntary agencies, they said, simply could not carry out such a gigantic task "were their resources ten times what they are, and ten times what they can be made."

American Philanthropy

It took more than a year of further agitation by the freedmen's aid societies and other interested groups before Congress, in March, 1865, authorized establishment in the War Department of a Bureau of Refugees, Freedmen, and Abandoned Land. Lincoln died before naming a commissioner for the Bureau. His successor, Andrew Johnson, acting on the advice of Secretary of War Stanton, gave the post to Major General Oliver O. Howard, a West Pointer of distinguished piety. The novelty of the federal government's assuming responsibility for the welfare and protection of large numbers of people whose rights had been little regarded either in the North or in the South assured the Bureau of a troubled existence. The act establishing the agency gave it wide but vaguely defined powers, and few of the Bureau's critics—numerous both during and after Reconstruction—charged Howard or his subordinates with failing to interpret their authority broadly or to exercise it vigorously. As a relief agency the Bureau operated on an unprecedented scale, assisting whites as well as Negroes. It leased land to freedmen, helped them find work, and supervised labor contracts with employers. It maintained courts to hear minor civil and criminal cases involving Negroes, and established hospitals, orphan homes, schools, and colleges. The relief activities of the Bureau brought the usual fears of pauperization, but Howard's policies in this sphere were prudent to the point of harshness. He decreed that help should go only to the "absolutely necessitous and destitute." In theory, at least, the Bureau attempted only to put the freedmen on the road to self-support in a free labor system.

The relation of the Freedmen's Bureau to the freedmen's aid societies (of which there were nearly thirty) provided an example, unfortunately soon forgotten, of the possibilities for fruitful co-operation between a government welfare agency and private philanthropy. The Bureau's relief activities eventually made it possible for the societies to concentrate their energies on education, the work in which they were really most interested. The Freedmen's Bureau was also interested and active in education, but such competition as developed was not between it and the private societies but between rival groups within the philanthropic ranks. Some, like the American Missionary Association, in which the Tappans were active, used education to spread religion and strengthen denominational interests. On the other hand, the Freedmen's Union Commission, a coalition of non-sectarian aid associations, stressed education pure and simple and reminded its teachers that they were not "missionaries, nor preachers, nor exhorters." The Freedmen's Bureau did not succeed in getting these rival groups to unite, and it could not ease the friction between them; but it discouraged duplication of effort in communities already supplied with schools, and it stimulated further philanthropic interests in the education of the freedmen by calling the attention of charitable organizations to those areas where need for teachers and schools was still great.

The Freedmen's Bureau did more than point out that education, prohibited under slavery, was the most urgent want of the freedmen: it provided about half the money spent on Negro education between 1865 and 1870. The Bureau leased, repaired, built, and helped build hundreds of schoolhouses. It protected schools maintained by benevolent societies, furnished transportation and quarters for teachers employed in the schools, and, although not specifically authorized to pay teachers' salaries, found means to assist the societies in meeting this expense. By the late 1860's teachers were in shorter supply than school buildings. The Bureau therefore suggested that the philanthropists establish teacher-training institutions for Negroes, and it encouraged this work by making grants to twenty normal schools, colleges, and universities. The assistance rendered by the Bureau in starting Fisk, Atlanta, and Howard Universities, as well as other institutions of higher learning for Negroes, constituted one of its most important and lasting contributions. General Howard was interested in quality as well as quantity and at one point he declined to help the American Missionary Association found more normal schools on the ground that the Association was already trying to operate more schools than it could support well.

By 1870, when the Freedmen's Bureau ceased its educational activities, the idea of Negro education had taken root in the South. The real question was not whether Negroes should be educated, but how and under whose control. Southern whites resented the Freedmen's Bureau and detested the northern teachers imported by the benevolent associations. They were not willing to allow the education of Negro children to remain permanently in the hands of persons who believed in racial equality and radical Republicanism. However, with few exceptions, such as the devoted women who spent their lives among the Negroes of the Sea Islands, Yankee teachers had gone home before the end of Reconstruction. Recognizing that the South was not yet in a position to make adequate provision for instructing any of its children, northern philanthropists such as George Peabody, John F. Slater, and Robert C. Ogden continued their efforts on behalf of Negro and southern education. But after the 1870's this assistance was accepted, and, as a matter of fact given, with the understanding that it would not violate southern institutions and traditions.

VI

"Scientific Philanthropy"

In the bestowal of charity and in prevention of
misery, the world has reached a new epoch.
DANIEL COIT GILMAN

The twenty-five or thirty years after the Civil War seemed,
to Americans living at the time, an era of stunning achievement in all fields of philanthropy. Later generations, accustomed to smile or wince at the social crudities of the Gilded
Age, have been slow to recognize that generosity and altruism
were as characteristic of the period as acquisitiveness and
self-seeking. Granted that philanthropists and those who write
about them have a tendency to dwell on what has been done
and to pass over things left undone, there was a certain foundation of fact in Robert Treat Paine's boast, made in 1893, "This
last quarter of a century has witnessed a noble outburst of
the energies of good men to help suffering brethren."
Charitable directories published in the 1880's needed as many
as a hundred pages to list and describe the numerous agencies

alleviating misery and combating disease, pauperism, ignorance, and crime. At least a part, and sometimes a generous part, of vast fortunes made by fair means or foul found its way back to the community in gifts to hospitals, libraries, art museums, churches, relief societies, orphan asylums, homes for the aged, seminaries, colleges and universities, and specialized institutions for training engineers, farmers, businessmen, physicians, dentists, pharmacists, and nurses.

When charity reformers and civic leaders of the post–Civil War generation spoke of the arrival of a new epoch in philanthropy they had something more fundamental in mind than the quantity and variety of their countrymen's giving. The magnitude and multiplicity of the outpouring for benevolent purposes rather alarmed than pleased them. What they hailed was the development of a more scientific spirit and method in philanthropy. And it was the spread of this scientific approach, bringing reforms in public welfare and private charity, that impressed them as the great humanitarian achievement of their day. At long last, or so they thought, the charitable impulse was being disciplined, the head was triumphing over the heart, the "machinery of benevolence" was coming to be understood and usefully operated, and "philanthropology," the study of the scientific principles of philanthropy, would soon be as well recognized as any other branch of learning.

The basic principles of the "new charity" would hardly have struck Joseph Tuckerman or Benjamin Franklin as novel, and the almoner who said in 1874, "I can ruin the best family in Boston by giving them a cord of food in the wrong way," spoke in the accents of Cotton Mather. The new charity was actually quite traditional in its point of view and already

"Scientific Philanthropy"

outdated in some of its assumptions and attributes. The scientific philanthropists of the late nineteenth century took the "do's" and "don'ts"—especially the latter—handed down from generations of charity reformers, organized them into a comprehensive system of rules, and applied them more rigorously than ever before in American history.

Although the ultimate sources of scientific philanthropy were remote, experience during and just after the Civil War provided the immediate background for its emergence. The relative success of the Sanitary and Christian Commissions gave new prestige to voluntary action. The Sanitary Commission, in particular, with its emphasis on visitation, inspection, and advisory functions, influenced the development of both official and voluntary agencies in the postwar years. The public health movement benefited from the wartime interest in camp and hospital improvement. A committee of sanitarians, which likened the poor population of New York City to "an immense army in camp, upon small territory, crowded into old filthy dwellings, and without the slightest police regulations for cleanliness," secured a reorganization of health services in the metropolis which was ultimately copied in other cities. Similarly, the belief that veterans were involved in the wave of crime and disorders that followed the war revived enthusiasm for prison reform and stimulated fresh interest in all branches of social science. War commissions and relief associations gave countless men and women of philanthropic disposition a taste for service and an experience in authority they were reluctant to surrender after hostilities were over.

One of those who was not ready to quit was Reverend Henry W. Bellows of the now defunct Sanitary Commission. Another was Miss Clara Barton, who had conducted her battlefield relief operations independent of the Sanitary Commission or any other authority. In 1866 Bellows and some of the men who had worked with him in the Sanitary Commission organized the American Association for the Relief of Misery on the Battlefield. For five years they sought unsuccessfully to obtain American ratification of the Geneva Convention of 1864 providing for neutralization of aid to the wounded in time of war. The connection between the Sanitary Commission, the Association for the Relief of Misery on the Battlefield, and the Red Cross movement is plain, but it was Miss Barton, not the Bellows group, who eventually established the American Red Cross and secured the adherence of the United States to the Geneva treaty.

Clara Barton was a unique character in her own or any generation. Had she chosen to do so she might have qualified for Dorothea Dix's corps of Civil War nurses, for she met the standards of maturity and plainness. She was born in North Oxford, Massachusetts, on Christmas Day, 1821, and once said of herself, "I was never what the world would call 'even good looking.'" Yet she was, by her own account, and despite a stature of little more than five feet, an "imposing figure." She had a magnetism that commanded loyalty and an imperiousness that led one of her close and devoted associates to call her "the Queen." Miss Barton had a remarkable talent for dramatizing herself. "I wrung the blood from the bottom of my clothing before I could step, for the weight about my feet," she wrote in one of her Civil War letters. She took herself and her work very seriously. These are useful qualities for leadership in any public enterprise—and Clara Barton had in addition the *sine qua non* of all the great humanitarians: "What is nobody's business is my business," she said, and believed.

"Scientific Philanthropy"

After the Civil War Miss Barton occupied herself for several years in lecturing on her battlefield activities, in checking hospital and burial records to obtain information for answering inquiries from relatives of missing prisoners of war, and in identifying and marking the graves of thousands of soldiers. She happened to be in Switzerland in 1870 and there met officials of the International Committee of the Red Cross. Work with the German Red Cross in the Franco-Prussian War brought her new laurels and popular identification with the Red Cross movement. In 1877 the Russo-Turkish War summoned her out of semiretirement and fired her ambition to found an American Red Cross society that would centralize and systematize relief activities in such emergencies. It was an uphill struggle, but in 1881 she incorporated the American Association of the Red Cross, and in the following year she had the immense satisfaction of seeing the long-delayed American ratification of the Geneva Convention become a reality.

Clara Barton's success in these campaigns stemmed in part from her ability to explain the provision of the Geneva treaty and the functions of the International Committee of the Red Cross in such a way as to allay American suspicions of foreign involvements even in humanitarian undertakings. But more important, both in the short and the long run, was her conception of the American Red Cross as an agency for rendering assistance in times of peace as well as war. In her propaganda as well as in the constitution of the new society she emphasized opportunities and responsibilities for service in plague, fire, flood, drought, and accident. As the historian of the American Red Cross has pointed out, her idea of what the Red Cross could and should do in peacetime made sense to people who saw no danger of war but who had recently raised large funds for victims of the Chicago and Boston fires and who were all too familiar with the havoc wrought by natural disasters, epidemics, and appalling railway and mine accidents. For most of the twenty-five years that Miss Barton dominated the American Red Cross, disaster relief was the organization's major activity. Although sixty years old in 1881 when her service with the Red Cross began, she administered relief in person and on the spot both in domestic catastrophes such as the Johnstown flood of 1889 and the Sea Island hurricane of 1893, and in foreign crises such as the Armenian massacres of 1896.

The peculiar nature of disaster relief, not to mention Miss Barton's vigorous personality and individualistic methods of operation, put the American Red Cross, in its formative years, outside the mainstream of late nineteenth-century philanthropy. To say this implies no discredit to Miss Barton or to the organization she founded. The Red Cross, which in practice meant Clara Barton, was not engaged in charity as the word is usually interpreted. Miss Barton had a sensible aversion to pauperizing recipients of Red Cross aid, but she was not as hagridden by the fear of pauperism as so many of her contemporaries were. She wanted to give temporary help to normal people who were victims of abnormal misfortune and to render such assistance as she could to restore them to their normal way of life. That, it must be said, was all that those she aided seem to have wanted or expected. As Miss Barton's critics within the Red Cross were to point out, she had no taste and small talent for organizational or administrative refinements. But surely her singular and endearing characteristic was lack of interest in reforming anything or anybody. She did not launch crusades to end wars, famines, plagues, fires, or floods; she simply met emergencies as they arose and to the

best of her abilities. Thus, although the comparison is somewhat strained, she belongs in the tradition of Stephen Girard
rather than of Benjamin Rush.

Miss Barton once served briefly as superintendent of a
women's reformatory in Massachusetts, but her Red Cross
work hardly touched the problem of greatest concern to advocates of scientific philanthropy. This was the treatment of
people who, even in normal times, were dependent on public
or private bounty for all or part of their support. Massachusetts,
the pioneer in so much nineteenth-century social legislation,
took a step toward more intelligent handling of the problem in
1863 by creating a Board of State Charities. In the next decade
ten other states followed Massachusetts' example. As a general
rule the members of these state boards had no administrative
responsibilities; they served without pay (in order to make the
offices unattractive to spoilsmen); and their duties were to
inspect, report upon, and make recommendations for improving public welfare institutions and such private ones as received
state assistance. In an era not notable for the excellence of its
public servants, the members and secretaries of these boards
—Samuel G. Howe, Franklin B. Sanborn, Josephine Shaw
Lowell, and Frederick H. Wines, to mention but a few of
a distinguished company—set high standards of integrity and
competence.

The task of bringing greater efficiency and more humanity
into state welfare services required persistent effort. In New
York and New Jersey the state boards of charity received
strong backing from State Charities Aid Associations, voluntary
organizations whose membership and program had some resemblance to the wartime auxiliaries of the Sanitary Commission. The National Conference of Charities and Correction,

a creation of the state boards, grew into a late-nineteenth-century version of the Benevolent Empire of the 1830's and became one of the most powerful agencies for spreading the doctrines of scientific philanthropy. Even so, progress was slow. The boards and their allies represented informed opinion, but legislatures were not bound to follow their recommendations, and they exercised only shadowy supervision over local poor-relief officers. Nevertheless the boards began the work of policing almshouses, insane asylums, orphanages, and schools for the blind and deaf. They resumed the struggle to obtain state care for the pauper insane and secured establishment of new asylums, training schools, and reformatories. They worked diligently to get dependent children out of almshouses and into state schools, county or private orphanages, or foster homes.

The care of the dependent classes, burdensome enough in normal times, became an even more serious problem when periods of depression vastly increased the number of people needing and demanding assistance. The hardship and destitution caused by the depression of 1873–78 were like the effects of a nationwide natural disaster. Private citizens, the older charitable organizations, and public authorities responded by setting up soup kitchens, breadlines, and free lodging houses, and by distributing coal and food to the poor in their homes. In the emergency little attention was paid to investigation of need, tests of destitution, or safeguards against the possibility that some of the needy might be receiving help from several sources at the same time. First come, first served, was the rule.

Persons of substantial means and enlightened opinion who worried in normal times about the financial cost and social consequences of improper care of the dependent classes were horrified by the excess of "kindly but mistaken charities" during the depression. They deplored the "profuse and chaotic" distribution of private charitable assistance to the "clamorous and impudent," and they complained that much of the municipal expenditures for poor relief went to impostors or grafting politicians and that such doles as did reach the needy had a bad effect on their character and willingness to work. This "peevish fault finding," as contemporary critics called it, was little appreciated in the early stages of the depression. "Are we to let people starve because the means of relief which are attainable are such that we may not regard as altogether the best possible?" asked the New York *Daily Graphic* in 1874. When charity reformers criticized James Gordon Bennett's gift of $30,000 to a soup kitchen, the *Graphic* pointed out that Bennett's scheme gave "all soup and no salary," whereas professional philanthropy proposed "all salary and no soup."

It was not salaries that the so-called professional philanthropists demanded (although paid charity agents began to be employed during the depression) but something better than soup and alms for the poor. They wanted better organization of relief operations, more discrimination in the bestowal of assistance, and more attention to the individual needs of the persons helped. Much of their emphasis, it must be admitted, was negative. They did not urge improved administration of public relief but cessation of all public aid to the poor outside of institutions. Outdoor relief, defined by one of its opponents as "the paying out of funds raised by taxation from provident men to support the improvident in their homes" had long been in ill repute, and toward the end of the depression taxpayers in Brooklyn and Philadelphia were sufficiently aroused and well organized to put an end to it. The saving of money effected by this action in the two cities, and the beneficent results it was thought to have in compelling would-be paupers to become self-supporting, confirmed charity reformers in the belief that outdoor relief was both undesirable and unnecessary. Private charity, properly organized and administered, could do all that needed to be done for the poor who did not require institutional care.

First, however, private charity must be purged of its sentimentality and organized into an effective force. Jewish welfare agencies had joined in Philadelphia in 1870 and in New York in 1874 to form the United Hebrew Charities, and during the depression charitable societies in the larger cities made some efforts to co-operate in detecting impostors and rounders. But it was the example of the London Charity Organization Society, founded in 1869, which most impressed those Americans who were seeking (as a Philadelphia group said) "a method by which idleness and begging, now so encouraged, may be suppressed and worthy self-respecting poverty be discovered and relieved at the smallest cost to the benevolent." Societies patterned after the London C.O.S. began to be organized in the United States in the late 1870's and multiplied rapidly in the 1880's. For the rest of the century, "charity organization" and "scientific philanthropy" were virtually synonymous.

Charity organization meant just that. As originally conceived it emphatically did not mean the granting of relief by the charity organization societies. The founders of these societies believed that there were already too many agencies engaged in giving alms and old clothes to the poor. "No RELIEF GIVEN HERE," announced signs at the entrance to the Buffalo C.O.S., and Josephine Shaw Lowell of the New York C.O.S. did not hesitate to advise prospective donors that all the organization's funds went for administrative expenses and not one cent to the poor.

The basic idea of the charity organization movement was to promote co-operation and higher standards of efficiency among the older relief-dispensing agencies. This objective was regarded as presumptuous by some firmly intrenched agencies who were well satisfied with their own methods and jealous of their prerogatives. With varying degrees of success, therefore, the charity organization societies acted as clearinghouses and bureaus of information. They maintained registries of all applicants for relief, with detailed records of the assistance given or refused by co-operating societies, and they undertook searching investigation of the need and worthiness of the "cases" referred to them. When they discovered a "helpable" applicant, they attempted to find employment for him, or referred him to the relief-dispensing agency best suited to meet his particular need. Through force of circumstances, and not without qualms of conscience, some of the charity organization societies actually became purveyors of relief. Usually, however, they preferred to help the poor by providing such services as penny savings banks, coal-saving funds, provident wood-yards, day nurseries for the children of working mothers, and workrooms where women could be trained to become nursemaids, laundresses, or seamstresses.

In theory, "friendly visiting" of the poor in their homes by volunteers working under the supervision of paid agents was the core—or better, the heart—of charity organization. By this means ties of sympathy and personal interest were to be established between the rich and the poor, and the poor were to be permanently improved and uplifted. The visitors were not to be almoners, for almsgiving was counterfeit philanthropy. Instead of stray coins, visitors were to bring encouragement and advice to the people they visited. From the writings of Octavia Hill, an English philanthropic worker, American C.O.S. leaders culled the following suggestions for volunteer visitors:

> You want to know them,—to enter into their lives, their thoughts; to let them enter into some of your brightness; to make their lives a little fuller, a little gladder. You who know so much more than they, might help them so much at important crises of their lives. You might gladden their homes by bringing them flowers, or, better still, by teaching them to grow plants; you might meet them face to face as friends; you might teach them; you might collect their savings; you might sing for and with them; you might take them into the parks or out for quiet days in the country, in small companies, or to your own or your friends' grounds, or to exhibitions or picture galleries; you might teach and refine and make them cleaner by merely going among them.

Miss Hill conceded that the poor, in their turn, might teach the visitors patience, vigor, and content. But in general hardly anyone active in the movement at the start questioned that the visitors were morally as well as materially superior to the visited.

This conviction of superiority, like most of the original charity organization program, rested on certain assumptions about the causes of poverty and dependency. As a rule the charity reformers were so preoccupied with pauperism that they gave little serious thought to poverty. To the extent that they did think about poverty they accepted the view that it was caused by weaknesses of character, body, or intellect, and curable by reform of the individual. Josephine Shaw Lowell (1843–1905), the principal founder of the New York C.O.S.,

"Scientific Philanthropy"

is a case in point. As she saw it, building character rather than relieving need was the true aim of the society's work. It is not "the poor" but "our brothers" who are our concern, she said. She took it for granted that those brothers were a young and untutored lot who needed stern discipline and careful training.

Mrs. Lowell was a woman of the leisure class who devoted forty years of her life to public service. But to say this does scant justice to the force of character and sturdy good sense that won the respect of her contemporaries. Born into a family of wealth, culture, and liberal leanings, she was the sister of one war hero and the wife of another. All the circumstances of her life, from fortunate birth to tragic widowhood, thrust her into a career of service. She brought to her work self-discipline, matter-of-factness, and a kindness which, if not indulgent, was all embracing. Kindness in her case was based not on sentimentality but on a religious conviction that each human being deserved good from every other because all were sons of God and had an eternal future. Mrs. Lowell was made of sterner stuff than some philanthropists. Although she wrote often of the duty of charity, she did not make a point of stressing, as Cotton Mather, Amos Lawrence, and many others had, the pleasures and privileges of giving.

As Mrs. Lowell saw it, the world was made up of two classes: workers and idlers. Workers might do or be many things, provided their activities were useful; idlers, in her succinct definition, were people who lived off the workers. Unfortunately, workers had a natural inclination to become idlers. The mass of men and women, Mrs. Lowell maintained, needed the pressure of necessity to force them to exercise their faculties. Hence it was dangerous to do too much for anyone lest he lose the ability and appetite for work. Like other charity reformers of her generation Mrs. Lowell also believed that certain undesirable social traits were transmitted from generation to generation and that some groups had a hereditary tendency toward pauperism and crime. Neither Mrs. Lowell nor her co-workers accepted the conclusion of the extreme Social Darwinists that all acts of mercy to the weak in body and mind tended to degrade the human race, but they did advocate putting chronic paupers into strictly supervised institutions so that the vicious and degraded would not perpetuate their kind.

It is not surprising that Mrs. Lowell and other founders of the charity organization movement should have been influenced by the notions of political economy and natural science current in the 1870's and 80's. More significant is the fact that those ideas seem to have had little effect on the actual working of the societies. Charity organization best demonstrated its claim to be scientific by allowing the demands of reality to override the hypotheses with which it began. Investigations, originally undertaken as a species of detective work to discover fraud came to be regarded as diagnoses to ascertain facts needed to treat distress intelligently. Salaried workers, although outnumbered by volunteer friendly visitors, played an increasingly important part in the work of the societies. These paid workers, who supervised and trained the volunteers, were already numerous enough in the 1890's to suggest that a new profession was in the making. In practice, charity organization societies became centers to which people in trouble applied for help in locating agencies that could assist them. Odd and indirect as this service sounds, it was a useful one in large cities where the very abundance of specialized benevolent associations made for confusion. The societies never gave up their efforts to improve and co-ordinate charitable work, and they proved their value in the depression of 1893–97, when new societies were founded, faltering ones revived, and flourishing ones took on new vigor.

Because scientific philanthropy insisted on gathering the facts about the specific causes of each applicant's need, C.O.S. case workers had to report and deal with poverty-producing factors that had little to do with the sufferers' characters. The caseworkers attributed as many as possible of these situations to moral lapses, but even before the gray nineties they were well aware of environmental causes of distress. The labor disputes of the eighties and nineties made some leaders of the "new charity" wonder whether the newest might not be justice in work and wages. Mrs. Lowell resigned from the New York State Board of Charity in 1889 because she felt that the interests of the working people were of paramount importance. "It is better to save them before they go under, than to spend your life fishing them out when they're half drowned and taking care of them afterwards!" she said. "I must try to help them, if I can, and leave the broken down paupers to others."

For at least three-quarters of a century charity reformers had been seeking to prevent pauperism. They had often expressed the opinion that the first duty of the community was not to feed the hungry and clothe the naked but to prevent people from becoming hungry and naked. By 1893 Robert Treat Paine, president of the Associated Charities of Boston since its founding, was of the opinion that the social order itself needed housecleaning. "Pauperism cannot be wisely considered alone," he said, "but the problem of how to uplift the general level of life must be studied as *one whole problem.*" The remedies proposed were still less fundamental than the language of those who advanced them suggested. Scientific philanthropy and social reform had not yet quite joined forces but they were drawing closer together.

VII

Benevolent Trusts and Distrusts

> If a combination to do business is effective in saving waste and in getting better results, why is not combination far more important in philanthropic work?
>
> JOHN D. ROCKEFELLER

The most famous document in the history of American philanthropy—although the word philanthropy does not appear in it—is an article entitled "Wealth" published in the *North American Review* in June, 1889. The author was the "Star-Spangled Scotchman," Andrew Carnegie. Born in a weaver's cottage in Dunfermline, Scotland, in 1835, Carnegie had come to the United States in 1848. As the eldest son of a poor family, he was old if not large for his years, and at the age of twelve cheerfully and self-confidently assumed the responsibilities of breadwinner. "Anybody can get along in this Country" he wrote in 1852. "If I don't it will be my own fault." Andrew Carnegie, likable, alert, shrewd, and able got along famously. By 1889, thirty times a millionaire, he had been a rich man for more than twenty years. For him the question had long been not how to gain wealth but what to do with it. He had reached some conclusions on the problem as early as 1868 and in 1887 had told his friend William E. Gladstone that he considered it a disgrace to die rich. Now, in his famous essay, he proposed that millionaires, instead of bequeathing vast fortunes to heirs or making benevolent grants by will, should administer their wealth as a public trust during life.

The year of Carnegie's birth was also the year in which Tocqueville published *Democracy in America*. Of all the changes that had swept over American society in the fifty-odd years since 1835, one of the most striking was the arrival of that race of rich men whose absence Tocqueville had noted. Carnegie certainly did not doubt that there was a "millionaire class" in the United States. It was to this class that he addressed himself. In assumption of superiority Carnegie went far beyond the charity reformers. His view resembled that of John Winthrop and William Penn, except in one important respect. Carnegie did not say, as those men had, that the great ones owed their distinction to peculiar arrangements ordained of God. He attributed the eminence of the millionaire class to fitness to survive and triumph in the competitive struggle. The trusteeship Carnegie proposed thus differed from traditional doctrines of stewardship. The millionaire, a product of natural selection, was an agent of the public, of the forces of civilization, rather than a servant of God. Trusteeship devolved on the man of wealth because he was fittest to exercise it. In the exercise of his trust he was responsible only to his own conscience and judgment of what was best for the community.

An English critic, astounded by the brashness of Carnegie's scheme, named it the gospel of wealth to distinguish it from the gospel of Christianity. With customary good humor Carnegie accepted the label, and, as usual, he won the encounter; for who can deny that "the gospel of wealth" sounds better and stronger than ' wealth"? As a matter of fact there were religious overtones in Carnegie's gospel. He was willing to have the scriptural passage about the difficulty of rich men entering the kingdom of Heaven interpreted strictly, and he believed that laboring for the good of one's fellows was the essence of Christ's teaching. But, as Carnegie frankly admitted, he did not believe that under modern conditions much good could be accomplished by imitating the life or methods of Christ. Let the laws of accumulation and distribution be left free; let the able and energetic dispose of their surplus as they saw fit; the millionaire class, working toward the same objectives as Christ, but (as Carnegie said) "laboring in a different manner," would someday bring "Peace on earth, among men good will."

According to the gospel of wealth, philanthropy was less the handmaid of social reform than a substitute for it. Wise administration of wealth was an antidote for radical proposals for redistributing property and a method of reconciling the poor and the rich. Carnegie spoke of "the temporary unequal distribution of wealth"; however, like his mentor, Herbert Spencer, he thought that it would take eons, an overturn of natural laws of economics, and an almost inconceivable revolution in human nature to erase that inequality. He believed it was a waste of time to challenge evolutionary processes, and he was firmly convinced that the only alternative to the system that rewarded millionaires with palaces and laborers with cottages was one that would condemn all to hovels. But Carnegie was no less convinced that "administrators of surplus wealth"—his term for philanthropists—had it in their power to bestow benefactions of lasting benefit on their weaker and poorer brethren.

Had Carnegie chosen to do so, he might have said simply that men possessed of more wealth than they could possibly use would be well advised to employ it for the public good. Possibly that was all he really meant. The arrogance of his language and the despotic tendencies of his philosophy should not blind us to the fact that his solution for the problem of surplus wealth was neither entirely new nor inconsistent with American traditions. Although Carnegie preached and practiced giving on an undreamed-of scale he did not propose that philanthropy should shoulder the whole burden of welfare. Far from it. Recognizing the responsibility of the state to care for the destitute and helpless, he urged the millionaire class to concentrate its philanthropic efforts on the able and industrious. His advice suited the temper of the times and the inclinations of self-made men. Coming after so many years of emphasis on the cause and cure of pauperism it infused new vigor into philanthropy.

Carnegie was as contemptuous of almsgiving and as fearful of impulsive generosity as the most doctrinaire charity reformer. "To assist, but rarely or never to do all," was the rule he laid down. Although he made a few bows in the direction of reforming the character and improving the morals of the poor, the assistance which had seemed most valuable to many nineteenth-century philanthropists, he was not really interested in those who needed this kind of help. The uplift he favored was of a different and less direct variety: libraries, parks, concert halls, museums, "swimming baths," and institutions such as Cooper Union and Pratt Institute, both of

Clara Barton. (From Clara Barton, *The Red Cross*, Washington, D.C.: American National Red Cross, 1898.)

Dorothea Dix. (From a portrait in the New Jersey State Hospital, Trenton; reproduced by permission.)

Andrew Carnegie. (From *Life Magazine*, April 13, 1905.)

which he greatly admired. Significantly he called these agencies "ladders upon which the aspiring can rise."

At the start of the 1890's the New York *Tribune* figured the number of persons in the millionaire class at 4,047. Few of these men and women seem to have taken literally Carnegie's assertion that it was a disgrace to die rich. Some of them, however, already were and long had been distributing a part of their surplus during life. Just how many were so disposed and exactly how much they gave it is not now possible to say. An investigation of their giving habits made by the *Review of Reviews* in 1893 reached the sensible albeit equivocal conclusion that cities would be poorer without the parks, museums, libraries, and technical institutes provided by generous millionaires, and considerably richer if more men and women of wealth followed the example of those who gave. This interesting, although not necessarily reliable, survey indicated that the percentage of millionaires who "recognized their obligations" varied from city to city. Baltimore, with 49 per cent of her millionaires listed as active givers, ranked highest on the list and New York, where millionaires were most numerous but apparently least generous, was at the bottom. Donors in different cities had distinct preferences: Cincinnati's millionaires supported musical and artistic ventures; those in Minneapolis gave to the state university and the public library; and Philadelphians were interested in overseas relief, Arctic exploration, and the education of Indians and Negroes. Boston, surprisingly, made a poor showing. "Our Boston millionaires," reported the local investigator, "give money when it is solicited (properly), and they all include in their wills some bequests to Harvard and to Massachusetts General Hospital. That is all."

American Philanthropy

Of all the ladders for those who aspired, free libraries and educational institutions with a practical slant struck capitalists of the 1880's and 90's as most inspiring. Carnegie's own benefactions, like those of so many philanthropists, began with the donation of a library to his home town, and he ultimately gave a library building to almost every community which provided a site and promised to maintain the building. He regarded Enoch Pratt, donor of the Pratt Free Library in Baltimore as "the ideal disciple of the gospel of wealth." Carnegie and other businessmen gave generously to Negro industrial schools, such as Hampton and Tuskegee, which elevated manual and domestic training into character-building disciplines. They were much less generous toward Negro institutions of higher learning. Only a trickle of philanthropic aid, mainly furnished by church groups, went to these struggling, poorly housed and equipped colleges, but, meager as it was, this assistance helped keep them alive. Students at Fisk University took financing into their own hands. Through concert tours in Europe and America the Fisk Jubilee Singers raised funds which permitted the institution to move from dilapidated army barracks to a new building appropriately named Jubilee Hall.

Although some business leaders thought higher education almost as detrimental to whites as to Negroes, colleges and universities continued to be beneficiaries of the millionaires' surplus wealth. "Here is a noble use of wealth," Carnegie said of Leland Stanford's audacious plan to build a university in the Far West, a project which in 1889 was believed to involve the greatest sum ever given by an individual for any purpose. Stanford's avowed purpose was to create a new kind of university which would give a practical rather than a theoretical education. Albert Shaw observed admiringly that the donor was going about the task in the same businesslike fashion he had employed in building the great stock farm where his fast horses were bred.

John D. Rockefeller (1839–1937) was an old hand at giving when, in May, 1889, a month before the appearance of Carnegie's "Wealth," he made an initial contribution of $600,000 toward founding the new University of Chicago. He was then approaching fifty and had been rich, and getting richer, for twenty-five years. But Rockefeller did not wait until he had a surplus before beginning to give. His account book for 1855, the year he went to work, recorded small but frequent contributions to charity, Sunday school, and missions. In the 1850's the amounts sometimes totaled a tenth of his income, and they increased over the years. Even so Rockefeller's benefactions were hard pressed to keep up with his accumulations. Thus in 1888, when he donated $170,000 to various good works, dividends from the Standard Oil combination were returning millions. Not even the rising University of Chicago, to which he gave $1 million in 1890 and a like sum in 1892, the latter "as a special thank-offering to Almighty God for returning health," could drain off his surplus.

The responsibility of wealth pressed as heavily on Rockefeller as on Carnegie. If possible, Rockefeller felt the burden even more than Carnegie, since he adhered to the old-fashioned religious doctrine of stewardship rather than to the new gospel of wealth. Amos Lawrence might have said, as Rockefeller did, "The good Lord gave me the money," but Carnegie certainly did not. As archaic as the sentiment sounds, there is no reason to doubt that Rockefeller sincerely believed it. He thought that the good Lord had given him the money for a purpose and expected him to handle it with care. The steward was faithful to his trust. Rockefeller was quite willing to give, but he felt an obligation to inquire into the worthiness of the causes to which he was asked to contribute. By 1891 he complained that these investigations were taking as much of his time and energy as the affairs of Standard Oil. Help came in the person of a thirty-eight-year-old Baptist clergyman, Frederick T. Gates, who agreed to assist Rockefeller in his benefactions by interviewing supplicants, making inquiries, and suggesting action. As a former fund-raiser Gates was wise in the ways of money-seekers. In his charge, as Gates himself recalled, Rockefeller soon found himself "laying aside retail giving almost wholly, and entering safely and pleasurably into the field of wholesale philanthropy."

Rockefeller's entry into the field of wholesale philanthropy set off a controversy—mainly one-sided, since Rockefeller did not reply to the attack—that continued for at least a quarter of a century. In 1895 Washington Gladden, minister of the First Congregational Church in Columbus, Ohio, and a leader of the social gospel movement, published an article, "Tainted Money," in which he outdid Emerson and antedated Thorstein Veblen in denouncing the ways of trade. Although Gladden did not mention any multimillionaire by name, his attack on the benefactions of "robber barons," "Roman plunderers," "pirates of industry," and "spoilers of the state" was thought to be directed at the Rockefeller philanthropies. Gladden had stated in a sermon delivered to the National Conference of Charities and Corrections in 1893 that the central consideration of charity should be the effect of the gift upon the character of the recipient. Now he raised the question whether a church or university could take offerings of money made in morally reprehensible ways without condoning the methods and accepting the standards of the donor. "Is this clean money?" he asked. "Can any man, can any institution, knowing its origin, touch it without being defiled?"

This was a hard question and it was taken seriously in the 1890's and 1900's when nearly every issue seemed at bottom a moral one. It came up again in 1905 when Gladden and other liberal clergymen objected to the acceptance by the Congregational Board of Foreign Missions of a $100,000 gift from Rockefeller. The controversy simmered down after it was revealed that the Board had solicited Rockefeller for the money. Moral questions are notoriously difficult to resolve and in this case no consensus could be reached because Rockefeller's character was defended as ardently as it was attacked, and eminent moralists pointed out that the purpose of the gift was as worthy of consideration, and easier to judge, than the origin of the money.

Jane Addams (1860–1935) of Hull House, who was already beginning to occupy an unenviable distinction as "the conscience of the nation," was one of the few public figures who viewed the tainted money issue with detachment. In the 1890's she rejected an offer of $20,000 for a Hull House project on the grounds that the donor's bad record as an employer made it unthinkable to accept his sponsorship of the undertaking, a co-operative boarding house for working girls, but she refused to become embroiled in the public debate over tainted money. Her conscience was sensitive and she was accustomed to drawing fine ethical distinctions. As a rule, however, she avoided passing moral judgments on people. It was the unrighteousness of conditions that troubled her, and movements for the fulfilment of democracy that excited her.

Miss Addams had founded Hull House, the best known of

the early settlement houses, in the same year—1889—that Andrew Carnegie enunciated the gospel of wealth. Like him, she hoped to establish ties of sympathy between rich and poor, but her purpose and methods differed from his. She made those differences clear when she confessed that the settlement movement was based on emotion as much as conviction, that it represented an outlet for sentiments of universal brotherhood, and that it appealed to persons who had "a bent to express in social service and in terms of action the spirit of Christ." While Carnegie proposed building ladders upon which the ambitious poor could rise, Miss Addams and other settlement leaders went to live with the poor. The settlement houses were designed to offer educated young men and women a means of getting in touch with the "starvation struggle" of the masses. Once the settlement workers had established friendly relations with their underprivileged neighbors and learned their needs, they could join with them in efforts to improve the common life. Perhaps this was a species of uplift. Jane Addams called it "the arousing of social energies."

Settlement houses were only one manifestation of the current of religious humanitarianism stirring in churches and among individuals of all faiths. Around the turn of the century other forces and a host of voluntary associations were at work or organizing to strengthen the social framework of democracy and to restore and extend the principles of self-government. But settlement residents, as Miss Addams pointed out as early as 1892, were "bound to see the needs of their neighborhoods as a whole, to furnish data for legislation, and to use their influence to secure it." Uncommitted to any particular program except flexibility and experimentation, the settlements contributed to nearly all the social movements of the early twentieth century. Settlement leaders including Miss Addams, Lillian Wald, Mary McDowell, Eleanor McMain, Mary Kingsbury Simkhovitch, and others of equal prominence, were formidable champions of the interests of women, children, and immigrants, and effective campaigners for improved housing, health, and recreation. The common attribute of these women was ability to reduce abstract issues to human terms and to translate high ideals into prosaic practice. In working with and for their neighborhoods they came to realize that "prevention," so long the watchword of the reformer, was not enough. There were unsatisfied needs in every community, whether for playgrounds, nurseries, or some closer approximation of social justice, which could be met only by positive action.

It was a sign of new ways of thought that after the 1890's the term "social work" began to replace "scientific philanthropy." The change was related to the growing number of paid workers in welfare agencies and to the development of training courses in applied philanthropy which, by 1910, had become schools of social work. Meanwhile new leaders such as Mary Richmond (1861–1928) and Edward T. Devine (1867–1948) had assumed direction of the charity organization movement. Miss Richmond, who occupied important positions in the Baltimore and Philadelphia charity organization societies and the Russell Sage Foundation, strove to put casework on a professional basis. Through her book *Social Diagnosis* (1917), she exercised a dominant influence on both the philosophy and methods of social work. Devine, as secretary of the New York C.O.S. and editor of the influential social work magazine, *The Survey*, brought the new profession into the forefront of the social reform movements of the Progressive era. In the 1900's social workers retained the old dislike of relief and cautious attitude toward charity. But where scientific philanthropists of an earlier generation had deplored charity seekers, social workers criticized the conditions that made charity necessary. Poverty rather than pauperism was now the bugaboo, improvement of the general standard of living the remedy.

Inspired by new hopes and visions, but still struggling with the old problem of misery, social workers sometimes expressed misgivings about the nature and tendencies of philanthropy. Was the benefactor-beneficiary relationship a denial of the equality democracy implied? Did charity perpetuate the conditions that created poverty? Could philanthropy, tied as it was to the purse strings of the classes who benefited most from the existing order, accomplish anything of importance in building a better society? The same or similar questions were being raised by critics outside of social work, although not so much in inquiry as in/condemnation. To practicing philanthropists who were also democrats and social reformers these were matters of grave import. If answers were not immediately forthcoming, the very fact that the questions were raised and thoughtfully considered had a wholesome influence on philanthropic developments.

Developments of great significance were under way. Rockefeller and Carnegie had retired from business in 1897 and 1901, respectively, but they still faced the problem of what to do with mounting fortunes. By 1901 even wholesale philanthropy of the sort each had been practicing for a decade was inadequate to dispose of accumulations totaling not tens but hundreds of millions. Some more effective method of organizing and conducting what Rockefeller called "this business of benevolence" must be devised. To Rockefeller the answer was plain. Put your surplus money in a trust, he advised the "men of worth and position" gathered to celebrate the tenth anniversary of the founding of the University of Chicago: "Let us erect a foundation, a trust, and engage directors who will make it a life work to manage, with our personal co-operation, this business of benevolence properly and effectively."

In the dozen years after 1901, as if to prove that philanthropy could be made a successful venture, Rockefeller, Carnegie, and other donors established a series of foundations that made earlier philanthropic ventures seem somewhat amateurish. The Rockefeller Institute for Medical Research (1901), General Education Board (1902), Carnegie Foundation for the Advancement of Teaching (1905), Milbank Memorial Fund (1905), Russell Sage Foundation (1907), Carnegie Corporation of New York (1911), and Rockefeller Foundation (1913) do not exhaust the list of foundations organized during the period, but their number, and even the size of their capital assets, was less significant than the boldness of the enterprise to which they were committed. Most earlier charitable trusts had been established for some narrowly defined purpose. The smaller Carnegie funds, designed to promote the donor's particular philanthropic interests, continued in this tradition. The major trusts founded by Carnegie and Rockefeller, however, were limited only to the advancement of knowledge and human welfare. Relieving the needy was not their objective. They would attack misery at its source through the weapon of research.

The advent of the foundations coincided with the era of muckraking and trustbusting, with a leftward trend in politics, growing militancy in the ranks of labor, and a general fear of bigness. According to popular legend John D. Rockefeller, alarmed by muckracking attacks such as Ida M. Tarbell's

History of the Standard Oil Company (1904), employed a public relations counselor, Ivy Lee, who advised him to increase his benefactions in order to buy public favor. Actually Lee did not become associated with Rockefeller until 1914, more than twenty years after Rockefeller had become a wholesale philanthropist. Frederick T. Gates, the principal architect of Rockefeller's benefactions, was aware of and presumably not averse to allaying popular animosity toward his employer. Gates, however, was a clergyman and businessman rather than a public relations expert. He was mainly concerned with helping Rockefeller administer a vast fortune wisely and beneficently.

Interestingly enough, the organization of large philanthropic trusts aroused little opposition until 1910. In that year a bill to incorporate the Rockefeller Foundation was introduced in Congress. By this time anything bearing Rockefeller's name or financed by Standard Oil money was bound to provoke controversy. Opponents revived the slogans of the tainted-money debate and likened Rockefeller's gifts to the Trojan horse and the kiss of Judas. The move was all the more resented because the federal government was prosecuting the Standard Oil combination for violation of the Sherman Antitrust Act. In 1911 the Supreme Court ordered dissolution of Standard Oil of New Jersey, the center of the Rockefeller empire. The decision made it unlikely that Congress would charter a new Rockefeller trust, even a benevolent one. The opposition of the Taft administration further weakened the foundation bill's chances for passage. Attorney General George Wickersham called the measure "an indefinite scheme for perpetuating vast wealth." President William Howard Taft also expressed disapproval of "the proposed act to incorporate John D. Rockefeller." In 1913, rebuffed by the federal government, Rockefeller incorporated the foundation under the laws of New York State.

The next two years were difficult ones for the foundations. In 1914 several members of the United States Senate attempted to prohibit the Department of Agriculture from accepting grants provided by the General Education Board for farm demonstration work in the South. Meanwhile, the United States Industrial Relations Commission, a body established by Congress to study the underlying causes of industrial unrest, broadened its investigation to include the operation of philanthropic foundations. The newly organized Rockefeller Foundation was a particular target of attack, but in 1915 the Commission's director of research arraigned all foundations for their wealth, loosely defined powers, exemption from federal taxation, freedom from public control, subserviency to donors, and benumbing effect on smaller philanthropic agencies and individual giving. None of this criticism led to legislative action against the foundations. But since the attitudes of beneficiaries are as important in philanthropy as the desires and purposes of benefactors, it is significant that the early foundations began their work in a somewhat hostile atmosphere.

The fear, however, was mainly of possible abuse of power in the future. Even as this suspicion was expressed, other voices were calling attention to the present need for the foundations and to their possibilities for good. The Russell Sage Foundation had already proved its usefulness to social work and social reform by financing the Pittsburgh Survey and by assisting the National Tuberculosis Association begin its educational exhibits. The Rockefeller Sanitary Commission, organized in 1909 and later absorbed by the Rockefeller Foundation, demonstrated that hookworm disease could be eradicated. In the course of this campaign the Commission advanced the entire movement for public health. The General Education Board co-operated with the Department of Agriculture in efforts to increase the productivity of southern agriculture. The Board made valuable contributions to secondary education in the South and to higher education in all parts of the country. The Carnegie Foundation for the Advancement of Teaching inaugurated pensions for college teachers which furthered interest in pensions for other workers, and it sponsored and published Abraham Flexner's epochal *Medical Education in the United States and Canada* (1910). As early as 1912 Edward T. Devine denied that foundations would inhibit the normal springs of benevolence. On the contrary, said Devine, the effect of the foundations had been to stimulate both public appropriations and private giving for education, health, and welfare.

"You have had the best run for your money I have ever known," Elihu Root once told Andrew Carnegie. Carnegie, a cheerful and impulsive giver in spite of his theories, managed to dispose of $350 million. John D. Rockefeller, less impulsive than Carnegie, also had a good run for the $530 million he conferred on benevolent causes. "We must always remember that there is not enough money for the work of human uplift and that there never can be," he said in 1909. "How vitally important it is, therefore, that the expenditure should go as far as possible and be used with the greatest intelligence!" The advice, although sound, was commonplace. It was the application that was difficult. Rockefeller's and Carnegie's chief contribution to philanthropy was to found institutions capable of distributing private wealth with greater intelligence and vision than the donors themselves could hope to possess. The great philanthropic trusts they established climaxed the long effort to put large-scale giving on a businesslike basis.

VIII

The Business of Benevolence and the Industry of Destruction

> I suppose we had to do it, and I suppose it was
> worthwhile, but think of the creative job we could
> have done with that money in a world of reason
> and sanity!
>
> GEORGE E. VINCENT

While administrators of great wealth were devising new methods to dispose of surplus millions, promoters of good causes offered the general public unparalleled opportunities for relieving pockets and bank accounts of spare dollars. And what a variety of goods "retail philanthropy" displayed! Churches, home and foreign missions, temperance organizations, church-related or non-sectarian colleges, hospitals, orphanages, and homes for the aged always needed money. The plight of newsboys, working girls, distressed immigrants, tenement dwellers, and southern mountain children was held up for all to see. Disasters at home or abroad brought appeals

The Business of Benevolence

for aid from the Red Cross and special relief committees. In good times and bad local relief associations, charity organization societies, settlement houses, babies' milk funds, free dispensaries, children's aid societies, societies for the prevention of cruelty to children and animals, the Y.M.C.A., Y.W.C.A., Y.M.H.A., Salvation Army, and Volunteers of America advanced their respective, and separate, claims for support.

Opportunities and importunities for giving, already numerous in 1900, increased enormously in the next decade and a half. The continuing vitality of the voluntary principle and a broadening sense of responsibility for improving the social environment led to the formation of a host of new national organizations maintained by dues, donations, and subscriptions. These were the years when the Boy Scouts, Girl Scouts, Campfire Girls, National Tuberculosis Association, American Cancer Society, Goodwill Industries, the Lighthouse, National Association for the Advancement of Colored People, National Urban League, American Association for Labor Legislation, National Child Labor Committee, and a hundred other leagues, associations, and committees came into being. Incomplete as the listing is, the names suggest the diversity of interests supported by private giving. After 1914 the situation was further complicated by the necessity of relieving war-sufferers in Europe.

In 1914 American philanthropy, if judged by the standards of a Rockefeller, Carnegie, or Morgan, was still conducted in a distressingly unbusinesslike way. This was less true of the internal operation of philanthropic agencies, many of which were professionally managed and efficiently organized, than of the relations of the different societies to each other. Both locally and nationally benevolent activities were poorly coordinated. Partly because of the rapid expansion in the prewar

123

years, partly because of the nature of voluntary enterprise, there was duplication or overlapping of effort, rivalry for public favor, competition for funds. Fund-raising in particular was in a chaotic condition. As Mathew Carey had pointed out many years earlier, those who gave were solicited time and again, while many potential givers were either ignored or approached in ways not calculated to stimulate generosity.

These defects were obvious to social workers, and progress toward correcting them was being made before the war. Even in a nation of joiners social workers displayed remarkable ability to find or create organizations to join. They formed conferences within conferences, and established federations, councils, and committees to improve and promote special fields and methods of social work. In a few cities representative councils of welfare agencies took over the task, earlier attempted by charity organization societies, of raising standards and co-ordinating charitable efforts. Federated fund-raising, first tried in Denver in 1888, realized among Jewish charities in Boston in 1895, and adopted in a broader scale in Cleveland in 1913, was shortly afterward put into effect in fifteen other cities. Meanwhile a Danish innovation, the sale of special stamps at Christmastime to "stamp out" tuberculosis, had been taken up in the United States. After 1910 when the Christmas seal campaign became a joint responsibility of the Red Cross and the National Tuberculosis Association, it proved a relatively painless method of raising money and also demonstrated the possibility of co-operation between national voluntary agencies. Sums raised in Christmas seal campaigns ($450,000 in 1913) were small, however, compared to those garnered each year by the Y.M.C.A. The Y.M.C.A.'s leadership in fund-raising went back to the days of the evangelist, Dwight L. Moody, but in the decade after 1905 practice made near-perfect the hard-hitting, highly publicized "Y" drive to attain a specific dollar goal in a limited period through professionally directed teams of volunteer collectors.

Of all American philanthropic organizations the American Red Cross, by tradition, the terms of its charter, and international agreements, was most directly concerned by the outbreak of war in Europe. In 1914 the Red Cross had fewer than 150 chapters and only about twenty thousand members; but even these modest figures reflected an appreciable growth in size and strength in the decade since the reorganization that accompanied Clara Barton's resignation. Its unofficial leader from 1905 to 1915 was Miss Mabel Boardman, a woman of inherited wealth, established social position, high ideals, and fixed opinions who, in making the Red Cross a national organization, shaped it after her own comely image. When war came, Miss Boardman and Red Cross officials promptly offered assistance to sister societies in Europe and called on the chapters to raise funds for war relief. At the time (August, 1914) and for more than a year thereafter, Miss Boardman and her advisers interpreted Red Cross charter obligations strictly and assumed that war relief could legally be extended only to sick and wounded combatants. In September, 1914, amid fanfares of publicity, a Red Cross "mercy ship" sailed for Europe bearing 170 doctors and nurses and supplies and equipment to establish hospital units in the warring nations. Partly because of the expense involved in maintaining these units, they were withdrawn in October, 1915, but, to the extent that the Allied blockade permitted, the Red Cross continued to send medical and hospital supplies to the fighting forces of both sides.

In fact, as events in the very first months of the war proved, medical assistance for combatants was much less needed than relief to civilians in occupied countries, to refugees from war zones, and to sufferers from disease and famine caused by military destruction, blockade, and the disruption of normal life. Belgium was the immediate problem. There, in the space of a single month, an industrious, thriving, populous nation was reduced to destitution, its industry, trade, and transportation destroyed. By autumn, with stores and warehouses empty, and factories closed, almost the entire population, numbering some 7,500,000, was in desperate straits. On October 16, 1914, Brand Whitlock, the American minister in Brussels, cabled President Wilson, "In two weeks the civil population of Belgium, already in misery, will face starvation." That Belgium did not starve was due almost entirely to the efforts of an unofficial, unincorporated organization set up in London about a week after Whitlock sent his message to Wilson.

The Commission for Relief in Belgium grew out of an attempt made by a Belgian relief committee to buy food in England. The Belgian group sent Millard K. Shaler, an American mining engineer then living in Brussels, to London to make the purchase. In London, Shaler sought out another mining engineer, Herbert Hoover, who had recently won fame by directing the relief and repatriation of thousands of American travelers stranded in Europe at the start of the war. When British officials refused to grant Shaler a shipping permit for the goods he had bought, Hoover and Shaler appealed for assistance to Ambassador Walter Hines Page. In co-operation with other neutral diplomats, Page obtained a guarantee from Germany that Belgian relief supplies would not be requisitioned by the occupation forces and arranged with Allied governments to allow those supplies to pass through the blockade. And, with the help of a Quaker conscience, Hoover made a wise decision. He exchanged a $100,000-a-year business career for the difficult and unremunerated post of chairman of the Commission for Relief in Belgium, a step which was to lead him, leap by leap, into positions of helpfulness and power such as few men have known.

The task of the C.R.B. was to acquire, by purchase or gift, the tons upon tons of food and clothing needed to sustain the people of Belgium, and later of German-occupied portions of northern France; to assemble and transport these supplies from all over the world; and, as a neutral agency, to oversee their distribution or sale (to those who could afford to buy) by Belgian and French relief committees. In the best of circumstances the task would have been immense, and the difficulty of performing it in the midst of war can scarcely be imagined. Fortunately, in addition to the brilliant leadership of Hoover and his staff—which included, among others, a contingent of Rhodes Scholars—the C.R.B. had the co-operation of the belligerents and the warm support of world opinion. In the two and a half years of American neutrality no philanthropic cause found wider favor in the United States; but supplies and money came from other countries, too, and in proportion to population New Zealand made the largest contribution. The Commission could not have accomplished its work, however, had it depended solely on voluntary contributions of philanthropic individuals or groups. All told these amounted to about $52 million, while the monthly expenditures of the Commission ran from $5 million at the outset to a high of $30 million in 1918. By far the greater part of the approximately $1 billion spent by the C.R.B. between November, 1914, and August,

1919, came from Belgian government funds on deposit abroad, subsidies by the British and French governments, and, after 1917, United States government loans. After the United States entered the war the work of the Commission continued under Dutch and Spanish sponsorship.

One of the agencies which assisted the C.R.B. at the start of its operations was the Rockefeller Foundation. The Foundation, just beginning its mission of promoting "the well-being of mankind throughout the world," had not contemplated entering the field of direct relief. It had intended to "go to the root of individual or social ill-being or misery" and had assumed that its proper work lay in the advancement of public health through medical research, education, and demonstration. Nevertheless, in the autumn of 1914 the Rockefeller Foundation provided a depot for the use of the C.R.B., purchased almost a million dollars worth of food for the Commission, chartered ships, and advanced funds for freight charges. Meanwhile, the Foundation appointed a War Relief Commission, headed by Wickliffe Rose, who had been in charge of the Rockefeller Sanitary Commission's campaign against hookworm, and including Ernest Bicknell, on leave from his position as national director of the American Red Cross. This Commission investigated relief needs in all the nations at war, established a European headquarters in Switzerland, conducted a variety of relief programs on its own, and provided funds to assist other agencies in their work.

In all, one hundred and thirty American agencies were participating, directly or indirectly, in war relief at the end of the period of American neutrality. They had sponsored activities ranging from sewing classes for Belgian refugees in Holland to educational, recreational, religious, and welfare services of Y.M.C.A. secretaries in prisoner-of-war camps. The Red Cross conducted a successful campaign against typhus in Serbia in 1915 and, at the end of that year, reversing its earlier policy, became active in civilian relief. The American Committee for Armenian and Syrian Relief raised money to feed and shelter refugees in Turkey, Persia, and Russia; and the American Jewish Relief Committee attempted against insuperable odds to get aid to Poland, where hundreds of thousands of civilians—facing the same problem as the Belgians —perished from disease and starvation. Nowhere were humanitarian efforts conducted on as large a scale or as generously supported as in Belgium. Even there, and to a much greater extent elsewhere, the tightening Allied blockade—which at last declared contraband even such items as rubber gloves for surgeons—interfered with the flow of supplies. Voluntary philanthropy was at best but a feeble weapon to oppose the engines of war, and all that could be done by American agencies met but a minute part of an overwhelming need.

James T. Shotwell, general editor of the *Economic and Social History of the World War* (a 150-volume work which was not completed until the eve of World War II), observed in 1929 that the most remarkable thing about the war was not that it involved so many people but that it involved them so completely. For Americans the period of total involvement was far shorter than for other major participants. Brief though the experience was, it accelerated and accentuated tendencies that were to give twentieth-century American civilization a distinctive character. This was as true of philanthropy as of other aspects of American life.

The changes worked by war were most obvious in the American Red Cross. In April, 1917, President Wilson summoned a conference of businessmen and financiers to discuss the financing of the Red Cross war program. These men promised the Red Cross increased support from the business community, providing its administration was strengthened by appointment of a War Council. In May, 1917, the War Council occupied the newly completed national headquarters building and transformed the Red Cross from an agency of neutrality and humanity into an auxiliary of the United States armed forces. The War Council selected as its chairman Henry P. Davison, a member of J. P. Morgan and Company, and he in turn named other leading bankers, corporation executives, and, inevitably, a public relations expert, to top positions in the organization. At the time of Davison's appointment it had been said that he was the kind of man who could make the Red Cross a "50 million dollar proposition instead of a 5 million dollar one." Davison did more than that. One of his first decisions was to set the goal for the 1917 fund drive at $100 million.

This figure—a sum fifty times as large as the Red Cross had spent for war relief between 1914 and 1917, and much larger than any voluntary organization had ever before attempted to raise—is as good a symbol as any of the daring and vision Davison brought to the Red Cross. The campaign to obtain it was no simple appeal to chapters for funds. It was a carefully planned undertaking to convince the public that every dollar given to the Red Cross was a demonstration of patriotism and a contribution to victory. To assist in conducting the campaign the Red Cross borrowed Charles S. Ward, the Y.M.C.A.'s most successful money-raiser, and seventy-five experienced Y.M.C.A. secretaries. Campaign leaders, working with amazing speed, assigned quotas to individual cities and towns, rallied community and business leaders to the cause, organized thousands of volunteer workers, and prepared the countless forms, posters, advertising layouts, and publicity releases to be used in the drive. Conducted in June, hard on the heels of the First Liberty Loan, the campaign not only achieved but exceeded the goal. Similar methods applied with more time for planning carried the 1918 drive to the astonishing total of about $175 million. In all the Red Cross collected $400 million during the war and postwar years, and membership, which stood at about a quarter of a million at the start of 1917, had reached twenty-one million by the start of 1919.

With vastly increased funds and members the Red Cross was in a position to render effective assistance both to American troops and to civilians and fighting men in the Allied countries. From the outset aid to the Allies, especially France, loomed large in Davison's program for the Red Cross. The organization ultimately spent considerably more in assisting refugees, children, the families of French soldiers, and the French anti-tuberculosis campaign than in services for the American Expeditionary Force. In World War I the Red Cross supplemented Army and Navy medical departments much more directly than in World War II. It recruited men for the ambulance corps and nurses for the Army, Navy, and Public Health Service; and set up, equipped, staffed and sent overseas numerous base (1,000-bed) hospitals and smaller hospital units.

While the Red Cross had exclusive responsibility for supplementary relief for the sick and wounded, it shared responsibility —that is, competed with—a number of other philanthropic agencies in serving able-bodied soldiers and sailors. The Commission on Training Camp Activities maintained some semblance of order in the United States by permitting the Red Cross to distribute supplies and perform social work through field directors attached to military units, and authorizing the Y.M.C.A., Knights of Columbus, Jewish Welfare Board, War Camp Community Service, and Y.W.C.A. to develop educational and recreational services in camps and surrounding communities.

Overseas, however, the situation was more confused because the Army did not attempt to co-ordinate the work of the private societies engaged in military relief. The agencies themselves, eager to be helpful and anxious to prove the worth of their services, set up hotels, clubs, canteens, "huts," and "dugouts" wherever they could, jockeyed for position and favor, and became embroiled in unwholesome religious and institutional rivalries. The result was spotty and uneven service, some areas being oversupplied with facilities, while others received not so much as a baseball, chocolate bar, or magazine from the societies. Agencies like the Y.M.C.A. which attempted to do most suffered criticism for sins of omission and commission; those like the Salvation Army which attempted relatively little won extravagant praise. In the long run the confusion and competition produced by what Raymond Fosdick of the Commission on Training Camp Activities called "the present policy of laissez faire" was to convince the Army that the morale services attempted by the societies should not be left to private agencies. "Morale," as Fosdick stated in his final report to the Secretary of War, "is as important as ammunition and is just as legitimate a charge against the public treasury."

The competition of the private agencies extended from the field of action to the crucial area of fund-raising. Here, how-

The Business of Benevolence

ever, the pressure of public opinion and the influence of Secretary of War Newton D. Baker and John D. Rockefeller, Jr., eventually forced the seven national organizations (other than the Red Cross) that were participating in soldier relief at home and abroad to join in a united fund drive. The United War Work campaign of November, 1918, although inaugurated amid impressive demonstrations of unity, was conducted under peculiarly difficult conditions. The great influenza epidemic, which reached its peak in October, was still in progress and incapacitated both solicitors and contributors. More important, the war was coming to an end. John R. Mott, the saintly secretary general of the Y.M.C.A. stepped into the breach with the startling message that peace was more dangerous than war. "We need not be solicitous for our soldiers and sailors when they are drilling and fighting and confronting the great adventure of life and death," he announced. The real danger and need lay ahead when relaxation of discipline and more leisure would expose the troops to increased temptations. A nation in the process of adopting the Prohibition amendment responded enthusiastically to this and similar moral arguments. Moreover a 1917 amendment to the income tax law encouraged individual giving by permitting deduction of charitable contributions up to 15 per cent of taxable income. This provision, combined with the 60 per cent surtax levied on high incomes, enabled the very rich to give generously of money that would otherwise have gone to the Collector of Internal Revenue. Once again the goal was oversubscribed. In what was then called "the largest voluntary offering in history," the United War Work Fund raised $200 million "to prevent the period of demobilization becoming a period of demoralization."

Peace in truth did present problems, and problems much

graver than the leisure-time activities of American soldiers and sailors. The chief problem was to get food, clothing, and medicine to millions of men, women, and children in central and eastern Europe who were suffering from the worst famine in three hundred years. Fortunately the United States had quantities of agricultural commodities which it was more than willing, for humanitarian, economic, and political reasons, to send abroad. If helping suffering humanity also helped American farmers dispose of surplus corn and wheat, so much the better. The important thing was that assistance was needed and provided in enormous quantities.

Throughout most of 1919 European relief needs were far greater than voluntary agencies could meet. This was the period when Mr. Hoover, simultaneously head of the United States Food Administration, Grain Corporation, American Relief Administration, and also director general of relief for the Allied governments, performed his most remarkable feats of financing and executing international aid. Toward the end of 1919, while governmental relief agencies were being liquidated, American philanthropy assumed the task of feeding and caring for millions of European children left orphaned, crippled, homeless, and undernourished by war and attendant catastrophes. At the suggestion of Mr. Hoover, who had transformed the once official American Relief Administration into a private charitable organization, the numerous groups interested in this field organized the European Relief Council; the Council conducted a joint fund drive in the winter of 1920–21 to which foundations, school children, and community chests contributed $30 million.

Cotton Mather's observation that the reward of doing good is an increase in opportunities to be helpful was borne out

The Business of Benevolence

later, in 1921, when the Russian writer, Maxim Gorki, appealed to "all honest European and American people" for food and medicine for famine-stricken Soviet Russia. Previous proposals to send aid to postrevolutionary Russia had come to naught because of suspicion on both sides. However, in the summer of 1921 Mr. Hoover, now Secretary of Commerce but acting in the capacity of chairman of the unofficial American Relief Administration (the beneficiary of the assets of the Grain Corporation, which Hoover had headed during the war), was able to negotiate an agreement with Russia. The Soviets agreed to give A.R.A. personnel freedom, protection, and assistance in relief operations, and the A.R.A. undertook to extend such assistance as it could and guaranteed that its workers would not participate in political activities. The Russian and American governments, the A.R.A., the Red Cross, and organizations as various as the Volga Relief Society, Southern Baptist Convention, American Friends Service Committee, and Laura Spelman Rockefeller Memorial helped finance the program. A businesslike undertaking conducted to the mutual satisfaction of both the Soviet government and the A.R.A., Russian famine relief constituted a hopeful precedent for the future as well as a successful capping of the international relief activities of the war era.

Nearly all the foundations contributed heavily to the war and postwar fund drives. In the sentence quoted at the head of this chapter George E. Vincent of the Rockefeller Foundation expressed the point of view of foundation executives: war relief was necessary and presumably worthwhile, but it was not the creative job that the foundations hoped to perform. Education and research were the real concerns of foundations, and even during the war they continued active in these fields.

American Philanthropy

Public health, medical research, and medical education—all three, of course, closely related—were the particular interests of the Rockefeller philanthropies. Between 1913 and 1929 the International Health Commission of the Rockefeller Foundation, operating on a world-wide scale and always working in co-operation with governmental agencies, lent its assistance to campaigns against hookworm, yellow fever, pellagra, malaria, and tuberculosis. Foundation philanthropy is often regarded as impersonal, but four scientists serving the Rockefeller Foundation, including the renowned bacteriologist Hideyo Noguchi, died of yellow fever while fighting that disease in Africa or South America.

The Rockefeller Foundation and the General Education Board, in what was perhaps their most important service, made large grants to medical schools in the United States and abroad. The key figure in obtaining and distributing the $50 million which Rockefeller contributed to the cause was Abraham Flexner (1866–1959), secretary of the General Education Board for a decade after 1917. Funds supplied by Flexner, whom Hans Zinsser dubbed "the uncle of modern medical education in America," were not free gifts, but hardheaded investments, made on condition that the recipient would raise an equal or larger sum from other sources and institute improvements in facilities and instruction. The emphasis was on improving the quality rather than on expanding the number of medical schools. Through the assistance of these grants, and as a result of the stimulating effect they had on giving by other donors and appropriations by state legislatures, medical education—backward and neglected in 1910—had been virtually revolutionized by the end of the 1920's.

The Business of Benevolence

A more difficult task, and one much less completely effected, was improvement and expansion of educational facilities for southern Negroes. "The only purpose for which the Negro has asked or received philanthropic aid has been for the support of education," said Booker T. Washington in 1912. Northern philanthropists had been furnishing this aid ever since emancipation. At the turn of the century, interest in the education of Negroes merged with the efforts of the Southern Education Board and the General Education Board to promote the public school movement in the South. "We have no thought of colonizing northern teachers in the South, or of propagating northern ideas at the South," said Wallace Buttrick of the General Education Board to a joint session of the Georgia legislature; "quite the contrary; we believe that . . . your schools must be organized and maintained by you in harmony with your institutions and traditions." This approach was based on the philosophy that progress in the education of Negroes depended on further education of southern whites. In practice it meant acquiescing, at least for the time being, in the development of segregated and unequal school systems. But Negro education, although subordinated to white, was not entirely neglected. Philanthropy continued to provide opportunities for Negro youth that southern states and communities could not or would not undertake on their own initiative. In the two decades after 1911 Julius Rosenwald of Sears, Roebuck, and Company, through various personal gifts and grants made by the Rosenwald Fund, contributed to the building of more than five thousand rural schools. Toward the end of the 1920's the Rosenwald Fund, the General Education Board, the Carnegie Corporation, several other foundations, and Negro philanthropists (such as James and John Burrus of Nashville) displayed greater interest than formerly in higher education for Negroes.

Two events at the end of the war—the doubling of Yale's endowment through the Sterling bequest and Harvard's successful, professionally directed campaign to raise $14 million—augured well for higher education. In the next decade foundations and individual donors, including Edward S. Harkness, George Eastman, and James B. Duke made conditional or outright gifts to colleges and universities that enlarged endowments, created new departments, altered the appearance of campuses, and (in the case of Duke) changed the name of the institution. The Carnegie Corporation gave so exuberantly in the early 1920's that by 1924 it had pledged $40 million in future income to various institutions. Conditional grants made by the General Education Board had by 1925 added an estimated $200 million to the endowments of three hundred institutions. A newer development, fostered by the growth of foundations, was the promotion of scholarship by means of fellowships and grants for advanced research. Some foundations were operating agencies, conducting investigations and performing services through their own staffs. The larger number, however, were fund-dispensers and used part or all of their income to finance studies undertaken by individuals or groups independent of their control. The latter course, as the Rockefeller Foundation early learned, was especially necessary in controversial areas, such as the social sciences, where the objectivity of the investigation must be clearly demonstrated.

Even in the 1920's questions were raised whether foundation-financed research could be objective and whether institutions accepting aid from foundations and corporations could maintain their integrity. There was a flare-up of the old tainted-money debate in 1925 when the board of regents of the University of Wisconsin, in an action both praised and derided, resolved not to accept gifts from "incorporated educational endowments"—although it continued to accept donations from the Wisconsin Manufacturers' Association, public utility companies, and other corporations. Generally speaking, however, scholars were more interested in securing adequate support for research than in quibbling about its source; and obtaining funds from foundations for fellowships, grants-in-aid, and other research subsidies became one of the tasks of the American Council of Learned Societies and the Social Science Research Council. In addition to research projects of individual scholars, foundations supported such large-scale co-operative ventures as the *Encyclopedia of the Social Sciences* and the *Economic and Social History of the World War.* It was not a foundation, however, but the New York Times Company which financed preparation and publication of the original twenty volumes of the *Dictionary of American Biography;* and it was a private citizen, John D. Rockefeller, Jr., who gave the Library of Congress $500,000 to begin the enormous task of reproducing material relating to American history in the archives of foreign countries.

Whether performed by great donors such as Mr. Rockefeller, Jr. (whose personal benefactions included gifts for the resurrection of Colonial Williamsburg and toward the restoration of Versailles, Reims Cathedral, and Fontainebleau), or by men and women of lesser means, individual giving remained the mainstay of philanthropy. Foundations had increased to two hundred by 1930 and annually poured millions of dollars into selected channels of benevolence. Their aggregate endowment, however, approximately $1 billion, was only about half what Americans gave each year for philanthropic purposes. Habits of giving and techniques of raising money developed during the war continued in the 1920's. Each year the springs of charity poured out a golden flood: $1.75 billion in 1921, $2 billion in 1924 and 1925, almost $2.5 billion in 1928.

During the 1920's the business of benevolence developed professionals, not only in the arts of casework, but in the specialty of fund-raising. The former were notoriously underpaid; the latter were well rewarded for their services. Social workers, influenced by contemporary trends in psychiatry and interested in techniques of helpfulness, became increasingly concerned with complex problems of individual adjustment to social stress. Professional fund-raising companies counseled and otherwise assisted fund-seeking institutions to reach their goals, charging a flat fee or a percentage of the collection. By the end of the 1920's there were twenty firms of this sort in New York City alone; their clients included leading colleges, churches, and community chests.

Spurred by the success of the war drives, the community chest movement spread from 40 cities in 1919 to about 350 a decade later. At the outset federated financing had been opposed both by strong agencies which had no difficulty in raising money and by those who saw in it another example of business domination. Acceptance of the community chest idea, which of course was by no means complete, reflected the force of the "New Era" concept of co-operation in all areas of enterprise. The community chest reduced competition and promoted rational distribution of charitable profits. It expanded the number of givers, increased the amount of money available for social work, and ultimately released social agencies from dependence upon a few well-to-do givers. The chest, sometimes called "the budget plan of benevolence," made giving less an act of personal charity than a form of community citizenship, almost as essential as the payment of taxes.

The outpouring of money for philanthropy was matched only by the praise heaped on it. From time to time, it is true, doubts were expressed about the wisdom of undue reliance by society upon private benefactions. But critics of business civilization seldom questioned American generosity and defenders frequently boasted of it. In 1928, a year which saw five hundred lump-sum gifts of $1 million or more, the *Saturday Evening Post* characterized the charitable zeal of business leaders as a "practical application of the golden rule." "We work, and we work hard, not for the money itself but for the good that may be done with it," said the *Philadelphia Inquirer* early in 1929. And a sober historian, Marcus W. Jernegan, writing in a learned journal in March, 1929, affirmed the popular view: "Never in the world's history have such unprecedented amounts of money been granted by private and public agencies to alleviate human suffering."

Professor Jernegan's inclusion of public agencies was significant. Even before the depression public expenditures for welfare were growing more rapidly than private contributions to charity. State after state had adopted special relief programs for dependent children, the blind, and the aged. State appropriations for mental hospitals and schools for blind and deaf children increased; so also did local outlays for public health nursing, baby clinics, dispensaries, hospitals, and sanatoriums. Nevertheless, at the very crest of prosperity, aid to the needy was already straining the budget of family welfare societies. In April, 1929, the *Survey Graphic* devoted an entire issue to problems raised by what was then called technological unemployment. All too soon—although not soon enough—the normal business of benevolence would yield the stage to the grim business of relief.

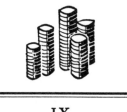

IX

A Time to Remember

The effort to make voluntary charity solve the
problems of a major social crisis . . . results only
in monumental hypocrisies and tempts selfish people to regard themselves as unselfish.

REINHOLD NIEBUHR

Almsgiving, a practice long out of fashion in philanthropic
circles, came back into style in the first two years of the great
depression. Little was heard in 1930 and 1931 of the old warning that an excess of benevolence would debauch and pauperize
the poor, although a great deal was said about the soul-destroy-
ing effects of governmental doles. Financiers and corporation
executives threw themselves into the work of raising funds for
the unemployed and discovered, as one of them said, "There's
a spiritual side to helping those who must have help this
winter." Industrialists lent warehouses for use as shelters for
the homeless. Al Capone, Y.M.C.A.'s, newspaper publishers,
and Catholic nuns supported breadlines. A society woman—
so the story went—admiring the breadline run by Mrs. X,

American Philanthropy

"Lady Bountiful of the Bowery," said to a social worker: "Please find out what it costs. I'd love to have one."

These charitable labors were carried on with the blessings of the President of the United States. No one was more disturbed by the paradox of poverty in the midst of plenty than Herbert Hoover. No earlier President recognized as fully the responsibility of the federal government to take vigorous action to promote economic recovery. And none of his predecessors was more firmly convinced that responsibility for relieving distress lay with individuals, voluntary organizations, and local governments. In speech after speech Hoover sought to drive home the obligation of individuals and communities to prevent those "in honest difficulties" from suffering hunger and cold. Time and again he attempted to stimulate the nation's spiritual energies to greater charitable efforts. "Charity is the obligation of the strong to the weak," he said in February, 1930. "Works of charity are the tests of spiritual development of men and women and communities." As the months and years passed, Hoover's praise of charity, "the loftiest of all spiritual qualities," became more fulsome. His speeches usually included some reference to "community service" or "mutual self-help" through the responsibility of local government, but he never waxed as eloquent about tax-supported assistance as about voluntary benevolence.

The President's approach placed heavy burdens on community chests and the American Red Cross. The former, in Hoover's opinion, stood for the sense of charity in individual cities; the latter, which he called "one of the most beautiful flowers of the American spirit," represented "our people in their most generous, unselfish and spontaneously warm-hearted character." Both institutions, to the best of their abilities, lived

144

up to the trust the President imposed in them. Community chests in a number of cities, including hard-hit Detroit, reached their goals in the autumn of 1930 and in some instances raised larger sums than in previous years. "In every city," reported the Association of Community Chests and Councils in November, 1930, "a large part of the increase has come directly from job-holders—persons who may at any time have to turn to the chest for aid." Meanwhile, in one of the most curious and characteristic episodes of the early depression period, the American Red Cross spurned a proposed congressional grant of $25 million and undertook to relieve two and a half million drought sufferers in twenty-three states with $5 million from its disaster reserve funds and $10 million raised in a special campaign. "All we pray for is that you let us alone and let us do the job," the chairman of the Red Cross central committee told Congress in January, 1931.

President Hoover enthusiastically indorsed the Red Cross's rejection of the government's tainted money. The immediate problem was famine, but, as he saw it, the basic moral issue involved was vastly more important. "We are dealing with the intangibles of life and ideals," Hoover said. "A voluntary deed by a man impressed with the sense of responsibility and brotherhood of man is infinitely more precious to our National ideals and National spirit than a thousandfold poured from the Treasury of the Government under the compulsion of law." Statistically minded critics estimated that the Red Cross drought-relief program, the largest peacetime operation in which it had ever engaged, brought those aided an average of 42 cents of assistance per week.

As the depression worsened and the nation, in the President's words, passed through another Valley Forge, the administration launched its most ambitious effort to alleviate distress through benevolence. In August, 1931, Hoover announced the appointment of Walter S. Gifford as head of the Organization for Unemployment Relief. Gifford, described by *Time* as "a 'clean desk' executive" whose only hobby was charity, was president of the American Telephone and Telegraph Company and also of the New York Charity Organization Society. To assist Gifford in the task of mobilizing and co-ordinating the charitable resources of the country Hoover enlisted the services of one hundred leaders of business, industry, finance, and philanthropy. The organization distributed model relief plans to cities and towns across the nation and prepared a nationwide campaign to raise an undisclosed sum—unofficially reported to be $175 million—for community chests and other private relief agencies. By an unfortunate coincidence United States Steel, Ford, General Motors, and other large corporations—many of whose executives were members of the President's Unemployment Relief Organization—announced wage-cuts of 10 per cent or more just before the campaign was scheduled to begin. In the circumstances Hoover's speech opening the fund drive sounded even more cloistered than usual. He dwelt on the "God-imposed responsibility of the individual man and woman to their neighbors" and urged Americans to be their brothers' keepers.

No fund appeal since the war drives of 1917 and 1918 received wider publicity or had a more professional flavor than the campaign of October–November, 1931. Movie theaters and college football teams gave benefit performances. Radio broadcasts carried messages of inspiration and hope to millions of homes. Advertising agencies contributed a series of high-powered advertisements which appeared, free of charge, on billboards and in newspapers and magazines. If anything the campaign was oversold. Although there were no representatives of the unemployed in the President's Relief Organization the first advertisement purported to be an open letter from "Unemployed, 1931." Tightening his belt, as well he might, "Unemployed, 1931" said, "I'll see it through if *you* will!" The second proclaimed, "Between October 19th and November 25th America will feel the thrill of a great spiritual experience." Give liberally, the copy writer urged, "And know that your gift will bless yourself; it will lift your own spirit." Another advertisement, which looked very much like those for toothpaste, declared, "The world *respects* the man who lives within his income. But the world *adores* the man who *gives* to the LIMIT of his ability." Finally, "In one month . . . every city and town in the land will raise the funds that will be necessary to banish from its borders the fear of hunger and cold. . . . Just one month, and our biggest job will be over."

Twenty years later Hoover recorded in a volume of his *Memoirs* that the drive was a success both in raising funds and in "awakening" a sense of national responsibility for being " 'my brother's keeper.' " Contemporary evidence and opinion, although divided, was less reassuring. The campaign did raise a great deal of money, but the total was closer to $100 million than $175 million, and this was nowhere nearly enough to banish from the nation either the fear or the actuality of hunger and cold. Those who chose could take comfort from the fact that 200 community chests, reached or slightly exceeded their quotas and 179 increased previous totals by 14 per cent. On the other hand, those who were so inclined, and they included the executive director of the Association of Community Chests and Councils, could point out that one-fourth of the chests had failed by 10 per cent or more; that only 35 per cent of chest funds would be spent for relief and that this represented only 30 per cent of the total conservatively estimated need for relief in the chest cities. The other 70 per cent was supposed to come from tax-supported agencies. Chest success did not accurately reflect a community's ability to meet the crisis, since exhausted resources or limitations on taxing and borrowing powers made it impossible for many cities to raise the public share of relief funds. In practice a chest goal was more likely to be an estimate of the amount which could be raised than an indication of the sums really needed by welfare agencies. Moreover, the campaign had no effect on sorely distressed rural areas, mining villages, and mill towns where there were no local charities and only the most rudimentary public provisions for poor relief.

While the campaign receipts were still being totaled, a Senate committee began hearings on two bills proposing federal appropriations for unemployment relief. Mr. Gifford was unable to provide the committee with definite information on the extent of unemployment, the number of persons in need, the number then receiving aid, or the standards of assistance furnished the needy. He gave the impression, however, that matters were well in hand. With unintended humor he observed that federal appropriations might be a disservice to the unemployed, since "Individuals would tend to withdraw much of the invisible aid they are now giving."

A number of social workers also appeared before the Senate committee. These witnesses, in close touch with the relief situation in their communities, were much less confident than Mr. Gifford that matters were well in hand, and they were less disturbed by the prospect of federal aid. Two years of depression had wrought changes in social workers' thinking. There was no tendency now to magnify the extent of private benevolence or to dwell on the superiority of charity to public relief. On the contrary, witness after witness maintained that even in normal times private organizations relied on public agencies to carry the major burden of assistance and that in the present emergency it was public responsibility and public appropriations, not private giving, that required stimulation. Walter West, executive secretary of the American Association of Social Workers, testified that the country's existing relief system was primitive. It forced the jobless and their families to bear almost the entire cost of unemployment, since neither public nor private agencies relieved them until they were destitute. One advantage of federal relief, said West, would be to "take off some of the curse of charity." Another witness, J. Prentice Murphy of Philadelphia, advised the committee: "If the modern state is to rest upon a firm foundation, its citizens must not be allowed to starve. Some of them do. They do not die quickly. You can starve for a long time without dying."

Hoover's speech opening the emergency fund drive had implied that philanthropy was on trial. Actually the trial was over. Philanthropy stood condemned, convicted not only of bankruptcy but of more heinous offenses. The fact that private relief organizations, Red Cross chapters, and religious groups such as the American Friends Service Committee were doing what public bodies found it impossible or inconvenient to do received little notice. Philanthropy, according to its critics, was a dodge of the rich to escape taxes and hold on to power. This was an old charge that gained new force each time business tycoons asked others to be their brothers' keepers. "Riot insurance" was the name scoffers gave the businessmen's and bankers' relief efforts. Theodore Dreiser, who had once written with weird objectivity of the curious shifts of the poor now, in *Tragic America* (1931), denounced all charity as a racket, controlled like everything else by Wall Street. Paul Douglas, Stuart Chase, and other liberal economists marveled at the mentality of men who abhorred the "dole" of unemployment insurance and cherished breadlines, handouts, and relief drives as the American Way. It remained for Abraham Epstein, a pioneer crusader for public old-age insurance to commit the supreme heresy. He denied that Americans were generous. In a widely quoted article published in the *American Mercury* in 1931 Epstein declared: "The myth of our unparalleled generosity has no firmer base than the benevolence of a very few men who have distributed small parts of their extraordinarily large fortunes."

That Hoover's homilies on charity should have contributed to bringing philanthropy into disrepute was unfortunate, ironic, and understandable. History abounds in examples of humanitarians who were ahead of their times. Hoover belonged to a different breed: the humanitarian behind the times. In his public addresses he seemed to envisage American society as a sentimental jungle in which the overflowing hearts and tender consciences of the strong would minister everlastingly to the wants of the weak. He revered charity too highly and attached too much virtue to casual giving—so much, in fact, that he was tempted to place the interests of the benevolent before the needs of the necessitous. Possibly because of experience in war and famine relief he tended to equate philanthropy with succor of the suffering. This was an old and respectable view, and tenable in time of war or natural disaster. It was not adequate or appropriate, however, in an era of economic crisis; and it conflicted with a long-established tendency in American philanthropy. For years Americans had boasted of their generosity but almost in the same breath they had decried the need for charity. The constant effort of American humanitarians since the days of Cotton Mather had been to restrain and discipline, not to expand, the charitable impulse. With the assistance of great givers like Carnegie and Rockefeller they had sought and all but succeeded in turning the main stream of philanthropy from ameliorative to preventive and constructive tasks. It was too late to reverse the direction. As the governor of New York observed in August, 1931, the time for platitudes had passed.

To the despair of friends and foes Franklin D. Roosevelt usually managed to avoid either getting too far ahead of or lagging too far behind public opinion. In his attitudes toward charity, as in so many other matters, he revealed an understanding of abiding tendencies in the national character. Instead of exaggerating the moral significance of neighborly kindness, he attempted to prove, as Tocqueville would have said, that virtue was useful. Even in acknowledging gifts to a favorite charity, the Warm Springs Foundation, Roosevelt went to some pains to point out that every disabled person restored to useful citizenship added to the assets of the nation. "By helping this work," he said, "we are contributing not to charity but to building up of a sound nation." Similarly, in calling for state aid to the unemployed in 1931, Roosevelt declared that such help should be offered "not as a matter of charity, but as a matter of social duty." Subsequently he was to defend vast federal appropriations for unemployment relief as a means of promoting business recovery; and still later he argued that federal minimum wage, maximum hour, and child labor laws were necessary to conserve manpower, increase purchasing power, stabilize markets for farmers' products, and make business more profitable. Ironically enough, Roosevelt's insistence —sometimes strained and occasionally comic—on finding practical justifications for humanitarian action appears to have been an important factor in convincing an adoring electorate that his heart was in the right place.

Under Roosevelt's leadership New York became the first state to offer assistance to local governments in the financing and administration of unemployment relief. A number of other states followed New York's example but in others timidity, disinclination to burden taxpayers, constitutional prohibitions, and in some cases sheer lack of resources precluded effective state action. Nevertheless a break had been made with the outdated assumption that relief was a purely local responsibility. After that not even the Chamber of Commerce of the United States and an organization called Sentinels of the Republic (which sponsored a series of radio broadcasts in which prominent conservatives addressed the nation on "Too Much Government," "Government Interference in the Home," "The Menace of Paternalism," and "Our Vanishing Freedom") could block the drift toward federal participation in relief. Hoover stood firm as long as he could. But in the spring of 1932 he asked the Red Cross to supervise the processing and distributing of surplus wheat and cotton to the needy—a task which the organization accepted and performed with dispatch and credit—and in July he gave his approval to a measure authorizing the Reconstruction Finance Corporation to make grants thinly disguised as loans to state for unemployment relief and public works. After Roosevelt entered the White House the tentative steps already taken in the direction of greater governmental responsibility for welfare turned into something resembling a march. The tempo varied from time to time but generally the movement went forward.

When the emergency was over—it lasted for the better part of ten years and was ended only by the greater crisis of World War II—the nation had not only survived but in doing so had entered a new social era. The ransoming of capitalism had cost more money than any government had ever before spent in time of peace. Enormous expenditures for public welfare required borrowing on a scale that only war had previously justified, and the adoption of a revenue program that compelled wealthy persons and large corporations to carry a larger share of the tax burden than they were accustomed to bear. As a result of grants-in-aid to states and federally administered work and relief projects the unemployed were better provided for than in any previous depression. Admittedly this was not saying much. Social workers, not to mention the unemployed and the so-called unemployables, recognized needs which, if they had been met, would have required still larger appropriations than Roosevelt and his oddly assorted supporters were willing to sanction. It is significant that both at the time and later the New Deal was as often criticized for attempting too little as for doing too much. In all likelihood a comparable emergency in the future will be met by prompter and more, rather than less, governmental action.

Incomplete though the New Deal relief and security programs were, they registered a striking advance over the inhumane, archaic, and unsystematic methods of treating distress practiced before the depression. By 1941 the United States had a start toward social insurance systems that would protect workers against some of the hazards of age and unemployment.

It had a considerable start toward federal-state partnership in caring for the aged, the blind, and dependent children. Federal leadership, supervision, and financial assistance had strengthened the states' welfare services and had encouraged states to adopt measures such as unemployment insurance which they had previously been hesitant to put into effect. Preventive measures to forestall or minimize dependency and promote security had been inaugurated, had been approved by the Supreme Court, and had seemingly become accepted as permanent obligations of government. Most surprising of all, in the midst of depression, organized labor had grown in numerical strength, legal status, and aggressiveness. Assisted by the generally sympathetic attitude of the federal government, larger numbers of Americans than ever before had won and were vigorously exercising the right to improve their economic conditions through collective bargaining.

The entry of the federal government into relief financing and the consequent expansion of public welfare activities at all levels of government took some of the pressure off philanthropy. Throughout the 1930's there remained ample need for the services private agencies could offer millions of families on relief and the millions more who, although hardpressed, were not yet receiving relief. No one pretended, however, that private charity played more than a subordinate and supplementary role in the alleviation of distress, and the common assumption was that its responsibilities in this area would continue to decline. Philanthropy was almost rid of the unwelcome task of relieving destitution and almost free to return to more congenial occupations: "pioneering," development of experimental programs, promotion of research, enrichment of cultural life, and improvement of techniques of helpfulness applicable to individuals and families at any income level.

The only problem was money. "Where are the millions of the 1920's?" was a familiar lament. The springs of charity by no means dried up, but they ran at only about half their usual volume. The stock market crash reverberated through the corridors of art galleries and music halls, for even in normal times museums, symphony orchestras, and opera companies operated at a deficit and relied heavily on a few very rich and generous patrons. Proud organizations like the New York Philharmonic and the Metropolitan Opera Company now had to pass the hat to ordinary music lovers. Saving the "Met" became almost a yearly event, nearly as exciting as opening night. The Red Cross, the National Tuberculosis Association, and hundreds of private agencies represented in local community chests retrenched.

Even richly endowed foundations felt the squeeze of hard times. The Julius Rosenwald Fund, for example, could not meet pledges made when the market was high; its endowment was invested in common stock of Sears, Roebuck, and Company, which dropped from $200 a share in 1928 to $10 in 1932. The Fund was saved from premature liquidation by the cooperation of the General Education Board and the Carnegie Corporation, which took over some of its responsibilities, and by changing its program from making grants to engaging in research. Other major foundations, although not as seriously affected by the depression, also adjusted programs to meet the emergency. Grants became smaller and more varied and were directed more toward fellowships and support of specific research projects than to increasing institutional endowments.

The Carnegie Corporation, like the Rosenwald Fund, operated under the burden of commitments made in freer spending days. Nevertheless, the Corporation was able to contribute almost $2 million to emergency relief and social service agencies in 1932–33, and throughout the depression period it found the means to assist art museums and to promote art and musical education. The Carnegie Corporation also supplied the American Foundation for the Blind with funds to develop recorded or "talking books" for those of the blind who could not use Braille (about 80 per cent). The venture offered a classic example of the way philanthropy is supposed to work, because in 1935, after the foundations had perfected the program, Congress began to appropriate money to the Library of Congress to permit nationwide extension of the service.

The depression caught the Rockefeller Foundation in the throes of reorganization and in the midst of replacing old leaders with new. The new officials were less medical-minded than their predecessors, more willing to support research in the social sciences and humanities, and less averse to "scatteration," the foundation expression for retail philanthropy. In 1933 the trustees appropriated a million and a half dollars to expedite discovery of remedies for the depression. No very striking results flowed from this emergency measure, but the grants the Foundation made to the National Bureau of Economic Research and similar agencies contributed to advances in methods of studying economic problems as well as to the accumulation of more precise knowledge of income distribution and related issues. Hardly less valuable, in a time of increasing governmental responsibilities, was the Foundation's aid to the Public Administration Clearing House. This agency, still operating in Chicago, brought together organizations representing public officials in city management, welfare, public works, finance, and personnel administration. The Rockefeller Foundation bore out its claim to be a pioneering institution by lending support to the extension and improvement of instruction in the Russian, Chinese, and Japanese languages in the early 1930's, long before the necessity for such work was popularly recognized.

Despite the scaling-down of benefactions as the economic crisis became more serious, some of the millions and some of the millionaires of the 1920's remained active in the 1930's. Several of today's larger foundations, including the A. W. Mellon Charitable and Educational Trust (1930) and the Kellogg (1930) and Sloan (1934) Foundations, came into being during the darkest years of the depression. The great individual givers, Edward S. Harkness and John D. Rockefeller, Jr., while contributing generously to emergency relief drives, also gave on an even more generous scale to the kinds of projects in which they had long been interested. Harkness, like the younger Rockefeller, devoted his life to disposing of the fortune his father had made in Standard Oil. His princely gifts went to princely institutions: Harvard, Yale, Columbia, Phillips Exeter, Lawrenceville School, the Metropolitan Museum of Art, and great hospitals and medical centers. Rockefeller's benefactions rivaled his father's in size and outdid them in variety. The restoration of Williamsburg, the colonial capital of Virginia, International House at the University of Chicago, the Cloisters Museum, and preservation and development of park sites from Mt. Desert Island and New York City to the Grand Tetons were among his philanthropic interests in the early 1930's.

Restoration projects also appealed to the master tinkerer,

Henry Ford. His attitude toward charity— "Give the average man something and you make an enemy of him"—smacked more of the cracker barrel than of the gospel of wealth, and it was a cracker-barrel world that Ford attempted to reincarnate at the Ford Museum and Greenfield Village in the industrial city of Dearborn, Michigan. The Museum was a replica of Independence Hall that spread over acres and contained relics of old-fashioned ways of doing business, making things, and going places. Surrounding the Museum was Ford's reproduction of an early American village. It revealed, in one fascinating, inharmonious whole, the birthplaces of Ford, Noah Webster, William A. McGuffey, and Luther Burbank, a seventeenth-century stone cottage from England, a steamboat from the Suwannee River, the schools Ford had attended as a boy, a tintype studio, a windmill from Cape Cod, a village green, a colonial church, Thomas A. Edison's workshop and laboratory, the Wright brothers' cycle shop, and the building in which Ford had built his first automobile. Opened in June, 1933, the Museum and Village enshrined themselves in the hearts of countless visitors whose country was even then moving ahead, so Franklin D. Roosevelt said, toward the goal of a self-supporting and self-respecting democracy.

Philanthropy could survive the depression. But could it survive the New Deal? That was the question conservatives worried about, especially after the advent of the new and more aggressive New Deal labor, social security, and tax policies of 1935. Community chest leaders scored a victory that eventually proved to be important when, over Roosevelt's mild objections, they amended the Revenue Act of 1935 to permit corporations to deduct charitable contributions up to 5 per cent of taxable income. Those who professed to believe

MORALE

It wins wars.

It beats depressions.

It lays the firm foundations for prosperity.

AMERICA is engaged in a mighty enterprise of morale building. In one month—October 19th to November 25th—every city and town in the land will raise the funds that will be necessary to banish from its borders the fear of hunger and cold.

Just one month, and our biggest job will be over. Just one month, and we shall have met the worst threat the Depression can offer; and we shall have won!

You can help. Give to the funds that your community is raising. Give generously.

Feel the thrill that comes with victory. Go forward with America to the better days ahead.

The President's Organization on Unemployment Relief

Walter S. Gifford

Director

Committee on Mobilization of Relief Resources

Chairman

The President's Organization on Unemployment Relief is non-political and non-sectarian. Its purpose is to aid local welfare and relief agencies everywhere to provide for local needs. All facilities for the nation-wide program, including this advertisement, have been furnished to the Committee without cost.

Advertisement of the President's Organization on Unemployment Relief. From *The Saturday Evening Post*, November 14, 1931.)

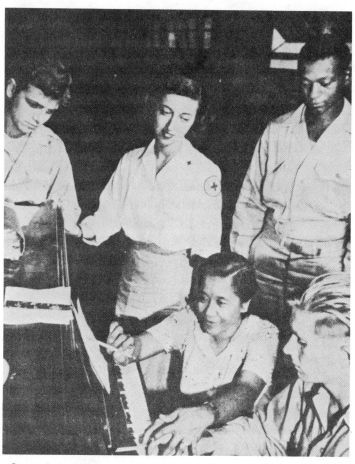

Scene in ARC Roosevelt Club, Manila, 1946. (Reproduced by courtesy of American National Red Cross.)

that business was conducted for no other purpose than to support charities continued to express grave doubts about the effect of higher estate, income, and corporation taxes on giving, and about the implications for philanthropy of the New Deal's allegedly leveling tendencies. Soon there will be no more millionaires, ran the argument. With the goose will go the golden egg. And then what will happen to churches, colleges, museums, and hospitals? The *Saturday Evening Post* warned that government might go on piling up taxes but it need not expect benefactions to pile up too. As if to prove the point the widely publicized will of Jesse Isidore Straus, president of Macy's department store and former chairman of the New York State Temporary Relief Administration, contained a codicil revoking gifts to eighteen philanthropic institutions because of high estate taxes levied by the state and federal government.

As events were to prove, it was possible for both benefactions and taxes to pile up. Since the days of Amos Lawrence large donors had been in the habit of describing their charitable gifts as investments; in the face of higher income and inheritance taxes, the richer the donor, the sounder his charitable investments became. The economic uses of philanthropy were not exploited to the full until the war prosperity of the 1940's. Even in the 1930's, however, it was recognized that a person in the higher income brackets, if so inclined and properly advised, could make useful contributions to philanthropy with little sacrifice of spendable income, and occasionally to his own advantage. In making income tax returns donors could deduct charitable gifts up to 15 per cent of taxable income; they could avoid the capital gains tax by giving appreciated stock to a foundation or recognized philanthropic institution (and, as trustee, continue to vote the stock); and they could reduce the amount of inheritance taxes their heirs would have to pay by bequeathing judicious portions of their estates to incorporated foundations. It was also possible, as Edsel and Henry Ford demonstrated, to arrange matters so that the foundation would pay the inheritance tax imposed on the portion of the estate left to members of the family.

Philanthropy remained in bad repute in liberal and radical circles throughout the 1930's, and for reasons which, if not new, were vigorously and cogently argued. "Philanthropic and business interests are not merely complementary, they are identical," observed one critic in 1938. "Just as you can't run a steel mill without machine guns, so you can't run a capitalist democracy without a pretense of philanthropy." Eduard C. Lindeman, of the New York School of Social Work, whose *Wealth and Culture* (1936) was a study of the operation of one hundred foundations during the 1920's, offered an economic interpretation of modern philanthropy: it was disintegrating capitalism's way of distributing, in its own interest, wealth which could not be spent on luxuries, was not needed for reinvestment, and could not profitably be employed for speculation. Foundations, and by implication all large-scale benefactions, denoted the development of a rudimentary social consciousness in the donors, but they also represented the donors' determination to control social thought and expression. Lindeman's judgment of the trustees of the great philanthropic foundations was even more damning than his interpretation of the motivation of donors. Taken as a group the trustees represented "social prestige, financial success, and middle aged respectability." These were exemplary attributes, but were they adequate or proper qualifications for leaders of organizations supposedly dedicated to pioneering, pathfinding, opening-up of new frontiers of social well-being? Lindeman did not think so. "Nothing," he said, "is so repugnant as the arrogance of those who presume to impose cultural norms upon a society on no basis of warrant other than . . . pecuniary success under . . . a competitive economy."

Since Americans have seldom been disposed to obey the proverbial advice to refrain from looking gift horses in the mouth, it is not surprising that in the 1930's, of all times, they should have cast wary and suspicious eyes on the benefactions of millionaires. The gifts were accepted but with slight thanks. In 1936 the *Christian Century*, recalling Charles Lamb's fable, reflected that to perpetuate the present system in order to keep up the flow of million-dollar gifts would be like burning down a house to roast a pig. The *Nation* observed in 1934 that the best thing that could happen to American universities would be an inability to find rich men to beg from and to put on their governing boards. The broker Charles Hayden's bequest (1937) of $50 million to endow a foundation for educating American youth mentally, morally, and physically prompted the *New Republic* to remark, "If these are the best uses to which vast fortunes can be put it might be better not to permit such accumulations at all." "It is a good thumping gift but it is not enough to justify the existence of swollen fortunes," Heywood Broun said in 1937 of Andrew Mellon's offer to give the federal government both his collection of old masters and the money to house the collection.

Mellon's gift, announced in December, 1936, was a thumping big one indeed, the biggest single benefaction of the decade, and the largest gift that had ever been made to the United States government. The grand total for the collection, the

National Gallery building, and an endowment fund contributed by the Mellon Educational and Charitable Trust was in the neighborhood of $80 million. There was no disposition to reject Mellon's offer but the fact that the aging financier had made it while a suit involving his 1931 federal income tax return was pending received due, or perhaps undue, notice. In the spirit of the time critics deplored the conservative design of the gallery building and worried lest the self-perpetuating board of trustees might discriminate against living American artists. The National Gallery, which opened in 1941 *was* classic in style, but its permanent collection contained works by living American artists as well as masterpieces by dead Europeans. The Index of American Design, a gift of the federal government, comprised 20,000 water colors and drawings of folk and decorative arts prepared by artists employed on WPA art projects.

There were other evidences of the New Deal's patronage of the fine arts, music, drama, scholarship, education, and recreation. Not only in relief but in many other fields the taxpayer of the late 1930's was supporting activities once regarded as primary concerns of the philanthropist. But larger governmental expenditures, instead of stifling neighborly kindness, seemingly stimulated it. As early as 1935 the nation's total contribution to private benevolence, estimated as $2.5 billion, slightly exceeded the pre-depression peak. By 1938, in spite of conservative fears and radical jeers, philanthropy again ranked as one of the leading American enterprises.

If material as well as spiritual considerations contributed to the revival of private giving, it was nevertheless true that philanthropy emerged from the depression decade with a stronger base of popular support. The number of contributors to community chests rose even when chests failed to reach their goals. Annual Mobilizations for Human Needs, the nationally conducted publicity campaigns for community chests, were carried out with all the fervor and dedication of war drives—which in fact they soon became. The Red Cross experienced no difficulty in raising a $25 million relief fund at the time of the Ohio-Mississippi floods of 1937, and, in furnishing assistance, did not hesitate to work with numerous federal agencies, including the W.P.A. and the C.C.C. The President's Birthday Balls and the March of Dimes campaigns of the National Foundation for Infantile Paralysis brought philanthropy into the hearts and price-range of the multitudes. Those who disdained traditional charity had abundant opportunity to contribute time and again to committees, leagues, and alliances fighting militarism, fascism, racial injustice, and violations of workers' rights.

As the 1930's drew to a close, philanthropy still faced difficult problems. It had lost its sentimental aura and it remained to be seen whether the public could be induced to give as generously for preventive and constructive tasks as for emergency relief of suffering. It also remained to be seen whether philanthropy could, in fact, provide the leadership, imagination, and understanding necessary to devise happier social relationships. Meanwhile, as Roosevelt observed in paying tribute to the work of volunteer and official agencies in the floods of 1937 and the New England hurricane of 1938, there was no conflict between private and governmental welfare service. There was more than enough work for both, he said, not only in meeting disasters, but in "our national effort to lift up the lower one-third of our nation to a standard of living that will conform with decency and comfort and self-respect." Before that task was completed another war and a continuing emergency widened the horizons of both government and philanthropy. The problem was not one-third of the nation, but something like one-half of the globe.

X

A Voyage Is Now Proposed

A voyage is now proposed to visit a distant people
on the other side of the globe; not to cheat them,
not to rob them, . . . but merely to do them good,
and make them, as far as in our power lies, to live
as comfortably as ourselves.

BENJAMIN FRANKLIN

World War II was an expected war in which the United
States was not expected to participate. War had been so often
forecast and so long anticipated that the German invasion of
Poland in September, 1939, came almost as an anticlimax. A
decade of crises had familiarized the world with the politics of
terror, violations of treaties, subversion of established governments, seizure of foreign territories, and bombing of civilians.
In the prewar years and continuing at least until the middle of
1940, American policy, as expressed in neutrality legislation,
official statements, and public opinion polls, was to deplore aggression and to affirm that the mistake of 1917 would not be
repeated. Whatever happened American boys would not be

sent overseas to fight other nations' battles. Munitions makers, international bankers, and foreign propagandists would not again be permitted to draw the United States into a war to save democracy.

In this climate of opinion philanthropic efforts to relieve victims of war and oppression multiplied but rarely flourished. Throughout the 1930's American Jews gave unstintingly to finance the Joint Distribution Committee's far-flung, desperate labors to save Europe's persecuted Jewry from extinction. Pacifist, youth, and church groups tirelessly solicited for China and Spain. "We dance that Spain may live," read placards announcing dances sponsored by college students sympathetic to the Loyalist cause. There was no lack of organizations seeking funds for overseas relief. The trouble was that they all appealed to the same relatively small segment of the American people who were genuinely concerned about Fascist aggression. Attempts to obtain broader popular support made little headway. In 1938 the American Red Cross tried and failed to raise $1 million for Chinese relief. The Committee for Impartial Civilian Relief in Spain had even less success in attempting to collect $300,000 so that the Red Cross and the American Friends Service Committee might supply limited quantities of surplus American foodstuffs to both sides in the Spanish Civil War. The events of 1939 brought little change in public attitudes except to heighten suspicion of actions which might conceivably endanger the neutrality of the United States.

The Neutrality Act of 1939, adopted shortly after the outbreak of the war, recognized the possibility that the overseas operations of American relief organizations might affect the foreign policy and national interests of the United States. The

A Voyage Is Now Proposed

Act, in addition to numerous restrictions on American economic activity in nations officially declared to be at war, required voluntary agencies which wished to engage in civilian war relief in belligerent countries to register with and submit monthly reports to the Department of State. The Act specifically excluded the American Red Cross from the registration and reporting provisions and it did not apply to agencies operating in nations such as China, the Soviet Union, and Finland, which were not technically belligerent. During 1940 and 1941 the number of both registered and unregistered foreign relief agencies increased rapidly as the war spread to more and more countries. In the approximately two years of American neutrality in World War II, about seven hundred American organizations raised a total of $90 million for civilian and refugee relief overseas, and Congress appropriated an additional $50 million for distribution to refugees by the Red Cross. The fall of France in the summer of 1940 made assistance to nations still fighting the Axis powers seem less a form of charity than one of the measures "short of war" contributing to the defense of the United States.

At the same time that agencies for overseas civilian relief were increasing in number (there were seventy for Great Britain alone), national defense measures at home brought a boom in domestic welfare services. Aid to American armed forces, only recently in bad repute, regained its traditional popularity after adoption of the Selective Service Act of 1940. "Swing into patriotic note," the vice-chairman of the Red Cross advised chapter leaders in the autumn of that year. Early in 1941 the Red Cross swung into the blood donor program, its major contribution to national defense and one of the notable achievements of voluntary activity in the war years.

Meanwhile, profiting from experience in World War I, the Y.M.C.A., Y.W.C.A., National Catholic Community Service, National Jewish Welfare Board, Salvation Army and National Travelers Aid Association combined their military welfare programs and fund appeals in the United Service Organization for National Defense (U.S.O.).

Unfortunately the co-operative approach represented by U.S.O. was the exception rather than the rule in 1941. Groups in every community wanted to do something for the draftee and were determined to do it by themselves. There were no bottlenecks in the organization of war charities. The President's Committee on War Relief Agencies, appointed in 1941, studied the problem of duplication and encouraged combination of agencies engaged in the same or similar lines of work. The Committee, however, lacked authority to exercise effective supervision. The war relief picture, confused before Pearl Harbor, became chaotic afterward. By the summer of 1942 the President's Committee reported that the number of war relief agencies could only be estimated, that those operating in the domestic field were subject to no co-ordination, supervision, or control, and that the public was therefore subjected to far too many solicitations by agencies which duplicated work performed by others. "We were fairly falling over each other in a complex and undirected effort to organize, to publicize, to solicit, and to give," recalled Winthrop Aldrich, who was president of the British War Relief Society and active in U.S.O.

By an executive order issued in July, 1942, President Roosevelt transformed the earlier Committee on War Relief Agencies into the President's War Relief Control Board and greatly increased its authority. The Board now had power to control all solicitations for voluntary war relief, both foreign and domestic; only the American Red Cross, church, and other non-war charities remained outside its jurisdiction. It had power to license and withdraw licenses from war relief agencies and, in the interest of economy and efficiency, to eliminate or merge organizations. The Board scheduled the various national fund appeals and prevented competing campaigns during the periods set aside for the Red Cross, National War Fund, United Jewish Appeal, and War Bond drives. The staff of the Control Board sharply scrutinized overhead costs and made reasonable economy of operation a requirement for continued licensing. It found that in a few agencies overhead costs consumed 50 per cent, 70 per cent, and in extreme cases, all of the funds raised for relief. When the members of the Board (Joseph E. Davies, Charles P. Taft, and Charles Warren) made their final report in 1946, they could point to impressive achievements: the Board had cut the number of war relief agencies from seven hundred to ninety had promoted a remarkable degree of co-operation among the survivors, and had improved the services they offered. It had played a part in reducing overhead costs from an average of 10 per cent in 1942 to just over 3 per cent in 1945; and it had helped bring the National War Fund into existence.

The National War Fund, a private non-profit corporation established late in 1942, was the most ambitious venture in united fund-raising the United States had yet seen. In three national campaigns conducted in 1943, 1944, and 1945 the Fund combined the appeals of local non-war charities (mainly community chests) and the major war-related service and relief agencies including U.S.O., British War Relief, United Service to China, and American Aid to France. The union of war and non-war charities was fortunate for all concerned. Local welfare organizations, which might otherwise have suffered from the competition of the more glamorous war agencies, received considerably more than half of the $750 million total raised in the three War Fund drives. "The chests had the organization, and the war agencies had the appeal," the general manager of the National War Fund later remarked; "as long as the war lasted it was a winning combination."

Even while this winning combination was operating, it was obvious that larger funds than voluntary organizations could muster would be required for postwar relief. In November, 1943, fifty governments organized the United Nations Relief and Rehabilitation Administration (UNRRA) in a co-operative effort to meet the immediate postwar needs of war-devastated countries. At the close of the war this international agency sold or gave the governments of liberated countries immense quantities of food, clothing, medical supplies, livestock, and other relief materials. To the extent that it was possible to do so UNRRA returned exiles, prisoners, and refugees to their homes. For those who could not or dared not go home it operated displaced persons camps. UNRRA was financed by the non-invaded countries which provided commodities and cash to the extent of 2 per cent of their national incomes in 1943. The United States share of the $4 billion expended by UNRRA was $2.6 billion. In addition to money and goods from governments UNRRA received $210 million in cash, clothing, food, and livestock from individuals and associations in the United States, Canada, Australia, and New Zealand. Needless to say, this hopeful experiment in sharing resources on the basis of "from each according to his means and to each according to his needs" did not survive very long in a divided, distrustful world. UNRRA lasted long enough, however, to tide nations in bitter need over the worst of the postwar crisis and to help avert widespread famine and epidemic.

Neither the work of UNRRA nor the lend-lease and economic recovery programs launched by the United States government during and after the war diminished the eagerness of the American people to extend sympathetic assistance to people in foreign countries. After 1943 the American Council of Voluntary Agencies for Foreign Service, comprising the larger foreign relief agencies registered with the President's Control Board, planned and co-ordinated non-governmental programs. CARE, the Cooperative for American Remittances to Europe (later Everywhere), which began sending food parcels from Americans to designated recipients overseas in 1946, was one of the Council's creations; CRALOG (the Council of Relief Agencies Licensed to Operate in Germany), LARA (Licensed Agencies for Relief in Asia), and ARK (American Relief for Korea) were others. All of these alphabetical agencies, as their names indicated, were federations of numerous organizations which pooled their energies for a common cause.

The bureaucratic character of postwar relief was the product of several factors: the number of people and organizations wishing to help, the hard realities of fund-raising, and the extraordinary complexities of relief operations after 1945. Programs had to be approved by and correlated with those of official agencies. In occupied areas clearance had to be obtained from military authorities. Elsewhere, agreements had to be negotiated with governments regarding protection of property, exemption of relief supplies from customs duties and other taxes, and freedom from ration control. These difficulties, however, did not prevent fifty or more voluntary agencies from entering the field. Between September, 1939, and December, 1945, American voluntary agencies sent more than $500 million in goods and funds to war sufferers overseas; in the six years after the war private philanthropy raised approximately $2 billion for relief, reconstruction, and social services abroad. The aid furnished by voluntary organizations, impressive though it was, was insignificant in comparison to the appalling need. Nevertheless it reflected the light of American kindliness and good will, a candle if not a beacon in the stormy night.

Philanthropic contributions to postwar relief supplemented the much larger expenditures made by official agencies. In the period immediately after the war the American army spent as much as $500 million a year for civilian relief in countries where United States troops were stationed. Under the Marshall Plan, or European Recovery Program, which began in 1948 and continued until 1951, the United States helped nations of western Europe bolster their economies by means of grants and loans totaling $12.5 billion. The Marshall Plan was a form of prudent investment rather than a display of loving kindness and even ardent supporters of tax-supported foreign aid acknowledged that "person to person" giving possessed virtues that "government to government" assistance could never attain. Parcel post packages sent to friends and relatives in foreign countries accounted for a large share of personal giving. CARE and religious organizations such as the Roman Catholic War Relief Services and the Protestant Church World Service provided additional channels through which private citizens contributed relief supplies to individuals, churches, and charitable institutions overseas. In 1946 American Jews, numbering less than five million, collected $105 million for the

A Voyage Is Now Proposed

United Jewish Appeal, and in 1948 they raised $150 million for it. With funds supplied by U.J.A. the Joint Distribution Committee, United Palestine Appeal, and United Service for New Americans took European Jews out of displaced persons camps, assisted Jewish emigration and resettlement, and helped the new state of Israel in its fight for life.

War needs and war prosperity contributed in about equal measure to the generous support accorded assorted philanthropic causes in the 1940's. War taxes, although reaching levels which might reasonably have been expected to inhibit voluntary giving, did not in fact have that result. Charitable contributions reported in income tax returns were five times as large in 1945 as in 1939; corporation gifts increased nine times during these same years. Possibly the amounts given to charity might have been larger if taxes had been lower, but in the opinion of J. K. Lasser, the nation's favorite income tax adviser and author of *How Tax Laws Make Giving to Charity Easy* (1948), the taxing system fostered "the natural impulses to give to charity." The tax laws recognized the necessity and desirability of private contributions to charitable, religious, and educational institutions by permitting individuals and corporations to make tax-deductible gifts for philanthropic purposes. Progressive rates virtually assured that persons whose incomes were subject to surtaxes and corporations in the excess profit bracket would make contributions at least up to the limit of tax deductibility. For wealthy people and profitable corporations charity was a bargain, because what was given was mainly forgiven taxes. In the upper income brackets the question became not whether one could afford to give but whether one could afford not to give. It was not necessary for large givers to seek "tax loopholes" in order to take advantage of the inducements the revenue code offered donors. Their benefactions, although hard on the Treasury Department and presumably burdensome to other taxpayers, accorded with the letter and spirit of the law.

Income, inheritance, and corporation taxes, which continued at a high level in the decade after World War II, also contributed to a great increase in the number of foundations, one of the striking philanthropic developments of the postwar and Cold War era. Out of consideration for the social utility of foundations the revenue code conferred various privileges upon them. Subject to certain restrictions, foundation income from investments was tax exempt; contributions to foundations were deductible; and the gifts and bequests they received were subject neither to gift nor estate taxes. Quite aside from tax benefits, the foundation provided a convenient method of channeling the gifts of large individual and corporate donors to beneficiaries; with tax advantages, and in the face of high income and estate taxes, the foundation was irresistible. In the late 1940's there was evidence that some foundations served the donors' business interests better than they served philanthropy. In 1948 a congressional investigation conducted by Senator Charles W. Tobey of New Hampshire uncovered some of the curious uses to which foundations might be put. They could and were being used to provide venture capital for industry, to safeguard dynastic control of business enterprises, and to permit ruthless operators to plunder and wreck going concerns. Of course the unscrupulous businessman could not pocket the foundation's tax-free profits but, as trustee, he could use them for further piratical ventures. As one observer noted, there might even be something left over for occasional gifts to charity.

A Voyage Is Now Proposed

Separating foundation goats from foundation sheep was not easy, and eradicating those which were simply tax-evasion schemes without hurting legitimate foundations was even more difficult. A complicated revision of the revenue code adopted in 1950 dealt with the worst abuses. Under the new law, foundations might lose tax-exempt status if their records showed they existed mainly for the accumulation of capital or if they engaged in certain transactions which diverted income or principal to the donor or his associates. In any case income obtained by conducting a business unrelated to the foundation's ordinary purpose was subject to taxation. Nevertheless the legal or not yet prohibited forms of tax benefit enjoyed by foundations remained sufficiently appealing to encourage further growth. By the mid-1950's their number exceeded 5,000 by conservative estimate and approached 7,500 by some counts.

In the early 1950's the larger and more reputable foundations, whose financial affairs were conducted with such probity that they expressed willingness to operate in a fishbowl, were subjected to a different kind of scrutiny. Had they made grants to support un-American or subversive activities? If so to whom? When? Why? How much? Since government offices, universities, public schools, churches, motion picture studios, and radio and television networks were under attack for harboring subversive elements, and since philosophical systems, methods of scholarship, textbooks, folk tales, and works of art were widely suspected of spreading un-American attitudes, it was only natural that foundations should also be subjected to congressional investigation.

There were two probes. The first, held in 1952 under the auspices of the Select (Cox) Committee of the House of

Representatives, asked the larger foundations to answer a searching 100-item questionnaire, and through public hearings, interviews, and correspondence gathered additional material on foundation operations. The Committee reported that in a few instances foundations had made grants to individuals or associations subsequently "cited or criticized" by congressional committees, but that the general record of the foundations was good. The second or Special (Reece) Committee investigation of 1954 was less judiciously conducted. Its chairman, paid staff, and practically all the witnesses permitted to testify reiterated that foundations, educational institutions, and research organizations were involved in a "diabolical conspiracy" to foist socialism on the American people. By a majority vote the Committee ended the hearings without permitting the foundations to reply, except through written statements. In a minority report two members of the Committee called the proceedings "an ugly stain" on the record of the House of Representatives. Whatever disservice the Committee rendered the House, it did no serious harm to foundations. Editorial reaction to the Reece Committee was distinctly unfavorable. Foundations were already unpopular with extreme rightists; nobody else took the majority report seriously—least of all, apparently, one of the members of the Committee who accompanied his signature of the report with a statement expressing disapproval of its principal findings and conclusions.

Foundation officers have long maintained that it is extremely difficult to give money away wisely. In the late 1940's and 50's they did not suffer from lack of advice. Edwin R. Embree, formerly president of the Rosenwald Fund and an old Rockefeller Foundation hand, warned the foundations against "scatteration." William H. Whyte, Jr., the anti-organization man, reminded them of their obligation to support the individual researcher. The Cox Committee made it plain that foundations were expected to check on the "loyalty" of scholars, musicians, artists, and research institutions before making grants to them. Seymour Harris, a distinguished economist, advised foundations and non-profit research organizations to avoid public policy issues and to concentrate on collecting and organizing facts. Congressman B. Carroll Reece, who regarded "empiricism" as a dangerous, un-American "ism," wanted to know why foundations did not support "pro-American projects" such as "studies regarding the excellence of the American Constitution, the importance of the Declaration of Independence, and the profundity of the philosophy of the Founding Fathers"? William H. Whyte, writing in *Fortune*, a comparatively safe platform from which to make the suggestion, urged foundations to exercise "their ability and will to contribute to changes in the status quo of American life." All these recommendations implied dissatisfaction with current foundation practices. The most serious was Edwin Embree's charge that foundation giving was becoming "conventional and stereotyped" and that there was "an ominous absence of that social pioneering that is the essential business of foundations."

The principal recipient and target of this advice and criticism was the Ford Foundation, which was the newest face and had the fattest purse in the foundation world. Although organized in 1936, the Ford Foundation concentrated on local and family affairs until after the death of Henry Ford in 1947 and did not become active nationally until the early 1950's. Then, in possession of 90 per cent of the stock of one of the nation's greatest corporations, it was in a position, and necessarily obligated, to spend on a larger scale and broader front than any other foundation. Its resources, counted in billions rather than millions, comprised one-third of the combined assets of all foundations, and by 1954 its annual appropriations represented between a fourth and a fifth of total foundation spending.

The most striking thing about the Ford Foundation was its announced decision to spend money "in the difficult and sometimes controversial task of helping to realize democracy's goals." This meant problem-solving, not in the relatively safe and approved areas of medical and biological research, but in the social sciences, education, and the field of international understanding. To solve its own problem of rapidly accumulating funds the Foundation set up a number of autonomous organizations such as the Fund for the Advancement of Education, Fund for Adult Education, Fund for the Republic, Resources for the Future, Center for Advanced Study in the Behavioral Sciences, and the National Merit Scholarship Corporation. Some of the Foundation's direct grants for research in the social or behavioral sciences supported teams of scholars engaged in efforts to solve problems which, in the opinion of critics, were scarcely problems and hardly worth solving. On the other hand the Foundation's largest gift—the largest ever made by a foundation—was universally praised. This was a special appropriation of $560 million announced in December, 1955, to assist privately supported colleges and universities to raise teachers' salaries, to help privately supported medical schools strengthen instruction, and to enable privately supported non-profit hospitals to extend and improve services. Toward the end of the 1950's, in addition to conducting foreign aid and fellowship programs, supporting experiments in educational television, and supplying venture capital to both the more and less venturesome areas of scholarship, the Foundation began to make grants to novelists, poets, artists, musicians, composers, and dramatists.

Even after the advent of the Ford Foundation individual donors continued to provide roughly 75 per cent of the nation's total contribution to philanthropy. The foundations' share was about 8 per cent, which was slightly more than the percentage from charitable bequests and somewhat more than that of corporation gifts. The total—half of which went to religion—was unprecedentedly high: $5.4 billion in 1954, $6.7 billion in 1957, and proved to be well in excess of $8 billion in 1960. Of course these amounts would not buy as much in the 1950's as in earlier decades, and they were drawn from and had to be spread over a constantly growing population. On the other hand, some charitable obligations were declining because social insurance, buttressed by industrial health and welfare programs, pension plans, and unemployment benefits had strengthened the economic security of workers and their families. Neither governmental nor private welfare programs actually assured the American people against want, but it was certain that never again would voluntary benevolence be expected to play the dominant role in relieving sheer economic need. For this very reason philanthropy's role became more complex, and its responsibility for devising and demonstrating helpful services was heavier than ever before.

Private welfare agencies were no longer supported only by the rich and they no longer catered only to the poor. They were community enterprises offering counsel, guidance, and opportunities for growth to people at all economic levels. In a real but new sense the old charity organization motto, "Not alms but a friend," was the program of philanthropy in the 1950's.

Alms, if not being distributed to the needy, were still being collected by a variety of organizations through house-to-house and direct mail solicitations. Some of these were frauds which, in the 1950's, took an estimated $120 million a year from unwary givers. The vast majority, however, were legitimate and a great many had to do with health—or rather disease. It was a rare week (some said night) which did not find mothers marching up and down Main Street armed with collection kits supplied by one or another of the fifty national and innumerable local disease-combating associations. The National Foundation for Infantile Paralysis set the pace, not only in fund-raising but in accomplishing its mission. After scoring a brilliant victory over paralytic polio with the Salk vaccine in 1955, the agency shortened its name to the National Foundation and turned toward the conquest of rheumatic diseases, birth defects, and disorders of the central nervous system.

Social workers and public health experts, without disputing the great service rendered by the National Foundation, American Cancer Society, American Heart Association, and similar groups, questioned whether separate attacks on different ailments added up to an effective program for fighting disease and promoting health. As long as salesmanship and emotional appeal were the tests of support, comparatively rare diseases received as much or more attention than the more serious and prevalent ones. Meanwhile businessmen, labor leaders, newspaper editors, and housewives, became resentful of the ever recurring drives. At the end of the 1950's it seemed probable that the United Fund (a combined community chest and national agency campaign) or some variation of it (such as one drive for local agencies and another for national organizations) would sooner or later cut down the number of separate solicitations by agencies in similar lines of work.

At mid-century the most difficult, vital, and in many ways most traditional tasks of American philanthropy lay in the field of foreign aid. Helping those in need wherever they might be was no new experience for the people of the United States. The obligation was as old as belief in the stewardship of wealth and the gospel of doing good. Distance was no barrier to neighborly kindness in an era of instantaneous communications and swift travel; and even if Americans had been less disposed toward benevolence than they were, considerations of self-interest and national security would have required them to pay serious attention to the plight of the three-fifths of the world's population living in near-misery. The poverty of these people, as President Harry S. Truman warned in 1949, was a handicap and a threat both to the sufferers and to the rest of the world.

The "Point Four" program whose outlines President Truman sketched in his Inaugural Address of January 20, 1949, envisaged a co-operative attack on world poverty through technical assistance and capital investment in underdeveloped or overexploited areas. In 1950 Congress implemented the technical assistance features of this "bold new program" by adopting the Act for International Development. In the Mutual Security Act of 1957 Congress provided for the establishment of a new and potentially important lending agency, the Development Loan Fund. Meanwhile, supported in part through funds supplied by the United States, United Nations' agencies such as the Food and Agriculture Organization, World Health Organization, International Children's Fund, and International Bank for Reconstruction and Development, expanded their efforts to help undeveloped areas increase the productivity of their soils and workshops and improve the health and living standards of their people.

This was the kind of work in which American missionaries had been active for a century or longer. At the start of the Point Four program religious organizations and other voluntary agencies were operating approximately 2,500 social service, medical, educational, agricultural, and even industrial projects in Latin America, Africa, the Middle East, and Asia. In the 1950's organized philanthropic efforts overseas (as distinguished from assistance sent by individuals to relatives, friends, and strangers abroad) were co-ordinated by the American Council of Voluntary Agencies for Foreign Service, and mildly supervised by the Advisory Committee on Voluntary Aid (successor to the President's War Relief Control Board), which operated under the United States International Cooperation Administration. In one fairly typical year, 1956, private gifts for foreign relief totaled $535 million or about 8 per cent of all American philanthropic expenditures. The money was used to sow corn and dig wells in Mexico, develop improved varieties of wheat in Colombia, plant trees in Italy, take mason jars to Greece, found a library school and an institute of business administration in Turkey, set up social work demonstrations in Indian villages, and send fishing equipment to co-operatives in Hong Kong. All these and many other projects undertaken by philanthropy continued in the familiar pattern of encouraging self-help and building ladders for the aspiring. The Rockefeller and Ford Foundations were engaged in this work. So was CARE. But it was significant that a great deal of foreign relief and technical assistance was sponsored by religious groups and conducted by employees and volunteers in the service organizations of the various denominations and faiths.

Quantitatively, American philanthropy played only a minor role in the crusade to promote the economic and social development of the poorer half of the world's population. Attempts to measure philanthropy by monetary standards, however, result either in cynicism or complacency and are bound to be misleading. The relatively small share of foreign aid expenditures borne by voluntary agencies did not accurately indicate either the actual or the potential contributions of philanthropy to the work at hand. Limited budgets, as organizations like the American Friends Service Committee regularly proved, were no barriers to useful service. Voluntary agencies supervised the distribution of American food surpluses. They participated, sometimes on a contractual basis, in technical training and agricultural demonstrations. But, as always, the contribution of philanthropy lay less in specific deeds than in a tendency to influence social policy toward responsible action and humane goals. Religious organizations and periodicals were among the most vocal and vigorous champions of Point Four, and the churches were perhaps the most important influence in building up popular support for foreign economic aid.

During the 1950's, partly as a result of the Korean War and the intensification of the Cold War, governmental spending for "mutual security," or military assistance to foreign countries, consumed the lion's share of appropriations for foreign aid. The Point Four program, however, was not abandoned. In 1957, when the total outlay for foreign aid was $8 billion, roughly 20 per cent or about $1.7 billion was designated for economic and technical assistance. Critics denounced Point

Four as a "giveaway," "global charity," and "compulsory benevolence." Supporters viewed economic assistance as an endeavor in which national self-interest coincided with national idealism and asserted that appropriations for it should be doubled. Others, sympathizing with the objectives of the program, questioned its organization and methods of operation. There was room for wide difference of opinions on these points. Some observers, consciously or unconsciously adopting the point of view of scientific philanthropy, suggested that the multiplicity of governmental, intergovernmental, and voluntary agencies participating in technical assistance, the short-term, project-by-project approach followed by most of the operating agencies, and the confusion caused by lack of central leadership and direction were more serious handicaps than inadequate financial support. At the end of the decade the whole foreign aid program, military as well as economic, was under review by Congress.

The voyage Franklin proposed in 1771 was still, almost two centuries later, a very chancy venture. In addition to and quite as important as the question of support or opposition at home, there was the problem of reception abroad. If those who supplied the money were restless, those who received the assistance were proud, suspicious, fearful of being bought. Since technical assistance was essentially an effort to help people help themselves, its effectiveness depended as much on the initiative of the recipients as on the generosity of benefactors. Yet even with the best of intention on both sides there were complicating factors. Every improvement in health and reduction in mortality in undeveloped areas increased the pressure of population on food supplies. Unless production of food kept pace with increasing population, achievement of decent levels of consumption would be impossible. In spite of problems of this sort one school of thought maintained that modern knowledge made human want obsolete. According to other experts the gap was widening, poorer countries growing relatively poorer, hungry continents becoming still hungrier.

Everyone agreed that the extraordinary needs of the age demanded knowledge as well as good will. It was frequently said that fostering economic growth under conditions of freedom was the most challenging task of the twentieth century. Certainly it was one of the most difficult assignments modern man had consciously attempted. The outcome was admittedly a gamble. Whether the risks involved in the undertaking were greater than the possible consequences of failure to act was an unsettled issue.

As the United States entered the second half of the twentieth century, problems that had formerly troubled a few wealthy philanthropists had become the common concern of all citizens. This was true not only because services previously supported by private benevolence were now maintained by taxation but also because the United States had the largest national and per capita wealth of any nation. In facing the problems of a revolutionary epoch the American people had the advantage of great material resources wrested by labor and intelligence from a once underdeveloped continent. They could draw upon the knowledge and skills acquired, and profit from the mistakes made in three and a half centuries of hard-fought struggle to win justice, education, security, and opportunity for all. The American record abounded in men and women sensitive to the misfortunes of their fellows and willing to make others' causes their own. Americans had a long experience in founding voluntary agencies to perform tasks which individuals could not accomplish alone and which public bodies, for one reason or another, were not able to undertake. They had had long experience with charity, too. They knew that charity was subject to abuse, by the giver as well as the taker, and that the most effective and acceptable form of benevolence was not endless, soul-satisfying almsgiving but sensible efforts to help people become independent and prepared to work out their own destinies.

Important Dates

1601   Statute of Charitable Uses, cornerstone of Anglo-American law of philanthropy, and Elizabethan Poor Law, basis of English and American public poor relief, enacted by Parliament

1630   John Winthrop (1588–1649) preaches "A Model of Christian Charity" to Puritans bound for New England

1638   John Harvard (1607–38) bequeaths library and half of his estate to newly founded school at Cambridge, Mass.

1646   John Eliot (1604–90) begins missionary work among Indians of Massachusetts

1649   Society for the Propagation of the Gospel in New England established by Parliament; rechartered in 1661 and continued to support Indian missions until Revolution

1657   Scots' Charitable Society, first American "friendly society," founded in Boston; reorganized 1684

1675   Massachusetts legislature provides relief for frontier settlers driven from homes by King Philip's War, thus departing from principle of exclusive local responsibility for relief

1682   William Penn (1644–1718) comes to America to launch a "holy experiment"

1702   Cotton Mather (1663–1728) publishes *Magnalia Christi Americana,* one of earliest celebrations of American philanthropy

1710   Cotton Mather publishes *Essays To Do Good,* a popular do-it-yourself book

1715–18   Elihu Yale (1649–1721) sends gifts to Collegiate School of Connecticut (chartered 1701); school changes name to Yale College

1727   Franklin and friends organize "Junto," a mutual and community improvement society

1729   First orphan home in present boundaries of United States established at Ursuline Convent, New Orleans

1730   St. Andrew's Society founded in Charleston, S.C., "to assist all people in distress, of whatsoever Nation or Profession"

1731   Anthony Benezet begins half-century of teaching and promoting good causes in Philadelphia

James Oglethorpe advances a number of reasons, some philanthropic, to show why a colony should be planted in Georgia

1737   Jean Louis makes gift for founding Charity Hospital, New Orleans

1739–41   George Whitefield, on second visit to America, finds religious revivals in progress and helps turn them into Great Awakening; founds orphanage in Georgia in 1740

1751–52   Dr. Thomas Bond, assisted by Benjamin Franklin and others, founds Pennsylvania Hospital, the first general hospital in the U.S.; building opened 1756

1760   New York, Virginia, Maryland, Pennsylvania, New Hampshire, and Rhode Island collect and send assistance to Boston fire sufferers

1767   Philadelphia Bettering House, sometimes called "Pauper Palace" opened

1774–75   Parliamentary act closing Boston Port creates greatest relief problem in colonial period; other towns and colonies send money, grain, and livestock to aid Boston

1776   Society for Alleviating the Miseries of Public Prisons, earliest prison reform society, organized in Philadelphia; reactivated in 1787

1780   Pennsylvania, first state to take such action, passes Act for the Gradual Abolition of Slavery

1790   Free mulattoes of Charleston, S.C., organize Brown Fel-

Important Dates

lowship Society, one of several aristocratic charitable associations of that city

Death of Benjamin Franklin; will establishes Franklin Funds in Boston and Philadelphia to lend money to "young married artificers of good character"

1793   Yellow-fever epidemic in Philadelphia; worst disaster of kind in American history

1808   Andover Theological Seminary founded; popular cause among orthodox Congregational donors

1809   Mother Elizabeth Bayley Seton establishes order of Sisters of Charity of St. Joseph at Emmitsburg, Md.

1810   American Board of Commissioners for Foreign Missions organized; sends first missionaries to India in 1812

1811   Massachusetts General Hospital, favorite beneficiary of Boston philanthropists, founded

1816   American Bible Society, oldest of national benevolent societies, established; American Tract Society (1825), American Society for Promotion of Temperance (1826), and similar organizations founded in 1820's

1817   Thomas Hopkins Gallaudet (1787–1851) establishes in Hartford, Conn., America's first free school for deaf; one son to continue active in education of deaf until 1917

1818   Postwar depression prompts establishment of New York Society for the Prevention of Pauperism; similar societies in Baltimore and Philadelphia

1819   Supreme Court decision in Dartmouth College Case strengthens legal position of incorporated endowments

1821   Amherst College opens and receives liberal support from conservative Congregationalists

1824   Louis Dwight founds Boston Prison Discipline Society; controversy over relative merits of "Congregate" and "Separate" prison systems

1824–30 Samuel Gridley Howe takes part in, raises funds for, and administers relief in Greek War for Independence

1825   Founding of New York House of Refuge, first reformatory for juveniles; similar institutions in Boston and Philadelphia

Robert Owen (1771–1858) opens co-operative community in New Harmony, Ind.

189

American Philanthropy

1825-30   Boston Unitarians support Joseph Tuckerman's ministry to the poor

1829   Mathew Carey (1760-1839) attempts federated fund-raising in Philadelphia

1831   Arthur (1786-1865) and Lewis Tappan (1788-1873), New York dry goods merchants, become active in antislavery and manual-training college movements

Death of Stephen Girard; left largest fortune any American had thus far accumulated to charitable purposes

Amos Lawrence (1786-1852) retires from business to devote full time to benevolent interests and spiritual welfare

1832   Samuel Gridley Howe opens New England Asylum (later Perkins Institution), leading American institution for instruction of the blind

1835   Alexis de Tocqueville comments on American disposition to organize and join voluntary associations in *Democracy in America*

1836   John Lowell bequeaths $250,000 to found and support Lowell Institute, Boston; annual lecture series begins in 1840

1837   Samuel G. Howe begins instruction of Laura Bridgman, blind and deaf girl

Horace Mann begins work as Secretary of Massachusetts Board of Education

Depression opens; lasts until 1840's

1841   Dorothea L. Dix (1802-87) begins crusade for better treatment of insane; submits *Memorial* to Massachusetts legislature in 1843; publishes *Remarks on Prisons and Prison Discipline*, 1845

1843   Robert Hartley and other charity reformers organize New York Association for Improving the Condition of the Poor

1845   Establishment of first American conference of Society of St. Vincent de Paul, charitable organization of Roman Catholic laymen

1846   After decade of debate Congress passes act creating Smithsonian Institution

1846-47   Large American contributions for Irish famine relief

Important Dates

1847   Abbott Lawrence makes gift of $50,000 to Harvard; gift helps support work of Louis Agassiz

1848   Girard College opens in Philadelphia; most famous orphanage in United States and classic example of the "dead hand" in philanthropy

1851   Y.M.C.A. movement spreads to the United States

1853   Charles Loring Brace founds Children's Aid Society of New York, important child welfare agency

1854   Congress passes, President Pierce vetoes, Dorothea Dix's bill granting public lands to states to assist in financing care of insane

1859   Peter Cooper (1791–1883), one of best-loved American philanthropists, opens Cooper Union in New York City as center for free instruction in art and science

1861   United States Sanitary Commission, forerunner of American Red Cross, organized

1862   Freedmen's aid societies established in North to send teachers and relief supplies to former slaves

1863   Massachusetts establishes first central agency for supervising public welfare institutions

Catholic Protectory, largest institution for children in the United States, founded in New York City

1863–64   Sanitary Fairs in northern cities raise money and collect supplies for United States Sanitary Commission

1865   Freedmen's Bureau founded; active in relief and education in the South until early 1870's

1867   Peabody Fund, first of modern foundations, established by George Peabody (1795–1869) to assist southern education

1868   Opening of Hampton Institute in Hampton, Va.; best endowed school for Negroes

1869   Founding of London Charity Organization Society, which served as a model for American C.O.S. movement

1871–72   Fire sufferers in Chicago and Boston relieved by contributions from other cities

1874   Organization of National Conference of Charities and Correction, now National Conference on Social Welfare

1876   Opening of Jubilee Hall, Fisk University, Nashville,

Tenn.; money raised by concert tours of Fisk Jubilee Singers

1877   Buffalo Charity Organization Society established; similar organizations founded in other cities in next few years

1881   Clara Barton (1821–1912) organizes American Association of the Red Cross (name changed to American National Red Cross in 1893)

Booker T. Washington (1858–1915) organizes Tuskegee Institute for Negroes in Tuskegee, Ala.

1882   United States ratifies Geneva Convention of 1864, which provided for neutralization of aid to wounded in time of war

John F. Slater Fund founded to support Negro industrial schools and teacher training institutions

1884   Toynbee Hall, first social settlement, opened in London; visited by many Americans and served as model for American settlement houses

Hebrew Sheltering and Immigrant Aid Society organized to receive and assist Jews emigrating to the U.S.

1885   Stanford University chartered (opened 1891); gifts of Leland Stanford thought to be of unprecedented size

1887   Helen Keller (1880——), blind and deaf, begins study with Anne Sullivan

1888   Denver experiments with federated fund raising

1889   Andrew Carnegie publishes "Wealth"

John D. Rockefeller gives $600,000 to help found new University of Chicago

Jane Addams (1860–1935) establishes Hull House

1891   Rockefeller employs Frederick T. Gates as assistant in charitable matters

1892   New York *Tribune* counts 4,047 millionaires in the United States

1895   Washington Gladden publishes article on "tainted money" Jewish Charities in Boston adopt federated fund-raising

1898   New York School of Philanthropy inaugurates formal training courses for social work

1899   First American Juvenile Court established in Chicago

1900   American National Red Cross obtains charter of incorporation from Congress

1901   Rockefeller Institute for Medical Research incorporated

Important Dates

and begins work on small scale; eventually received $60.5 million from Rockefeller

1902 General Education Board established by John D. Rockefeller; his total gifts to it were about $130 million; Board in process of liquidation in late 1950's

Carnegie endows Carnegie Institution of Washington to encourage investigation, research, and discovery

1904 National Tuberculosis Association organized

1905 Carnegie Foundation for the Advancement of Teaching established

Resumption of tainted-money controversy

1907 Russell Sage Foundation, important in development of social work, organized

1909 First White House Conference on the Care of Dependent Children recommends establishment of federal Children's Bureau and declares that poverty alone should not be grounds for removing children from families

1910 Boy Scouts of America founded (Campfire Girls, 1910; Girl Scouts, 1912)

1911 Carnegie Corporation, Carnegie's largest foundation ($125 million), established

Missouri and Illinois enact "mothers' pensions" laws permitting assistance from public funds to maintain small children in own homes

1912 Congress establishes U.S. Children's Bureau "to investigate and report upon all matters pertaining to the welfare of children and child life among all classes of our people"

1913 Rockefeller Foundation chartered by State of New York "to promote the well-being of mankind throughout the world"

American Cancer Association founded

Modern community chest movement begins in Cleveland

1914 Red Cross "Mercy Ship" takes doctors, nurses, and hospital equipment to Europe at start of war

Commission for Relief in Belgium organized

American Jewish Joint Distribution Committee organized to co-ordinate Jewish war relief activities

Cleveland Foundation, first community trust, established

American Philanthropy

1915–16 U.S. Industrial Relations Commission investigates foundations

1917 Julius Rosenwald Fund established; active in field of Negro education

Income tax law permits individuals to deduct charitable contributions up to 15 per cent of taxable income

Publication of Mary Richmond's *Social Diagnosis*, landmark in social work

American Friends Service Committee begins operations

Red Cross asks—and gets—$100 million, largest sum raised by voluntary organizations up to that time

1918 Harkness family establishes Commonwealth Fund "to do something for the welfare of mankind"; active mainly in health field

United War Work campaign raises $200 million for seven national war relief agencies

Bequest of John W. Sterling doubles Yale's endowment

1919 Death of Andrew Carnegie, benefactions total $350 million

Harvard uses professional fund-raising counsel in $14 million endowment fund drive

Community chest in about 40 cities; spreads to 350 in 1929

Herbert Hoover (1874——) director of American Relief Administration; also Director General of Relief for Allied Governments

Twentieth Century Fund established by Edward A. Filene; specializes in economic research

1921 American Foundation for Blind founded; Helen Keller helps raise endowment

1921–22 Russian famine relief supervised by American Relief Administration, private organization headed by Herbert Hoover

1924 Total annual charitable contributions in United States reach $2 billion

1925 John Simon Guggenheim Memorial Foundation organized to aid young scholars and creative workers

1927 Restoration of Williamsburg, Va., financed by John D. Rockefeller, Jr. (1874——), begins

1928 Philanthropic peak of 1920's; 500 Lump-sum gifts of $1 million or more

Important Dates

Edward S. Harkness (1874–1940) gives $11 million to Harvard for house plan

1930 Kellogg Foundation organized; interested in health and education in rural areas

Louis Bamberger and Mrs. Felix Fuld donate $8 million to found Institute for Advanced Study, Princeton, N.J.

Edward S. Harkness makes large gifts to Yale and Phillips Exeter Academy

1931 Red Cross refuses to consider congressional grant for drought relief

President's Organization for Unemployment Relief conducts publicity campaign for local fund appeals

As a "temporary emergency" New York State assists local communities in financing unemployment relief

1932 Dedication of Folger Shakespeare Library, Washington, D.C., gift of Henry C. Folger

Red Cross processes and distributes surplus wheat and cotton to needy

Reconstruction Finance Corporation authorized to lend money to states for unemployment relief

FERA established to make emergency grants for unemployment relief

1933 Philanthropy at depression low point

Henry Ford opens Ford Museum and Greenfield Village

Rockefeller Foundation appropriates $1.5 million to expedite discovery of remedies for the depression

1934 First President's Birthday Ball for relief of polio victims

1935 Social Security Act, beginning of a permanent welfare program by national government

Heavier income and corporation taxes; corporations permitted to deduct charitable contributions up to 5 per cent of taxable income

Total contributions to philanthropy slightly exceed predepression peak

1936 Ford Foundation organized; not active nationally until about 1950

1937 Congress accepts Andrew Mellon's offer to give art collection and National Gallery building to public

Death of John D. Rockefeller; benefactions total $530 million

1938   National Foundation for Infantile Paralysis begins concentrated program of research into the cause, prevention, and treatment of poliomyelitis

1939   Neutrality Act requires agencies engaged in relief activities in belligerent countries to register with Department of State

1941   Red Cross adopts blood-donor program
        U.S.O. organized

1942   National War Fund, Inc., organized to collect funds for both war- and non-war agencies

1943   United Nations Relief and Rehabilitation Administration (UNRRA) founded to plan and supervise postwar emergency relief on international basis
        American Council of Voluntary Agencies for Foreign Service established by approximately fifty agencies to plan and co-ordinate private efforts

1945   CARE begins sending food parcels to Europe

1946   Voluntary agencies begin sending aid to Germany
        War Relief Control Board succeeded by Advisory Committee on Foreign Aid
        John D. Rockefeller, Jr., gives seventeen acres of downtown Manhattan land as site for United Nations headquarters
        Congress passes Full Employment Act, recognition of government's continuing responsibility to promote economic security

1946–48 United Jewish Appeal raises very large sums to assist refugees, immigrants to Israel, and government of Israel

1948   Senator Charles Tobey investigates use of foundations by business firms for non-philanthropic purposes

1949   President Truman announces Point 4 plan of technical assistance to underdeveloped nations
        United Fund movement begins in Detroit

1950   Revision of Internal Revenue Code subjects foundations engaged in certain prohibited practices to loss of tax exemption

1951   U.S.O. reactivated

1952   Select (Cox) Committee of House of Representatives investigates foundations

Important Dates

1953   Carnegie Endowment for International Peace opens International Center on United Nations Plaza, New York

Decision of New Jersey Supreme Court in *Barlow et al. v. A. P. Smith Manufacturing Co.* clarifies legal right of corporations to make contributions to higher education

1954   Special (Reece) Committee of House of Representatives widely criticized for tactics employed in investigation of foundations

1955   Ford Foundation announces largest grant in foundation history: $560 million to privately supported colleges, medical schools, and hospitals

National Merit Scholarship Corporation organized to assist talented students attend colleges of their choice

Development of Salk vaccine against paralytic polio climaxes seventeen years of work by National Foundation for Infantile Paralysis

1958   National Foundation for Infantile Paralysis becomes National Foundation; will combat rheumatic diseases, birth defects, and disorders of central nervous system

1959   Disc jockey Peter Tripp stays awake longer than anyone in history: performs for 200 hours without sleep (in Armed Forces recruiting booth, Times Square) "in the interest of science and the March of Dimes"

Suggested Reading

GENERAL

Although a great deal has been written on topics falling within the range of philanthropy, American historians have only recently begun to regard philanthropy itself as an interesting and profitable subject of research. The logical starting place for advanced students is the Russell Sage Foundation's *Report of the Princeton Conference on the History of Philanthropy in the United States* (1956), which suggests areas needing to be explored and contains a useful annotated bibliography prepared by Margaret M. Otto in consultation with F. Emerson Andrews. Merle Curti, in his article "The History of American Philanthropy as a Field of Research," *American Historical Review*, LXII (January, 1957), 352–63, assays past research in the field and also points out new paths of inquiry.

The standard encyclopedias include useful articles on charity or philanthropy. C. S. Loch's "Charity and Charities," *Encyclopaedia Brittanica*, V (11th ed., 1910), 860–91, is a classic; and Kenneth L. M. Pray's "Charity," *Encyclopedia of the Social Sciences*, III (1930), 340–45, and Edward Grubb's "Philanthropy," *Encyclopedia of Religion and Ethics*, IX (1928), 837–40, deserve notice. The index volumes of both the *Dictionary of American Biography* (1928–37) and *National Cyclopaedia of American Biography* (1893——) list subjects of biographies by occupation and happily include "Philanthropist" as an occupation. W. D. P. Bliss (ed.), *The New*

Suggested Reading

Encyclopedia of Social Reform (1908) covers a broad range of topics and is still helpful. For contemporary welfare problems, the best reference work is Russell Kurtz (ed.), *Social Work Yearbook* (1957, new ed., 1960). The *Yearbook* contains an excellent concise history of "The Development of Social Welfare Programs in the United States" by H. L. Lurie, articles ranging from "Administration of Social Agencies" to "Youth Services"—many with historical sections and all with bibliographies and a comprehensive directory of international, national, and voluntary welfare agencies.

F. Emerson Andrews', *Philanthropic Giving* (1950), an informed, witty, and sensible book is the best introduction to the complexities and technicalities of philanthropy. Walter A. Friedlander's *An Introduction to Social Welfare* (1955) is a superior textbook with helpful bibliographical suggestions. Nathan E. Cohen, in *Social Work in the American Tradition* (1958), relates trends in the profession of social work to general historical developments. Henry Winfred Thurston's *The Dependent Child* (1930) surveys methods of foster care of children in England and the United States. Public efforts in relief and welfare from the colonial period through the New Deal are traced in Arthur P. Miles's *An Introduction to Public Welfare* (1950). Sophonisba P. Breckinridge's *Public Welfare Administration* (1938) and Edith Abbott's *Public Assistance* (1940) are collections of documents with helpful introductions and, in the latter book, papers on the incongruities of the American poor law system.

Merle Curti's "American Philanthropy and the National Character," *American Quarterly*, X (Winter 1958), 420–37, provides a great deal of information on American attitudes toward philanthropy. Professor Curti is now preparing a history of American overseas aid. Edward C. Jenkins' *Philanthropy in America* (1950) deals mainly with the organization and financing of philanthropic agencies in the twentieth century but also gives some attention to the role of philanthropy in American life. Two studies by professional fund-raisers, Arnaud C. Marts, *Philanthropy's Role in Civilization: Its Contribution to Human Freedom* (1953), and John Price Jones, *The American Giver: A Review of American Generosity* (1954), offer practical and inspirational insights into the business of giving. Irvin G. Wyllie, in "The Reputation of the American Philanthropist," *Social Service Review*, XXXII (1958),

215-22, examines public reaction to philanthropic gifts. Professor Wyllie is currently studying the ideology of American philanthropy. Ralph E. Pumphrey's "Compassion and Protection: Dual Motives in Social Welfare," *Social Service Review*, XXXIII (1959) 21-29, analyzes two broad themes in philanthropy.

Lynn Thorndike's "The Historical Background" in Ellsworth Faris *et al.* (eds.), *Intelligent Philanthropy* (1930) sketches ancient and medieval antecedents of modern charity and poor relief. W. K. Jordan's *Philanthropy in England, 1480-1660* (1959) is the most important and authoritative work on the English background of modern philanthropy. Professor David Owen is completing a study of English philanthropy in the Victorian period. Two older books by B. Kirkman Gray, *A History of English Philanthropy* (1905) and *Philanthropy and the State* (1908), contain thoughtful passages on the uses and limitations of philanthropy. Karl de Schweinitz' *England's Road to Social Security* (1943) is a stimulating book by a leading American social worker. Sir William H. Beveridge's *Voluntary Action: A Report on Methods of Social Advance* (1948) is a warm tribute to philanthropic activity by one of the greatest advocates of the twentieth-century welfare state.

CHAPTER I

The writings of John Winthrop, William Penn, and Cotton Mather are primary sources for philanthropic thought in the early colonial period. Winthrop's "A Model of Christian Charity" (1630) is available in the Massachusetts Historical Society's, *Winthrop Papers*, II (1931), 282-95, and in abridged form in Perry Miller (ed.), *The American Puritans: Their Prose and Poetry* (1956). Samuel Eliot Morison's *Builders of the Bay Colony* (1930) has a good chapter on Winthrop; the best recent study is by Edmund S. Morgan, *The Puritan Dilemma: The Story of John Winthrop* (1958). Frederick B. Tolles and E. Gordon Aldefer (eds.), in their *The Witness of William Penn* (1957), provide selections from *No Cross, No Crown* (1669, 1682, 1694), *Some Fruits of Solitude* (1693), and *More Fruits of Solitude* (1702). Edward Beatty's *William Penn as Social Philosopher* (1939) and Auguste Jorns's *The Quakers as Pioneers in Social Work* (1931) are standard interpretations of Quaker humanitarianism. Cotton Mather's *Bonifacius, or Essays To*

Suggested Reading

Do Good (1710, often reprinted) is required reading. *Magnalia Christi Americana* (1855 ed.), I, 102, contains Mather's advice to Bostonians on the conduct of charity. Kenneth B. Murdock's introduction to his *Selections from Cotton Mather* (1926) helped revive respect for Mather; Perry Miller's *The New England Mind: From Colony to Province* (1953) offers the most learned recent analysis of Mather's thought. Elizabeth Wisner, in her article on "The Puritan Background of the New England Poor Laws," *Social Service Review*, XIX (1945), 381–90, examines Mather's charitable activities from the standpoint of modern social work.

Among Benjamin Franklin's numerous essays on charity and poor relief the following are especially interesting: "On the Price of Corn, and Management of the Poor" (1766), "On the Laboring Poor" (1768), and "On the Institution in Holland to Prevent Poverty" (1772). These are all in Albert Henry Smyth (ed.), *The Writings of Benjamin Franklin* (1907), as are Franklin's *Autobiography* and *The Way to Wealth*. Carl Van Doren's *Benjamin Franklin's Autobiographical Writings* (1945) is a handy anthology; and the best brief biography is Carl L. Becker's "Benjamin Franklin," in the *Dictionary of American Biography*, VI (1931), 585–98. Bradford Smith's *A Dangerous Freedom* (1952) is one of several works which comment on Franklin's use of voluntary associations.

Marcus W. Jernegan's pioneering work, *Laboring and Dependent Classes in Colonial America, 1607–1783* (1931), contains chapters on poor relief in Virginia and New England. The problems of urban poverty and its treatment are well covered in Carl Bridenbaugh's *Cities in the Wilderness: The First Century of Urban Life in America, 1625–1742* (1938) and *Cities in Revolt: Urban Life in America, 1743–1776* (1955). Both Robert W. Kelso's *The History of Public Relief in Massachusetts, 1620–1920* (1922) and David M. Schneider's *History of Public Welfare in New York, 1609–1866* (1938) are particularly useful for the colonial period. Verner W. Crane's *The Southern Frontier, 1670–1732* (1929) and Daniel J. Boorstin's *The Americans: The Colonial Experience* (1958) deal with the philanthropic motive in the founding of Georgia. The latter attributes the failure of the project, in part, to philanthropy's want of an experimental spirit.

American Philanthropy

Ola Elizabeth Winslow's *Jonathan Edwards, 1703-1758* (1940) and William Warren Sweet's *Religion in Colonial America* (1942) draw attention to the social results of the Great Awakening. Stow Persons' *American Minds* (1958) dissents from the view that the Awakening subsided rapidly after 1742. Stuart C. Henry's *George Whitefield, Wayfaring Witness* (1957) is the most recent biography of the English evangelist. Although mainly concerned with English developments, Eric McCoy North, in his *Early Methodist Philanthropy* (1914), includes material on Whitefield's orphan house in Georgia. James Dow McCallum, in *Eleazar Wheelock, Founder of Dartmouth College* (1939) and a compilation of *The Letters of Wheelock's Indians* (1932), records the various trials of another colonial philanthropic enterprise. William L. Sachse's *The Colonial American in Britain* (1956) contains data on attempts of colonial colleges to raise funds abroad.

George S. Brookes's *Friend Anthony Benezet* (1937), a loving biography, includes letters to, from, and concerning Benezet and Benezet's minor writings. Anthony Benezet's *Some Observations on the Situation, Disposition, and Character of the Indian Natives of the Continent* (1784) is characteristic of the author. *A Word of Remembrance and Caution to the Rich* (1793), written about thirty years before publication and originally entitled "A Plea for the Poor," is John Woolman's best essay. Frederick B. Tolles's *Meeting House and Counting House* (1948) gives an excellent picture of the Quaker society in which Benezet and Woolman lived.

Carl and Jessica Bridenbaugh, in *Rebels and Gentlemen: Philadelphia in the Age of Franklin* (1942) discuss the Pennsylvania Hospital and other benevolent institutions. Richard H. Shryock's *The Development of Modern Medicine* (1936) relates medical developments to humanitarian movements and shows the relationship between European and American activity. This relationship is the subject of Michael Kraus's "Eighteenth Century Humanitarianism: Collaboration between Europe and America," *Pennsylvania Magazine of History and Biography*, LX (1936), 270-86. Merrill Jensen's *The New Nation* (1950) has a chapter surveying humanitarian progress during the Confederation period. Benjamin Rush's *Essays, Literary, and Philosophical* (1806) is a fascinating miscellany by

Suggested Reading

one of America's greatest humanitarian reformers. George W. Corner's edition of *The Autobiography of Benjamin Rush* (1948) is valuable and L. H. Butterfield's *Letters of Benjamin Rush* (1951) is priceless. John Harvey Powell, in *Bring Out Your Dead* (1949), deals with Philadelphia's reaction to the yellow-fever epidemic of 1793 in a manner both vivid and scholarly. John Bach McMaster, in *The Life and Times of Stephen Girard* (1918), makes Girard's career dull; Harry Emerson Wildes's *Lonely Midas: The Story of Stephen Girard* (1943) overcompensates for McMaster's defects but is more satisfactory. Neva R. Deardorff's "The New Pied Pipers," *Survey*, LII (1924), 31–47, 56–61, comments on Girard's legacy and its influence on other donors.

CHAPTERS III AND IV

Two volumes in the "History of American Life" series, John A. Krout and Dixon Ryan Fox, *The Completion of Independence, 1790–1830* (1944) and Carl Russell Fish, *The Rise of the Common Man, 1830–1850* (1927), provide the social background for philanthropic developments in the first half of the nineteenth century. John Bach McMaster's *A History of the People of the United States*, IV (1895) and V (1900), and Edward Channing's *A History of the United States*, V (1922), give more space to philanthropy than do most of the general histories. The fullest treatment is in Emerson Davis' *The Half Century* (1851). *Niles' Register* (1811–49), which is indexed, contains a surprising amount of material on poor relief. Nearly all European travelers' accounts, including those of Tocqueville and Dickens, devote space to American philanthropic institutions. One of the lesser known but valuable accounts is George Combe's *Notes on the United States of North America* (1841). George Wilson Pierson's *Tocqueville and Beaumont in America* (1938) presents a panorama of the United States in 1831–32.

Edith Abbott's *Some American Pioneers in Social Welfare* (1937) contains biographical sketches and selections from the writings of Thomas Eddy, Stephen Girard, Samuel Gridley Howe, Dorothea L. Dix, and Charles Loring Brace. Joseph Tuckerman, *On the Elevation of Poor* (1874) reprints selections from Tuckerman's reports on his ministry to the poor in Boston. Mathew Carey's proposal for federated financing in Philadelphia in 1829 is reprinted in

American Philanthropy

the *Social Service Review*, XXIX (1955), 302–5. *The Works of William E. Channing, D.D.* (1887) includes "Remarks on Associations" and other relevant essays and addresses. William R. Lawrence's *Extracts from the Diary and Correspondence of the Late Amos Lawrence* (1855) is illuminating; and Lewis Tappan's *Is It Right To Be Rich?* (1869) follows in the pattern of Mather's *Essays To Do Good*. Both Emerson and Thoreau made pointed observations on philanthropy in their journals and essays. "Self-Reliance" (1836–39), "Man the Reformer" (1841), and "New England Reformers" (1844) give Emerson's views. *Walden* (1854) is salted with Thoreau's peppery comments.

Franklin Parker's "George Peabody, Founder of Modern Philanthropy" (Ph.D. diss., Peabody College, 1956) is a detailed study of an important figure. Helen E. Marshall's *Dorothea Dix, Forgotten Samaritan* (1937) and Harold Schwartz's *Samuel Gridley Howe, Social Reformer* (1956) are both excellent. Many of the philanthropists and reformers of the middle period still await their biographers, but Daniel T. McColgan's *Joseph Tuckerman* (1940), Benjamin P. Thomas' *Theodore Weld* (1950), and R. V. Harlow's *Gerrit Smith, Philanthropist and Reformer* (1939) do their subjects justice.

A number of topical studies are particularly useful for the pre-Civil War reforms: Albert Deutsch, *The Mentally Ill in America* (1949); Blake McKelvey, *American Prisons* (1936); Merle Curti, *The Social Ideas of American Educators* (1935) and *Peace or War* (1936); Ishbel Ross, *Journey into Light: The Story of the Education of the Blind* (1951); Harry Best, *Blindness and the Blind in the United States* (1934) and *Deafness and the Deaf in the United States* (1943). More specialized studies include: John R. Bodo, *The Protestant Clergy and Public Issues, 1812–1848* (1954); Clifford S. Griffin, "Religious Benevolence as Social Control, 1815–60," *Mississippi Valley Historical Review*, XLIV (1957–58), 423–44; and Irwin G. Wyllie, "The Search for An American Law of Charity" *Mississippi Valley Historical Review*, XLVI (1959), 203–21. Gilbert Hobbs Barnes's *The Anti-Slavery Impulse, 1830–1844* (1933), Henrietta Buckmaster's *Let My People Go* (1941), and William H. Siebert's *The Underground Railroad from Slavery to Freedom* (1898) are convenient sources for philanthropic participation in the antislavery movement. The work of Charles Loring Brace is

Suggested Reading

discussed in Thurston's *The Dependent Child*, pp. 92–131; Brace's own book, *The Dangerous Classes of New York and Twenty Years' Work among Them* (1872), is a fascinating account of "child saving."

CHAPTER V

The chapter on charity in Emerson David Fite's *Social and Industrial Conditions in the North during the Civil War* (1910) is still useful; Ellis Merton Coulter, in *The Confederate States of America, 1861–65* (1950), throws light on war relief in the South. There is a wealth of material on charitable fairs and Lincoln's support of them in Carl Sandburg's *Abraham Lincoln: The War Years* (1939). William Quentin Maxwell's *Lincoln's Fifth Wheel: The Political History of the United States Sanitary Commission* (1956) is admirable; George Worthington Adams' *Doctors in Blue: The Medical History of the Union Army in the Civil War* (1952) offers additional information on the working of the Sanitary Commission. George R. Bentley's *A History of the Freedmen's Bureau* (1955), the latest full-length study, can be usefully supplemented by John and La Wanda Cox's "General O. O. Howard and the 'Misrepresented Bureau,' " *Journal of Southern History*, XIX (1953), 427–56. The best treatment of the freedmen's aid societies is in Henry Lee Swint's *The Northern Teacher in the South, 1862–1870* (1941).

CHAPTER VI

Allan Nevins' *Emergence of Modern America* (1927) and Arthur M. Schlesinger's *Rise of the City* (1933) have proved their worth to a generation of students. Howard D. Kramer has two helpful articles on a somewhat neglected topic: "The Beginning of the Public Health Movement in the United States," *Bulletin of the History of Medicine*, XXI (1947), 352–76; and "Effect of the Civil War on the Public Health Movement," *Mississippi Valley Historical Review*, XXXV (1948), 449–62. Two studies of unusual value are Leah H. Feder, *Unemployment Relief in Periods of Depression* (1936), which covers the years 1857–1922, and Emma O. Lundberg, *Unto the Least of These* (1947), a history of social services for children.

Frank D. Watson's *The Charity Organization Movement in the*

United States (1922) is still the standard work in its field, but a new study by Verl S. Lewis is in progress. The best study of the origin and development of the family service movement is Margaret E. Rich's *A Belief in People: A History of Family Social Work* (1956). Amos G. Warner's *American Charities* (1894) is indispensable for an understanding of the point of view of charity reformers in the late nineteenth century. Robert H. Bremner, in "'Scientific Philanthropy,' 1873–93," *Social Service Review*, XXX (June, 1956), 168–73, gives citations to the voluminous contemporary literature on the subject. There are interesting comments on the "new charity" in Samuel Rezneck's "Patterns of Thought and Action in an American Depression, 1882–1886," *American Historical Review*, LXI (1955–56), 284–307. Jane Addams *et al.*, *Philanthropy and Social Progress* (1893), present the attitude of more advanced social workers in the 1890's. William Rhinelander Stewart's *The Philanthropic Work of Josephine Shaw Lowell* (1911) is still the only full-length study of one of the most important women of the late nineteenth century. Frances A. Goodale's anthology, *The Literature of Philanthropy* (1893), describes in winning fashion the work of women volunteers in many undertakings.

Boris D. Bogen's *Jewish Philanthropy* (1917) is still a valuable reference. A more recent survey is Herman D. Stein's "Jewish Social Work in the United States (1654–1954)," *American Jewish Year Book*, LVII (1956), 3–98. Barbara Miller Solomon, in *Pioneers in Service* (1956), provides a detailed study of the organization and work of the Associated Jewish Philanthropies of Boston. John O'Grady's *Catholic Charities in the United States* (1931) is comprehensive and authoritative. Daniel T. McColgan, in *A Century of Charity* (1951), records the history of the Society of St. Vincent de Paul in the United States. Both Charles Hopkins' *History of the Y.M.C.A. in North America* (1951) and Foster Rhea Dulles' *The American Red Cross* (1950) are readable and objective. The newest and most acceptable biography of Clara Barton is *Angel of the Battlefield* (1956) by Ishbel Ross.

CHAPTER VII

Andrew Carnegie's "Wealth," *North American Review*, CXLVIII (1889), 653–64, and "Best Fields for Philanthropy," *North American Review*, CXLIX (1889), 682–98, are reprinted in his *The Gospel*

Suggested Reading

of Wealth (1901). Burton J. Hendrick, in *The Life of Andrew Carnegie* (1932) sketches the background and reception of the gospel of wealth and gives some information on Carnegie's major gifts. Carnegie's benefactions are summarized by Robert M. Lester in *Forty Years of Carnegie Giving* (1941). John D. Rockefeller, in *Random Reminiscences of Men and Events* (1909), states his philosophy and program for giving. Allan Nevins' *Study in Power: John D. Rockefeller, Industrialist and Philanthropist* (1953) describes the difficulties Rockefeller encountered in carrying out his stewardship. *American Heritage*, VI (April, 1955), 65–86, contains the memoirs of Frederick T. Gates, Rockefeller's adviser on philanthropy, with an introduction and postscript by Allan Nevins. Raymond B. Fosdick's *John D. Rockefeller, Jr.* (1956), one of the most distinguished biographies of recent years, shows the broadening influence exerted on the younger Rockefeller by Gates and others with whom he was associated in managing the family benefactions.

Albert Shaw, in "American Millionaires and Their Public Gifts," *Review of Reviews*, VII (1893), 48–60, surveys the extent to which the gospel of wealth was being practiced by millionaires in the 1890's. Sarah K. Bolton's *Famous Givers and Their Gifts* (1896) deals with several almost forgotten donors as well as with many well-known ones. Edward C. Kirkland's *Dream and Thought in the Business Community, 1860–1900* (1956) and Irvin G. Wyllie's *The Self-Made Man in America* (1954) are useful on businessmen's attitudes toward philanthropy. Washington Gladden, with his article "Tainted Money," *Outlook*, LII (1895), 886–87, opened a celebrated controversy. E. Franklin Frazier's *Black Bourgeoisie* (1957) and Louis R. Harlan's *Separate and Unequal: Public School Campaigns and Racism in the Southern Seaboard States, 1901–1915* (1958) are critical of the influence of northern philanthropists on Negro education; Horace Mann Bond, *The Education of the Negro in the American Social Order* (1934) is a balanced account. Gunnar Myrdal *et al.*, in *An American Dilemma* (1944), II, 887–93, offer a quick survey of philanthropic activity in the field of southern education.

In *When Social Work was Young* (1939) Edward T. Devine records the variety of causes in which social workers were active around and after the turn of the century. The anti-tuberculosis crusade, which touched on many other issues, is treated in Richard H. Shryock's *National Tuberculosis Association (1904–1954)* (1957).

American Philanthropy

Robert H. Bremner, in *From the Depths: The Discovery of Poverty in the United States* (1956), discusses the role of social workers in reform movements of the Progressive era. Jane Addams' *Democracy and Social Ethics* (1902) and *Twenty Years at Hull-House* (1910) illumine the practical idealism of the settlement movement. Another settlement leader is memorialized in R. L. Duffus' *Lillian Wald* (1938). Florence Kelley's "Labor Legislation and Philanthropy in Illinois," *Charities Review*, X (1900–1901), 287–88, is a characteristic article by a formidable reformer. Her biographer is Josephine Goldmark, *Impatient Crusader: Florence Kelley's Life Story* (1953).

The Long View (1930) brings together some of the writings of Mary E. Richmond, an important figure in the development of social work. Miss Richmond's *Social Diagnosis* (1917), a description of the casework process, is one of the classics of social work. A biography of Miss Richmond by Muriel Pumphrey is forthcoming. Ernest V. Hollis' and Alice L. Taylor's *Social Work Education in the United States* (1951) contains a chapter on the history of schools of social work.

CHAPTER VIII

Dulles, *American Red Cross*, and Hopkins, *Y.M.C.A.*, are essential for war relief activities in World War I. Portia B. Kernodle's *The Red Cross Nurse in Action, 1882–1948* (1949) is thorough and unsentimental. Raymond B. Fosdick, in *Chronicle of a Generation: An Autobiography* (1958), describes the confusion resulting from the desire of numerous private agencies to serve the soldier. Frank M. Surface and Raymond L. Bland's *American Food in the World War and Reconstruction Period* (1931) is a methodical account of relief operations directed by Herbert Hoover in the decade after 1914. Two studies deal with special phases of Hoover's work: Suda L. Bane and Ralph H. Lutz, *Organization of American Relief in Europe, 1918–1919* (1943), and H. H. Fisher, *The Famine in Soviet Russia, 1919–1923: The Operations of the American Relief Administration* (1927). Frank Alfred Golder and Lincoln Hutchinson, in *On the Trail of the Russian Famine* (1927), report the observations of two A.R.A. investigators. Hoover's *An American Epic* (1959——), a "history of American enterprises of compassion," begins with a volume on the C.R.B.

John R. Seeley *et al.*, in *Community Chest: A Case Study in Phi-*

lanthropy (1958) focus on Indianapolis but present the historical background and development of the community chest movement. Willford Isbell King's *Trends in Philanthropy* (1928) studies patterns in giving in New Haven, 1900–1925. Henry S. Pritchett's "A Science of Giving," in Carnegie Corporation of New York, *Report of the Acting President* (1922), pp. 13–20, is a foundation executive's presentation of the difficulties of giving. A foundation founder discusses the same problem in Julius Rosenwald, "The Burden of Wealth," *Saturday Evening Post*, January 5, 1929, pp. 12–13. Cornelia Cannon's "Philanthropic Doubts," *Atlantic Monthly*, CXXVIII (1921), 289–300, critical of the philanthropic approach to social problems, received wide attention in the 1920's. "Giving—the Great American Game," *Saturday Evening Post*, December 28, 1928, p. 28, and "The New Gospel of Wealth," *Literary Digest*, November 30, 1929, pp. 22–23, are examples of the celebration of American philanthropy in the late 1920's.

CHAPTER IX

The availability of Arthur M. Schlesinger, Jr.'s *The Crisis of the Old Order, 1919–1933* (1957) makes it unnecessary to cite many works on the early depression years. Jonathan Leonard's *Three Years Down* (1939) preserves some of the flavor of the period. U.S. Senate Committee on Manufacture, 72 Congress, 1 session, *Unemployment Relief: Hearings on S. 174 . . . and S. 262* (1932), contains a mine of information. R. M. MacIver's *The Contributions of Sociology to Social Work* (1931), Reinhold Niebuhr's *The Contributions of Religion to Social Work* (1932), and Philip Klein's "Social Work," *Encyclopedia of the Social Sciences*, XIV (1935), 165–73, are all important sources for the orientation of social workers' thought in the early 1930's. Rich, *A Belief in People*, is particularly good on the impact of the depression on family welfare agencies. Abraham Epstein, in "Do the Rich Give to Charity?" *American Mercury*, XXIII (May, 1931), 22–30, discusses the inadequacy of philanthropy as a means of meeting social needs.

Harris G. Warren, in *Herbert Hoover and the Great Depression* (1959) attempts to do justice to the Hoover administration. The former President presents his own case in *The Memoirs of Herbert Hoover: The Great Depression, 1929–41* (1952). William Starr Myers' *The State Papers and Other Public Writings of Herbert*

American Philanthropy

Hoover (1934) is the standard source for Hoover's statements on charity and other subjects. Bernard Bellush, in *Franklin D. Roosevelt as Governor of New York* (1955), and Frank Freidel, in *Franklin D. Roosevelt: The Triumph* (1956), trace the development of Roosevelt's policy on unemployment relief. Dorothy Kahn's *This Business of Relief* (1936) is good on the situation in the mid-thirties. Josephine C. Brown's *Public Relief, 1929–1939* (1940) is the best guide to a complicated problem. Mabel Newcomer, in "Fifty Years of Public Support of Welfare Functions in the United States," *Social Service Review*, XV (1941), 651–60, records and comments on the changes in the financing of public welfare, 1890–1940. Marguerite T. Boylan's *Social Welfare in the Catholic Church* (1941) shows the impact of the depression and New Deal on organized Catholic charities.

CHAPTER X

There is an immense and growing literature on foundations. The best guide to it (and the best book on the subject) is F. Emerson Andrews' *Philanthropic Foundations* (1956). Wilmer Shields Rich, in *American Foundations and Their Fields* (1955) provides a comprehensive directory. Frederick P. Keppel's *The Foundation: Its Place in American Life* (1930) reflects the thoughtful and humane outlook of the author, who was president of the Carnegie Corporation. *Funds and Foundations* (1952), by Abraham Flexner, a foundation pioneer, is critical of foundation policies since the mid-1920's. There are histories of a number of the major foundations. The best is Raymond B. Fosdick's *The Story of the Rockefeller Foundation* (1952); the least reverent is Dwight Macdonald's *The Ford Foundation* (1956). Eduard C. Lindeman, in *Wealth and Culture* (1936), and Horace Coon, in *Money To Burn* (1938), emphasize the conservatism of the foundations. Joseph C. Kiger's *Operating Principles of the Larger Foundations* (1954) is a judicious study by the director of research for the Cox investigating committee. *Hearings before the Select (Cox) Committee to Investigate Tax-Exempt Foundations* (1953) is well worth consulting. Edwin R. Embree's "Timid Billions: Are the Foundations Doing Their Job?" *Harper's Magazine*, CXCVIII (March, 1949), 28–37, is the most challenging of the many articles criticizing the foundations in the late 1940's and early 1950's.

Suggested Reading

Other articles, too abundant to list here, are cited in *Report of the Princeton Conference.* Joseph C. Hyman's *Twenty-Five Years of American Aid to Jews Overseas* (1939) is a modest and moving record of the work of the Joint Distribution Committee. David Hinshaw's *Rufus Jones, Master Quaker* (1951) contains material on the American Friends Service Committee in the 1920's and 30's. *Voluntary War Relief during World War II* (1946), a report by the U.S. President's War Relief Control Board, is a useful summary. A history of the National War Fund, *Design for Giving* (1947) by Harold J. Seymour is particularly good on fund-raising. George Woodbridge's *UNRRA: The History of the United Nations Relief and Rehabilitation Administration* (1950) is a distinguished official history. Edward Mc-Sweeney's *American Voluntary Aid to Germany, 1945–50* (1950) is a short summary. The Congressional (House) Special Subcommittee of the Committee on Foreign Affairs, in its *Final Report on Foreign Aid* (1948), concludes that Americans can afford to send private assistance overseas and cannot afford to discontinue it. Walter R. Sharp, in *International Technical Assistance* (1952), attempts to inventory and evaluate United States government, United Nations, and regional assistance programs. William Adams Brown, Jr., and Redvers Opie, in *American Foreign Assistance* (1953), appraise twelve years (1941–52) of overseas aid. The private agencies' tasks are explored by the American Council of Voluntary Agencies for Foreign Service in *The Role of Voluntary Agencies in Technical Assistance* (1953). Alvah Myrdal, Arthur J. Altmeyer, and Dean Rusk describe the challenge of *America's Role in International Social Welfare* (1955). Max F. Millikan and W. W. Rostow, in *A Proposal: Key to an Effective Foreign Policy* (1957) argue for expanded, long-term American participation in economic development of undeveloped areas. Grant S. McClellan's *United States Foreign Aid* (1957) presents arguments pro and con; and *Current History*, XXXIII (1957), 129–67, devotes an entire issue to an objective review of foreign-aid problems.

J. Frederic Dewhurst and Associates, in *America's Needs and Resources: A New Survey* (1955), pp. 430–68, describe the domestic welfare scene in the 1950's. Ida C. Meriam's "Social Welfare in the United States, 1934–54," *Social Security Bulletin*, XVIII (October,

American Philanthropy

1955), 3–14, presents developments since the New Deal. There are many helpful insights in Max Lerner's *America as a Civilization* (1957); the section entitled "The Sinews of Welfare," pp. 123–39, is particularly rewarding. Marion K. Sanders' "Mutiny of the Bountiful," *Harper's Magazine*, CCXVI (December, 1958), 23–31, deals with financing of voluntary health organizations. Wayne Mc-Millen, in "Financing Social Welfare Service," *Social Work Yearbook* (1957), pp. 260–67, discusses the United Fund movement, and in "Charitable Fraud: An Obstacle in Community Organization," *Social Service Review*, XXIX (1955), 153–71, he describes the more common charity rackets and examines their direct and indirect costs. The American Association of Fund-Raising Counsel's *Giving, U.S.A.* (1961) is a handy guide to the distribution of philanthropic giving. Harold L. Wilensky and Charles N. Lebeaux, in their *Industrial Society and Social Welfare* (1958), pp. 148–67, survey and analyze contemporary welfare programs and expenditures.

Acknowledgments

This study was supported in part by a grant-in-aid from the Ohio State University Research Foundation. It was written while I was associated with the History of American Philanthropy Project at the University of Wisconsin. I wish to express my appreciation to both institutions, and also to the staffs of the libraries of the Ohio State University, Wisconsin Historical Society, and University of Wisconsin. It was my good fortune to be able to discuss the work while it was in progress with Merle Curti and Irvin G. Wyllie of the University of Wisconsin. Mr. Curti and Mr. Wyllie have read the manuscript and have given me the benefit of their criticism, but they are not responsible for my interpretations, errors, or omissions. I also wish to thank Merle Rife and Richard Thomas, who helped me begin research for the book, and Mrs. Mildred Lloyd, who put the manuscript in shape for publication. Daniel J. Boorstin's suggestions háve improved the readability of the book without altering its content or conclusions. Mrs. Catherine Marting Bremner made helpful comments on style, assisted in compiling the table of dates, and, like Sue and Ann Bremner, provided unfailing encouragement.

Index

Index

American Missionary Association, 87, 88

American National Red Cross, 78, 82, 122, 128, 133, 135, 144, 149, 155, 166, 169, 192, 193, 194; blood donor program of, 167, 196; Christmas seal campaign of, 124; and disaster relief, 94; and distribution of surplus commodities (1932), 152, 195; drought relief program of (1931), 145, 195; founding of, 92–93; and fundraising in World War I, 130–31, 194; membership in, 125, 131; in Ohio-Mississippi floods (1937), 163; and War Council, 130; and war relief (1914–17), 125–29, 193; in World War I (1917–18), 129–32

American philanthropy. *See* Philanthropy

American Philosophical Society, 18

American Red Cross. *See* American National Red Cross

American Relief Administration, 134–35, 194. *See also* Russian famine relief

American Revolution, 23, 30, 31, 33–34, 36, 38

American Society for Promotion of Temperance, 46, 189

American Sunday School Union, 46

American Telephone and Telegraph Co., 146

American Tract Society, 79, 189

American Tuberculosis Association, 119, 123; Christmas seal campaign of, 124

Amherst College, 51, 52, 189

Andover Theological Seminary, 51, 66, 189

Appleton, Nathan, 49

Appleton, Samuel, 52

Appleton, William, 46

"Arbella" (ship), 7

ARK (American Relief for Korea), 171

Armenian massacres, 94

Asia, 182

Association for the Relief of Respectable Aged and Indigent Females, 46

Association of Community Chests and Councils, 145, 147

Associations, voluntary, 4, 7, 14, 18–19, 47, 114, 185, 196

Astor, John Jacob, 44, 46, 55

Astor Library, 55

Atlanta University, 88

Auburn, N.Y., 64

Augustus, John, 65

Australia, 170

Bahama Islands, 5

Baker, Newton D., 133

Baldwin Locomotive Co., 80

Baltimore, Md., 50, 55, 109, 115, 189

Bamberger, Louis, 195

Barlow et al. v. A. P. Smith Manufacturing Co., 197

Barton, Clara, 125, 192; characterized, 92; in Civil War, 78; as Red Cross leader, 94–95; and Red Cross movement, 91–93

Bates, Joshua, 55

Beekman, James, 49

Belguim, relief of, in World War I, 126–28

Bellows, Henry W., 77, 80, 83, 91–92

Benevolent associations, 47, 87, 88, 103

"Benevolent Empire," 47–48, 96

Benezet, Anthony, 67, 188; antiwar tracts of, 28–29; charitable activities of, 26–27; defends Indian rights, 29; struggle of, for Negro rights, 29–31

Bennett, James Gordon, 97

Bible, 13, 32, 33, 47, 79

Bible Society of the Confederacy, 79

Bickerdyke, "Mother" Mary Ann, 78

Bicknell, Ernest, 128

Index

Index

Index

Index

Foreign aid, 4, 56, 173, 181, 183; as economic and technical assistance, 181–85; as military assistance, 183–84. *See also* European Recovery Program; Overseas relief; Point Four Program

Fort Sumter, 77

Fortress Monroe, 84

Fortune, 177

Fosdick, Raymond, 132

Foundations, philanthropic, 117–21; contributions of, to education and research, 135–39; contributions of, to southern education, 137; investigations of, 119, 174–76, 177, 196, 197; Lindeman on, 160–61; number of, 139, 175; "scatteration" of, 156, 176; and taxation, 159–60, 174–75, 196; views on, in 1950's, 176–77

France, 38, 127, 167

Francke, August Hermann, 12, 22

Franco-Prussian War, 93

Franklin, Benjamin, 11, 54, 72, 90, 185, 188, 189; antislavery views of, 31; attitude of, toward charity and poor laws, 17–18; influences on career of, 15–16; philanthropic and civic activities of, 16–19; quoted on foreign aid, 165; social views of, 16; will of, 18

Franklin, James, 15

Franklin Funds, 189

Frauds, charitable, 180

Frederick the Great, 27, 28

Freedmen's aid associations, 84–88

Freedmen's Bureau, 191; activities of, 86–88; relations with freedmen's aid associations, 86–88

Freedmen's Inquiry Commission, 85

French and Indian War, 26

French West Indies, 38

Friendly Societies, 25

"Friendly Visiting," 99–100

Friends, Society of, 11, 15, 29–30. *See also* Quakers

Fugitive Slave Law, 73, 74, 75

Fuld, Mrs. Felix, 195

Full Employment Act (1946), 196

Fund for Adult Education, 178

Fund for the Advancement of Education, 178

Fund for the Republic, 178

Fund-raising, 132, 163, 166, 171; for Bunker Hill and Washington Monuments, 55–56; in Civil War, 77, 78–79, 82–84; by European Relief Council (1920–21), 134; and federated financing and community chest movement, 47, 124, 140–41, 192, 193, 194; for Greek relief, 56, 84; by Harvard endowment fund drive (1919), 138, 194; and health organizations, 180–81; for Irish famine relief, 56–57; for Irish famine relief, 56–57, 84; by President's Organization for Unemployment Relief (1931), 146–48, 195; profession of, 140; Red Cross war drives for (1917, 1918), 130–31, 194; for relief of Boston (1774–75), 26; by United Fund, 180, 196; by United War Work Fund (1918), 133; Whitefield and, 22–23; in World War II, 169–70; by "Y" drives, 124–25

Gallaudet, Thomas Hopkins, 66, 70, 189

Garrett, Thomas, 75

Garrison, William Lloyd, 49, 50

Gates, Frederick T., 112, 118, 192

General Education Board, 117, 119, 120, 136, 138, 155, 193

General Motors Corporation, 146

Geneva Convention of 1864, 92, 93, 192

Georgia, 23

German Pietists, 12

Germany, 126, 196

Gettysburg, battle of, 78

Gettysburg address, 83

Gifford, Walter S., 146, 148

Index

Index

Index

Index

Index

Philadelphia Bettering House, 25, 188
Philadelphia Dispensary, 34, 35
Philadelphia Inquirer, 141
"Philanthropology," 90
Philanthropy: Aim and functions of, 2–3, 154–55; American attitudes toward, 1, 2, 45, 120, 141, 145–50, 159, 160–61, 185–86; atonement theory of, 44–45; and charity, 3; in colonial period, 24–26; "dead hand" in, 191; and democracy, 2, 57, 116; European backgrounds of American, 6–7; and foundations, 120–21; founders of American, 7; and gospel of wealth, 107–8; influence of Great Awakening on, 21; motives of, 3, 45, 118; and Negro and southern education, 88, 137–38; and New Deal, 154, 158–59; objects of, 3–4, 45–46, 51–52, 55, 90, 109–10; and overseas aid (1939–45), 172; program of, in 1950's, 179–80; and public relations, 118; and reform, 3, 4, 59–61, 71, 104; "retail," 122–23; Rush and Girard as representative of trends in American, 41; scientific, 17, 89–104 *passim*, 115, 184; sources of, 139–40, 179; as subject of research, 4; and taxation, 97–98, 133, 159–60, 173–74; and the technical assistance program, 182–83; tendency of, in U.S., 17, 151; training courses in, 115; "wholesale," 112, 116; World War I influence on, 129–40 *passim*
Phillips Exeter Academy, 157, 195
Phrenology, 72
Pierce, Franklin, 69–70, 191
Pilgrim's Progress (Bunyan), 35
Pittsburgh Survey, 119
Pius IX, 84
Plymouth, Mass., 6
Point Four Program, 181–82, 183–84, 196

Poland, 129, 165
Poor, the, 3, 14, 16, 17, 25, 70, 97, 143, 180; and charity reformers, 60–61; Franklin on, 17–18; "friendly visiting" of, 99–100; Mrs. Lowell on, 101; Mather on, 14–15; Whitefield's concern for, 22
Poor relief, 16, 17, 23–24, 79, 148, 154; criticism of, 61, 97–98; Elizabethan Poor Law (1601), 187; in England, 7, 61
Poor Richard's Almanack (Franklin), 16
Poughkeepsie, N.Y., 61
Poverty, 17, 72, 100, 116; in underdeveloped or overexploited areas, 181–85
Pratt, Enoch, 110
Pratt Free Library (Baltimore), 110
Pratt Institute (Brooklyn), 108
President's Birthday Balls, 163, 195
President's Committee on War Relief Agencies, 168
President's Organization for Unemployment Relief, fund appeal (1931), 146–48, 195
President's War Relief Control Board, 168–69, 182, 196
Princeton University, 23, 32
Prison reform, 35, 64–65, 91
Prisons and reformatories, 42, 64–65; institutions for juveniles, 62–63, 64, 73
Progressive era, 115
Prohibition amendment, 133
Protestant Church World Service, 172
Providence, R.I., 74
Public Administration Clearing House, 156
Public health movement, 91
Public land, 69, 70
Public welfare, 70, 95–96; before Great Depression, 141; during Great Depression, 152–54
Puritans, 7, 9, 187

Index

Index

Index

Index

Index

Wisconsin, University of, 139
Woolman, John, 29
Woolsey sisters, 77
Worcester (Mass.) Asylum, 68
World War I, 125, 131, 168; influence of, on American philanthropy, 129–40 *passim;* war relief in, 125–35
World War II, 129, 131; overseas aid and war relief activities in, 165–71
WPA (Works Progress Administration), 162, 163

Yale, Elihu, 188

Yale University, 12, 78, 138, 157, 194, 195
Yeatman, James, 85
Yellow fever epidemic (1793), 36–40, 189
Young Men's Christian Association, 79, 123, 130, 132, 133, 143, 168, 191; fund-raising drives of, 124–25
Young Men's Hebrew Association, 123
Young Women's Christian Association, 123, 132, 168

Zinsser, Hans, 136

THE CHICAGO HISTORY OF AMERICAN CIVILIZATION

DANIEL J. BOORSTIN, EDITOR

* Available in cloth only. All other books published in both cloth and paperback editions.

Now? "I've always known where you live. It's in your file."

"Someone turned an antique automobile, a Bentley, around in my driveway."

His petulance made me smile. I ran my hand across the Bentley's soft leather, and said, "That happens on my street, too. Some joker knocked my mailbox down last month."

"That doesn't happen where I live. It's rather exclusive. You see, Miss Dru, I pay dearly for my privacy and that of my child. I do not want curiosity seekers sightseeing my place."

"I haven't compromised your privacy, Mr. Whitley. If somebody sicced the sightseers on you, it wasn't me."

"Is it possible the authorities are watching my home?"

"In a Bentley? It's possible you're being paranoid."

"I don't think so. Now tell me what's happened on my case."

I suddenly got an attack of the giddies. "I've got to shake more trees, get some ducks in a row, before I can open up the peanut gallery."

Silence on his end.

I added, "Speaking metaphorically."

His voice sounded hollow when he said, "My question is, whose trees are you shaking, and whose ducks are you getting in a row?"

"What are you talking about?"

"I heard on the news that a car registered to an ex-policewoman was blown up last night. They said it might be related to the suburban children's murders."

"I'm not investigating those murders, Mr. Whitney. It was coincidence. The lead detective is a friend of mine."

Silence.

Bastard. He could yank me from the case for all I cared. I'd just as soon work solely with Portia, even pro bono.

His sigh wavered dramatically on the cell current. "Call me when you get to California. I expect to hear from you with every new development. Of course, I'll want a written report, too."

"When hell freezes—"

"What did you say?"

"Whatever pleases . . ."

I'd packed my suitcases and was finally in bed, half asleep, when the phone rang. It was going on midnight.

"Hello," the voice called down the line. "Can you hear me?"

"I can. Who is this, please?"

"Arlo Cameron."

Cameron was one of those who thought the distance between Georgia and California called for shouting. "Good evening, Mr. Cameron. Thanks for returning my call."

"Who you working for?"

"The state of Georgia, and Bradley Whitney."

He seemed to be mulling this over. "You know what's happened?"

"Eileen, your wife, and her daughter, Kinley, have disappeared. Have you heard from them?"

"No."

"Anything new on the case?"

"No, nothing. The cops here haven't a clue. I'm about to go crazy with this."

"I'm booked on a flight tomorrow. We need to talk."

"When you get in?"

"One-ish, your time. I'm at the Palkott."

"Come out at three. Little Tuscany, near the old Racquet Club."

I wrote down the address on North Via Las Palmas.

Back to sleep.

At three, the motion sensors in the back yard lit the spotlights. My one-car, detached garage was at the end of the driveway inside a four-foot picket fence.

I flew into the kitchen, to the bay window. Everything was quiet outside, nothing stirring. Yet I *knew* someone was out there. I ran from the kitchen to the dining room—another room that overlooked the back yard. I studied every blade of grass, every shrub, every shadow. It was eerily ordinary, too eerily ordinary. As if someone watched and didn't breathe.

Half an hour later, I shut the lights and continued to watch the yard by a slice of the moon. I thought about calling Lake. Or taking a flashlight and checking inside the garage.

Yeah, like I'm a one-woman bomb squad. Or one of those heroine-too-stupid-to-live types the romantic suspense writers always laugh about.

The hell with it. If a bomb went off inside my new old car, the insurance company could sort it out. Maybe I'd get used to Portia never speaking to me again.

I never got back to sleep and was relieved when the sky lightened. At dawn, I slipped outside, pulled open the garage door, and looked through the Bentley's windows.

A dark *thing* lay on the back seat. I called Lake. The bomb squad was there in seven minutes.

They presented me with Lake's binoculars.

A good laugh was had by all.

Even exhausted me.

Eleven

The Coachella Valley is at the northern end of the Colorado Desert. As the 757 lowered toward Palm Springs, I studied the rippling sand dunes that flowed into the Salton Sea, while people across the aisle looked at rippling sand dunes flowing away from the Little San Bernardino Mountains.

Palm Springs, my computer told me, is a hundred miles south of LA and has a population of forty-five thousand. A hundred thousand people, mostly Native Americans, call the Coachella Valley home. Because of the growing population in the desert, the environmentalists were worrying themselves silly about the sand dune ecosystem.

The tires bumped down on the runway, and I could finally take a deep breath. After the insanity at Atlanta's mess of an airport, it was nice to deplane to soft music and murmuring voices. The walk to the rental car booths didn't take a minute. Two people were in line ahead of me. A tall, dark-visaged man came into my sight line waving a sign. MORIAH DREW. The pronunciation was right, if not the spelling, but I was used to it. I waved and called out, "Mister." He turned. "I'm Moriah Dru."

He strolled toward me wearing a grin as wide as the Grand Canyon. He tossed the cardboard in a trash can. We shook hands. "I'm Dartagnan LeRoi."

"Your mama really named you Dartagnan?" I asked, looking down into his merry eyes. I'm tall; he's not, but he had a large deep voice.

He laughed. "My Louisiana mama heard the name from a travelin' salesman from Georgia."

Behind me, the rental car guy called, "Miss?"

"Let me take that bag," Dartagnan said, taking hold of the handle on my rolling suitcase.

I signed the papers for the rental, and as we walked through the automatic doors, I said, "I like Dartagnan."

He drawled, "I'm used to it."

Truth was, he looked like a Dartagnan. Wiry, nimble body, coal black hair, a mustache, swarthy skin dotted with two of the darkest eyes ever to come out of Louisiana, swashbuckling arms, and a belt buckle shaped like California. As we walked, he talked. Dartagnan was a man who liked to talk, and he talked fast. I learned that his mother's name was Josephine and his father's name was Alain. They were originally from the Grand Bayou Blue, but he was raised on Lafourche Bayou in Pointe-aux-Chenes in Lafourche Parish. His daddy worked at the sugar mill and sold Spanish moss on the side. Alain and Josephine never went to school because when high water came, it cut off the only school, which was in Mongegut. "Besides," he said, "we kids were part of the family work force." After high school, he became a cop in Houma, and, after burnout, he headed West, to The Springs.

All that info in less than five minutes.

Outside, the desert heat attacked my skin and lungs, and Georgia isn't exactly Alaska. My neck felt clammy. "Hot," I said, fanning myself with the rental papers.

"You get used to it."

"I won't be here that long."

He stopped walking and looked at me. "You think you're gonna find that mama and daughter that fast?"

"That's my goal."

"Then you better start lookin' somewheres else. You won't be finding them 'round here."

"In LA, maybe?"

He clucked his tongue. "Not likely."

We were at the Rent-a-Car parking lot. My luck, I thought, the car I get will be black. I said, "I should have picked a color."

Dartagnan smiled. "You can change cars, if you want."

Sure enough it was black, and I changed.

"You want to go to your hotel first?" he asked. "Or would you like somethin' to drink."

I looked at my watch. One-twenty. Four-twenty in Atlanta. Close enough for a cocktail, but I had a lot on my plate, including talking to this cop. "A nice cold beer sounds good," I said, rolling down the windows to let the broiling temperature inside the car meld with the hundred-and-ten degrees outside it. "I'm meeting someone at three."

"Where you stayin'?"

"The Palkott."

"Downtown. Let's go."

I followed his white unmarked late-model Camry. He made a right on Vista Ciero. Dartagnan didn't drive slow and covered the fifteen-minute drive from the airport in nine. The Palkott had been constructed on North Palm Canyon Drive.

"I'll be in the bar," Dartagnan said, leaving me with the bellboy.

"I'll be quick," I said.

My suite was a deluxe—complete with a sleeper sofa in the sitting room. The AC iced the desert tan walls. White spreads and drapes made me want to crash. I'm not one who can go without sleep. I ripped the drape cord and stepped out on the balcony. What a view. The San Jacinto Mountains are just as majestic as the websites say.

I splashed water on my face, dried off, lathered with moisturizer, and went downstairs. The brass-toned bar was down a hall, tucked in a corner. Dartagnan had an audience for some story he was telling. Two waiters and the bartender were laughing heartily, and I was five steps into the room when he turned to salute me. "I ain't been in here since I busted up a fight between Will Phillips and a reporter," he said.

"Heartthrob Phillips?" I asked.

"The one and the same."

"What was his problem with the reporter?"

"Takin' pictures."

"That's what reporters do."

"This is The Springs—Ol' Blue Eyes' stomping ground." He paused for effect. "Literally." The waiters and bartender snickered appreciatively.

"Things change," I said. "Still no reporters allowed?"

"It's a tradition. No reporters snooping, or taking pictures. Phillips is a married man."

"Uh-oh. He wasn't with the missus?"

"Never is."

The bartender asked, "What'll you have, Miss?"

"Amstel Light," I said. "Put the drinks on my tab. Room seven-twenty."

"You got it."

"Thanks," Dartagnan said, and we took our beers to a table well away from the bar. He motioned his head toward the bartender. "His ears're always open." Once we settled into our seats, he said, "Eileen's disappearing won't be kept quiet for long. Our press boys eventually get 'round to missing persons, once they sober up."

Who did the sobering up, the reporters or the missing persons? "It's not headlines in Atlanta, either. My client wants it kept that way."

"So does Arlo." Dartagnan hoisted his dark draft. "We'll do what we can."

65

"Tell me what you know. From the beginning."

"It's Sunday afternoon," he said, wiping his mouth after the chug. "Arlo Cameron's on the phone. I know him pretty good. We play racquetball sometimes—when he can't get another partner. You know how that goes." I nodded. Cops aren't the usual partners of millionaires. "Anyways, he says that Eileen wasn't home, and that Kinley's father just called to say she hadn't gotten off the plane in Atlanta. Arlo said he'd called around to a few of Eileen's friends and found out Eileen missed her afternoon with the girls at Mission Hills. That's where she plays golf, but this Sunday she wasn't playing because she was putting Kinley on the plane. But she told them she would be there afterward. You know, drinking the afternoon away. That was the plan."

"When did Arlo get back from LA?"

"Sunday afternoon. He said he wasn't surprised Eileen wasn't home because Sundays are her days for herself." Dartagnan stopped speaking, and I sensed a punch line coming. "So are all the other days, if you ask me."

What did I see in his face? Dislike? Disapproval? "What are you saying?"

"Eileen's a lot younger than Arlo." He wiped his nose with the back of his hand. "Hell, I'm a lot younger than Arlo."

I figured Dartagnan was forty. "How old's Arlo?"

"High sixties."

"Eileen's thirty-five."

"Typical for their crowd," he said.

"What else can you tell me about Eileen?"

Shrugging, he looked at his beer. "Pretty lady." Then he looked at me. "It's hard to be flashy out here. Everybody out-flashes everybody else. But Eileen—she stood out from that crowd—she was sure something."

Cops are supposed to be observant, but this one had a

personal interest in Eileen or I'd have to take my instincts to task. "What *else?*"

"She wasn't a phony. Her blonde hair was natural—like a Swedish blonde is. Her skin was like pale gold, and her eyes were pure cobalt."

He hushed, and I studied him for an instant. "You fell for her."

"I guess," he said with a shrug. "Any man would." He took a deep breath. "But—she was Arlo's. She adored him."

"What's Arlo like?"

"Hale, hearty guy. Smarter than he sounds. Mr. Hollywood."

"What type of stuff does he direct?"

"Westerns and Dirty Harry stuff. TV specials. He's not famous like Ford or Spielberg, but he turns out the films and makes big bucks."

"Where's he from, originally?"

"Texas, somewhere. The border. He calls himself a half-breed."

"Mexican?"

"Nah, Colombian and something."

"How long's he lived in Palm Springs?"

"More'n thirty years. He and Frank were buddies. He palled with Dinah and Joey."

"So he's the old crowd. People like Will Phillips are the new crowd, aren't they?"

"Yep. Parties are divided along those lines. The old crowd drinks up a storm, the new crowd snorts up a storm."

"Eileen did drugs, according to her ex."

"I wouldn't know," he said, too quickly.

"Eileen'd be in the new crowd, wouldn't she?"

His brow wrinkled as he thought about that. "If she went with them, I didn't know about it."

I doubted that. "No signs of foul play in the Cameron house?"

He looked askance, at something interesting on the wall. I'd caught him off guard. He shook his head, then met my eyes. "None I saw. There's nothing like that with this case. She took the kid and went into hiding. Nothing to do but wait till she comes back. They always do."

"Did you give it a thorough forensics go-through?"

"Enough. The place is always immaculate. Maids, and all. I would of noticed anything out of the way when I went there to check out Eileen's closets. See what she took with her."

"According to the report, Arlo couldn't say what she took."

"Her car's gone. So's her sable coat."

"She took a sable coat in August?"

Dartagnan raised his shoulders. "Who knows with women."

I thought of something I'd read. "The high desert gets cold at night, doesn't it?"

For a moment, he appeared to be analyzing me. "That it does, Miss Dru. That it does."

TWELVE

Heading north on Palm Canyon Drive, I wound through a few streets starting with "Via" and came to Via Las Palmas. The street forked, south and north. I wanted North Via Las Palmas. The streets of Italianate mansions, which went back to the thirties and forties, were known as Little Tuscany. The Camerons lived in a two-story pink stucco with a mission ridge roof and white plantation shutters. Two large acacias stood sentry at each end of the house. Traipsing up the adobe walk, I passed a koi pond surrounded by smoke trees.

Arlo Cameron jerked the door open before my finger touched the bell button. He stepped back so I could enter the high-walled foyer. A tiered Waterford chandelier cascaded from the coffered ceiling and tinkled lightly. Arlo—short, muscular, caramel-colored face, eyes large and liquid, hair wiry and silvering, eyebrows as wiry—had on an Arnold Palmer golf outfit and Birkenstocks. He affected a shadow of gray whiskers.

"Miss Dru, so good of you . . ." He offered his hand, and I placed mine in his. He slid his fingers over my palm rather than shaking, then spun me lightly and put his hand at the back of my waist. "Let's go this way." I felt like an actress he was positioning on a set. We moved over burnished copper tiles, through cool, refreshing air made possible by costly air-conditioning units and humidifiers. We passed through French doors, walked five paces down a hall and into the kitchen. It gleamed with stainless steel appliances and black granite counters. The Mexican pavers seemed too beautiful to walk on. But the smell. My God. I twitched my nose. Rotten fish?

He didn't apologize for the odor when he paused and faced me. "Miss Dru?" he said, rubbing his gray whiskers. "Or can we be less formal?" He spoke with a wet, nervous tongue.

"Dru is fine."

His pressed lips turned up at the corners. "Arlo." He bobbed his head as if this determining parlay was the reason for pausing, then waved a hand meaning for me to precede him. At another set of French doors, we passed into the covered patio where palm fans rotated lazily. White wicker sofas sported cushions the color of apricots and lemons. It wasn't hot out here, although walking up his driveway not five minutes ago, the afternoon sun had burned into my eyeballs. I looked around for air-conditioning ducts and found them. Below one duct, on a back wall, a circular bar had been built of some exotic wood. Six matching bar stools surrounded it. Walking behind the bar, Arlo looked at me. "I'm pouring rum and ginger ale. Want one?"

"Not too strong."

"No, no." He carefully measured the jiggers and poured the bubbly ale. "Please. Sit anywhere you wish."

Before we got comfortable, I wanted to ask. "Do you have any idea where Eileen could have gone?" I didn't want to drift into side bars. I walked to a wicker chair and sat.

He didn't answer until he'd placed my drink on a table by my right arm and seated himself across from me. "No idea. None at all."

"Can you think of anything you haven't thought of before?" Sometimes questions don't come out quite right.

He looked mystified. "I—no."

"Would she go to Los Angeles?"

"Eileen wasn't crazy about LA." He sipped his drink, looking at me over the rim. "She liked it here."

"Does she have friends who she might stay with?"

He looked as if that was out of the question and shook his head.

"Where did she go to think things out?" I reached for my glass.

He rubbed the rim of his. "Eileen didn't do that. Too many ghosts." He hesitated a tick. "You know about her parents and kid sister?"

"Yes."

"She liked to be with people. To rid the dreads."

"I'd like a list of her friends."

He canted his head to one side. "I don't know of anyone she was real close to. She was too new out here. She wasn't old Palm Springs with the women, if you get my drift." He tried on a smile. The gap in his front teeth reminded me of Ernest Borgnine. "Hell, I'm not an old Springer, either."

"Is society here that stratified?"

"You bet."

"I'd like to talk to people she might confide in, who might have an idea where she would go."

"That'd be me."

"I'm sure," I said and sipped. "I was thinking of a girlfriend."

"I wouldn't put a lot of hope in getting Eileen's inner thoughts from anyone."

"Do you think Eileen will come home eventually."

"If she can."

"What do you mean by that?"

"I don't know what happened." He spread his hands. Big, strong hands, one holding a nearly empty drink glass. "All I know is I came home Sunday, and no sooner got in the door than that asshole in Atlanta started calling. Excuse me, Miss Dru. I told the no-good-so-and-so that maybe they missed the flight, maybe Kinley's on the next flight. The jerk calls back.

The airlines says she wasn't on the flight, or any flight. I called some people where Eileen might be. I come up empty. I got hold of Dartagnan." He waved the air. "That's it."

"Did you and Eileen talk much about her ex, Bradley Whitney?"

"As little as possible."

"What did she say about him?"

"I don't pay any attention to the bad-mouthing. I been divorced twice. I been lied about, too."

"Did you think she was lying about him?"

"Don't know. Didn't care."

I looked bewildered for his benefit.

He leaned forward, gripping the glass with both hands. "I married her because I loved her. I didn't care where she came from, or who she was married to, or why she divorced the guy. I live in the present. Or the future."

"I guess making movies keeps you moving on."

"You got it."

"What was your relationship with Kinley?"

"I liked the kid. She was doing all right. She was smart."

"Was she unhappy in Atlanta?"

He sat back. "Who knows with kids that age?"

"Did you know that Eileen was determined to get custody?"

"Sure. It's all she thought about."

"Was that okay with you?"

"Sure." He hefted himself out of his seat, looked at my glass that had one sip taken from it, and headed for the bar.

"How was she going to do it?" I asked. "Get custody?"

Walking away, he spoke. "Hire a shrink for the girl. Go back to court."

"When?"

"As soon as she found a lawyer she liked." He rounded the bar and faced me. "Couldn't stand the one she had." He puckered his lips. "In the palm of the fuckin' judge's hand. Excuse me."

"I know the judge. Portia Devon is fair."

He leveled unwavering eyes at me. "Not to Eileen she wasn't."

"Eileen's an addict."

"She's not a sleaze like that stripper she married." He looked as if he could bite his tongue and jerked the tongs from the ice bucket.

"Stripper?"

He dropped ice cubes into the glass and uncapped the rum. "Now don't go and quote me." He splashed rum over the ice. "He once worked in this club. He told Eileen he was a gofer, and then a bartender. That was when he was in college. It was a boy-girl strip club. That's all I know." And, obviously, that was more than he had intended to say. He filled the glass with ginger ale and came back to his seat.

I said, "Working, even stripping in a club, is not criminal in Georgia. Smoking pot and snorting coke is."

"Look, Miss Dru—"

"Hey, I thought we were Dru and Arlo?"

"Okay, Dru." He looked at my glass, which was still mostly full. He sucked down half his drink, sat back, and gave a dismissive wave of his hand. "Eileen kept her feelings to herself. She was secretive. She was nervous as a whore in church most of the time. The pot evened her out. Nothing wrong in that."

"The judge told me if Eileen shook the habit, she'd reconsider custody. Between you and me, Portia's not crazy about Bradley Whitney. And any judge likes to give little girls to their mamas."

Arlo's right shoulder wriggled from his inner mirth. "If Eileen comes back, I'll tell her. It'll be news, I'm sure."

If? He'd sounded sarcastic, but he looked so forlorn my eyes wandered away to the sparkling pebble tech pool.

He said, "I wish I could be more help."

73

"Did Eileen withdraw more money than usual from her bank? Did you see any maps around the house, packed suitcases? Anything unusual like that?"

His gaze skimmed my face. "What are you talking about?"

"If she took off with Kinley, she had to have a plan, money, things to take, a place to go."

He looked as if the thought hadn't entered his head. "I didn't find no maps around the house or plans or suitcases. She took out some money from her account on Thursday. Twenty-five grand. She had a tip about a stock. I said good luck." As he watched the glittering water in the pool, he said, "I was good to Eileen, gave her whatever she wanted, but maybe I didn't pay enough attention."

"Who is her stockbroker?"

He took a deep breath. "I didn't ask her. Think it was some scam artist at the club. They hang around the women, mooching like that."

"You have a stockbroker?"

"In LA Eileen knows nothing about my business."

"Except you're in movies," I said. He nodded, finished his drink, and rattled the ice. He looked at my glass. Half full.

Time to broach the unspeakable. "Any reason to think your wife and stepdaughter could be dead?"

A sob exploded from the back of his throat. His glass hit the floor.

I said, "Sorry."

His head bowed to his chest, sadness seeping from his pores. Then he shook his head like he was trying to invalidate the present and relive a better moment.

Somewhere deep in the mansion, a gong sounded, as if timed to interrupt a bad moment.

"Hold on," Arlo said, getting up. I got up, too, picked up the glass and went to place it on the bar.

Some time went by before he came in with a woman. She was about forty and looked like someone you'd expect to see in Palm Springs: white blonde hair pulled back in a casual pony tail, nearly anorexic and very tanned. She had on an orange sundress, sandals, gold rings, and a locket. Her toenails and fingernails matched her sundress. "Arlo, my God," she exclaimed, little-girl breathless. "What's stinking up your house?"

I perked my ears. Arlo looked perplexed. "Stinking up my house?"

"In the kitchen."

"Oh, that," he snorted. "Eileen bought some sushi sometime before—sometime last week. I had to throw it out. Fifty-five bucks and nobody opened the cartons."

The woman said, "Eileen sure loved her sushi."

They both looked at me, the woman's head at a perky angle, Arlo uncomfortable. He pointed at the woman. "This is Heidi. From next door."

Heidi's eyes were as blank as a mannequin's. I said, "Nice meeting you."

She said in a pout, "I still can't believe Eileen's missing. I look out all the time, expecting to see her in the garden."

"Kinley's missing, too," I said.

Heidi's eyes grew extraordinarily wide. "I never thought for the tiniest second Eileen would skip like that." Arlo suddenly remembered he was the host. "Hey, ladies, let's sit. My back's killing me."

Heidi wriggled into a chair. Once settled, she said, "Arlo here thinks I probably was the last to see Eileen—and her little girl—before, before whatever they did."

"What time was that?" I asked.

She batted her lashes at Arlo, who got interested in the hair on the back of his hands. She said, "Late afternoon Saturday, I think, I thought they probably were going for dinner. It was about that time."

"Did you talk to them?"

"No. I was driving by to go to a cocktail party."

"That would have been around five?"

"I don't look at clocks."

"But you saw Mrs. Cameron and Kinley?"

She looked tested to the limit. "No, I didn't—not exactly. I saw the car—the back of it—and someone was there. Moving, like. It had to be them."

While Arlo studied his hands, Heidi kicked a foot and let a sandal fall to the floor. I asked, "Were you and Eileen good friends?"

I knew by the look on her face they weren't. She said, "Kind of. We talked. But I played tennis. She golfed."

"So, she wouldn't have confided in you?"

"Oh no, she wasn't . . ."

"Wasn't what?"

"She didn't—she wasn't the kind to tell her secrets."

"Did you think she had secrets?"

An odd smile distorted her mouth. "Everyone does."

"You, too?" I said, smiling. Her lips pressed as she looked at Arlo, who was still finding his hands more interesting than our conversation. "How long have you lived next door?" I asked.

"A year and a half."

"Are you married?"

At once, Arlo and Heidi sat upright and looked pissed. Arlo said, "Miss Dru, I asked Heidi over because she saw Eileen that day, not to tell her life's story."

I'd hit the hot button. "Sorry," I said. "Force of habit."

Heidi was on her feet, tripping toward the double French doors. Not rising to let her out, Arlo called over his shoulder, "Thanks, Heidi." She looked back and gave him a little-girl wave. He wasn't pleased when he looked at me. He waited a few beats before he said, "You got something in mind?"

"No," I lied.

"Heidi's a nice woman. A nice neighbor. She tends the fish in the pond when I'm gone. She tells the gardeners what to do. Knows every desert tree there is."

"Handy, when you live in the desert."

His mouth twisted while he appraised me. "As to your question, Heidi is not married now. She's a widow."

What else could I say, or ask? Then I thought of something. "Who's Eileen's hairdresser?"

The muscles of his face eased somewhat, and he sat forward. "You got to have something to chew on, don't you? That's the kind you are." I spread my lips to indicate a smile. He said, "Theodosia's on Ramon. She knows every hair on Eileen's head—as well as everyone who's anyone in The Springs. But if she knows what went on inside that pretty head of my wife's, I'd be damned surprised."

He rose and headed for the French doors. At the front door, he looked at his watch. "Supper time." He looked at me. "There's a great restaurant downtown. Used to be Frank's favorite place. Tourists now. You can ask me tourist questions, if you want."

I smiled sweetly. "But I'm not a tourist, Arlo."

I think he was going to say, "Call me, Mr. Cameron," but he nodded and said, "Good evening, then."

The door closed on my derriere—softly, but firmly.

THIRTEEN

I waited until I got to the hotel to look at the missed calls logged in my cell. Lake had called. So had Whitney. So had Portia. And so had Dartagnan.

Immediately, Mozart played. Whitney. He was the last person I wanted to speak to. He was strumming my one last nerve, and, I, apparently, his. He was not happy that I hadn't pulled the rabbit, Eileen, out of a hat. I said, "I'm a quick learner, Mr. Whitney. Palm Springers keep their mouths closed and their secrets to themselves."

"I don't care about those California weirdos. Someone out there has to know something about where she might have taken Kinley. She didn't vanish into thin air."

"The air here is very thin, literally and figuratively, Mr. Whitney."

"And what the hell am I to make of that observation?"

"I told you I'd find Eileen and Kinley, and I will."

"The longer this investigation lasts, the more vulnerable I become to curiosity seekers." With that, he cut the conversation.

It was ten-thirty at night in Atlanta, but I called Portia anyway. She never sleeps. I told her about Arlo's startling blab about a possible stripper past for the academic Mr. Whitney.

She observed, "Interesting, but too long ago to count for much."

"Maybe not," I said, thinking of The Cloisters.

"Keep at it, Moriah."

As if I wouldn't. As for Lake, it was hard to tell where people were when you called their cells, but the background noises didn't sound like he was in Frankie's. I heard honking horns. "You got the traffic gig tonight?" I asked.

"I wish I was directing traffic sometimes, but right this minute I'm heading downtown. A grandmother walking her pup said she saw a man dart from some bushes. She found a d/b, or rather the curious pup did. Woman was dead only minutes. Grandma's helping the artist draw a facsimile of the bush-darter. What's up with you?"

I told him all I knew, emphasizing the give-and-take between Arlo and Heidi.

"You think they got something to do with this?"

"They're being coy. Whether they're lying or being careful, I don't know. Heidi didn't actually see Eileen and Kinley—just the car. I'll have to verify that Arlo was in LA during the time they vanished."

"You can bet he was, because he'd be the likely suspect if they turned up dead. What's the cop Dartagnan saying?"

"He's a buddy of Arlo's. Taken with himself, but doesn't know anything."

"They been gone a week and this Dartagnan doesn't know shit yet?"

"He thinks Eileen's headed for Georgia with the girl. Maybe taking in the sights of Alabama."

"Thinks? What makes him *think* that?"

"He's playing the jurisdictional football game. Let somebody else handle it."

"Well, they haven't made it back here," Lake said. "Might be helpful if we put out a bulletin. A picture of them."

"Whitney'd have a stroke."

"It's a matter of time before the reporters get hold of this, you know. The FBI likes to put CAC cases on their website."

CAC was the bureau's Crimes against Children unit.

I asked, "How does Whitney look so far?"

"Squeaky. He doesn't miss his classes. He writes learned papers on his computer at home. Students, and other profs speak well of him. No scent of wrongdoing. We still haven't nailed down where he got his money."

"Well, I got something you can look into." I told him what Arlo'd told me about the stripping.

Lake gave his trademark whistle. "The mannequin has a blemish, huh?"

"It was a boy-girl strip club. There's only one that I know of in Atlanta."

"Sass Shay's," he said. "Two stages, one for the boys, one for the girls."

"Bet someone's still around from fifteen years ago."

"Is that a marching order?"

"A mere tap dance for you. What's fifteen years?"

I returned Dartagnan's call. As I'd expected, he asked me to dinner. I hemmed and hawed about exhaustion and finally let him insist.

The Ristorante Italia was in Cathedral City, a hop and a skip southeast of Palm Springs.

The maître d' led us through the crowded little foyer, past the cozy bar, into a large green room—light green carpet, green upholstered chairs, gold linen table toppers over green under-skirts, white napkins shaped like flowers in crystal water glasses.

This was Dartagnan's place, all right. Half the room hailed him as he was led to "his table."

He forbade shop talk—to assure proper digestion—for the hour it took to dine. And, furthering his initiative, he ordered for us. Not even Lake dared do that for me.

Cakebread sauvignon blanc, '01. We talked wines.

Pappa al pomodoro, which is Florentine tomato and bread soup. We talked soups. People should know more about Italian soups than *pasta fagioli,* he grumped.

Insalata saporita, that is, mixed greens with walnuts, pears, and Gorgonzola. Cheeses—I learned a lot about Italian cheeses.

Paillard di vitello, which was grilled veal topped with fresh arugula. We compared recipes for *osso buco.*

Tiramisu soufflé, spiked with Amaretto. He maintained a soufflé was better than heavy cakes and pudding desserts after three courses. Stuffed to the eyeballs, I had to agree.

Finally, a Moët & Chandon Brut-Impérial champagne. The French, he said, couldn't be beat for champagnes.

He patted his mouth and laid his napkin aside. Rising, he said, "Now we go and talk about the case."

Sated with food and wine, all I wanted to do was go to my room and pass out. "You'll be interested in where we're going and it's right in your back yard," he said.

On the way, while he drove fifteen miles an hour over the speed limit, he explained that on Thursday nights street traffic was closed between Baristo and Amado Roads on Palm Canyon Drive for VillageFest. "You know who Sonny Bono was?" he asked.

"Sonny, of Sonny and Cher," I said, almost too tired to answer.

He glanced at me, then back at the road. "As mayor, Sonny started the festival, and it continued. Most of the time, everything goes okay. Sometimes people drink too much."

I drank way too much. "I can't do a street festival tonight," I said.

He apparently didn't hear me. "You'll be interested in some of the Mission Hills exhibits."

No use protesting further. "Maybe I can pick up a desert memento for someone I know who loves all things desert."

He was quiet for a moment, and I got the feeling he had planned an après-dinner tête-à-tête at my hotel. He'd insisted on paying the entire dinner check. He asked, "You're not married, are you?"

"See a ring?" I said, holding out my left hand.

"Means nothing."

"It would to me."

We parked off the street. The first thing I caught was the smell—the wonderful food odors mingling with leather and five-hundred-dollar-an-ounce perfume. Food carts lined the street on each side. A person dressed as a long chocolate donut held a tray loaded with them. "Have a one," the Asian voice said through the chocolate frosting on his face.

"No thanks," I said.

"Hey Dartagnan," the man cried, "you no gonna pass me by, are you?"

"Not a chance, Zing," Dartagnan said, taking a sticky donut from the tray. "You know cops and donuts."

We walked on. Dartagnan explained as he chewed, "I eat at Zing's Donuts every morning I'm on duty, and that's seven days a week. Try the place unless you do room service."

"I don't."

"Zing's is next door to the casino. You can walk from your hotel."

Six pantomimes danced by—on stilts. A juggler followed, eight different objects flying from his hands. We wandered by booth after booth of crafts, of silver, and iron, and turquoise, and pottery. Dartagnan stopped at a weaver's booth. "You might pick out something for your special someone here."

I had in mind getting Lake an iron piece, not a basket. But the artistry was exquisite. A handwoven round tray with a lizard in the middle caught my eye. Not that I like lizards. It was just that lovely. The basket weaver had coiled the straw counterclockwise. I looked up to see Dartagnan talking to the woman behind the table. I swear to God I thought I was looking at a young Natalie Wood—dark eyes, wide full mouth, flawless warm skin in a perfect oval face. She looked at me and flipped her long black braid to the back of her neck. Something in the motion of her hand and her glance made me feel we'd be friends. And that feeling came seconds before Dartagnan introduced us. "Contessa Resovo, this is Moriah Dru of Atlanta."

She nodded, and her smile reached beyond her eyes. "Atlanta," she said. "Nice to have you here, Miss Dru."

"Just Dru," I said.

"You must call me Tess then. I see that you like the iguana tray."

"I must have it." I'd spoken before I knew the price and realized immediately that I couldn't afford it.

Dartagnan said, "Hope you've got a line of credit."

"That much?"

"Not for you," Tess said, grinning. "Half price. Five hundred for you."

I swallowed. "Sounds like a deal."

"It is," Dartagnan said.

The interplay between Dartagnan and Tess tantalized. Did he, like Lake, spawn groupies wherever he went? Dartagnan flirted clearly, but she didn't. Poised and rather standoffish, she might have been good at hiding her true feelings.

Dartagnan noticed that I noticed. He said to Tess, "Dru is an investigator for the State of Georgia. She's looking for a missing mother and child."

Tess's mouth turned down. "Here? Who?"

Dartagnan said, "Keep this quiet for the time being, but they are Arlo Cameron's wife and stepdaughter."

A hand went to her breast. "Eileen? Kinley? They are missing? When?"

"On Sunday morning they went for a hike in a canyon—we're not sure which one—but they never returned. It's so easy to get lost in the desert." There wasn't a hitch in his voice when he threw out this bold lie, unless he knew it to be true.

"Yes," Tess agreed. "For tourists. But in the desert, there are people. They will help you find your way back."

"Sure in Painted Canyon, but not in Lost Coyote Canyon—if they strayed there." He clutched my shoulder. "Kinley's father in Atlanta hired Dru here to find them."

One of her eyebrows cocked, and I understood why. An investigator from a southern city—hired to find someone lost in the desert? Dartagnan's lie stood out. She said, "Lost Coyote Canyon is forbidden."

Dartagnan turned to me. "The Canyon is sacred. And closed. But there are those who won't listen, especially if their child begs to go."

Tess's eyes danced when she looked at me. She grinned and said, "I am not simpleminded. Dartagnan brings you here because he thinks I might be able to help you find them—if they are really lost in the desert."

His laugh was hearty and full of teeth. "You couldn't find your way past Saks Fifth Avenue."

"Don't be so sure. You know Aunt Rosa is teaching me the old ways."

He looked at me. "Tess's aunt is famous in the canyons. She runs the reservation's casino in Mission Palms, but she's also a shaman who's found lost souls before."

Tess said, "I am going to visit her tomorrow afternoon late." Her eyes traveled from him to me. "Perhaps if Eileen doesn't return by the time I leave, we can go together."

"I would like that," I said, wishing tomorrow were now.

Tess wrapped the tray in brown paper and put it in a simple woven shopping bag—a handsome freebie. She took my credit card. For the next couple of months there'd be no wine purchases at Murphy's Wine Shop.

Tess and I made an agreement. If she didn't hear from Dartagnan or me that Eileen and Kinley had returned, we'd meet at the Palkott tomorrow. We hugged our goodnights, and Dartagnan led me back the way we'd come.

"Hey, Monsieur Dartagnan," a man called from the curb.

He stood outside a food booth. The sign hung above it read: "Too Busy to Cook?" The man wore a chef's crepe paper tall hat. He had a pencil-thin moustache that curled at the ends. I blinked a couple of times. *He can't be for real.*

We ambled over to the booth. Dartagnan exaggerated a stage whisper that the man could hear, "Philippe tests out his goodies on the unsuspecting for free."

The man tittered with his hand to his mouth. "They *l'amour* the sushi, the California rolls," he said. I wondered about his French and noticed he wasn't as wispy as he affected. He towered over Dartagnan, and he seemed familiar—the movie Frenchman in a chef's hat, perhaps.

Dartagnan explained, "Philippe's got five stores from Rancho Mirage on up the valley. He personally flies his tasty trays everywhere."

"All sushi?" I asked.

"*Non,*" he said. If he was French, I was Chinese. He went on, "Trays of *merveilleux* cheeses and wines. *Le monde des saucissons.* Eggplants, the *couleurs,* they take your breath away." He spoke with his fingers together. "Caviar, smoke salmon, oysters in season, foie gras, escargot, truffles. *Boeuf* so divine you would never want any but Philippe's." He kissed his fingers, so *de rigueur.* "You call ahead, I make what you want."

"How's that for service?" Dartagnan asked, then realized he hadn't formally introduced us. "Philippe, this is Moriah Dru. She's visiting from Atlanta."

"Ah, you want the fried chicken"—he pronounced it *shik-can*—"and the okras?"

"You bet," I said. "Lunch tomorrow, before I shop?"

"My pleasure, *mademoiselle.*"

Strolling back the way we'd come, dodging dawdlers and sellers packing up, I said to Dartagnan, "Where did you come up with that wild idea? A hike in the canyon? Eileen and Kinley? Sounds far-fetched for leisure-loving folks." I waited for an answer, but Dartagnan appeared not to have heard the question. "Or was it a wild idea?"

His mouth twisted like a man who thinks before he speaks. "If Eileen and Kinley aren't in Palm Springs, and they're not, according to my grapevines, and if they're not in Georgia, then we've got to look elsewhere. I'm thinking they may have hauled out across the desert, up toward the windmills, heading east toward Joshua Tree. They'd have to stop and eat, get gas, sleep. The Mission Hills Indians own most of The Springs and most of the Coachella Valley. There are about six or seven subgroups, but they're all Mission Indians. The name was given to them by the Spanish. There's some differences in their cultures, but they all speak the same language. Shoshone. They use cell phones like us white folks, but their ancient communication system still can't be beat."

"Smoke signals?" I jested.

"Gossip."

I was almost asleep when Lake called to say that they'd positively identified the man who owned the white Cadillac. "Brody McCracken, age forty. Lives in Ackworth, disbarred lawyer. His father was a lawyer, his grandfather was a judge, his uncle was a state senator. He has an arrest record for child molestation. Law license surrendered; money paid out for not going to trial and jail."

"Sounds like your man," I agreed.

"We'll know in our next life. His DNA's off to the crime lab. There's about a million tests ahead of his."

"No hurry. He's dead."

"Unless he didn't do the crimes. Then we still got a sicko out there."

"Any more bodies turn up?"

"No," he said. "You can't see, but my fingers are crossed."

"Cross a couple more that I find Kinley quick."

"Get Dartagnan off his ass."

"I'm trying."

FOURTEEN

Zing's energy could give a beaver a headache. His skinny oriental body flicked and flipped back and forth serving donuts and pouring coffee. When I entered, he smiled and gestured toward the round seat at the end of the counter. I suspected that was Dartagnan's usual place. Zing slid coffee toward me and grinned an apology for being too busy to serve me immediately.

After he'd taken care of a dozen customers, he ran to a large glass door through which I could see five Asian men frying donuts. He jerked it open and spoke fast and incomprehensively. Two men left their donut-frying duties and rushed out to take on the customers. Talk about a Chinese fire drill.

Zing came toward me carrying a pot of coffee. He poured, ran back to the burner, and replaced the pot. On the way back to me, he snatched a French cruller from a display, placed it on a plate, and sat it before me. "My compliments."

I had to eat it.

"You new in town?" he asked.

"Temporarily," I answered. The sugar melted in my mouth. "Tasty."

"You are a friend of Dartagnan's?"

"Just met him yesterday."

"I see."

"We're working together."

"Ah, working. Good."

"Why good?"

"No good to be girlfriend."

"I sense a secret here."

"Tess, the artist, she would scratch your eyes out."

Tess, jealous? But then I think I hide my jealousy well, too. "She doesn't have to worry," I said. "Are they serious?"

"Serious? No. Tess is engaged to someone else."

"Her fiancé doesn't mind?"

"He is busy with his other pleasures."

"Engagements out here sure are different than where I come from."

"Well, you see this. Tess, she was married before. She is half-Indian and her aunt and uncle follow the old way. Her husband, he dies in the accident. Now she is engaged to his brother, but his brother is too young to marry by California laws."

"How old is he?"

"Fifteen, sixteen. Too young."

"You're kidding. She's engaged to marry a teenager? How old is she?"

He shrugged his shoulders. "When he turn eighteen, off they go into abode house and stay for three days. They come out married."

"In the meantime, Tess and Dartagnan carry on."

"It is the way of the world."

Somehow I didn't believe him.

FIFTEEN

Theodosia's hair salon looked like Rodeo Drive come to Palm Springs. Her sign said that she had shops in LA, Palm Beach, New York, and Chicago. Getting out of the rental, I thought, this is fruitless—the entrepreneur proprietress isn't going to be here.

But I was wrong. She met me as I entered the salon.

"You're surprised, aren't you?" she said. If Theodosia was Greek, then her name fit. She was tall, strikingly dark, and very handsome.

"I bet Arlo called ahead," I said.

"Arlo and I are longtime friends," she said, puffing her bing-cherry lips. "He asked that I speak with you and that's what I'm doing. I am very discreet." She smiled, showing large straight teeth as she turned to lead me to the back of the salon. "Not all hairdressers are busybodies," she said, with a backward wave of her hand. "I am sorry for Arlo's—shall we say—momentary loss."

I looked around the spacious office where elegant antiques vied with salon clutter. Theodosia sat in a leather chair. I sat on a small couch beside her. I felt like a television talk-show guest.

"I started my career in Atlanta," Theodosia said, tapping her red nails on the satinwood arm. "Small world."

"Did you have a shop there?"

"No, dear. I started at Cut 'n' Curl in the Avondale Mall. I scissored hair for seven dollars. A buck tip, if I was lucky."

"A modest beginning," I said.

"Very, but I am ambitious." She reached to pick up a silver cigarette case and a matching holder from a table in front of us. "I quit and came out to Los Angeles. Guess where I went to work?" She pushed the cigarette into the holder.

"A Cut 'n' Curl in a mall?"

"Smart girl." She lit the cigarette and blew a stream of smoke toward the ceiling. That's when I knew for certain she'd started life as a man. She said, "Then I was discovered."

"Isn't everybody here?"

"I adore sardonic humor," he/she said. "The angular cut made Sassoon famous, and I improved on it." She ran a hand over a wig that made her look like Cleopatra. She then glanced over my mass of dark curls. "Your hairdresser doesn't do you justice," she purred. "You should have glamour. I would cut your hair to your shoulders, feather it just a bit. Then I would iron it straight and curl it into loose spirals. Very chic. Very sexy."

My hairdresser had tried spirals, but my lifestyle didn't allow for hour-a-day hair maintenance. I said, "From photographs of Eileen, looks like she had good hair to work with. Did you personally style it?"

"Not always, but when I was in the salon I did. Her hair was divine—thick and silky—the perfect texture for anything I wanted to create. I keep a photograph of her on the board. People wanted a style like hers." She sniffed and waved the cigarette holder. "Most asked the impossible."

"When did you last see Eileen?"

"I checked my book to reassure my memory. It was last Thursday. She brought her little girl, too. I didn't do the little girl's hair, but it is just like her mother's."

"Did Eileen come in every week?"

"At least, depending on her social schedule," she said and

took an unhurried drag on the cigarette. "She missed her standing appointment yesterday. I was very perturbed, because I was planning on making a few suggestions on the cut of her hair. Eileen was so good to experiment on." She tapped the cigarette holder against a crystal ashtray. "So she has disappeared, huh? Arlo said that's why you've come to The Springs." I opened my mouth to tell her how important it is to keep it quiet, but she held up a finger. "When Arlo wants the world to know Eileen left him, he can be the one to broadcast the news."

"Trouble in paradise?"

She looked amused. "Now what do you think I'm supposed to say to that?"

"The truth?"

Through half-closed eyes, she looked upward, at the cigarette smoke swirling toward the ceiling. "You want to know about Eileen and Arlo as a couple?" Her performance heightened my anticipation. I couldn't wait to hear the dirt. She apparently read me and guffawed. "Eileen loved him; Arlo was devoted to her."

"That's it?" The smoke surrounded me, and I coughed into my fist.

"He's very romantic beneath that rather rough veneer. You know, men don't have to be handsome to be sexy."

"You think he's sexy?"

"Oh, yes. Money, you see."

"I understand the money part."

She wrinkled her nose "You disapprove?" I shrugged. She said, "The handsome men here—most don't have money and are gay. By money, I mean *lots*, and by gay, I mean *very*."

"Then there are no rumors about troubles between the Camerons?"

"I didn't say that, did I? There are always rumors. That's what makes life fun."

Theodosia enjoyed acting—and baiting me. "How about a hint?" I asked.

"Arlo has been here a very long time. Eileen has been here, oh, four, five years. Arlo had a life before Eileen. He enjoyed the companionship of many women. A few turned up with unexpected bonuses in their pouches. But they were paid handsomely, and there are many discreet clinics in LA. He'll always be a pussycat for a pretty ingénue."

She stubbed the cigarette out and opened the case for another. I was about to gag. "And Eileen?"

"If she ran off with another man, I don't know who he is. She hangs around Dartagnan. They say she knew him before she came here."

"He didn't tell me that," I said.

She clicked the lighter shut. "Don't you wonder why not, with all that talking he does?"

"The man can talk."

"He could talk about a lot of things, but he won't. Not if he values living in The Springs."

"Where did Eileen know him from?"

"He didn't tell me. Nor did she. It's just something people . . . think."

I let that sink in. "Think about the last time you saw Eileen—was she nervous, did she say anything peculiar?"

Her lips pushed the smoke out. "Nothing that sticks in my mind. I'd say she seemed happier than I'd seen her in a while. She loved showing off her little girl. The child could be in commercials or in the movies. Arlo could get her a contract in a heartbeat."

"What was Eileen's idea about that?"

A sound came from her nose. "Never mind what her idea was. There was the father in Atlanta. Bradley Fucking Whitney." She sucked on the cigarette.

It was useless holding my breath since I had to talk. "I take it Eileen discussed Whitney with you?"

Blowing smoke, she said, "Eileen couldn't wait to fry his ass for lying in court."

"What did he lie about?"

"Himself."

"Did Eileen go into detail?"

"Just to say she found out he had secrets."

"What kind?"

"What kind of secrets can a man have, dear? Sexual secrets. From her description, I'd say homosexual secrets."

I nodded that I agreed. "You lived in Atlanta. You know the city. Even if Whitney was homosexual, the court wouldn't necessarily take the child away. The times, they have a-changed."

She studied the tip of her cigarette. She outdid Portia when it came to using a cigarette as a conversational prop. "Depends," she said, and stubbed it out. "How did he comport himself? What were his . . . inclinations?"

"Do you know anyone in Atlanta who might know about him?"

She sat back. "It was a long time ago, but I keep in touch with my old friends. If he's out and about, I can learn about him, yes."

"He may not be. He's an educator."

"Still closeted, huh?"

"It would appear."

She snorted as only a he can do. "He sneaks out. He must. Temptation. Compulsion."

"Have you heard of The Cloisters?"

She eyed the cigarette holder. "That place where rich people go by the sea?"

I laughed. "Not hardly. It's an exclusive men's club in Atlanta."

She picked up the holder and gripped it between her teeth. "The Cloisters, huh. I'll ask my friends about it. It intrigues me."

Me, too.

Sixteen

Philippe's shop stood out on Ramon Road—white ceramic tile and glass block. I figured Philippe came from New York originally. Everyone in Palm Springs, except Native Americans, comes from somewhere else.

I expected a bell to peal when I entered the shop, but none did. Philippe stood at a computer, totaling a woman's purchases. Seeing me, he raised his chin and held up a finger. The lady took her bags and left. Philippe flashed out of sight, but, seconds later, came from behind a dairy case that was chock-full of cheeses.

He held a white shopping bag bearing a logo for the fanciest takeout place I'd ever been in—and Atlanta's no slouch for takeout places. The logo was a caricature of Philippe cavorting above the name of his shop: Too Busy to Cook? Underneath that, it read: "Philippe Wischard—Cordon Bleu Chef."

Philippe placed the shopping bag on the counter and said proudly, "I have your shik-can, fried creesp. A few secret spices to savor *le* palate. Also, I have for you a fried okra salad. Arugula and spring greens. And for dessert, a nice anise cheesecake."

I don't like licorice or cheesecake. "Monsier Philippe," I said, "you have outdone yourself."

"Not so, *non*. For my friend, Dartagnan, and for you. A friend of my friend is my friend." I'd heard it said, an enemy of my enemy is my friend. I liked that better.

He fiddled with numbers on his computer while I watched

his assistants, two women and two men, clad in all white and wearing floppy chef's hats, waiting on expensively dressed customers. My eyes roamed over the interior, which contained foodstuffs, wine, coffees, flowers, and very expensive utensils. The aroma overwhelmed, each individual aroma lending its fragrance.

"Fabulous," I said when he handed me my check. I had my American Express card ready. The cost of this lunch was going on Whitney's tab. "Anybody else in Palm Springs run a place like this?"

"*Non.* I, alone, have *les coeurs et les ventres dans le* Springs."

I grinned at him. "Monsieur Philippe, you ever been to France?"

His laughter was over the top. Then he replied in unaccented English, "Everyone wonders. No one but you has asked."

"I'm inquisitive."

"And very beautiful, too. Beautiful people can get away with being, er—*quoi?* Outrageous? But *oui*, I have indeed been to France. I studied in Paris. I will tell the truth to you. I was born in New Brunswick, New Jersey. My mother named me Philippe. *Pourquoi? Je ne sais pas.* I speak comic-strip French because it is what people here want. They want to make fun of the Phony Frenchman. That is what they call me behind my back. But this is Palm Springs. Everybody is an actor." He paused, then resumed his role. "*A l'instant meme, pourquoi?*—why are you in our little counterfeit oasis in the desert?"

"That is the question, *n'est-ce pas?*" That was about the extent of my French.

He held up his hands, palm out. "I pry no more."

"I will tell the truth to you. I am on a mission."

"Ah, no better place, *mademoiselle*. I am right, am I not, that you are not a madam?"

"I am not a madam."

"You still have the freshness. So many young women, they marry, and they lose that look of naïveté."

"You're observant."

"It helps me to make suggestions for madams who are looking for just the right thing to take the boredom out of food, and for mademoiselles who want to court a lover."

"Tell me, what does it say to you when a woman orders sushi—raw squid, mackerel, abalone—for herself?"

His face segued through various aspects—frowns, smiles, wry grimaces. "Does your mission have to do with sushi?"

"Maybe."

He looked suddenly as if I were competition come to town. "But you are not a cook, a chef?"

"Don't I look like a chef?"

"*Non*," he said, holding up his gnarly hands. "Your hands. They are not calloused, nor are they scarred. Look at mine. The burns, the knives."

"You're right, I'm not a cook."

"I can tell you this. Women who eat raw sushi—the squid and the mackerel and the abalone—they are experimental, or . . ." he bowed his head from his neck, "they are Japanese."

"Not everything's raw, is it?"

"Few fish from *la mer* are served raw. The eel, the squid are *en vinaigre* or *vin blanc*. It is more *délicieux* to those who eat at McDonald's." He shuttered.

"I was visiting Arlo Cameron the other day—"

"Ah, the movie man. *Oui*." His eyes slid sideways before he said, "Monsieur Cameron has asked me some discreet questions, I must tell you, *mademoiselle*, but I will not repeat our conversation. I am sworn."

"All right, *monsieur*. Arlo Cameron didn't strike me as a sushi person, yet—"

"Oh, *mademoiselle*, he is not. He devours steak tartare I make especial for him. Filet mignon ground with onions, Worcester-shire, and some secret spices. On pumpernickel, you mound it, and make a hole, and put in a raw egg and capers. *Délicieux!*"

"Eileen is the sushi eater. Arlo said—"

"Ah, the beautiful madam. Yes. I fix especial for her last weekend."

"Saturday?"

"Yes. Three dozen assorted."

"Expensive."

"They who come into my *magasin* can afford, you see?"

"I see."

"I make California for the little girl. For Madam Cameron, hake and abalone and eel. She bought caviar and champagne. I say, 'Monsieur Cameron's cellar is full of champagne,' but she says, 'I like the Moët & Chandon—you know, the cheap stuff.' I laugh. Fifty-nine a bottle isn't *that* cheap."

"Too bad the little girl had to go back to Atlanta. She seems so happy with her mama." Philippe's head tilted to one side like a sad mime.

I went on, "And probably Eileen looked so let down at the thought of sending her home. Did she seem that way to you, Monsieur Philippe?"

"*Oui, mademoiselle.* That Saturday, Madam Cameron is with her little girl. The little girl picked out some trifles she wished to take on her outing—to be the last of her vacation. They go to the skate park that afternoon."

"Arlo was in LA."

"*Vraiment, mademoiselle.* Madam Cameron asked that I deep-fry a turkey and prepare my special slaw for Monsieur Cameron when he returned from Los Angeles on Sunday. She paid me up front."

"Tell me how Eileen seemed."

"For your mission?"

"In part."

He cast his eyes over my shoulder. "Madam looks around my shop." I turned my head to follow Philippe's eyes—to the flower section. He said, "Madam's attention was *las fleurs*. I hear her gasp a little. Her mouth, it drops like this." He mimicked the look of shock or surprise. He continued, "When I look over there, a man was buying *le bouquet*. I asked Madam if she knew him. She said, 'No, oh no.' But I wonder. *Oui*, I wonder. The man, he paid, and walked out. Madam lingered, looking out of the window until finally she called to the little girl and they left."

"What did he look like?"

"I never saw his *visage*. He wore *le chapeau*." He reached up and patted his chef's hat and laughed. "Not like this, more like golf players wear. I could not see much about him, but I asked Nicole, who sells *las fleurs et les bonbons*. She said he was average. Polite. *Moyen*."

"Think a bit, *monsieur*. Dark, tall, short, blond?"

He shrugged and flipped up his hands in a familiar Gaelic gesture. "Average."

"Did he ever look directly at Eileen?"

"Not that I saw."

"Or Kinley?"

"It is probably the imagination of mine. I think to myself, Madam is just not herself. As you say, she had to send *la jeune fille dans sa ville*. I don't think the little girl wanted to go home, either." He shook his head. *"Triste."*

I returned my attention to the flower section. "Nobody's tending to the flowers today?"

"My girl is out this week. She goes to *le festival* up north."

"Is this festival far from here?"

"Who knows?" he said. "*Les festivals* are everywhere. She is young. She goes where *la jeune* go."

"Monsieur Philippe," I said, having fallen into the habit of addressing the imposter by a legitimate courtesy title, "I told you that I was on a mission. You perhaps have guessed it. But, please, let's keep what we've been talking about to ourselves."

"*Mon dieu!*" Philippe's hands flashed up. "*Non* do I expose my clients." He slapped both cheeks. "My business! I would be *en ruine.*"

I picked up my lunch, and hurried away leaving Philippe the picture of offense.

SEVENTEEN

From my hotel to the Swim and Skate Park, it took seven minutes and two wrong turns to reach Pavilion Road at Sunrise Plaza. The parking ticket–taker took my ten bucks and looked at my shopping bag as if he were about to tell me I couldn't bring it in.

"Lunch prepared by Too Busy to Cook?" I said.

He said, "We have food and beverages inside."

I held up the bag. "Can I?"

He tilted his head. "Go ahead."

It's a California thing—big-time skateboarding. I stood at an iron fence and gnawed chicken—which was wonderful—and watched skateboarders do impossible things on concrete ramps. They named the various sections: the Combi Bowl, the Flow Bowl, and the Nude Bowl—like a kidney-shaped pool.

"What do you think?" came a voice I recognized.

"Noisy," I said, turning to look at Dartagnan. He wore shorts, golf socks, and a hat that had the Mission Hills logo tree on it. "You played golf."

"Me and Arlo," he said, watching the kids on their boards. "He said he needed to get his mind off Eileen. He wasn't very good at it—getting his mind off of Eileen, or golf."

"You took his money?"

"Fifteen dollars. Five a bet. Max three."

"You should be ashamed," I said as I chewed.

"I see you got lunch from Philippe."

"It wasn't his treat." I dug into the heavy plastic cup of okra salad with an equally heavy plastic fork.

"It never is."

"You order from him?" I asked, savoring the crispy greens and okra.

"Never. I go by at closing. He gives me what he would throw out if I didn't take it."

"Poor thing." I took another bite.

"You finding out anything?"

"Zip. Nada."

"Zing said you came in."

"You following me?"

"Somebody's got to watch out for you."

"Why?" I'd finished the salad and dug further into the bag. I brought out a square flat container, opened it, and saw the cheesecake. I held it out to Dartagnan. He shook his head, and I threw it into the bag. "Why?" I said again.

He'd looked up, his back to the sun. His stare didn't go a thousand yards, but a hundred, maybe. He said, "Palm Springs is a place where everyone has secrets. A bunch of money brings a bunch of secrets. You don't, if you're in your right mind, go asking questions about those secrets. See what I mean?"

"If anybody I talked to let a cat out of the bag, I didn't pick up on it."

"See?"

"Did Eileen have a stockbroker?"

He laughed. "Even Arlo didn't buy that one. She was using the money she took out to go shopping. Bet it was gone by Friday. She bought clothes for her kid."

"Rich people use credit cards."

He wagged his head. "Who knows. When you going with Tess?"

"You want me out of Palm Springs?"

"What you're after isn't in The Springs, but no, I like you here."

"What I'm after is two whos," I said, wadding up the shopping bag. "Those whos are somewhere, and I aim to find them." I headed for the trash bin.

He skipped up next to me. "Didn't mean to put your nose out of joint. I mean for you to believe me. Eileen and Kinley aren't anywhere near here."

"You keep saying that."

"It's 'cause I know it." His cell phone rang. " 'Lo," he said. "Yep. Nope. Leavin' now."

He studied me for a moment. "You doing anything interesting tonight when you get back from the desert?"

"Sleeping. I'm still hung over from last night."

"Say the word when you want to go at it."

"To go at what?"

He waved. "Say the word; you'll see."

EIGHTEEN

Tess waited under the hotel's canopy in a sun-faded Jeep. Somebody had smacked into the passenger door. It creaked when I opened it. On the back of my seat, an eagle had been etched into the leather. A patch of leather with a skinny cactus painted on it dangled from her key chain. Tess wore a million-dollar smile and a long-sleeved blue-jeans outfit. A jungle hat perched impertinently on her head.

I stretched my naked legs under the dash. "Am I going to freeze?" I asked, rubbing my sleeveless arms.

Her foot eased down on the gas pedal. "It gets cold in the desert in the evening, but I have a box of things in the back. You'll be warm enough."

I leaned back and raked my mass of hair back with both hands. Call it premonition, but I had a feeling that Tess's shaman aunt would provide a clue to Eileen's disappearance. The sun was at our backs as we headed east. Tess said, "It is good to get out of the city."

"You ever been to Atlanta?"

"I have not. I talked to Russell Wolf. He said the streets there were poisonous."

"He's right. Have you traveled much outside Palm Springs?"

"I lived in Texas when I was a girl."

"Where?"

"El Paso. On a rez."

"How'd you get to California?"

"I was born here. My mother took me away from here when . . ." Her mouth turned down. "I don't remember my father. Then my mother died when I was thirteen. I came back here."

Many people I've gotten to know have lost someone close. The grim reaper hangs over me much too much. "How well did you know Eileen?" I asked.

"Okay," she answered.

"You two ever do girls things together, like lunch, or have fun?"

"No. I'd see her when she was with Dartagnan. They were friends. And Dartagnan and I are friends."

Interesting trois. "And Arlo? Where was he?"

"Making movies. Doing deals."

"Too busy for his wife?"

"He is a busy man," she said, keeping the car at an even speed. "You know, he is like an unofficial mayor now that our beloved Mr. Hope is gone."

The road had gone from smooth to uneven. "Were Eileen and Arlo a happy couple?"

"Very happy, very good together."

"Where would Eileen run with Kinley?"

Her elbows tightened into her sides. "I know of no place."

"Dartagnan said there are many shelters in the desert."

Her forehead winkled. "I have heard that."

"You think she could have gone to one?"

"It is possible, yes."

"Would your people know of some of these places?"

"Maybe."

We turned south on a newly paved asphalt road. It ribboned up the valley and my ears began to fill—and soon to pop. An awesome sight lay before me—the desert, powerful and romantic. To my right, vertical black obelisks reminded me of

Stonehenge. On my left, black rocks topped hillocks. Pebbly, wide gulches made me think we'd landed on the moon. Tess began to talk of the land and called the ditches "arroyos."

"It's magnificent," I said. "But it would be easy to get lost. Everything looks alien, one arroyo like another."

"Living here, you find markers."

"But no Gas-n-Go to mark your way."

We rode past what she identified as Joshua trees and yuccas and rock cairns. "All of this land you see, it is *our* land." She spoke like an oracle of the ancient gods. I felt like an interloper, insignificant. She turned onto a dusty road, and said, "My uncle is head of our tribal council. As the elder, he was given his own reservation—where we are going. We have twenty-eight families living there. My aunt is the medicine woman for our rez, and the larger rez next to us."

We bounced through cholla cacti, and when I thought my words wouldn't shake in my throat, I asked, "Do your people still speak the old language?"

"Mine do. A lot of our people, those who have remained in the desert, have kept our traditions—like the Bird Songs."

"Bird Songs?"

"They are for ceremonies. My uncle is a Bird Singer, and I dance like the birds of our ancestors, who, like us, went south for the winter." I noticed that her silver earrings were birds in flight.

"What kind of ceremonies?"

"Burials. In the old days, my people were cremated. Three days for cremation, three days for the ashes cooling. We sang and danced for the spirit to soar. It is a happy thing, to die. We visit with our dead and let them see that we do not forget."

Three days to burn. "Do your people still cremate?"

"If it is a personal choice, it is allowed, but we cannot use the old ritual. When the Spanish Catholics came, they made us bury our dead uncremated. After a couple of centuries, and given the laws of California, we are content with Christian rites."

"You lost a lot of your heritage to the white man's idea of Manifest Destiny," I remarked.

"Not only then," she said. "You also lose your heritage when you go to Sacramento every month and line up for a handout check. But that was before we were allowed to build casinos. Now we can afford to retrain our young in our language and culture. We are looking forward to fall fiesta. I hope that you will attend."

"I don't think I'll be here then," I said hopefully, "but, if I am, I'm sticking with you. I adore your passion for your land and your people." I'm not usually that gushy.

She said, "When I was in El Paso, as a little girl, I dreamed of one day coming home."

We were going due south and I figured we'd soon come to the Salton Sea.

"Our big casino is in Mission Palms," Tess said. "My aunt and uncle run it. The casino—it has given us the money to bring back our pride. We are buying banks and hotels. We own your hotel."

"It's very fine."

The sun was suddenly gone, although it wasn't near nightfall. Outside my window, a wall of black rock rose skyward. Tess said, "We are in Lost Coyote Canyon, my home. We are riding on a tuff bed. See ahead to our left? That cave leads into an abandoned gold mine."

A sign read: FORBIDDEN. NOT RESPONSIBLE FOR DISASTERS!

Tess said, "People come who are not welcomed. You can see, we have no fences or gates, but we do not take responsibility for people looking for gold. They are fools."

"I hope Eileen wasn't foolish enough to come this way."

"Eileen knows this land."

"Has she been here with you?"

"Not so much, but Dartagnan liked to picnic by the mine and weave tall tales."

Dartagnan again.

We bumped along the tuff road, passing sandstone rock outcrops and desert junipers that clung to the sparse soil. She pointed to a slick rippling sandstone fracture that would have been a waterfall had there been a river above it. On either side of the sheer slope, circlets of darkly varnished rock cascaded to the desert floor. "That is a dry waterfall," she said. "We call it Ripple Rock."

"Looks treacherous."

"It is, when the monsoons come and water pours over it. When you see black clouds in the west, get to high ground. It is monsoon season, but this afternoon we don't need to worry. The air is not right."

We climbed higher into the desert, passing stone cairns. "Those are works of art and religious shrines," she said. "They are sacred. That is one of the reasons we forbid outsiders in Lost Coyote Canyon. Tourists strip the stones."

We came to a grove of palms. "The oasis surrounds a hot spring," Tess said, penetrating the trees and stopping the Jeep. It felt good to stretch the muscles after the grinding drive up the canyon. I followed Tess through the gentle palms. We were silent, as though the land beckoned but forbade chatter. The faint smell of sulfur rose on the dry breeze that bathed my skin.

Tess walked out of the grove and I followed her to a mound of pebbles in a cactus patch. It looked like children had constructed a stone castle. "The stones are geodes," she said. "They have crystals inside them. People come from all over the world to hike the canyons to find geodes."

We stood at the work of art for several moments before Tess

turned to lead us back the way we came. I took a step and my foot sunk into sand, halfway to my ankle. I freed it and looked at the sunken spot. Tess said, "Damned pocket gophers. Makes walking treacherous."

Back at the Jeep, Tess fetched a blanket. We stretched it out near the hot spring, which was a deep, dark pool of mineral water surrounded by large stones. Tess said such pools were abundant and were medicinal and sacred. She brought out a handsome oval picnic basket.

I coveted it. "That's a weird-looking cactus," I said, pointing to the design on the basket. It started on the front and flowed over the top.

"It's a boojum tree," she said. "It looks like an upside-down carrot, doesn't it? It was named for a character in a Lewis Carroll book." She took several lidded clay pots from the basket and arranged them ritually. Obviously they were art from the desert. She said, "We shall have a bite to eat here. My people have eaten their late meal by now."

"Did you make those?" I asked, pointing to the pots.

"I did, but they are not my designs. I borrowed them from the Navajo. Our people were weavers and woodworkers. I learned the old Navajo ways from my mother's friend in Texas."

I thought about modern pottery wheels and kiln furnaces. "Aren't the old ways laborious?"

"That which is worth it is," she said. "It takes hours to dig the clay, and grind it, and get it into shape. Then the wood must be gathered for the fire. Children gather pitch from the piñon tree. We coat the clay with hot sap and fire it in an open pit of juniper wood."

I took the lid off a squat pot. "Um-yum, guacamole."

Tess raised flat bread from the basket. The guacamole was divine, although I was still full of Philippe's food. Tess told me it was Lost Coyote Canyon guacamole. "The usual ingredients," she said, "plus some secret spices." She and Philippe had an affinity for secret spices.

She poured tea into small clay cups that were twenty subtle shades of blue and green. A stick bird had been etched on mine with symbols like hieroglyphics. Tess said, "Like the cairns, they are religious. I can't explain them. Bad luck."

No bad luck, please.

As beautiful as was the clay ware to the eyes, the tea tasted dreadful.

"Creosote and honey tea," Tess said, laughing at my puckered face. "It is made from the stems and leaves for a variety of ills. It works on horses. That's a good indication it has medicinal properties. No psychological influences with horses."

I set my cup down.

She said, "We must drink a full cup before we see my aunt, the medicine woman. She believes it rids the body of transmittable poisons."

Lifting the cup, I said, "I'll do it."

I wiped my mouth with the back of my hand, and, soon, it was time to go.

Back on the road, it wasn't ten minutes until we came to a vast three-storied, man-made, mud-brick structure, with rows of cutouts for windows. It looked deserted. Air compressed in my chest, and I shivered.

"Indian apartments," Tess said. "We call them the Adobe Flats. What do you see in them?"

"Sorrow, despair."

She nodded. "Decades ago, many families lived in them. Children starved. Women were old at fifteen. Men laid around and died of peyote poisoning. Many claim they hear the ghosts of those who lived there when they pass by."

I was glad to circle away from the haunted, mud-brick structure.

Nineteen

Stucco homes with Spanish tile hip roofs lined the reservation's upscale street. There wasn't a soul walking, sitting, or standing. "It is the time of day for introspection," Tess said. "And learning. Our children are studying now." She pointed out a mansion sitting well back from the street, surrounded by a six-foot security fence. I caught the movement of big dogs, or wolves. "The home of my aunt and uncle," she said.

Casino money, I thought. Like diamond merchants, they needed their fences and guard dogs.

We came to a street of small shops: a newspaper stand, a convenience store, a used-book emporium. "This must be downtown, the business district," I said.

Grinning, she said, "Our rez is a thousand acres. Next to it is the main rez, where we can go for groceries, gas, and the post office. But mostly, everyone goes to Palm Springs to shop. Or for real shopping, Los Angeles or Phoenix."

We both laughed. Tess was a shopper. But I wouldn't travel more than ten minutes from my home or office to buy anything, and she must have gleaned this about me.

After the last stop sign, the asphalt streets gave way to unpaved roads. The houses were squalid adobe with poorly thatched roofs. "We still have poor people," Tess said. "They seem to prefer not to enrich themselves, so we leave them to be as they'd like."

It was nearly dark when three dark men came running from a

house and got into an old car. Tess cried, "Those crazies."

We had traveled on for several minutes through cairns and cactus when a wood cabin on stilts emerged. She pulled up to a front porch that spanned the small house. "The Moon Lodge," she said.

Getting out of the Jeep, I rubbed my arms. "Cold now."

Tess handed me a soft, long-sleeved leather jacket that zipped at the waist, and we walked up the steps. A teenage girl opened the door. Inside the cabin, it was almost pitch dark. After several blinks, I made out people—girls—squatting. Older women sat on benches lining two walls. They didn't seem to notice our entrance; they were watching what went on in the middle of the dark, hot room.

Tess hugged the girl who opened the door, and whispered, "You have blossomed well, my cousin." She turned to me. "I want you to meet Windla, and Windla, I want you to meet Dru."

Windla's smile was as warm as her cousin's. "Dru. I like your name."

"Thank you. I like yours."

Windla closed the door, and immediately I began to sweat. I rubbed my neck. All the cabin windows were closed. An upright barrel stove burned in the corner. Tess whispered, "I will not introduce you at this time. My aunt is saying the moon ritual for her son's daughter."

"Moon ritual?"

"On a girl's first moon, she must remain on her back on a bed of herbs until the next moon phase. She is the moon maiden."

We sat on a bench near the door. It was hot as hell, and I wanted to crack it open. I reached my arms back to remove the jacket and caught the sleeve on a nail in the wall. I felt the rip with my fingers, and a scrap came off in my hand. Horrified, I showed it to Tess. She shook her head as if to say, *no matter*. I got the jacket off and laid it beside me on the bench. I put the scrap in my shirt pocket.

The moon maiden lay on a brush pile on a dirt floor in the middle of the one-room cabin. She had on a plain white long gown. She writhed as Tess's aunt ran her hands two inches above her body—from head to toe, back and forth. With each pass, the woman's hands would pause where the moon maiden's legs ended and her torso began. The medicine woman's eyes were closed and her head moved rhythmically to her incantations in what I assumed was an ancient tongue. My eyes roamed to the squatting girls, who sat silent and enchanted. That's when I saw one who looked like she didn't belong. Her skin glowed milky white. Her black hair lay askew atop her head. She was very young and appeared very scared. I turned to say something to Tess, but she laid her palm on my hand. I felt a bite, and then looked down. The onyx stone in her ring had twisted toward her palm. One of the prongs had pricked the back of my hand. She whispered, "I am so sorry."

I rubbed my hand. "S'all right." I looked at the moon maiden. "Can she eat or drink?" The words seemed to hover in the back of my head.

"Only warm water," Tess said. "Cold water causes cramps. She can eat no salt or hard food. Only mush."

A long white bone lay at the moon maiden's right hand. I asked, "Wass that for?" My tongue felt thick as I said the words. My eyes went to the young pale girl. My vision blurred.

Tess answered, "It is a buffalo leg bone. If she has an itch, she can scratch with that. She cannot touch herself."

Tess's aunt raised both her hands to the ceiling. The squatting girls rose from the floor. The white-skinned girl seemed at a loss and looked to Windla for guidance. Tess said, "The girls will dance around the maiden, and sing of their first moon."

Tess's aunt brought out a tambourine. The girls joined hands and circled the moon maiden, chanting and dancing. The small girl's lips moved, but she obviously didn't know the words, and when she stumbled she looked at Windla.

The young girl's face turned orange. All things around me began to glow. Black balls floated in front of my eyes. I rubbed them and green came into the orange. I was hot—on fire. Vomit flared up my esophagus. I slipped sideways. A woman's voice came from another land. "Dru! What's the matter? Dru!" She moved to catch me, but I fell from the bench and everything went black.

TWENTY

My lips felt thick, my tongue stuck to the roof of my mouth. My eyeballs were on fire. I couldn't shift my body for the pain in my bones and muscles. Hot deep inside, yet I shivered in the darkness. I moved my head and glimpsed a star through a small opening.

Cave. I'm in a cave.

I heard voices, one above the others, strange and guttural. *"Ahct, ahct, dyun, myun, wyck."* Then a series of "Oweeeeees." And laughter.

I knew the acrid smell. Marijuana.

I'm dreaming, or I'm dead and in limbo. So hot, so terribly hot. *I'm in hell. Oh dear mama, send the priest. I'll be good. I'll say rosary for every decade. Our Father, Who art in heaven. . . .* My lips slurred the lines. *Hail, Mary, full of grace, the Lord is with thee . . . pray for us sinners, now and at the hour of our death. Amen.* Hot water slipped down my temples.

"She's awake."

Who are these people?

A hand raised my head. A light blinded me. "Helth . . ." my lips and tongue tried to speak. "Pleath . . ."

I felt a prick in my right wrist, and then my mind fled again.

Somebody threw ice water on me.

"Dru, Dru, hurry," the voice said.

"Whoth . . . ?"

A pulling at my arm, but I couldn't move. My body felt like an iron beam.

"Come, hurry."

"Wherth . . . ?"

"It's Tess. We must hurry from here."

Tess? "Canth . . ."

"You must."

She hovered above me, straddling, bending, pulling my shoulders. I tried, oh how I tried, but I just couldn't. I couldn't and I couldn't understand why I couldn't. Finally, she had me sitting, but she hadn't the strength to lift me. She pulled me along a rough floor, then down steep steps. Every thump shot excruciating pain along my nerve paths until it became so unbearable I wanted to die.

"Listen," she said urgently, "I hear in the distance. They will be here soon." She dragged me outside. The cold air stung my lungs. She propped me against a wall. "Let your hands walk you up the wall." She sat and showed me how, and I tried. I seemed to gather some strength. "Good, you're moving up. Keep going up. No! Don't fall. We must hurry."

I was upright, but I stumbled. The wall held me up. "Legth, canth . . ."

"Quick!" she said, and threw her strong arms around my waist.

Her Jeep was near, but oh so far away for my immobile feet. Over the hood I saw pinpoint lights glow in the distance. I knew if I didn't get to the Jeep I would die. I didn't want to die here, like this. Lurching like a diver off a cliff, I got control of my feet and staggered toward the Jeep. With my last step, I banged my head on the plastic window. She opened the door and rammed me inside. She ran to the driver's side and revved the Jeep, hurtling us into the night.

Fear strengthened my aching sinews, and I rotated my

shoulders and head to look behind me. Twin lights drawing closer. Looking ahead again, I saw only darkness. She hadn't turned on the headlights.

"Where to?" I asked, aware of a powerful thirst.

"We'll go in circles. I can't brush the tire tracks, but that might confuse them."

"Who them?" My words sounded like they came from another galaxy.

"I don't know."

"Whhy?"

"They came to the lodge and took you away. You were ill."

"Where?"

"You don't remember?"

"I—no—Dar-canyon."

"Dartagnan? What about him?"

"Park—oasith—rock pool." I shook my head and slouched against the side door, my knees jammed against my chest.

"At Moon Lodge you passed out. My aunt called for help. They came from town to take you to the hospital. But you never reached it. Dartagnan went there. We started searching."

I willed myself to remember, but nothing . . .

She went on, "I thought about where you could be. The Adobe Flats came to mind. Nothing good happens there."

"You are—who?"

"Tess."

"Teth?"

"Yes."

"Member—men—hear voithez."

"They are after us now."

"Why?"

"Because something's happening—somebody's—some malign spirit has invaded our land."

"Huh?"

"I have dreams of strangers who come into our midst and steal our souls."

"Soulths?"

"You have been drugged. Datura. It is confusing. Your speech will get better."

"I ate . . . what?"

"Or drank."

My head lolled against the glass, and I saw a woman in my mind, laughing, drinking tea, telling about the boo-boo tree. We were in a place that was hot with stones and palm trees and pocket animals. Suddenly the lights behind us got brighter, and I raised up.

"Stay down," Tess said and jerked the wheel left.

Something hit the back of the Jeep. My head banged the window. Tess shouted, "Bastard!" The Jeep bucked. Its tires spun in the sand.

Whoosh! The explosion thrust the Jeep forward. "Out!" she shouted. "Out!" As she jammed the brakes, I fumbled for the door handle. I got it open and rolled face down onto the desert floor. Lifting my head, I felt the flames and dragged myself to my knees. My arms held my shoulders up, but my head lolled to the ground. I crawled. I paused to let my eyes roam over the strange land, now lit by fire. Ahead thorn scrub—trees and bushes. I crawled through my agony, collapsing twice. The second time, I couldn't raise my body. Smoke and effort stung my eyes as sweat flowed from my forehead down my temples and neck. With my elbows, I belly-dragged myself into the scrub and, clenching my teeth again in pain, rolled over to see what was happening behind me.

In the light of the burning Jeep, I saw people running and screaming. Was one of them the woman who called herself Tess? I wished with every living fiber in my body that I could jump from this hiding place and help her, but my legs wouldn't move.

My cheek brushed something prickly.

The shrieks sounded closer, curdling the night. I lifted and looked out from my cover. The woman—Tess—broke from the shadows of the fire, free of the men. She shouted over the fire's crackle and roar, and over the men's voices, as she ran flinging her arms above her head. The men tried to catch her. In that instant, I knew that she was obliterating my trail. They caught her when she was no more than a few yards from where I lay in the thorn scrub. Had they just looked down. . . .

They yanked her away, toward the burning Jeep. Although she cursed them, there was something oddly intimate in her voice—and their laughter. She called one of them Ro-all.

"Ro-all, stop! Stop this fucking minute!"

She knows who they are.

Tess and the men disappeared behind the Jeep, into the shadows of the night and the flames. I was afraid for her, but she knew who they were, and maybe she knew what she was doing. The jeep burned into the night, finally burning itself to a glow. I rolled onto my back and elbowed myself onto my butt. I must find water. I got to my knees, and that's when the last of the embers died, leaving me in a pit of darkness. The night never lightened, there was no moon, nor stars, only the blackness of a devil night. I would have to sleep and wake in the morning and find water. I crawled deeper into the scrub and fell forward on something that moved. "Ouch."

I wished I were with Tess, wherever she was.

I'd dozed for just a moment. That's all it seemed—just a moment. When I opened my eyes, a fierce light flashed above me, and I stared into a mass of roiling anger. The fearful storm from the west. In the next instant, an explosion rocked the sizzling atmosphere. I struggled to rise. Intolerable pain racked my arm. I lay back and touched it—swollen and hard as stone. Whatever happened to my arm, I knew it needed help. Struggling to sit, swallowing against the misery in my hard, hot limb, I surveyed the scattered rocks on which I'd lain. A slippery swell of horror filled my gut. I wasn't in thorn scrub. Where was I? Had I awakened and moved in the night?

Fear propelled me to my feet, and wind lashed my hair across my face. The ground shook to the incessant rumbling overhead. I couldn't tell west from east, but I had to get away from here. Wind-whipped, I stumbled into the storm. I turned away. Then away again. No matter which way I turned I was headlong into wind and rain. In the shards of lightning, I saw the stone cairn. High ground.

Rain-blinded, blood hammered in my veins. I tried to climb, but I needed both hands and arms to hoist my aching body. Forcing my injured arm upward, I couldn't close my fist. The wind tore at my tortured body and my dying soul. Seconds later, a wash of water moved my feet. I clung to the face of the rock. The water rose to my knees. Then my waist. The force was too strong. It ripped me from the cairn, thumped and swirled me into a downward spiral, and then slung me headlong down a steep cliff. People popped into my head, one after the other. A handsome man with dimples. A hawkish-looking woman. A man who said he was my fiancé. A French twit. A little girl who didn't look like an Indian.

And then nothing.

Twenty-One

I woke from oblivion thinking, *So hot. So hurt.*

Voices. Children. Close by. And shadows hovering. On my back, limbs splayed, like on a cross.

"Mama," a child called, "This is the coolest play yet. Look at the rips in her shirt."

Play?

I could turn my head. Adults hurried forward, toward me.

A man said, "They make these reenactments so real. Bet she's the miner's wife who got scalped for the gold."

"I don't know, Troy," the woman said. "She's got all her hair. She's wearing shorts, not old-timey clothes. And where's everybody else in this play?"

A shadow loomed closer. "Holy Christ!" the man said. "She's for real. She's injured."

"She got lost looking for the gold mine," a kid cried out. "And there it is. She almost made it."

The gold mine?

The man's face hovered closer. "Let's get her up." He touched my cheek. "Can you stand?" He was close enough for me to smell his yeasty breath.

"Look at her arm, Troy," the woman cried. "And her bruises. We better call for help."

"You can try nine one one," the man said. He touched my neck; his hand felt wooden. "Can you talk?"

My tongue stuck to my lips. "Bluhhh."

"You're wounded and dehydrated," he said. "I'm a dentist, but I know that much. Stay brave, we'll see to you."

Stay brave.

"Troy, I got through," the woman shouted. "They're coming."

"Help is on the way, Miss," he said. "Good thing we decided to hike off the trail and see the old mine."

Good thing. Yes.

Eventually men in green came and put me on a board, and strapped me down as if I were going to jump up and run away. They spoke, they asked questions, but all I could say was, "Bluhhh." They seemed to know me, and what happened, but my head knew nothing but pain.

Inside the ambulance, an Indian woman put a wet rag over my face and bathed my cheeks and lips. "Sun," she said, "much too much sun." I rolled my eyes back to see a man with a needle. My heart froze. Didn't I know him? A cop? I tried to struggle, but the woman said, "Quiet. You need fluids." The needle went into my arm and for the millionth time I lost my mind.

Twenty-Two

I was climbing a thousand spiral steps. It was agonizing, and I wanted to go back down—down, down, down into a black world where I wasn't thirsty. Or wrapped in pain.

"Awake," a far-off voice said.

Slim shivers of light came through my lashes. A cold hand touched my cheek. "Christ, she's hot," a woman said. The bed jiggled. A blurred image hovered in my half-open eyes. I saw a skinny dark-eyed woman. She took my hand. She said, "It's Portia. Can you remember?"

I tried to open my mouth. I couldn't find my voice.

She said, "Lake and I came as soon as we heard from Dartagnan that you were missing."

From the other side of my bed, a male voice said, "Dru, can you hear me?"

I could hear them. I just couldn't speak. And I didn't know who they were.

"You're going to be all right," he said.

The woman calling herself Portia said, "Of course she'll be all right." She laid a hand on my forehead. "Neither concussion, coyotes, nor snakes can defeat her."

Snakes?

The woman had backed away, and the man's face was close. "Dru," he said. "Can you hear me?"

I grunted. I just wanted water. And to get out of the bindings. I squirmed, and pain raged in my body. "Ma yarm."

"Your arm will be fine," the man said. "The swelling is already going down."

"Wha—hap?"

The woman said, "You have to tell us."

The man said, "A tourist family found you lying in the desert. The doc says you got a concussion going over the waterfall. And you had some weird poison in you." *Waterfall? Poison?* He continued, "It was a different kind of poison than that of the sidewinder—how he knows the breed of the snake is more than I know."

The woman said, "He's guessing because they aren't as venomous as other rattlers, otherwise she'd be dead."

Don't say more.

"Wa'er," I managed. "Pleee . . ."

Time passed; I don't know how many hours, or days, or weeks. Nausea was a constant companion. When no one was with me, I passed the time counting the dots on the ceiling and hating the rich smell of roses and lilacs and magnolias that surrounded me as if I were in a coffin. They told me a man named Arlo sent me flowers every day. Arlo, they promised, would come to see me when he got back from Los Angeles.

Often I drifted into never-never land where a man went with me. We laughed, and kissed, and he promised a life of infinite passion. An engagement ring circled the third finger of my left hand. When I woke, the ring wasn't there, and I knew that he was dead. My fiancé was dead. Why was I alive?

As time passed, the pain in my body lessened, but not in my heart. I spent endless hours thinking of my lost love.

They told me that I had been bitten by a snake, that coyotes gnawed my toes, and that I'd been caught in a monsoon and cracked my head going over a waterfall called Ripple Rock. It was a true-blue miracle, they said, because nobody had ever survived a fall over Ripple Rock. They told me this with joy in their voices.

But I cursed a lot.

They told me that I was an investigator from Atlanta. That I'd come to Palm Springs to find a child. They said that the child and her mother had not been found. I didn't know what they were talking about. I cried and tried to bring my mind back.

"Crying's okay," the man named Lake said.

His solicitude grated.

He also asked unfathomable questions like: "Remember telling me that Bradley Whitney had performed in a strip club?"

"What . . . ?"

"Well, I checked with Sass Shay. Lucky for us, the bartender was a longtime employee. He remembered Bradley Whitney. He stripped, all right. In a mask. He was billed as the Masked Mystique."

I looked at him, thinking, *So?*

He made a noise of frustration. "Darling, you must try harder."

Apparently, I'd known this man in another life, but not as good as he knew me. He called me Dru, and darling, and my love. He'd kiss me when he came into the room and wipe the sweat from my face. I felt a twinge of guilt that he irked me most of the time.

As time went by, I recalled more about Portia. She was a school mate and a judge. She gave me a car. Once she asked bluntly, "What the hell were you doing in the desert in a monsoon?"

I shook my head that I didn't know.

Lake said soothingly, "Don't force it."

Try harder, don't force it? A contradiction from him, but, in fact, traces of my life were returning. He was a policeman, and I used to be a policewoman. I liked my uniform. See, I am trying, and forcing.

Twenty-Three

Another day passed and another stranger came into my room. "Hey, brave girl!" he hailed. "How's our survivor?" His heartiness was strident, and I just stared at him.

"Oh, I forget," he said, his dark eyes and white teeth sparkling like he was in a low-budget pirate movie. "You don't remember a thing. Well, you survived one of the worst monsoons August has seen in a century. Over the dry waterfall in Lost Coyote Canyon. You're the talk of The Springs."

"Whoopee," I said.

My sarcasm didn't phase him. "They found you at the bottom where the mine is. The water volume must have cushioned you."

"What's your name?"

"You kiddin' me?"

"I don't know you. I don't know a lot of people who apparently know me."

"Damn. I didn't know you were that bad. The head bang and the jimsonweed done a number on you."

"Jimsonweed? Is that the same thing as datura?"

"Yep. Got a lotta names. Same ol' nasty stuff. Makes you wonder why folks get a kick out of smoking it."

"I don't smoke."

"How'd you get hold of it?"

"What's your name?"

"Dartagnan."

A trio of costumed men with swords flashed into my brain. "The Three Musketeers," I said. Another flash occurred, and I recalled a visit from the man who sent me fresh flowers twice a day. His name was Arlo. He was in the movies and told me his wife was the mother of the child I sought. I asked Dartagnan, "You an actor?"

"Nope. Cop. PSPD."

Lake came in and stared down at Dartagnan. "Anything new?"

"Nope," Dartagnan said. "Nothing on the woman and the girl. Nothing on why your lady friend here went missing in the desert."

Lady friend?

A woman came to see me. Her name, she said, was Tess Rosovo. An explosion went off in my head, I saw fire and my arm went numb. She said, "I know you don't know me now, but you and I became friends on our ride into the desert." *She's an Indian princess.*

She told me that she'd taken me to the desert—to her family's home on the reservation—because I suspected the woman named Eileen had taken her child to a woman's shelter. Together we would ask the residents where these places might be. Then she said I started feeling bad and went to sleep in a bedroom in her aunt's home. A couple of hours later she went to look in on me and saw that I had disappeared. She said the back door was never locked and neither was the gate. Her family concluded I had wandered away and began a search for me. She speculated that at some point in my wanderings, I fell into jimsonweed and got the toxin under my skin. And then along came a snake.

Later, Lake and Portia came to say they'd contacted a hypnotist who would help me remember. I sighed and asked if they thought I *should* remember. They exchanged glances—

again. It appeared I said a lot of odd things.

Another day came to a close, and when everyone left, I turned on the television. News programs bored me. I flicked past inane sitcoms and awful reality shows. PBS had on a charity auction; I was about to flick it off when I saw a basket sitting on a table. The camera closed in. I found myself sitting up suddenly. The auctioneer described the basket.

". . . The boojum tree is unique to the Sonora Desert and is named after a mythical creature in Lewis Carroll's book *The Hunting of the Snark*. Our gifted local artist, Contessa Rosovo, frequently weaves the strange plant into her designs. Let's start the bidding at fifteen hundred dollars."

I didn't breathe as the image of the basket sitting on a blanket in an oasis popped into my head. And guacamole. And disgusting tea.

I broke into a cold sweat as memories tumbled over each other. A cabin. Windla. Perspiration dripping down my neck. Chanting. A barrel stove with a fat pipe going through the ceiling. Words from Tess about girls getting their first moon. An older woman passing her hands over a young girl lying on dirt. A pale face that didn't belong. Dancing. My hand. A ring. Tess. Orange images. Black.

I fell back on the pillow, exhausted. Sleep came inside a blazing Jeep and over a waterfall and into a gold mine and down onto the belly of a snake. Then the Indian princess came and threw water on me.

I sat up shivering. It was all so clear now.

Then a nurse came in with a needle.

"No!"

Twenty-Four

I woke to familiar dawn shadows, sat up, and said aloud, "I remember. Everything." My clothes were in drawers, in a metal locker. My sluggish and weakened body wanted to rest, but the hell with that. I pulled out slacks and a shirt and was standing in my underwear when Portia and Lake came in together.

They stopped, drop-jawed.

I pumped my fist. "I remember."

Portia shot toward me like a black bullet. "What?"

"All of it," I said.

"Tell us," she demanded, throwing me a blanket to cover my nearly nude body.

I sat on the bed and hit the highlights of what happened.

"A ring poisoned you?" Lake asked.

"Had to be," I assured him. "Tess was wearing an onyx ring. It was turned around. A prong pricked me. I felt it just before I passed out."

Lake rubbed his nose with a forefinger, a gesture I knew. It spoke of doubts. Portia's eyes were kinder, less doubtful, but wondering.

I felt my face flush. "Don't look at me like that. I'm sure of what happened."

Lake said, "I hope you remember we have an appointment this morning with a hypnotist."

"Not me."

"Dru, I think it'd be best . . ."

"I don't need a damned hypnotist."

"You're telling us that Tess Rosovo—the pride of the Mission Hills Indians—poisoned you and left you to die in the desert?"

"She poisoned me, but then she saved me."

He folded his arms across his chest. "Who did she save you from?"

"I don't know, but the Jeep burned up." If I sounded abrupt and disconnected, that's the way I felt.

"Finish dressing, Dru. We'll get some fresh air before we get to our appointment."

"We? You can go. I'm not."

Portia intervened. "Moriah, it couldn't hurt."

"Who found this hypnotist?"

They looked at each other, and I knew it had been Tess. "No."

Portia gave in. "We can't make you, of course."

"No, you can't. Now get out, Lake. I'm getting dressed. Then I'm leaving."

"You can't. The doctors . . ."

"I'm through with the doctors, the nurses, the meds, and the goddamned needles."

My suitcases lined the window. I lifted one.

"Where are you going?" he asked.

"Check back into the hotel," I said, heaving the suitcase onto the bed with the arm that wasn't sore. "Find Eileen and Kinley." The painful effort reminded me of a snake-in-the-desert. "Backtrack to the desert and find out who wanted me dead."

"Let's talk to Tess first," Portia said. "And Dartagnan."

"Forget it." I turned to Lake. "Please—I'd like to get dressed without an audience." He moved stiffly out the door. "Ass," I said.

"There *is* one thing you don't remember," Portia said.

"What?"

"You and Lake—you were close friends—lovers."

"I remember." This morning, in that twilight time before fully awakening, the laughing man of my dreams died. I took a deep breath. Then I was with Lake.

"But you don't feel the same now, do you?" Portia said.

I considered my answer. I didn't feel the same, but I didn't want to admit it to Portia. It would cast doubt on my recovery. "Sure I do. I just—he's aggravating me."

"Even when you didn't remember shit, he aggravated you."

"It'll be all right," I said and looked at my longtime friend. "I need some time, that's all."

"He wants the best for you, the very best. And so do I."

"I know that."

"I have to go back to Atlanta. My trial schedule is backing up. I can't ask anyone else to fill in."

"I understand," I said. "I'm fine."

"Lake will be here to help."

"I don't need—"

"Moriah, you need his help. If you're right and you have enemies, you don't know who they are."

I looked at Portia feeling like a chastised child. "Okay, but how long can Lake be away from his job?"

"He's yours as long as you need him. The APD has a soft spot for one of their favorite ex-cops."

It was silly, but I felt elated.

"Go easy on Lake," Portia said, stepping close enough to hug me. "Let your heart remember, too."

I couldn't tell her that it was because my heart did remember and that it was sick because it had to forget once again the man I couldn't marry because he was dead.

TWENTY-FIVE

I'd just settled into Lake's rental Jeep and plugged my cell phone into the jack when the cell played Mozart. I looked at the panel. "Whitney."

"Welcome back to the real world," Lake said.

Whitney said into my ear bud, "Judge Devon informed me of your—mishap. We've lost valuable time."

"A simple, 'How are you doing?' would be a nice beginning," I said, hearing Lake's snigger as he drove us toward the Palkott Hotel.

"Well," Whitney said, "I assume you've recovered your memory or we wouldn't be talking. The judge said you were going to be hypnotized."

"Don't need hypnosis. Had an epiphany just in time."

"Ah, a sudden manifestation of the essence, or meaning, of something."

"Yeah, scholar, a sudden manifestation."

"The essence is, can you still investigate my case?"

"I'll find your child."

"This epiphany tell you where Kinley is—where Eileen is?"

"Not existential enough."

"Miss Dru, time is running out."

"Not *if* Eileen's got Kinley with her."

"*If?* You think she doesn't?"

"I didn't say that. I said *if.*"

"What else could have happened?"

"Mr. Whitney, that's obvious, but let's not go there now."

"Obvious? To whom?" He didn't bother to control his fury. "My little girl is gone, my ex-wife is gone. This is adding up to be a big zero, and I'm paying for it."

"Two and two don't always add up to four if somebody's fiddling with the numbers, Mr. Whitney."

"Are you sure you've fully recovered?"

"Very sure. Let's go with your assumption that Eileen kidnapped Kinley. No one here knows where she could have gone. She didn't confide in her friends. A neighbor saw them Saturday afternoon. She hasn't left a paper trail, so she hasn't run out of money. She withdrew twenty-five thousand from her account on Thursday before she disappeared."

"Twenty-five thousand? That's an hour's shopping for Eileen."

"At one time in her life she probably learned thrift."

"Arlo's helping her. She's likely hiding out in LA That's Eileen's style, not living in the desert with unkempt Indians. Did you check the airlines going to LA? Do I have to do that for you?"

My fist tightened, and my voice rattled like marbles stuck in my throat. "I checked. The cops checked. But you go ahead and check." Lake reached over and touched me on the shoulder. "Look, Mr. Whitney, Eileen's car's gone. If she's not hiding in Palm Springs, she had to take out across the desert. Native Americans own most of it. If she isn't hiding with them, then she had to stop and get gas, and eat, and sleep. The word is out."

"The word is out? You've been out there more than a week and all you can do is put the word out? You'll have the media on my ass. The last thing I wanted—the very thing I paid you to avoid."

"What are you saying, Mr. Whitney?"

His silence was loud enough to simmer through the ether. He

finally said, "I'm sorry you got hurt, but I have certain goals. . . ."

I finally got it. "You're firing me?"

He didn't say anything for a while. "Don't you think you've failed?" My body drew as tight as a bow string. He said, "Judge Devon talked to the policeman out there. He told her that Eileen's definitely not in Palm Springs. I don't think you need to be in Palm Springs, do you?"

I cut in, "I'll tally up the totals for you, Mr. Whitney. Naturally, the time I spent recovering will *not* be included."

I put on sunglasses and tucked the paper airline ticket in my purse. My work here wasn't finished, but I was. Failure does not sit well on my soul. As Lake and I walked from the ticket counter at the airport, I saw a familiar man duck behind a group of women, obvious tourists. The buzzing ladies were excellent cover for him. And because of them, I lost sight of him. "Someone's following us," I said.

Lake's shoulders slumped like he'd failed at something. "Who?"

Temper, I told myself. "If I knew, I'd have said his name."

"How do you know he's following *us?*"

"I've seen him before. He ducked behind those women."

Lake looked at the gaggle of females. Then he nodded toward a small man with a laptop who was hurrying toward the ticket counter. "That man?"

"Don't be an ass."

TWENTY-SIX

We had a cup of coffee at Zing's donut shop. Zing wasn't there. He was on vacation. Our next stop was at Philippe's Too Busy to Cook? I didn't see Philippe. Two men and a woman wearing floppy chef's hats were busy with customers. No one manned the flower and candy section. "Is Monsieur Philippe in?" I called to the woman.

"No," she said, not bothering with a phony French accent. "He's on vacation this week."

"Where is the girl who sells flowers?"

"Nicole?"

"Yes, is she around?"

"She never is," the woman grumbled. "She's a part-timer. I've told Philippe that we must get someone more dependable. But he goes for cheap."

Outside, I said to Lake, "Betcha Theodosia's also on vacation." He didn't comment. In doubting silence, he seemed content to take me wherever I wanted to go.

In the hotel bar, the bartender who'd jived with Dartagnan the night I arrived wasn't there. He was on vacation. I drank an Amstel Light and ate a corned beef sandwich while Lake drank Coke. No doubt he thought he needed a clear head—what with taking me into Lost Coyote Canyon where I *believed* there had to be evidence of a burned-out Jeep, where I *said* a torrent of water had nearly washed me into an abandoned gold mine.

We kept up the hush when we hit the road. I hugged the passenger door of the Jeep. Even with sunglasses, the desert light burned into my eyeballs. Ten minutes into the ride, the AC in the rented four-wheeler began pouring hot air out the vents. I agreed we should roll down the windows rather than go back and get another vehicle. I suspected the shocks failed, too, because we jostled up the tuff road—still with nothing to say to each other. We came to the gold mine. No tourists today. In silence, Lake and I walked over the place where I'd been found. He put an arm around me. I looked up at him, feeling like I was tumbling on a wall of water again.

He let his arm slip to his side and turned toward the head of the arroyo. "That Ripple Rock?"

"That's Ripple Rock," I said.

He looked west. "Those hightops could become thunder-heads."

Let the goddamn thunder roll, and the rains come down, I wasn't intimidated. "Let's go on."

The Jeep rocked and rolled onward, up the arroyo, past the apex of Ripple Rock and kept going up into the high desert. My head ached. Lake's polo shirt was soaked. So was my hair. We reached the cairn above the dry fall. I studied it. "I never had a chance," I murmured.

"For what?" Lake asked.

"Salvation," I said.

He looked at me and asked, "Do you want to go on?"

"Just drive."

The Adobe Flats rose on the skyline. Lake pressed the gas, and the four-wheeler dusted up fine desert dirt, which felt like sandpaper on my face.

"The famous Adobe Flats?" Lake said. *Sarcastic bastard.*

Wiping sweat beads laced with grit, I answered, "The very ones."

"People lived in those stacked hovels?"

"A hundred and some–odd years ago, after they'd been stripped of their land, and before the government allotted them a few acres for a reservation."

He spoke, and I listened to his mellow voice. "My ancestors didn't keep slaves, and they didn't run the natives down the Trail of Tears, but I often feel I should answer for those who did." I looked over at him. He put his hand on my knee. How awkward, I thought, but I smiled at him, at the memory of how I used to feel when he touched me. If only he believed me.

We drove in circles looking for a patch of dirt and spiny thorn scrub that had seen fire. I didn't expect to see a burned-out Jeep, but there had to be fire debris. Everything leaves a trace. "We've passed these same cactuses several times," Lake said. He pointed a finger over to his right where a few smoke trees and yuccas bunched together above desert brush. "There's a likely place you might have crawled."

We left the four-wheeler and stepped through the scrub. There wasn't a speck of evidence that I'd been in the flora cave. But then it had rained many days in a row.

I heard a tic-tic-tic.

"Snake," Lake said. He grabbed my jeans at the back belt loop to keep me from taking another step. "Sidewinder."

I watched, horrified, as it sidled and snapped away from us.

"Fascinating," he said. "What's a night hunter doing out now?"

I wondered if it had been the one. "Maybe he came out to say he's sorry."

It disappeared into the rocks while I rubbed my arm. It was nearly healed. So was my brain bruise, although I still had mild dizzy spells. Right now, I fought to keep one at bay.

Lake looked west. The bright clouds were coagulating. "You want to see other things before the rains come down?"

★　★　★　★　★

We rode through the main street of stylish ranch homes. Lake commented, "Looks like Twenty-One Oh One Suburbia Street, Alpharetta, GA."

"The casinos have made Native Americans rich," I said.

We stopped at Tess's family home. The shutters were tight. On the mailbox, the sign read: *The home of Casper and Rosa Rosovo. Please ring the bell. We will fetch the mail. Thank you.*

It was useless to press the bell button, and I knew it by instinct, but I did anyway. Two Dobermans ran forward, snarling and baring their teeth. As I waited—in vain—the smothering afternoon heat wrapped around me, and I felt eyes watching me through the shutters. *Maybe I'm round the bend and haven't realized it.*

Lake was drumming his fingers on the steering wheel when I got inside the Jeep. He backed onto the main street, and we rode quietly to Moon Lodge. It looked deserted. Glancing at Lake as he opened his door, I saw an impassive profile. My blood pressure dropped a couple of points. *He hates this.* I walked up the cabin's steps and tried the doorknob. Locked. I went to a window, looked in, held my breath, and stood back to let Lake see into the room. He looked at me. "Like you said, one room and a barrel stove."

Nothing else was as I'd described it, or remembered it. Benches didn't line the walls. The interior was furnished like a hunting lodge—a deer head mounted on the wall by the stove, a few early American chairs and a settee haphazardly placed, as if men had scooted them around to chat and drink and smoke with each other, animal skins on the wooden floor. The wood looked old. The night of the moon ritual, it had been an earthen floor. I looked at Lake's face where shadows shifted across etched lines. *Say something.*

"A deer in the desert?" Lake said.

"A mule deer," I muttered. "They've changed the cabin since I was here."

"To make it look like you don't know what you're talking about." His words were even and toneless.

Balling my fists, desperation giving way to anger, I was about to spout off when I heard engine noise wavering on the thin, hot air. We turned to see a Jeep trail dirt as it tore toward us. The Jeep was new. It might be Tess. Ten seconds later, I was disappointed to see a broad-shouldered, dark-complexioned man get out and walk up with a mild question in his expression.

"I hope we're not trespassing," I said, too fast. "I've been here before. I think I lost a bracelet inside the cabin."

He looked at his boots for a moment, then back at me. "You are not trespassing. We welcome all who wish to visit. When was it that you lost your bracelet?"

"A week ago, Friday night. Mrs. Rosovo was holding a moon ritual that night."

He scratched a cheek. "A moon ritual? Here?"

"I was with my friend, Tess Rosovo. You know Tess?"

He looked as if he smelled something bad. "Is this a joke?"

"No."

"This is not the house of moon rituals. This is a house for men and boys."

"But I'm sure . . ."

His eyes were hard, and equally sure. "You are mistaken."

"Can you tell me where I might find Tess Rosovo and where they hold their moon ritual?"

"To both, I cannot."

"It's important."

He looked at Lake as if seeing him for the first time—thus dismissing me. "Who are you?"

"Richard Lake."

"Tell your friend she is mistaken. This is a hunting lodge."

"I can see that," Lake said. "Where is Miss Rosovo?"

The man apparently decided to give in. "She lives in Palm Springs."

"She's not there. Dartagnan LeRoi said she was on the reservation."

"She might be. It's a big place. Her uncle's home is back on the main street."

"No one answered."

"Then they are somewhere else."

I looked out at the desert sky and wondered if I hadn't been transported into one of Arlo's cheap films.

Lake said, "Makes sense." He threw up a hand. "We'll be going. Sorry to trouble you."

"No trouble." The man turned for his Jeep.

I came down the steps after Lake and followed him to the four-wheeler. When we'd closed the doors, Lake didn't look at me.

"Well?" I said, a little more belligerently than I intended. When he didn't crank the engine right away, I said, "Look, I am *not* mistaken."

He turned the key and put the gear in drive. "Okay." He looked out his side window. "He's watching us."

I turned my head. The man in the Jeep looked as if he were going to get out and come toward us.

Lake pressed the gas. I said, "Drive back to town."

"What then?"

"I'll go my own way."

"I can't let you do that."

"I don't like your attitude."

"No attitude."

"You don't believe me."

"I didn't say that."

"I can read your face and your body language."

"My face and body language should be telling you that I'm concerned. That's all."

"Concerned for what? That I've lost my friggin' mind?"

That ended conversation until he said, "We're passing the Rosovo house again. Want to stop?"

It was still shuttered, but my sixth sense saw eyes following us up the street. "No one's going to answer the door. This is a setup."

"Why have these Native people set you up?"

"They're protecting Eileen and her daughter."

"Why?" he said. We were leaving the town, bumping along on an unpaved road.

"Arlo," I said, my butt bouncing on the bad shocks.

"Why?"

"Seems obvious."

"Not to me."

"It does to me."

"Are you going to tell me what's so obvious?"

"No."

"Well, where do you want to go?"

"To the Adobe Flats."

Lake constantly checked his rearview mirror. I checked the side view. No Jeep. No dust. Just a mirage of shimmering light in between the cacti and smoke trees. And the high clouds closing in. "Gonna come down," Lake said.

I shrugged, not caring, feeling invincible.

At Adobe Flats we got out. I scanned the horizon. There was an outcropping of rocks I hadn't noticed before. They were perhaps a hundred and fifty yards away, near the end of the building. "Over there," I pointed. "I thought I saw a flash."

Lake studied the rocks. He turned his palms up and let his gaze skim my face. We got out of the Jeep and walked over the sand-dirt to the stone steps. Ghost pain burned my rear end—Tess dragging me down those steps. The entrance was an upright rectangle smack in the middle of the long building. The wooden lintel brushed Lake's hair when he ducked to go inside. A narrow hall disappeared into murky light, presumably at the back of the building. Off this hall, narrower halls lead into tiny rooms. "Rabbit warrens," Lake said.

He inspected the ground, perhaps for real evidence that I'd been here, or maybe he was pretending to believe me.

I said, "I thought I was in a cave."

Nodding, he said, "I could use a flashlight."

We reached the back of the building where worn earthen steps led upward. It was dark as night, and I willed my visual purple to kick in. Halfway up, we came to a landing off which passages went right and left. The ancients who lived here had to be short. I was stooped, and so was Lake. He asked, "Could you have been kept in one of the rooms on this floor?" I had told him that the room I was in was near steps.

"No, there are no windows in these rooms. In one of my awakenings, I recall seeing stars from a window."

I followed him up to a third story where little rooms were carved out of the walls. "Jesus, people lived here?" Lake said.

Daylight shined through exterior windows, enough that I could see that the rooms were bare, except for signs of joint-smoking, beer-drinking and love-making. "Condoms," Lake said. "I thought this place was sacred."

"Articles for the sacred rituals, maybe?" I said. "If we ever find Tess, she can tell us."

"Why do you say *if?*"

"I have a bad feeling about Tess."

His dark eyes, though shadowed, sought mine. "I've always trusted your instincts, Dru."

He'd created another awkward moment. "You're talking

about the past."

"No," he said, taking my hand. "But I'm wondering if you remember *everything.*"

Did I remember *everything?* I said, "Nobody remembers everything about anything."

TWENTY-SEVEN

We came to a wide, shallow room. "Must be the penthouse," Lake said.

Looking around, I said, "I doubt the people living here would have called it that."

He shook his head. "You've lost your sense of humor, too."

That could be because one night my bones melted in this place.

The room had two earthen windows facing the western sky. Lake was drawn to a spot under one where a blanket was scrunched against the wall. He reached down to pick it up.

At that same moment, I looked out the second window and saw a man standing on the rock where I'd seen the flash. His arms were extended. I'm sure he held a rifle.

Terrified, I dived for Lake just before he stood up. The bullet whistled through the window. I rolled off Lake and sat, gasping for air.

"Shit!" Lake cried, reaching for the gun in his ankle holster. I didn't realize he wore his off-duty gun. He jumped to one side of the window and pointed the automatic toward the ceiling. He shoved his head out the window and drew it back quickly— twice. "Stand across from me," he said. When I positioned myself at the other side of the window, he knelt, put the gun on the floor, and shoved it toward me. "Watch for sudden move-ment, and shoot," he said. He backed away and crossed the open window.

I held the gun and took quick glances outside. No one stood on the rock, or lay on it. Nothing on the desert floor moved. Lake inched closer. "Lake," I said. "Get back." I held the gun, looking out, watching for movement.

"The shooter's gone," Lake said. He craned his neck for a quick glance out the window. "You say he was on that rock?"

"Standing up."

"You think he was deliberately calling attention to himself?"

"Could be," I said, "but why?"

"Didn't you say this was a forbidden canyon and outsiders aren't welcome?"

"Tess brought me here."

"That doesn't mean she extended an open invitation."

"So what are you trying to say, Lieutenant?"

"A warning shot—to run us off. Maybe the man at the cabin."

"More than one man wants to kill me, I think."

"He shot at me."

"You're in the way. They want me."

"Because you think the men's lodge had a moon ritual in it?" He spoke like his vocal chords were in a vice grip.

"No, because I'm looking for Eileen and Kinley."

"You said they drugged you after they kidnapped you from the cabin. Why didn't they just kill you then?"

"I don't . . ." I heard a noise. A quiet flap on hard ground. I turned to Lake. "I heard something down there, outside, coming inside."

Lake stuck his neck out the window, peering down. "I don't see anything."

"I heard—"

"Your hearing is astute these days," he said, and turned from the window.

I held the gun at my side, pointing at the floor. "And your skepticism seems to have affected your senses," I shot back.

He walked to the middle of the room, then looked back, "You coming?"

I flung past him into the hall. Something sparkling on the floor caught my eye, and I picked up a piece of silver. Birds in flight. I shoved it at him. "Tess's. She wore the earrings the day she took me to the moon ritual."

He glanced at the earring. "Nice workmanship."

A short, sharp scrape interrupted my retort. "Did you hear that?"

He put his finger to his lips. "Yes."

Then came the guttural whispers of angry or frightened men. I went ahead of Lake, to the top of the steps. "First floor front hall," I said. "Three at least. They could all have rifles. We are two, with one thirty-eight. Not good."

He reached for the gun hanging in my hand. "You don't know they *all* have rifles."

Before he could get his hand on the gun, I darted down the steps.

"Dru! Get back here." He clamored after me.

I fired rounds as I jumped down the steps. The Glock has seventeen in the magazine. Its retort echoed off the ancient mud walls, booming like a shotgun, bullets pinging into the landing wall. I reached the landing with Lake breathing on my neck. "Give me the gun, Dru. Now."

I scooted across the landing, gun held in both hands, cop style, aiming to head-shoot anyone who popped into view. Light rose from the first floor, and I ran down the steps, turned the corner into the main hall and saw three men dash from a side hall and pump their legs out the front door. Lake caught up with me, and I handed him the gun. "They're outside."

Grim-eyed, he grabbed the automatic and examined the magazine. I followed as he checked the side halls for sneak attackers. Outside, the three had reached the rock and rounded it.

A heavy truck started up. The engine pounded down the canyon, but we never saw the truck.

The gun in his hand, pointing at the sand, Lake aimed his stormy brown eyes at me. "What the hell did you do that for?"

"We were trapped, outmanned, and probably outgunned."

"I had a strategy."

"So did I."

"Some strategy. Get us killed."

"The best defense is an offense, ever hear that?"

"Some offense."

"Where are those men now?"

"Dru, what the hell's wrong with you?"

"Those men didn't know if we had guns, or how many. They're bad, but not stupid. They'd calculate the odds."

He waved the gun at the Jeep. "You got a plan to get us to the vehicle without getting ambushed?"

"They're gone."

"Your clairvoyance working overtime?"

"You're alive."

"You know what this looks like to me. Three little Indians out hunting one day and accidentally—or maybe on purpose—shoot at a window of the old ancestral flats. Like city kids shooting out street lights. Then they decide to come inside and smoke a joint. Lo and behold, a mad woman with a Glock comes running down the stairs, shooting up the walls."

"Earlier you thought someone was warning us to get out of the forbidden canyon. Now it's a joy-shooting bunch of kids." I ran for the four-wheeler.

"Dru," he shouted. Apparently he wasn't totally convinced of his rationalization, because there was terror in his voice. He caught up and shoved me inside. He turned on me. "What the hell's got into you? When we were partners, you never acted like you did in there. We shared the danger, and we watched each other's backs. Have you forgotten your cop training?"

"It's been a while since I was a cop," I fired back. "But I haven't lost my instincts. I knew how to save us. I didn't survive the worst the desert can throw at me and not have developed a sense of what I can do."

He snorted and put the gun in the holster. We rode back to town in hateful silence. He dropped me off at the airport, where I rented my own car, a little Honda.

TWENTY-EIGHT

I told Lake I was having a room service dinner and then getting a good night's sleep. Maybe later, I'd get a good night's sleep. I left for VillageFest. I wasn't surprised to see him walking in the middle of the crowd. He lifted his chin and gave me a smeary smile and sauntered ahead, never looking back. As irrational as it was, I took two shallow breaths and blinked away tears.

Zing didn't have a donut stand that night, and Philippe wasn't serving up trays of sushi. Tess didn't have a table booth, and Dartagnan wasn't anywhere to be seen. I ate an enchilada, a tamale, and drank a cold beer, and tasted nothing.

On the way back to my hotel room, I spotted a familiar figure. He was broad-shouldered and dark-complexioned. He wore sunglasses and a fedora-type straw hat. I was certain he was the man at the airport. And he was very like the man whom we met at the cabin. I ran to catch up to him, but he disappeared behind a green-striped tent. I circled it. No one was there.

Back in my hotel room, I looked at my missed calls. I almost threw the damned cell across the room. Lake's number appeared twice. Mozart played as I held the cell. The name on the display surprised me: Bradley Whitney. I was in no mood for a contentious conversation with my ex-client.

The concerto played again. Dartagnan. I answered, "What? You're not on vacation, too?"

"What're you talking 'bout, girl?"

"Zing, Philippe, Theodosia are all on vacation. They get a

free trip to Vegas?"

Dartagnan laughed. "It's August, Miss Dru. People leave this hellhole in August."

"Where's Tess?"

I thought he wasn't going to answer, but he said, "I believe she had a show somewheres up Twenty-Nine Palms way."

I said, "Her folks' house was shut up when I went there today."

"They go with her sometimes. Or they're at the casino in Mission Palms."

"Is it open all night?"

He laughed as if I'd asked a dumb question. "Hear you're going back east tomorrow."

"Where'd you hear that from?"

"The Springs is a small town, Miss Dru. Very small."

"I'm one hundred percent convinced."

"Sorry 'bout all that happened. Glad you're better."

"Me, too."

A three-hundred-pound casino bouncer told me that the Roso-vos weren't around. I was two paces from a door marked PRIVATE when three men walked out. Lights blazed inside a hallway behind them, and before the door closed, I saw someone else duck into a doorway.

The bouncer escorted me to the exit and watched as I drove from under the marquee. I had to wait for traffic in the road to clear before I made a left. A Jeep came flying up the road. Once it passed, I could pull out. The Jeep's right flasher came on, and the driver braked suddenly. Tess's face glowed from the windshield. My eyes trailed down to the passenger-side fender. It was dented. I gripped the wheel so hard, the muscles in my hands hurt. Tess made a right in front of me. I watched in my rearview mirror as she stopped beneath the marquee and jumped out. The bouncer followed her into the casino.

I yanked the Honda into reverse, backed up, and stopped in front of the Jeep. A valet came up as I got out. "Forgot something inside," I said and dashed into the casino. Tess had opened the door marked PRIVATE. The bouncer saw me. I pointed to Tess. "I'm with her."

"Tess," I called. But the door shut.

I banged on it until the brute caught my arm.

"Tell her I need to talk to her."

He looked at me as if I were a runaway lunatic.

Suddenly the door jerked open. Tess said, "That's okay, Harley."

Tess's cheekbones were more prominent than I remembered. Her hair tangled. I said, "I've been trying to find you." She didn't answer but tilted her head to beckon me inside. "Are you all right?" I asked. She closed the door on the bouncer and led me down the hall. "Tess? Answer me." She opened the door into an office and hung back for me to go in first. Rosa Rosovo sat behind a desk. Lake sat in a director's chair.

I felt weightless, like an astronaut untethered from his ship. "What's going on?"

Lake stood. "I found Tess for you."

Tess backed up against a wall and protested softly. "I wasn't lost. I had a showing in Joshua Tree."

I stared at Lake, my hands curled into tight balls. "You were sitting here while that bouncer threw me out."

He said, "I didn't know you were out there, Dru."

Liar. Tension hung like fog, and neither Tess nor Lake would look at me.

Mrs. Rosovo, however, drilled me with her prune-like eyes. "We are sorry for your misfortune, Miss Dru. Please accept our hope for a continued recovery and please have a safe trip back to Georgia."

"I've recovered," I said.

She brushed a hand back. "One day your memory will return."

"It has," I said.

She exchanged a cagey glance with Lake and Tess, then looked at me. "Datura lingers."

Tess said quietly, "Dru, I didn't take you to a moon ritual." She suddenly got interested in her torn cuticles. "I *told* you about a moon ritual. We hold them—in different places."

"I was there," I insisted. "The cabin, the girls, the heat. The dancing, the chanting, and then, being so dizzy . . ."

Nervous eye signals flashed between Mrs. Rosovo and Lake. "Go on, Tess," her aunt said.

Tess's words tumbled out. "I didn't rescue you from the Flats. My Jeep didn't burn up. You can see it sitting outside."

"Easy to re-create."

Tess plucked at a cuticle and glanced at her aunt. "I took you to see my aunt at our home. You got sick, you went outside and wandered away."

I stared into Mrs. Rosovo's eyes. "I've never been inside your home."

Lake took a step toward me and held out a hand. "Let's go."

I stared at him. "You go."

"Dru, this is going nowhere."

My eyes went to Tess, who seemed fascinated by photographs on the opposite wall. "Why are you doing this, Tess? I trusted you."

"Doing what?" Mrs. Rosovo intervened.

I walked toward her desk. "Trying to make Lieutenant Lake believe I'm delusional. You and I and Tess know better." I rounded on Lake. "Tell them about this afternoon, at Adobe Flats."

"I talked with Mrs. Rosovo before you got here," Lake said.

"I was right. Some natives shoot at interlopers."

"Bull."

Lake took my arm. "Thank you for seeing me, Miss Rosovo. Mrs. Rosovo."

"No," I said, trying to jerk my arm away. "I can't go. Not like this."

"We extend hospitality, Miss Dru," Mrs. Rosovo said, "but in the circumstances, it would be better . . ."

"That little girl in the cabin—"

"What little girl?"

"In the cabin. A little girl, with a wig. She—she didn't belong. She had the fair skin of a blonde."

Mrs. Rosovo had trouble keeping eye contact. She cleared her throat and said, "You are mistaken." She folded her hands on the desk. "I'm afraid you are a victim of stereotyping. Not all Indians are dark-complexioned with dark hair."

"I have photographs of Eileen and Kinley, and—"

"Please," Mrs. Rosovo said. "No more."

I looked at Tess's worried profile. "You've betrayed me, Tess."

Tess apparently reached into herself and found a defense, because she leveled a chilly gaze at me. "You are ill."

"That little girl, take me to her, prove to me who she is, then I'll believe you."

Mrs. Rosovo said to Lake, "Our conversation is ended."

"Yes," Lake said, gently tugging my arm.

I faced him. "No, I can't—"

He stepped me toward the door, saying quietly, "Dru, please. Can't you see? These people can't help you."

"Won't."

"Good day, Miss Dru," Mrs. Rosovo said.

I was barely out when the door closed forcefully. I turned on him. "What the hell were you doing here?"

"Trying to help you."

"By going behind my back?"

"Trying to find the truth."

"You know the truth."

He held my good arm and tugged me down the hall. I shook free. He spread his arms to block my retreat. "No, Dru." He caught me around the waist and pushed me to the door. The bouncer was holding it open. Once through, I said, "Let me go."

"Don't make a scene."

"You don't know what a scene is."

Outside, I looked over Tess's Jeep while Lake stayed close. Inside it, the key hung in the ignition on a boojum ring, but there wasn't an eagle etched into the leather of the passenger seat. I said, "Same year, and model, but Tess didn't have time to etch the eagle."

Lake's eyes were watchful as if he thought I might jump in it and take off. "A good night's sleep," he said. "Things will seem different in the morning."

"Not unless people decide to tell the truth, and you decide to believe me."

"I believe you believe."

I don't think I ever felt this bitter. "Go back to Atlanta."

"I am, in the morning. We both are."

No matter what I did, I couldn't lose his headlights all the way back to Palm Springs.

I tossed all night. Lake had pissed me off so thoroughly I could keep him benched at the back of my mind, but I couldn't stop wondering why the hell these people were trying to make me believe something that wasn't true. I began to make up scenarios. One made a lot of sense.

TWENTY-NINE

The FBI bureau office in Palm Springs is on East Tahquitz Canyon Way. The name on the office door read GILA JOE CORLEE. He opened the door. Tall for a Plains Indian, he was maybe forty-five, looking like a totem Indian without the war bonnet and ankle feathers, and when he introduced himself he pronounced his first name "Heela."

We shook hands, and I took a seat. I glanced around the small mess of a room. His desk took up most of it. I sat on the sort of straight wooden chair I call a butt throbber. The metal table to my right was loaded with papers and files.

Agent Corlee looked amiable enough, but there was an impatient edge to him. "Miss Dru, Detective LeRoi said he'd explained to you that I've been on vacation. Some vacation. On the border looking for illegals."

I appreciated his attempt to make small talk. "Surely FBI agents get vacations."

"We would if we could get away from cell phones and PDAs."

"What would we do without them?" I said with disinterest. Corlee made an acquiescent grunt, and clearly it was up to me to start the conversation. So I did. "Detective LeRoi said y'all had swapped information on the Whitney case. But I wanted to hear what you've learned in your words."

His head tilted left. "There's really nothing I can tell you that he hasn't. Truth is, he's more up on the case than I am."

"He said that, too."

His expression said, *Then why are you here?*

"I thought you might give me a different perspective," I said. "Do you know Arlo Cameron personally?"

"Everybody knows Arlo."

"And Eileen?"

He took his time answering. "Not well. They say she did drugs, but it wasn't my problem. She didn't deal or distribute, to my knowledge."

"You got snitches, don't you?"

His lips puckered. "Nobody's been snitching about Mrs. Cameron and her daughter."

I must have looked as bleak as I felt. He said, "Maybe we can get farther along when we get the photos and particulars up on our website." I almost laughed out loud. Whitney would have a hemorrhage.

Corlee said, "Look, Miss Dru, I know your credentials. You know that these cases of parental kidnapping are mushrooming. It's the nature of divorce and money and possessiveness. When I learned that your agency was investigating, I was overjoyed." He waved his hand toward the table where piles of case files seemed about to tumble onto the floor. "In those stacks are thirty-one cases of parental kidnappings." He smiled indulgently. "I'd hoped when you cleared this one, you'd take on some of my load."

I was supposed to feel a pat on the back and be happy about it. "The Whitney case took me into the desert, to the reservation."

He smoothed his black hair back with a large brown hand. "I heard that you were swept up in the monsoon. You okay now?"

"I am."

"You got snakebit?"

"My arm's almost back to normal," I said. "I believe Kinley Whitney's on that reservation."

"Why?"

"I saw her."

"When?"

"A week ago. Last Friday night."

He picked up a pen. "Where?"

"In a cabin where Mrs. Rosovo was holding a moon ritual." As he wrote, he bobbed his head. For all I knew, he could have been doodling. "When I got out of the hospital and went back to it, the cabin had been turned into a hunting lodge."

He stopped writing and raised his head. "You think somebody's playing games with you?"

"My mind."

"Detective LeRoi told me that you had amnesia."

"Temporary. From Datura and the knock on the head, but it's gone. However, there are those who want to make me believe I'm delusional." He put his pen down. "I'm not, I assure you."

He chewed the corner of his lower lip. "I've got to get over San Diego way, but I'd appreciate it if you'd write a detailed report of who you spoke with, where you went, what was said to the best of your recollection. In other words, write out your every movement since you got to The Springs. Will you do that?"

"It's something I do routinely," I said, looking at the table, at the heap of papers that looked unread.

"But you know," he said, smiling kindly. "there's a deep underground where these women take these kids. They can disappear for a long, long time. Or they can come back on their own next week."

"Eileen didn't disappear into any maternal underground, Agent Corlee."

"Did you know her?"

"Not personally, but my investigation shows she wanted custody of her child, but she also wasn't giving up her lifestyle. She was going through the courts like she should."

He made a moue of concession, and I wondered how well he knew Eileen. He asked, "In your opinion, what do you think prompted her to disappear with the kid then?"

I spoke before I should have. "In my opinion, she didn't disappear with her child. And I don't think they're together any longer."

"What makes you think that?"

Lord, I couldn't go near intuition—the laughable *woman's intuition.* As I thought of a way to word my suspicion, he asked, "You think Eileen Cameron's dead?"

"Likely."

"Why?"

"Little things." *Like a man buying flowers who frightened her the day she disappeared. Like her child in a moon cabin. Like people trying to make me believe I'm nuts. Like people following me, shooting at me.*

He rose, my signal to get up, too. "Have you told this to Detective LeRoi?"

"No," I said, sure that Gila Joe Corlee knew Dartagnan was a little too close to the principals.

He pulled a ten-gallon hat off a rack by his desk. "I've got terrorists to track down, homeland security issues piling up, illegals frying inside tractor trailers." He held the door open for me. "I need hard facts. If you find out something concrete, start with Dartagnan."

Thank you, Agent Gila Joe Corlee. For nothing.

And hell would freeze before he got a written copy of my report.

THIRTY

I sat in the back of the 747, and Lake sat at an emergency exit in the middle. I dozed most of the way to Atlanta, once snorting awake, embarrassing myself to the twenty-something man next to me. When I deplaned, I didn't see Lake in the crowded B Concourse.

The weekend came. I hadn't heard from him. My skin hummed like small sweat bees crawled beneath it. Except for working road trips, this would be the first weekend we hadn't seen each other in two years. Sure, we'd gotten sideways of each other, but he'd never disbelieved in me, nor I in him.

I spoke twice to Portia via phone. Although she chose her words carefully, I heard the worry in them, but then that was Porsh. I cleaned my house with an intensity that busted my knuckles but seemed to strengthen my healing arm. I baked pies and cakes and fancy casseroles that I wouldn't eat. The only time I went outside was to carry food to Peachtree Street and set it on sidewalk ramparts or trash cans for the homeless— for the free spirits who wouldn't set foot inside a shelter.

I drank too much gin—not Blue Sapphire, but something less expensive. I woke early Monday morning with a howling hangover, drank coffee and considered a bloody, but before I surrendered to temptation, Portia called. A troubled female teen in foster care had run away.

I sat in the courtroom gallery, watching Portia's lips move as she quietly talked to the foster parents, when Lake came in and

161

scooted across the bench to sit beside me. "Hi there," he said.

Hi there? "Lieutenant," I said, head and eyes straight ahead.

"I talked to Gila Joe Corlee in Palm Springs."

"Did he ask if I was in the nuthouse yet?"

"He told me that Arlo put his house up for sale. He's moving to LA."

"No surprise."

"He thinks the move is suspicious."

"Oh really now." I pretended to concentrate on what was going on up front with Portia.

"Arlo's lived in Palm Springs for twenty-five years. He's one of the town's most popular people."

"Movie types move to LA all the time."

"Corlee is waiting for your report. Didn't you tell him you'd share your notes with him?"

"Did I tell him that?"

"I wasn't there," he said. "Corlee said the neighbor woman's house is closed up, too. Heidi's her name. Corlee said people in town are talking about Heidi and Arlo."

"I saw them together," I said. "It didn't take five seconds to see what was going on. But then, I'm known to be delusional."

"Eileen hasn't been missing a month yet," he said.

"Eileen's dead," I said.

"You've thought that from the beginning."

"Arlo's selling the house only puts the monument on her grave." I looked at him for the first time and almost gulped. I'd never seen his achingly beautiful eyes so bloodshot. I looked back at Portia on her bench and whispered, "So detect, detective."

I felt his eyes taking inventory of my face. "I'm sorry, Dru."

"I'll be all right."

"I miss you."

His whisper spoke to idyllic memories of days long gone. I

looked to my right, at the wall where Portia displayed that part of the Ten Commandments she deemed proper for her court-room.

Honor your father and your mother.
You shall not murder.
You shall not commit adultery.
You shall not steal.
You shall not bear false witness against your neighbour.
You shall not covet your neighbour's house or anything that belongs to your neighbour.

I heard Lake rub the stubble on his face. I'd never known him to miss a day shaving. He said, "I've been thinking . . ." I looked at him, at the clouds in his eyes.

A sound intruded, and, when I looked ahead, Portia flapped toward us. In her long black robe, she resembled a scrawny crow wearing glasses. I loved her at that moment. She asked, "Any news on our runaway?" I gave her a brief negative shake of my head. She said, "I feel sorry for the foster parents. They're opting out of the system. I hate to lose good ones because of problem kids."

I said, "I talked to the runaway's grandmother in Memphis. She swears her granddaughter's not there. The grandmother also said, and I quote: 'Glory's sake, the chile's fourteen. Let 'er be. I wasn' but thirteen when my mama throws me out six months gone with chile. I learned to survive. Let my granbaby be.' "

Lake spoke without spirit. "Maybe grandma has a point. Not much you can do with a fourteen-year-old who doesn't want to be where she is."

Steely-eyed, Portia looked at me. "Find her."

"I will," I said, and then stared at Lake. "I'll find Kinley, too." *My heart screamed—for God's sake, take his hand.* But my mind was too damn stubborn to do it.

Portia waved toward the door at the back of her courtroom. "See you, Lieutenant."

Lake squeezed my arm, rose, and left.

"I see things aren't going any better," Portia said, sliding onto the bench where Lake had sat.

"*Things* are not going at all," I said.

"They sort out, they always do—with civilized people."

"Who defines 'civilized'?"

Her eyes were soulful. "You need to find Kinley," she said. "Fuck Whitney. I'm giving you the go-ahead."

"I thought the powers-that-be think I'm chasing a chimera and want to leave it to law enforcement."

"Per diem and expenses," Portia said. "If I have to pay from my own pocket. And for God's sake, leave chimeras out of it."

THIRTY-ONE

When the fat man came in, I was putting away the file on my fourteen-year-old runaway. I hate losing kids. I hate dealing with stupid adults. Best guess was my girl had been given a ride by a trucker heading east, leaving Memphis, where she'd been hidden by her grandmother. My runaway, like as not, had been raped and murdered and left on the side of the Pennsylvania Turnpike.

It was five o'clock, and I needed a drink. The intruder was prescient enough to see I didn't welcome him wholeheartedly.

"I won't take up a lot of your time," he said, rolling a cotton porkpie in his hands. "I knew you had an office here."

"And?"

He slid the soft hat under his arm. "Can I sit a spell?"

"Sure," I said, planting my trousered butt back in my chair. I looked more closely at him—ex–law enforcement, private now. "And you can tell me your name."

"Bellan Thomas."

"Where you from?" I asked. I knew the established PIs in Atlanta.

"Birmingham," he said. "Alabama."

"I didn't think you meant England." He smoothed his tie. That simple gesture told me I was way too testy. *Try nice.* "Look, Mr. Thomas how's about we have a drink, and you can tell me what's on your mind. It's after five."

"I don't drink," he said. "Anymore."

I knew what that meant—a perpetually recovering alcoholic, although he didn't have that gray, deprived look. He wasn't especially tall but he went at least two-fifty, had dirty blond hair and a bushy red moustache with waxed tips. Maybe fifty years old. Southern voice and careful mannerisms.

I went to the filing cabinet and pulled out a middle drawer. Inside I kept a bottle of cheap gin, tonic, and a stack of Solo cups. As I prepared the gin and tonic, sans ice, I said, "I hope a doctor never tells me my liver's shot. I wouldn't be good standing up at meetings and telling about the times I wore the lampshade."

"Them meetings aren't fun, you can take that to the bank."

"Okay," I said, sitting, taking a sip, and raring back in the swivel. I eased off my shoes and crossed my ankles on the desk. "What's on your mind?"

"Eileen Whitney Cameron."

My feet came off the desk and squared on the floor. "What?"

"She's a client of mine."

"Since when?"

"Three months ago."

"To do what?" As if I didn't know.

"Investigate her ex."

"She wanted you to dig into Bradley Whitney's past?"

"And present."

"What for?"

"She wanted dirt on him to use in court to get her kid back."

I felt the wind coming back into my sails. "Tell me you got some."

"I gave her my initial report. She asked me to keep digging. I'm a digger, Miss Dru."

My drink tasted fabulous. "Apparently she wasn't content to wait for your shovel to do its work. She and Kinley lit out for parts unknown."

"That's what I hear."

"You sound skeptical."

"I'm a *good* PI," he said. "I also found out you used to be with the APD, and that you have your own PI agency that specializes in kids. You were hired by Bradley Whitney to find Eileen and the kid."

"What else did you find out?"

"You got back from Palm Springs a couple days ago. Something happened out there."

"I didn't find Eileen, and I didn't find *the kid.*"

"I know. The kid's not with her daddy now, either."

"What did you find out about her daddy?"

"I can't tell you that."

"Why not?"

"Privileged."

"PI work isn't privileged, Mr. Thomas. And you said Eileen was your client."

"I make my work confidential. I don't tell no one what I've found out until I tell the client."

"But you reported to her once." He nodded. "Then you collected more information on Bradley." He nodded again. "But since then, you haven't heard from her, have you?"

After a moment's hesitation, he said, "She told me not to contact her home, but I did. I didn't identify myself, but the maid told me she was out on vacation. The maid had no idea when she'd be coming back. I suspected from the sound of her voice she was holding back."

"No one's heard from Eileen Cameron for nearly a month," I said.

"That doesn't mean *nobody* knows where she is," he said, a gleam in his eyes. He obviously thought that I was the *nobody.* He looked hopeful when he said, "I can pay for any leads you give me."

"I used up all my leads. They led nowhere."

"You telling me you got no idea what happened to Mrs. Cameron and the kid?"

"Tell me what you found out about Bradley Whitney."

"Can't."

I gritted my teeth. "Don't give me that. Why else are you here?"

He raised his chin. "I do good work for my clients. I get paid for my good work. You can take that to the bank."

"How much does she owe you?"

"Fifteen thousand bucks."

"Fifteen?"

"I do good work."

"I can tell you this, Eileen won't be paying you any time soon."

"If you know so much, why didn't you tell the PS cops?"

Why hadn't I told Dartagnan about my suspicions? Was it a question of trust? Probably. I said, "Like you, I don't get paid to do their job."

"Where's Eileen?"

"Probably dead."

He didn't look surprised. "But you can't prove it?"

"Nope, but maybe I could if you'd tell me what you've found out." He breathed in like a man resigned, but still spread his hands, palms facing down. I said, "The juvy judge can compel you."

He grunted out a laugh. "I'd open up like a busted oyster if she paid me." So he knew the judge was a she.

I took a long, scrutinizing look at Bellan Thomas. I liked him. Didn't know why, but I did. "Tell you what," I said, getting up and going to fix another drink. "Why don't we work together? You're out fifteen grand, and I'm out two people."

He thought about this. "What do you have in mind?"

"You go to Palm Springs. I've worn out my welcome there."

"You?" It sounded like he belched.

"I'll tell you the story, if you agree."

"Before I agree, we got to palaver about it."

Palaver? "Okay, but first tell me, did you get paid for your initial report to Eileen?"

"Yeah, she paid five thousand in advance, and I did five thousand worth."

"What did you report to her?"

"Uh . . ."

"Mr. Thomas—"

"Bellan."

"I'm Dru."

His mustache arced up his cheeks in a grin that had the waxed tips almost curling around both sides of his nose. "Mr. Whitney's an interesting character in case you don't know."

"I met him."

"He's slick and rich."

"I got that impression."

"He's also one corrupt cookie."

"I believe it, but I'd like proof." When he didn't continue, I said, "Summations are fine, but I want details."

"Look, Miss Dru—"

"Dru. We're almost partners, remember?"

"We need to talk money first."

"That's the kind of palaver you want?"

"For starters."

"Well, my client—your target—fired me," I said. He shoved back, grunting, apparently wondering why I'd wasted so much of his time. "But that doesn't mean I've given up the case. The juvenile judge will scrape up a few pennies from the state coffers to pay expenses if I can show I'm not chasing a chimera."

He grinned. "Is that like something my mama used to call

the boogeyman?"

"I think you know what a chimera is, Bellan."

"A spook. An incubus."

"A delusion."

"Your juvenile judge paying my expenses?"

"I can pay you. Not the fifteen grand, but for the work you do for me."

"You hunt down kids for a living on your own dime?"

"Idiotic, don't you think?"

He brushed off any altruism I might have implied. "Funny you bringing up chimera. You might call your ex-client that."

"A boogeyman? A spook and an incubus?"

"All that, and a dirtbag. I'll tell you what was in my first report to Mrs. Cameron. I'm keeping the second report to myself until I find out what happened to her."

"For which you'll reap many dimes."

"I don't drive a Bentley."

"You know what I drove before the Bentley?"

"No idea. Do you agree or not?"

"You want this agreement in writing?"

"I can tell you're a straight shooter."

"You can? Most con artists I've come across look like straight shooters. You look like a straight shooter, too." He bobbed his head. "But if what you're holding back, because of a few bucks, keeps me from saving Kinley, I'll bust your chops—personally."

The matter-of-fact way I said it made his eyes blink rapidly. He held his arms out in supplication. "No one wants to hurt that kid."

"But Eileen's a different story, isn't she?"

He sat back, sucked in air, and laced his fingers across his belly. "Bradley Whitney was born in the Arkansas backwoods. The Ozarks. His parents were killed in a feud." He shook his head. "Hard to believe this Hatfield and McCoy stuff still goes on, isn't it?"

"I see it every day—the big-city version."

"The people who killed his folks, they got killed five or six years later."

"By Whitneys?"

"Who knows? Anyway, there were ten little Whitney kids. All got scattered among the relatives. Bradley Whitney went to Little Rock to live with an uncle. He was nine or ten. Then when he's eleven, the uncle gets killed in fight, and Whitney becomes a ward of the state. He's put in a foster home and lives there until he's fifteen. He finished school and walked away. Nobody knows, or will say, where he went. Nobody tried to find him. Couple years later, he surfaces in Atlanta."

"Hmmm," I mused. "Not the typical background for an academic, is it?"

"Bradley Whitney is a genius. He never set foot in a schoolroom until his uncle died and they put him in a foster place."

"Hard to believe that the Little Rock schools didn't catch up to him."

"He was only with the uncle a while. When he went into the foster home, they gave him a test to show where he should be in school. They were thinking maybe first grade. Guess what?"

"He got high school equivalency?"

"College. He tested off the charts, but they stuck him in ninth grade. He graduated from high school three years later then walked away. Nobody knows where to, until Atlanta."

"Time to hit the big-time," I said. "Where'd he surface?"

"The clubs."

"What clubs?"

"Strips. Working as an underaged jack-of-all-trades."

"Where'd he live?"

"Here and there. Crashing mostly with people he could

171

charm out of a room and food. He enrolled in Georgia State."

"I get it, you worked backward starting with his college records. Naturally they would contain his high school records."

"There's all kinds of ways," he answered mysteriously. It made me think of Webdog's ways.

"Let's back up," I said. "Was he ever in trouble with the law in Arkansas?"

"No record. Model student. Model foster child."

"Too good to be true?"

"Smart people don't get busted. You can take that to the bank."

"So our boy's now in college, working in strip clubs; what's next?"

"So after he's—well—developed into manhood, he goes on stage."

I feigned shock. "What?"

"He worked his way through college stripping in a he-she joint."

Although I knew this, that primal slimy feeling wormed across my shoulders.

"You look funny," Bellan said.

I shook my shoulders. "First time I ever heard of someone who actually stripped their way through college—and it had to be a man."

He chuckled. "It's not something he puts on his résumé, you can take that to the bank."

The man had money and banking on the brain. "Did Eileen know all this?"

"She knew nothing. He told her he was from New York, The Hamptons. She sopped up his story like biscuits in molasses because he'd lost his Arkie accent and sounded very New-Yorky—her word. Smart people can do that."

I played with my empty plastic cup. Now was not the time

for another gin. "He's a poster child for bettering oneself."

"He also told Eileen that he'd lost his folks in a plane crash in the Alps in Europe and that their bodies were never found."

"Out with hillbilly feuds," I said.

"For a fact," he agreed. "He lives in a mansion now. He didn't when he lived with Eileen, but they didn't live poor."

"Where'd he get his money?"

"I'm still digging into that. I've unearthed his millions in stocks, bonds, mutual funds. Trouble is, where'd he get the seed money in the first place?"

"Did Eileen have a clue?"

"Insurance from the plane crash."

"We know that's not true. What's with his two academic jobs?"

"Up-and-up. Not a bad mark on his record. His students like him. The girls, especially."

"Which leads us to his sex life?"

"Cold as a mackerel, Eileen said. Too fastidious."

"Yet he strips?"

"Stripped. Years ago."

"Have you come across a place called The Cloisters?"

"Yeah," he answered vaguely.

"Whitney's a regular. An owner maybe?"

Bellan shook his head. "Being ex-cops, you and I both know these joints are owned and controlled by a very few—um—entrepreneurs. They're not your Fortune Five Hundred crowd, and they guard their territory like mama alligators on the nest."

"There's ways to unhide ownership."

Shaking his head, Bellan said, "That's as far as I go for now."

"Let me get this straight. For five grand you gave Eileen the sketchy details of a past life. Fifteen grand has to buy a lot more. Give me a hint."

His moustache climbed up his cheeks and circled his nose

again. "Let's talk about Palm Springs. Convince me why I should go there."

I told the story, more or less, as it happened.

"You got amnesia?" He frowned.

"Temporary. I'm back to being me."

"You telling me straight?"

"You can take it to the bank."

THIRTY-TWO

I live in Peachtree Hills. When I got to my street, I spotted Lake cruising south on Peachtree Street. He honked and waved with a grin that could melt ice in Antarctica. He made a U-ey, followed me, and pulled into my driveway. I sat in my car for a long moment. I knew my day would come down to this.

I'd planned to call him tomorrow, tell him about Bellan Thomas, ask him to verify the PI's bona fides. I opened my car door. He walked up the drive to the back gate. He'd shaved but that didn't make him appear less haggard. "What's cooking on Peachtree Street?" I asked, moving toward him. "Somebody jump off the Darlington?"

"How are you, Dru?"

His physical presence made my heart feel like a balloon full of helium. "I'm good. And you, Lieutenant Lake?"

"Lake. Just Lake." His dug both hands in his pockets and hunched his shoulders forward.

"I was about to call," I said. "Come inside?"

He walked through the gate into the back yard. I closed and padlocked the gate. I'd gotten careful since I'd glimpsed a Chevy Caprice a couple of times. Maybe my imagination—not a rare breed of car. Lake went to the concrete birdbath and scratched Mr. Brown's ear. Mr. Brown jumped down and wound himself around Lake's legs. The skin of a chipmunk lay in the birdbath bowl. "I see you had supper already," Lake said, and scratched the cat under the chin. I crossed my arms and felt a warm breeze

175

sweep my skin. Lake seemed about to speak, then closed his mouth as if afraid to blunder into a verbal morass.

I led him inside and punched the numbers on the alarm's keypad. "Good to see you locking up these days," Lake said.

"Comes from chasing chimeras." He looked away, not going near that one. I slipped my bag from my shoulder and threw it on the kitchen table. "I'm having a G and T, but not with Blue Sapphire." I went to the cabinet to get out the fixings.

"Got any beer?"

I used to keep it for him. "The liquor store's only a half mile up Peachtree," I said.

"G and T it is."

We sat across from each other at the stout oak table, our drinks on cocktail napkins, my nervous system whacked-out. But I steeled myself against his brooding gaze.

"I guess—I have to begin somewhere," he said.

"If you want me to, I will," I said, sipping my drink.

His eyelids blinked back tender pain. "Sure."

"I had an interesting visitor this afternoon."

The lines around his eyes eased. "Anyone I know?"

"Not unless you know a PI named Bellan Thomas."

He shook his head. "I thought I knew them all."

"He's from Birmingham. He was hired by Eileen Cameron to dig up dirt on Bradley."

His eyes widened at the news. "Smart girl, hiring from outside Atlanta."

"I want to know more about Bellan Thomas. You got any contacts in Birmingham?"

"I got contacts everywhere." As a cop, if he didn't, he could get them quick.

As I related Bellan's story, Lake curved his long, fit body into a more comfortable position. When I told him about the bargain I made, he sat forward, obviously dubious. He said, "I'd need to know more about this character before I'd go trusting him."

"That's why I've asked you to dig into his background."

"You think what he's holding back is that important?"

"Important enough to cost Eileen fifteen grand."

"Killers hire out to murder an entire city block for less than that."

"There's that, too."

He scratched the side of his neck. "Seems certain, Eileen's dead." I didn't mouth any of the sarcasms that occurred to me, and he continued, "I got to wonder if Whitney knew this guy was on his tail?"

"What do you want to bet he did?"

He placed the cocktail glass carefully on the table, rose, and dragged his chair close to me. He reached for both my hands and held them. "I'm glad to see you've got your enthusiasm back. It looks good on you."

"Feels good," I said, looking at his hands clutching mine.

"Susanna misses you," he said in a voice so sweet I felt like an ice cream cone on a hot summer afternoon.

"I miss her," I said, barely hearing my voice.

He lifted my chin. "We both miss you." I kept my eyes very still and relished this snapshot of a moment. He said, "I'd like you to come with us to the park Sunday."

Susanna's beatific face rose in my mind. "If I can," I said, hoping he couldn't hear my heart jamming like a rocker on stage.

"Sunday's a day of rest," he murmured, stroking my arm. "We both need a day of rest, and Susanna needs to see you. I think some of my worry has rubbed off on her."

"Your worry?"

"I've been concerned, Dru."

I couldn't control the tremble in my bottom lip. "About what?"

"I know you're physically healed, but—"

"But not mentally," I said, the muscles in my neck tightening.

"I don't mean that," he said, his fingers sliding between mine. "I mean spiritually."

"Has the great mystic come to give me that divine message?"

"Don't make fun of me," he said and leaned away from me. "I'm not as smart as you. I can't match wits with you."

Oh Christ, I thought. What in the hell is wrong with me? I laid my hand on his knee. "I'm sorry." I held my breath and looked into his face, now deflated, anxiety tugging his skin. "I feel like a prickly cactus. Maybe that's the desert's legacy. I can't shake the dreads. I'm nervous all the time, like my insides are ready to pop from my skin." I was talking too freely; I hadn't meant to confide my feelings, which were too chaotic even for me to understand. "We'll go to the park Sunday. Susanna will be a comfort."

At the door, Lake hugged my bowstring of a body and raised my chin. "I'll find out about your PI. Maybe he's the break we need."

We?

I tried to breathe past my heart, now in my throat.

THIRTY-THREE

The next day I began in earnest to investigate Bradley Dewart Whitney.

Curriculum Paradigms, Inc., was located in an industrial park in Alpharetta off Old Milton Parkway. Naturally I parked on the wrong side of the building and had to walk around the rectangular, two-story to get to suite 102. All the offices had identical vertical blinds. Some were opened, some closed. Many had "Laboratories" in their names. Secrets going on, I supposed.

Curriculum's blinds were open, and I went in. The clock on the receptionist's desk told me it was ten o'clock. No other items on the desk, nor a receptionist sitting in the chair behind it. The coffee on somewhere smelled as if it had been boiling down since yesterday. Despite that, the anteroom was as sterile as a lab—white walls, white furniture. The only color was a *National Geographic* magazine that lay on a white table.

A wispy-haired man came out of an office, evidently to see who had wandered unexpectedly into his parlor. He was short and thin and middle-aged, and altogether nondescript. An invisible, colorless man. An academic to his eyeballs. He looked perplexed, as if he couldn't figure out what I was doing here. "You lost?" he asked.

"I don't think so," I said. "This is Curriculum Paradigms, Inc., isn't it?"

Still skeptical, he said, "Yessss. Er . . . can I be of any assistance? I am, at present, the only staff member here. I am Dr. Brommer."

I held out my hand. "Dr. Brommer. Are you the director here?"

"I am that."

"Then you can help me," I said, taking out my leather identification wallet and handing it to him. "I'm from Child Trace. I look for missing children."

He looked at the ID. He looked at me. "Yes, I see," he said.

"You have an employee here, a Mr. Bradley Whitney?"

"Dr. Bradley Whitney. Yes."

"I'm investigating the disappearance of his ex-wife and child."

"Oh," he said, shaking his head. "So sad, yes. So sad. These things . . ." He stepped back, and waved vaguely toward his office. "Come this way."

His office was in keeping with the sterile outer office. He sat behind a Swedish modern desk, and I took a seat opposite him. His face was imprecisely kind. He said, "Miss Dru, I would like to help you, but . . ."

"I'm sure you would. Any little thing you can remember, you never know, it can help."

"I'm afraid I didn't learn anything to remember."

"I need to ask you about Dr. Whitney." He blinked as if I'd spoken Russian. "Hopefully, you can help me out in that regard."

His eyes slid past my right shoulder. "Well, I don't know that I know much."

"Let's start with how long he's worked here?"

"Well," he scratched his shallow chin. "That would be about six years."

"How did he get the job? How does one get a job writing aptitude tests?"

"Well, by applying, of course."

How stupid of me.

Before I could reply, he said, "That wasn't very specific, was it?" I smiled enough to show him dimples. "Well, you are not quite correct when you say that Mr. Whitney *wrote* aptitude tests. Mr. Whitney is a scientist."

It was my turn to look perplexed. "What kind of scientist?"

"We at Curriculum Paradigms, Inc., analyze data collected along lines of inquiry."

"What kind of inquiry?"

He seemed to forbear that he must expound. "The nature of our inquiries are on linguistic divisions irregular in unalienable linguistic divisions." He lost me and continued his high-blown linguistics until he came to the end. "Such is the nature of relative protocol."

"And Dr. Whitney is addressing this relative protocol?"

"Yes, to the extent that will afford the challenging facets of the underachieving pupil in context with nonalignment . . ."

My head reeled. "But that brings me back to my question: how does one get this job?"

The word *job* seemed to startle him. "Dr. Whitney is a genius. We recruited him while he was in college. His work in urban studies is exemplary. Quite outstanding."

"He teaches at Georgia State."

"He is excellent in the classroom—a quality that not all academics possess." He seemed to imply that perhaps he lacked this quality.

"How well do you know Dr. Whitney personally?"

He thought a moment. "He is a colleague. That is about all I can say. We have not associated socially."

"Does he associate socially with any of his colleagues here?"

"I do not believe so. Although we are a laboratory, and we share our findings, we work independently of one another. The scientists work alone, collecting their data, interpreting it, etcetera."

I joked, "No gathering around the old water cooler to talk football and wives and kiddies."

He laughed half-heartedly. "Our scientists hardly ever come here. They work at home; often they have related occupations like Dr. Whitney."

"Does the job pay much?"

He acted like I'd burped. "Excuse me?"

"What's the salary range for someone who does what Dr. Whitney does?"

"Salary?" *That old demon coin of the realm.* "That information, of course, is confidential."

"Let me ask you this: would he ever be in a position here to earn more than say two hundred thousand a year?"

He looked like he wanted to laugh out loud, but his face only lightened. "That would be a challenge *even* Dr. Whitney would find daunting."

He'd told me more than he thought he had. He knew Whitney a lot better than he was letting on.

THIRTY-FOUR

Georgia State University is an urban campus, founded in 1913 by the Georgia Institute of Technology as "the evening school of commerce." For decades, it had been a school noted for nonprofessional certification and competed with community colleges around the counties. Students worked during the day, and then took Marta—Atlanta's rapid transit system—to their night classes. Then GSU's status blossomed when Atlanta grew internationally and, as a consequence, the demand for a reasonably priced education did, too.

Bradley Whitney possessed a master's degree in urban policy studies and a PhD in educational policy studies. He officed on the fifth floor of the Educational Policy Studies building. Although it was lunchtime, I took a chance he'd be around. He wasn't in the classroom, so I found his office. I stood in the doorway and listened while he waved a sandwich in one hand and lectured an enthralled group of eighteen to twenty students who had crowded into the large room. Most were women.

He paced and said, "Educators are trapped in divergent schema. On the one hand they are asked to sanction all students' achievements. But, they are also asked to guarantee that apprentices expand and gain equal access to indistinguishable instructive probabilities."

He hadn't looked my way, but I thought he spoke to me.

He was saying, "Mobility theorists see the intellectual cream expanding in endowment, talent, and labor. Reproduction

183

theorists think that capitalistic civilization is menacing enough to stratify and quash itself to satisfy the demand for dutiful and consenting human resources."

His head turned, and he narrowed arrogant eyes at me. "I think there's another chair for a passing student hanging on my every word." The besotted laughed in unison. I twinkled fingers at them and went to lean against bookshelf.

Whitney went on like that for another fifteen minutes. I wondered how many ways you can say that the culturally disadvantaged are preyed upon by society. Countless ways, it seemed.

Eventually Whitney wound down and told his listeners that he'd answer their questions formally in class in an hour. They slowly trudged out, making jokes with him as they left. The girls thrust their boobs out more than was natural, and giggled when he bestowed a special smile or word on them.

Once we were alone, Whitney closed the door, picked up an apple from his desk, bounced it in his hand, and said, "An apple for the teacher. I never took an apple to my teachers. My mother thought it was *too terribly gauche*. Think of the irony." He slammed the apple into a wastebasket. "Sick of the damned things. You here for a reason?"

"I'm back on the case," I said, "and I'm back investigating everyone who has ever heard the name of Eileen Whitney Cameron."

It was hard to read his mannerisms, so maybe I just imagined that he was acutely pissed. After the pause, he said, "That's good to know. I've still got some credit on my fee advance—to my way of thinking. So check away. I've nothing to hide."

"Let's start with your résumé. Will you provide me with a copy?"

"My résumé?"

"Sure, you know that piece of paper that makes you out to be a genius, overlooking the lesser failings like getting fired, or—"

"Excuse me? I can assure you I've never been fired."

"I'm not speaking of you in particular."

He smirked. "You speaking about your own résumé?"

"I wish I were as good as what I've written down."

"Well," he said, looking smug, "I am."

"Then you won't mind if I have a peek."

"What do you want to know?"

"Where you're from. Where you went to high school."

"Is that stuff on résumés?"

"Should be. Marital status, birthplace."

"What about race, religion, gender, weight, height?"

"Not those. But hobbies, maybe. Employers like to know how well rounded you are, what you do in your spare time. You got any interesting hobbies?"

His eyebrows drew so close to each other they formed a straight line across his eyes. I wondered if he was pondering The Cloisters.

He said, "I play golf whenever I get the chance. It helps if you're in the business world, but actually, in academia, it's considered mundane."

"Where were you born?"

"I can't see that it matters in the least."

"Still, I'd like to see your résumé."

He looked as if he were about to explain divergent schema again. He said, "I think not."

"You see," I said, "according to the State of Georgia, the Open Records Law, I can request your personnel file from the university's Human Resources Department. It'll take a while to get a response, a couple days, but . . ." I shifted my backpack, "if I must, I must."

I waved and started for the door. He muttered, "Bitch!"

I glanced over my shoulder and grinned. "Evaluating the concepts, I'm happy that we share cognitive ethics, aren't you?"

THIRTY-FIVE

I drove the Bentley down Decatur Street, wondering if Whitney'd found out that the car which had turned around in his driveway that time was mine. Probably, like he'd *probably* known Eileen had an investigator on him. I looked in my side and rear mirrors and didn't see a Chevy Caprice. I slowed for a stop sign and saw Lake's unmarked parked at a meter. His butt leaned against a front fender, and his arms were folded. He unfolded them to wave, and I pulled up behind his cruiser. He met me at the window. "Care to get a bite? I got news."

"What news?"

"Lunch? On me."

"You're on." I gave in to the prospect of news. I hadn't thought about food in a while.

He got into the Bentley and pressed my hand. "Still hounding the scientists?" In a phone call earlier, I'd recounted my visit to Brommer at Curriculum Paradigms, Inc.

I pulled into the flow of traffic. "Dr. Whitney appears to be trapped in divergent schema. I can't figure if he's a mobility theorist or a reproduction theorist."

"Mobility. Upward."

I drove toward Thelma's diner. "What have you found out about him?"

"He's not Old Atlanta. Guarantee."

Lake's ex, Linda Lamont, *was* Old Atlanta. She knew the social register like the back of her cotillion dance card. "You ask

187

Linda?" I said, keeping my voice steady.

"She never heard of him. Where he lives, Old Country Place, sounds old money, but it's not. All new money." He put a finger under his nose and raised it in the air. "Sniff. Sniff."

I smiled. It was a tribute to Lake's charm and good looks that, ten years ago, he snagged Linda, the belle of the Piedmont Driving Club. Officer Lake had arrested her for DUI, but something happened to the ticket on the way to the courthouse. I'd never been jealous of Linda, even though I knew he was still fond of her. She couldn't hack being a cop's wife; he couldn't hack society—although I've seen him in a penguin suit. Simply fabulous.

I dropped the reverie. "Whitney doesn't want to part with his résumé."

"I'll drop by HR this afternoon," Lake said. "They'll hand over the résumé."

I parked in front of Thelma's. It's a meat-three-veg, carbo-loader—the kind of food Lake loves. I should talk, my plate was piled with mac-and-cheese, fried okra, and mashed potatoes. I selected banana pudding for dessert and added a big plastic glass of overly sweetened ice tea. Southern comfort foods.

After a bite of macaroni, I asked, "So what's the news?"

Ripping into his chicken, Lake said, "I can get into The Cloisters."

My temples began to pulsate. "What about me?"

"Wrong gender."

We'll see about that. "When?"

"When Mr. X can set it up." He stuffed hot white meat into his mouth. As if by infusion of protein, he looked his faultless self. "Guests are invited on select nights."

"When was the last time you ate?" I asked.

He savored the creamed corn. "Couple weeks ago."

"What select nights?"

He washed his food down with iced tea. "Don't know yet, but Mr. X said guests are vetted as possible members."

I pushed my plate away. "Who's Mr. X?"

"A rich pedophile turned snitch."

"Whose snitch?"

"Vice's." Lake dug into the mashed potatoes.

"What's he done?"

"Got caught in the men's at Chastain going after an under-ager. Dickheads like him are dumb. Can't they think maybe a sting is going down at two in the morning?"

"So Mr. X is coerced into getting you into The Cloisters? How'd he know you wanted to get in?"

More chicken followed the potatoes. "I spread the word around the shop, vice. When this guy was brought in, he says he's sorry for the *misunderstanding* at Chastain. Then he babbles on about being on the wagon about boys, but he can't help falling off. He cries. He says he spends thousands a week in The Cloisters to get over his addiction. That's when the vice cop says, maybe we can work a deal. The slimebag listens, then he says, 'Sure, I'll get your man into the The Cloisters. Just cut me some slack, and I'll be a sponsor.' "

I mused, "The slime's got money apparently."

"He owns his own company. It's a holding company that owns a slew of fast-food joints on the south side."

"Is he black?"

"No. Far's I know, The Cloisters is not an equal-opportunity leering joint."

"When'er we going in?"

Lake carefully put his fork down. It was full of mashed potatoes. "*I'm* going in when *I* get the invitation."

"Get your sponsor to issue two invitations."

"Wrong gender, Dru."

"That can change."

"A quick trip to Sweden?"

"No, a quick trip to Sircher's."

"Sircher's?" The proverbial light bulb lit in his face. He laughed. "That queen of switcheroo?"

"Cross-dressing is not a one-way street." Lake didn't look happy. "We need to find out what nights Bradley Whitney will be at The Cloisters?"

"Zone Two guys say he's there every night."

I'd never been into disguises. I could dress up or down as need be, or wear a pair of glasses, or a wig, or a hat, but that's the extent of changing my appearance for the sake of the job. But those simple things weren't going to convince anyone that I was a man. The person for the job was Sircher. Bless her contour-changing heart.

Her palace is on Peachtree Street just south of the Five Points Marta Station and Underground Atlanta. She shares the tacky commercial part of the famous street with cheap costume shops, makeup emporiums, sex toy joints, plastic-shoe stores, and other assorted holes-in-the walls.

I pulled up at a curb in front of Sircher's Contour Palace.

Sircher's shop took up three storefronts. The windows were painted white and black—in an opaque harlequin design. No one was getting a gander of what went on inside the contour palace. Sircher equipped the theatrical community and the transvestite community, which sometimes was the same thing.

I jangled the bell and heard the lock pop. Inside, the odor of perfume and wax overlaid the centuries-old smell of bricks and moldering lath and plaster. A hall went off to the left and another continued straight ahead. Behind doors were rooms in which clients were taught to alter their appearance—and pony up goodly sums to do so.

Tapping on the inner door, I waited. Sircher expected me.

I'd called an hour ago. She'd been surprised, more than a little suspicious, until I told her I wasn't on the force any longer. "I heard that," she'd said, her masculine voice cawing through the cell. "But y'all have a habit of resigning and going undercover."

"Not me, promise. I've got my own agency now. I'm not investigating you."

"Okay, so no one's been blaming me for their cock-a-doodle carryin's-on. So who're you investigating?"

"Now Sircher—"

Her laugh was a donkey's bray. "What you want from me, dear girl?"

"I want to be a man."

"Now you're talkin'." Many thought Sircher *was* a man. But not the APD. Sircher's real name is Ethel Wallace, and it's anyone's guess about her sexual orientation.

I said, "Just for a night."

"Just one? What if you like it?"

"Sircher, it's not a sex night."

"Every night's a sex night, even if you're not married—especially if you're not married."

An odd prickling crept under my skin, and I thought of my dead fiancé. Hell's bells, I couldn't even talk to an old farce like her without ghosts of the past haunting me. "Can I come see you?"

"Sure," she said. "When?"

"Now."

"As long as you don't have a search warrant."

"A thing of my distant past."

"C'mon girl, we'll get to work."

"Sounds like it's going to be an ambitious undertaking."

"Making a good-looking sliver of a female into a man's surely a challenge," she said, sounding as if she were rubbing her hands in glee.

Sircher filled the door when she opened it. At least six feet tall, she had to weigh three hundred. Her hair—which was done up in a mass of dark purple and held in check with several large combs—had originally been black, and sometimes still was. She wore a red-sequined muumuu, and I thought the cow pun was apropos. There were dozens of strands of beads around her corrugated neck. In a few past lives, she'd been a palmist, a crystal-ball gazer, and tarot reader.

I held out my palm.

Taking it, she said, "Sorrow." She looked at me—her large brown eyes abject. "You got troubles." Dropping my hand, she stepped aside and swept her hand toward her emporium.

"Then I sure as hell don't want to see the cards," I said, taking in the shelves of potions and lotions and jars and wig stands and pestle pots. MGM's makeup lab couldn't have been more extensive.

She shook her head sagely. *"When sorrows come, they come not single spies, but in battalions."*

Spies? Of all the sweet sorrows in Shakespeare, she'd chosen that one. I quoted back, *"When we are born, we cry that we are come to this great stage of fools."*

Sircher spread her hands, and cried, *"Out, out, brief candle! Life's but a walking shadow, a poor player that struts and frets his hour upon the stage and then is heard no more: it is a tale told by an idiot, full of sound and fury, signifying nothing."*

"I'm afraid I've exhausted my Shakespeare," I said.

"I could go on and on," she said. She put her large hands on her vast hips. "You need to tell me more. First off, why do you want to be a man?"

"Let's just say, for the fun of it." Sircher knew too many

people and too many places in this town, which could be small when it wanted to be. She stepped up to me, and, all of a sudden, ran her hands across my chest. I flinched and she laughed. "Don't have to camouflage much here."

A good look would have told her that, but I suspect she wanted a feel. She asked, "Are you going to be on a stage?"

"I hope not."

"I see," she said, and maybe she did. "So whoever you encounter in your new guise, you'll be up close and personal?"

"More or less."

"Which means we got to make you look natural." She wrinkled her brow. "Kissing involved?"

"Not that close," I said. "I told you. We're not talking sex."

She surveyed her shelves, then began pulling things off them. "Where's this deception taking place?"

"Not sure," I said, looking at the array of women's wigs. None for men.

Sircher asked, "Who you trying to fool—men, women, or both?"

"Men."

"Easier than women. What's the lighting?"

"Don't know. Dim, I would think."

"Where?"

"Don't ask."

"I am discreet. Very. Ask your partner."

"Former partner."

"Are we talking night, day, artificial light, candlelight?"

"Night, artificial light, rather dim, candles maybe. I don't know."

"Anybody there might know you in your former capacity?"

"As a cop? Doubt it."

"Ever been at this place before."

"Not inside. Now quit with the questions."

She got theatrical. *"Suspicion always haunts the guilty mind; the thief doth fear each bush an officer."*

"You're getting warmer," I said.

She lowered her eyes. I thought she was going to snort. "You need to change your nose. It's a nice nose for a woman. I've got some clients who'd die for it. Have, actually, in surgery. They didn't have Michael Jackson's surgeon." She walked to an easel beside her desk and picked up a piece of chalk on the rail. "Stay still for a bit," she said, her hand quickly sketching as she glanced at me.

She kept up the dialogue. "Three dimensional makeup builds on your own features. But you can't use it on moving muscles like your jaws and lower cheeks. It will fall off. But on your nose and cheekbones and forehead, you have a good foundation for it." She handed me the sketch. It looked like me. She moved to a shelf for a jar. "Nose putty," she said. "There are other substances that you can use to build up your nose like Plastici. It's a soft wax, but I don't like it for a lot of reasons. One, if you sweat, get nervous, or get overheated, it can slide right down your face. You wouldn't want that, would you?"

"Uh-uh."

"Might be dangerous, huh?"

"You're fishing again."

Shrugging, she said, "Remember this when you start practicing with this stuff, a little alteration can cause a big difference in your looks." She picked up the sketch. Below the caricature of me, she dashed off three smaller sketches, showing nose changes. Me, with a wide nose. Me, with a curved nose. Me, with a bulbous nose. I grimaced.

Sircher said, "Make it Roman. You nose is narrow and a bit long, so putting a slight curve on top of the bone will be effective. Remember, the less putty you use to get the job done, the more natural you're going to look. I'll give you a sheet of instructions."

I felt overwhelmed already.

"Now for skin changes. It would've helped if you'd had acne or chicken pox when you were a kid."

"You gonna put some pox on me?"

She grinned. "A few changes with liquid latex ought to do it. It's trickier than putty. But it can't be beat for creating skin texture and wrinkles. How old you want to be?"

I hadn't given it a thought before she asked. Finally, I said, "About forty will be fine."

"We'll get you into early middle age with this stuff. Pull your cheeks back, like this." She pulled hers back, as if she were try-ing out for a facelift. "Then apply liquid latex. After it's dried, let go. You'll see lines." Then she reached for my left hand. "Too damn delicate. My other clients would be green with envy. It's so much easier to add then take off, so use the latex to age your hands the same way. You don't have to make them larger. They're not as noticeable as a feminine nose." She tapped my fingernails. "And get these cut and squared."

"Should I change my eye color?"

"With that vivid blue, like headlights. I'll get you some contacts. You ever wear them?"

"No."

"Get used to them first. Add eyeglasses, those skinny rimless ones. When's this masquerade going to be?"

"I'm not going to slip up," I assured her.

Her eyes rolled in mock exasperation. "If you get back from this undercover job okay, let me know."

"You're my palmist, you should already know."

Surveying me again, she said, "You got good shoulders and your height's okay. But you could use two-inch elevators. What size you wear."

"Nine."

"Perfect. What apparel is appropriate for the occasion? It would help if I knew where you were going."

"Casual but elegant. I'll be shopping the upscale secondhand stores in Buckhead."

"No need. You need wardrobe, I got wardrobe. I usually charge a costume fee, but for you, nothing for one night."

She wrote down my measurements. "I'm adding a little to the coat. You should pad a little in the shoulders and around the waist." She took a wad of my hair in her hand and said, "Now for this luscious stuff."

"I hate going to beauty shops."

"We have an assortment of skull caps." She motioned to the wigs.

"I don't see many men's."

She swayed across the room, opened a drawer, pulled out a bald headcover, and then a salt-and-pepper man's wig. In another drawer, she rummaged the small boxes, and got the contacts. I cringed at the thought of the cost.

She said, "Try some putty on the bony parts of your chin. If you don't talk much, you can get away with it." She held up a bottle. "Use this spirit gum to hold the putty in place."

"No mustache?"

"You want to look phony?"

Out came a shopping bag. In went my new head and hands. She held up a tube. "I'm giving you this stoppel paste. It's adhering wax with stipple hairs to give you a closely shaven look. You might want a suggestion of whiskers."

She went to her computer and input numbers. A printer threw out the totals. I looked at the sum. Not *that* bad. I got out a checkbook, paid, and let her lead me down the hall with my shopping bag. "I'll courier the shoes and suit to you Monday, if that's soon enough," she said.

"Sounds fine."

At the door, Sircher said, "All this stuff has instructions. Use surround mirrors to see your profile. I got a funny feeling you need to look *real* natural."

"Isn't that what a disguise is for?"

"Just remember," she said sagely, *"False face must hide what the false heart must know."*

Thirty-Six

I normally didn't work in the office on Saturday, but a restless feeling that wouldn't be assuaged by cooking took me to the office. I showed my badge to the guard, took the elevator up, and unlocked the door to the reception room. I stepped on the envelope before I saw it. Instinct told me I wasn't going to like what was inside.

I lifted the envelope at its edges, and walked toward my office. I heard telltale, rapid clicking and stuck my head inside Webdog's office. "Hey," I said. "Just another work day for you, too? Or are you inventing vicious attack games?" The super computer belonged to Webdog.

Looking up, he smiled and shook his head. "Working for the woman."

I asked, "Who're you hacking into?"

"What's hacking?"

I held up the envelope. "You see this when you came in?"

He looked closely. "Nope. Who's it from?"

"Don't know yet," I said, examining the envelope. I gestured toward the computer. "Whatcha working on?"

He adjusted his heavy-framed geek glasses. "You might find this interesting." I sat in a metal folding chair next to him. He opened a file and continued, "Just got an answer twenty minutes ago from an e-mail I sent to the Houma Police Department. Seems they never had an officer there named Dartagnan Le-Roi." He pointed at the words on the monitor. I read them:

" 'In my twenty-five years here in records, I'd remember. Believe me, I'd remember that name.' "

"So our Detective Dartagnan lied," I said.

He opened another file. "Here's some more stuff on Dartagnan LeRoi. No records for a Josephine or Alain in Pointe-aux-Chenes. Or in Lafourche Parish. No Dartagnan LeRoi in Lafourche Parish or Mongegut. No records from Grand Bayou Blue Parish."

Getting up, I saluted Web. "Good work."

In my office, I slit the envelope with the scalpel I used as a letter opener. Two papers fell on my desk. One was a check. The other, a handwritten note. Whitney had written: "You'll see that this check is undated." I looked at the check. Indeed it was undated, and was made out to me for fifty thousand dollars. I read more: "If you agree to stop snooping into my life—for instance your conversation with Dr. Brommer at Curriculum Paradigms, Inc.—then you can date the check and cash it. I gladly do this because educators are targets for any kind of suspicion. Careers are ruined on whispers and innuendoes. For my daughter's sake, and mine, I beg of you to trust me. Regards, Bradley Dewart Whitney."

"Ha." *I progress.*

THIRTY-SEVEN

Sunday. A heavenly morning, the sun bathing the grass and trees and birds on the bath. I can swoon. I do when I think of Susanna—Lake's lovely daughter. And heart-stopping Lake.

Bellan phoned as I was packing food and drink into the willow basket for which Lake spent half a month's salary. We'd gotten big into picnics when we started going to Chastain Park on Friday nights—when work didn't interfere—for the open-air concerts. Like snobs, we figured to fit in with the ritzy crowd who showed off their pricey picnic trappings, candelabras included. A wine rack had been built in the top of the basket, and today I made sure we had the waiter-style wine pull and two crystal balloons for the nice pinot noir I selected to go with the fried chicken and red-skin potato salad.

With the land line phone receiver scrunched between my shoulder and chin, I said to Bellan, "It's eight in the morning out there."

"And hot as a two-dollar pistol."

"You Alabama boys don't have anything to complain about. Where are you staying?"

"Belleview Suites."

"What's going on?"

"I got an appointment with the real estate people to see the Cameron house this afternoon." Bellan didn't look like he could buy a multimillion dollar house. He seemed to sense my thoughts. "I told the real estate lady that I was a PI from

Alabama, and that I was lookin' for a place for my client, who is a Southern Company executive. I gave her my card and a number to verify. The phone exec is a real guy who I did some work for a while back. He's grateful enough to agree to help me with anything that isn't illegal."

I thought the story was thin. If I were Arlo, with a missing wife and stepdaughter, and a mad dad back East, I'd have him checked eight ways to Sunday.

Bellan went on, "The real estate girl made some phone calls to check me out, then she got real nice. She told me about other *properties* that she thought would suit, if the Cameron mansion didn't. Of course, she didn't say Cameron's name, but I'm just saying that for you."

"Yeah," I said. "Don't slip and say anything that gives us away. And watch yourself."

"This evening I'm having some supper with a PI here—tab's on me. Name's Larry Bell. Used to live in Montgomery. We shared a few times together."

"You trust him?"

"As much as my mama. She only went wrong on me a couple times."

"Remember, forget my name with these people."

"The story I tell him is, I'm looking for Eileen. She hired me and she didn't pay me. I don't know nothing about what people in Georgia are looking for—if he brings it up."

"Be careful, Bellan. Please."

"I'm not gonna get amnesia," he said.

The moment I got out of the car, Susanna ran into my arms. Her silky blonde hair felt like angel kisses on my face. She smelled wonderfully sweet, and I couldn't have clutched her closer.

"Darlin'," I said, finally putting her down and squatting at her level. "You have grown. You must be two whole inches taller than when I last saw you."

"Dr. Larson says I'm going to be a tall girl."

"I believe you are."

"Just like Daddy," she said. I dry-swallowed when I looked at him. I couldn't read his face in the dazzling sunlight. Susanna seemed to have picked up on our awkwardness. "Miss Dru, did you bring the basket?"

"Sure did, sweetie," I said, standing and going to the Bentley's trunk.

Did I imagine it, or did someone duck suddenly behind the wisteria that lined the sidewalk? I glimpsed back at Lake. Had he noticed my startled reaction?

He had. "You okay?" He was at my side, grabbing the wicker basket's handle and lifting it, while I took out the stadium blankets.

We walked three abreast. Lake carried the basket. I had the stadium blankets clutched in one hand and Susanna's weightless hand holding my other. Suddenly, she broke free and swept ahead.

"Stay close," I called to her. The canopy of hardwoods kept the sun from beaming on us. I looked around. Other couples with children were filling the picnic area. There were no tables, but we didn't use tables.

I told Lake about Bellan's call and his ruse to get into the Cameron mansion. "I like a PI with an imagination," Lake said. He glanced at me. "You and him make a good team."

You and I used to, I started to say, but just then Susanna came back with a handful of impatiens and held them up for me. "Thank you, they're lovely," I said.

We reached our place and spread out the soft waterproof blankets. We liked to sit on the ground with the ants and eat and drink and talk and watch the kids play softball. The teams were warming up as we got set. Susanna was hostess. She passed the linen napkins and ceramic plates, then my mama's sterling forks, knives, and spoons. Lake pulled the casseroles out, and Susanna plucked the lids off. She lifted out covered dishes—slaw, deviled eggs, pickles, olives. After everything was thus and so, she pushed a pickle stick in her mouth. The juices ran over her lips and down her chin.

"Oh, look," Susanna cried, pointing to little birds chasing one another.

I said, "Carolina chickadees."

"I call them blackcaps," she said.

"That's exactly what they're wearing," I said, and grinned at her.

"What are you two talking about?" Lake asked.

"We're being bird-ders," Susanna said. "It's my hobby with Miss Dru."

"All's I know is pigeons," he said.

The softball game began. We ate fried chicken with our fingers and watched the first inning.

"I'm going to play ball when I grow up," Susanna said.

"I thought you were going to play golf," Lake said. "Yesterday—"

"Golf *and* softball," Susanna said, swiping her mouth with her napkin.

After a second helping of potato salad, I leaned back on my elbows. The day was bright, but we were sun-filtered. The songs and chirps of birds on the air vied with the howls of ballplayers. A light breeze blew my hair and Susanna's. Lake's frolicked on his forehead and I watched his profile, thinking that it felt good to have peace dominating my spirit. Then I didn't hear birds. I sat up and turned my head. Where were the squirrels? They'd been chasing each other up and down the trees. Looking around, I caught his eyes. My mouth opened. He sat on the bleachers, opposite us—and stared.

"Lake," I said softly, touching his leg, "The man."

Lake faced me, his eyes troubled, doubtful. He looked at Susanna. So did I. She sat very still, looking at the bleachers. Lake raised his head toward the wooden benches. "Who?" he demanded. "Where?" His hand automatically went halfway to his ankle, where his holster was strapped, then it stopped.

I looked where the man had been. In the instant of Lake's distrust, the man had vanished.

I said, "The man from Palm Springs. Dark-complexioned. At the airport. At VillageFest."

"Let me remind you," he whispered, chin turned away from Susanna, "I've never seen this man."

"He was there," I said, searching the crowd for his face.

"Maybe he left to get a hot dog," Lake said, his voice so tight it went up half a tone.

A soft murmur escaped Susanna's lips. I looked at her. She was near tears. "What is it?" I asked, sorry that her daddy and I had let our cross-currents upset her.

She looked at Lake. "I saw him, too, Daddy."

A looked of consternation crossed Lake's face, and he turned his head and shoulders, scanning the panorama. He looked at his daughter. "What did he look like, sweetie?"

Her little mouth puckered. "I don't know. He was looking at me."

The idyllic afternoon had suddenly been ripped apart.

"When?" Lake asked, keeping his voice calm.

"When I was looking at the birdies," she said, then traced a finger across the sky toward the bleachers. "One birdie went that way. I saw the man. He looked at me."

"You think he's the same man Miss Dru saw?"

Susanna shook her head yes. "He was looking at her, too."

Lake and I looked at each other. My God, what had we

exposed her to?

"Can you describe the man?" Lake asked. "Was he a dark man?"

Susanna's eyes slid upward toward mine. I smiled. "Honey, just explain in your best words."

"I can't. Miss Dru, you saw him, too."

Lake's face muscles tightened in a look I couldn't nail down—afraid, frustrated, furious. He took Susanna in his lap. "Well, there's lots of people over there. And we're the only ones sitting right here for them to see. You know what I think?"

"No," she answered and rubbed an eye.

"A man saw a beautiful woman and a lovely little girl, and he couldn't help staring. When he got caught, he got embarrassed, and walked away. People are like that when they're caught looking at others."

I said, "Your daddy's right. Don't you get ticked when Michael looks at you?" Michael was her schoolmate, whom she liked, except when he "looked at me."

"I guess," she said, apparently losing interest. The chickadees were back. So were the squirrels.

Lake said, "About time for Mommy to come." His glance at me made me swallow against a shudder. "So, I guess we'll pack up."

Susanna was good at putting things away, and we let her. Get her mind off the man. At my car, Lake whispered, "Want me to come to your house?"

My blouse contracted and expanded with my breathing. "I could kick myself, not thinking about the danger . . ."

He moved closer and pulled me into him. "Shh," he said, "It's going to be all right. I'll keep watch." He pushed my hair off my forehead. "Susanna is very fond of you, you know. She'd take up for you over me every time."

I pulled back. "What are you saying? That she really didn't

see the man?"

He looked as if I'd slapped him. "How can I know, Dru? I've never seen anyone matching your description of him. I don't know who Susanna saw. Maybe—"

"Nobody."

"Please, don't," he whispered.

Susanna looked up suddenly.

Lake said, "Why don't I come by—"

"Don't," I hissed and bent to lift Susanna.

Kissing her, I said, "I love you, sugar."

"I love you, too," she said. Then she leaned in and whispered in my ear, "I *did* see him."

I believed her, but in my heart I wished Lake was right, and that we both were imagining the same stranger. "Don't ever, ever be out by yourself," I said.

"I never am."

That was literally true, because detectives' kids were watched like hawks if their parents had any regard for their well-being. Still, I wondered if I shouldn't call Linda Lake and ask her to be extra cautious. But no, she would call Lake and then he would call me—and it would all get very tedious.

THIRTY-EIGHT

Mr. Brown wasn't in the yard. No surprise. No doubt he was out for an afternoon snack. My cottage felt empty when I walked in and threw my purse and keys on the oak table. Standing in the middle of the kitchen, I felt one-dimensional—flat as a pancake. And alone. Pangs of regret, I had a few. I didn't like how Lake and I ended, but damn the man. How can you let someone come close when he doesn't trust and believe you? I was laden with exhaustion; my bed beckoned, and I entered my cool, pastel bedroom and drew the shades. I was asleep as soon as my head met the white satin pillow. A little girl and an evil man were the stuff of my daymares.

The phone woke me. It was still daylight.

"You okay?" Bellan shouted.

"Sure. Little drowsy. Having a nap."

"Good for you."

"What's cookin'?"

"I got showed around the Cameron property, like I said."

"And?"

"I had me this big ol' satchel filled with easel paper. The sales gal was curious, naturally. She told me right away that they didn't allow picture-taking. So I told her that I wanted to sketch the room and do the dimensions."

"She let you?"

"After a while. I told her that *her* dimensions were fine—as far as they went. I said I was measuring for my client's

207

furniture—which was high-priced antiques he'd move with him. You know, a chest for the foyer, a secretary for the office—that kind of stuff—*if it fit*. If the stuff didn't fit, I told her, he wasn't buying. That cured her of questions, and she got real interested when I talked antiques. I about ran out of my knowledge before she okayed the drawing and the measuring."

"This is in aid of what?"

"A big ol' fat ruse."

"Go on."

"The gal got tired of following me around, watching me measure, and went off to the pool with her cell phone. That's when I got busy with the Luminol."

"Luminol. Oh my God, you didn't."

"I surely did."

Luminol luminesces in the presence of blood. Once I was over the shock, I said, "What'd you find?"

"Blood everywhere."

Eileen was dead. I hoped it was only Eileen. "You didn't go spraying that stuff all over the house, did you? My God, talk about destroying a crime scene."

"I know better," he crowed. "I used a dropper. The likely place was the doorways. When bodies go down, they don't stay in the house. They got to be moved out. My way of thinking is, she was gunned down in the front foyer. They tried to clean it up with bleach, but it got down in the grout. You been there to the house?"

"Yes."

"The double doors in front got a glow on the wood facing. And in the key hole. They always forget the blow into the keyhole. Gunshot does that."

It wasn't hard to figure what must have happened. The man buying the flowers delivered the flowers and shot her when she opened the door. What didn't make sense was that she apparently knew the man, actually saw him in Philippe's shop. Was he the man at the airport, the man in the bleachers today? And where was Kinley? I couldn't make myself believe she might be dead, too.

Bellan went on, "I think I told you I'm having supper with Larry Bell, the PI here?"

"You did."

"Larry's got a nose for everything that goes on around him."

"I look forward to your conversation."

"Call you, then."

Hanging up, I let my hand rest on the phone for several seconds. "Murder in the Mansion": a good title for a mystery. But it wasn't a mystery, what happened. I wish I could have talked to the flower girl at Philippe's. Maybe she could recollect the man who'd bought the bouquet. But a lot of days of flower-selling had passed.

I called Bellan back and told him to find her. I hung up and peered outside. Rain poured through the sun rays. Mr. Brown wasn't sitting in the birdbath. Two blue jays were perched on the rim. From the bushes, Mr. Brown crept toward them. As they flew into the trees, Susanna's spritely figure suddenly flitted on the lawn, an ethereal picture of happiness as she clutched the brown cat, who, of course, had missed another opportunity at the birds. Lake appeared next to her, ruffling her silky blonde hair.

I shook the gossamer memories.

Lake. I should call him, tell him what Bellan reported. I hadn't called his loft since we came back from Palm Springs. *What's holding you up? This is business.*

I dialed the familiar number. After a dozen rings, I hung up. I punched the area code for his cell, then hung up when the image of a phantom woman named Jeannie climbed into my brain. Jeannie of the telephone answering machine sitting on a barstool talking to Lake at Frankie's—his favorite Sunday evening watering hole when we weren't making pasta together.

Quit!

I went for Sircher's makeup bag.

She was right, it took painstaking practice, and patience. More than I possessed. Altering my nose changed my face all right. I looked like a prizefighter who had taken twenty hits too many. The chin puttying was a disaster.

The phone rang while I was stripping the gunk, rubbing the latex into rolls.

I picked up.

"Hey," Lake said. "You called?"

"I did," I said peeling putty from my chin. I waited for a moment, but he didn't say where he'd been. "I talked to Bellan this afternoon. Remember I told you he was posing as a gofer for a high roller in Birmingham?"

"Uh-huh. Did he get into the house?"

"Long story short, he dropped Luminol on likely spots and got blood."

He was quiet for a moment. "Does that surprise you?"

"No. I think Eileen was gunned down at the front door by a man delivering flowers."

He didn't reply for a couple of beats. "That reminds me of— what was the name of that case?"

Rubbing my face with astringent, I said, "Don't recall at the moment, but it proves assassins borrow each other's tricks."

"You know that Bellan's actions compromise the case, don't you?"

"Bellan says he was careful, just a few drops here and there where he could use his light."

"The question is, did Arlo hire the hit?"

Thinking of Heidi, I said, "Either him or Whitney."

"What's Bellan's next move?"

"Meeting tonight with a PI that moved to Palm Springs from Alabama."

"Good luck to him."

"You sound worried."

"I didn't like it out there."

"Neither did I."

"See you at lunch tomorrow?"

"Not Thelma's," I said. "I've got a meeting with Portia and Whitney in the morning. How about Central Park—with the bums."

"My darling girl, 'bums' is not politically correct."

"The homeless, then."

"That's not PC either. They're urban campers."

That ended our conversation. I wondered where he'd been earlier in the evening. I could have asked him what he had for dinner, but I *knew*. He always had wings and celery at Frankie's. And curly fries.

THIRTY-NINE

A gray sheet of rain arrived with Monday's dawn. I'd been up long before then, practicing my putty lessons. Couldn't sleep, so might as well do something constructive. I was getting better, the prizefighter had only suffered a few blows. I washed the spirits from my face and went out to fill Mr. Brown's dish and the bird feeders. My neighbors think I'm fattening the tufted titmice for the cat. By eight, I'd drank a pot of coffee and read my e-mail. Dartagnan sent one saying the FBI had posted Eileen's and Kinley's pictures on their website.

As I gathered my keys, backpack, and umbrella, the phone rang.

"Hey, it's Bellan," he said, sounding excited.

"Bellan, what's up? I've got to leave for court."

"You meeting with that judge in Eileen's case?"

"Sure am."

"Witch of a woman."

"A witch of a woman with the brain of Einstein and the heart of a hooker."

He chuckled. "Don't judge a judge by her cover, eh?"

"What's up in The Springs? You have dinner with your PI friend?"

"Yeah. Larry's been out here five years and already he's got a bead on everybody who's anybody."

"Give me the highlights. Write up the details and e-mail them to me."

"Well, for one thing, just about everybody who wants to be is on Arlo's payroll."

"On Arlo's payroll?"

"He's a movie guy. He films all these westerns in the desert. Cowboys and Indians."

"He hires people out there to be extras?"

"You got it," he said. "You know how they name all the streets out here for the movie stars like Hope and Crosby and Dinah Shore?"

"Yes," I said, impatient, not wanting to be late.

"Well, out by the casino they got in the desert, they got a street named Arlo Cameron."

"I didn't know that."

"They got a sandwich in the casino named 'The Arlo Cameron.' Beefy, like a Philly steak. They got a horse race called 'The Arlo Cameron.' It's a stakes race."

"Bellan, I'm impressed all to hell, but I've got to run. What did you find out about Contessa Rosovo?"

"She had a lot of pretty good parts in Arlo's movies. You ever see any?"

"No, I'm not a fan of cowboys and Indians."

"I sure am. See all them on the Cowboy Channel when I'm home and relaxing. I never met Contessa yet, but I plan on it. I think I know which one she is in the movies. Hot little girl, romances the white guy, who usually gets killed. They're not the stars, you know."

"That'd be my guess."

"Her tribe owns the casino. Her aunt and uncle runs it."

"I've met the family."

"Tess is engaged to an Indian boy, brother of her dead husband," Bellan said.

"She told me. But there's something between her and Dartagnan LeRoi."

"Now, there a gent for you. Larry says if he ever arrested anybody, nobody knows about it. He's friends with people he needs to be friends with. Everybody else, he doesn't bother about."

"Is he in the movies, too?"

"You guessed it."

"You talk to him yet?"

"I called. He says he can't help me. He says Larry's reliable. End of conversation."

"What about the girl in Philippe's food boutique?"

"Not around much, part-timer. I'll catch up to her. They call him the Phony Frenchman, did you know that?"

"Uh-huh."

"He makes up exotic crap that won't see the inside of my mouth. Larry's gone crazy with this California shit."

"I must run," I said. "I'll call this evening. And get to Tess as soon as you can. The flower girl, too."

"You ever hear of an open secret?"

"What do you mean?"

"Everybody knows, but nobody says, because they figure everybody already knows."

"I get it. So?"

"It's worth the fifteen grand that Eileen owes me." He chuckled, and I could visualize his moustache curling up his cheeks.

"Wait a minute," I said. "You know something everybody else in Palm Springs knows, and you want fifteen thousand to tell me?"

"Well, it has implications, you see. And—I found it out. You didn't."

"You're not getting fifteen thousand dollars from me. I can't afford it, but you aren't getting it from Eileen, either. You got to know that after what you found in Arlo's house. Besides, what if

214

I told you that I'm pretty sure I know the open secret?"

"You could, if you talked to the right people. But you didn't tell it to me, and I think you would have."

"I have to go."

He didn't seem to hear, just said, "You making progress on who owns The Cloisters?"

"Take it to the bank."

"All I say is, don't get too close to Whitney. Bad things can happen to you."

"I'll be sitting beside him in the judge's chamber in about twenty minutes. Bye."

Bradley Whitney was enraged. He reminded me of a cartoon where steam pours from the nose and ears of the character. Portia laid out her reasons for going to the press. It was an obvious one: to bring awareness to anyone who might have seen or have knowledge of the missing persons.

"How much to keep this contained?" he asked. "Nobody looks at the FBI's website, but pictures on television will ruin me."

"Haven't you been listening?" Portia said, glaring at him. "This isn't about money, and don't ever infer again that I can be bought."

Whitney tried to look contrite. "I certainly wasn't inferring any such thing."

Her black beady eyes didn't let up. "Two people have vanished, one's a child in my jurisdiction. She's your child, and you should want everything possible done to find her."

Still, he was adamant. "Everything's being done that can be done. The police, the FBI. They're happy as hell that the Atlanta papers and nightly news isn't pressing them for results *yesterday.* I've learned that ninety percent of parent-child kidnappings go without media coverage, so why should I have *my* case blaring across the country." When he glanced at me, I snapped my mouth shut so he wouldn't jump down my throat. "Supposedly I've hired the *best* that money can hire."

"Miss Dru is not a magician, nor is she omnipotent."

I threw a bone to Whitney. "I agree that media attention *could get some results,* but I'd like to have a little more time to—"

Whitney visibly softened. "To what?"

"A colleague of mine in Palm Springs has come up with some promising leads, and—"

"What leads?"

Portia barked, "Would you let Miss Dru finish a sentence?"

"Who's this colleague?"

"A reliable investigator from—"

"Am I paying him?"

"You're not paying me, either, in case you've forgotten."

Portia wriggled in her seat. "If you need some time, Miss Dru, you can have two days before I talk with the newspaper and TV people. And," she looked at Whitney, "you will pay her a fee for those two days."

Whitney took out his checkbook. He made out a check without asking how much. When he'd finished, he rose stiffly and threw it on Portia's desk.

Picking it up, she looked at me. "Twenty grand enough?"

"Yes," I said, opening my purse. I extracted Whitney's undated check "Here," I said, "Let's trade. A bribe, for an earned fee."

Snatching it, Whitney looked from Portia to me. "You two are determined to ruin my life, aren't you?"

Portia's grimace was pure hellfire.

"Mr. Whitney," I said, "I'm determined to find out the truth about what happened to Eileen and Kinley."

When Whitney left, I told her what I wanted her to know, and her expression told me she knew that I wasn't telling her everything. I told her about Arlo and the Palm Springs movie extras, but I didn't tell her Bellan went into the house and found blood. That would have brought her chamber down around me. I didn't tell her, either, that Lake and I were plotting to get into The Cloisters. She might have wanted to go, too. She wouldn't need to fake a nose or a masculine chin or bushy eyebrows. A dark suit, and she was good to go.

FORTY

High noon, the sun stoking the fires of August, we stood in line at Joseph Wannamaker's Red Hots in Woodruff Park. We took our hotdogs to a concrete fountain filled with gunk and sat on the edge. The city of Atlanta had remodeled the park several times, but it always reverted to its former self: patchy grass, smelly benches, foul fountains. Ripping the top off a bag of chips, Lake announced that we were going to The Cloisters tomorrow night.

"Oh, no," I moaned, and felt mustard ooze from my mouth. I swiped the napkin across my lips. "I don't know if I can get my nose right by then."

"These places are dark," he said, munching the chip. "You know, I should have a problem with your not telling Portia about the blood in Cameron's house."

"But we don't know if it's Eileen's," I said, swallowing the last bite, and then chugging Coke. "We don't even know if it's human. Or suppose it was somebody at one of his parties who cut his finger on a champagne glass? And I noticed the tiles in the foyer had a copperish tint. Luminol fluoresces in copper or its alloys. Also in horseradish."

"Horseradish?"

"Saw it on the internet."

"That's why I said I *should* have a problem," Lake said. "What else is interesting about what Bellan told you is, half the town—those that are not already movie stars—owes Arlo for getting them in the movies."

"That makes Arlo a godfather."

"Let's say the flower man was the hit man," he said. "Where's the body? Hit men hit and run."

"Arlo's got Dartagnan in his pocket. God knows, he didn't do much investigating in that house. Neither did the FBI guy, Corlee. Suppose he's got movie credits, too?"

"Why not? FBI guys have private lives. They'll deny it, though." He munched down on the last of his dog, wiped his mouth, and said, "Professional responsibility compels me to tell Dartagnan that Bellan found blood in Cameron's house." He wadded the paper hot dog holder and the potato chip wrapper together and stuffed the ball into his Coke cup. "I'm not looking forward to imparting that bit of illegality."

"I'm not sure Dartagnan's really a cop," I said. "He seems to have lied about everything."

At the trash can, we tossed the debris and walked up Peachtree Street. Lake took three caramel candies from his pocket. These are meant to satisfy until the next pieces of cake or pie. He knows it's useless to offer me one.

"I think Eileen's buried in the desert," I said.

A capricious wind picked his tie off his chest and blew it across his face. His black hair swirled on his forehead. Being near him was like being near an open flame. He said, "Okay. So, who buried her?"

"Someone who's an extra in an Arlo Cameron production."

"Does this someone have a name?"

"I don't know it—yet."

"Where to from here?" he asked.

"I'll wait to hear what else Bellan turns up. So far, he's been successful. You can take that to the bank."

Lake flicked me a glance and grinned. "Well," he said, "at least *he* checks out. The cops in Birmingham say he's okay.

Never had problems with him. He cooperates—for a fee, or an exchange of info. Is that the bank you're talking about?"

"I got a check today for twenty thousand from Whitney. I can pay Bellan and get the juicy stuff he's found out on the genius."

"I wonder how juicy?" Lake said.

"We shall see."

The afternoon passed uneventfully. I studied Bellan's e-mails. He was a meticulous reporter, but after I'd read everything twice, I concluded his oral summary had been just as good as his written report, and the money grubber didn't hint at having learned an open secret. Oddly, the flower girl was keeping herself hidden. I wondered why. *Don't worry,* Bellan had said, *she's not dead, she's just not around.*

I played the tapes of the conversations I'd had with Dr. Brommer at Curriculum Paradigms, Inc., and of Whitney in his classroom. They hadn't known they were being taped, which is technically illegal, but I wasn't planning to use the stuff in any legal proceeding. I listened a second time with my hands poised over a computer keyboard, pecking out the gist of the conversation. Then I scissored the tapes.

My assistant, Pearly Sue Ellis, came in, waving papers. "Lieutenant Lake faxed Whitney's résumé. Our slime boy's on paper saying he was born in New York. But he went to high school in Little Rock. Graduated Central High School, straight As. BA, MA, PhD from Georgia State."

"Get onto Central High," I said. "Get a copy of his transcript. He wasn't born in New York, according to Bellan, but he did go to high school in Little Rock. Dr. Whitney is selective about his lies."

"He had to tell where he went to high school so GS could get his transcripts," Pearly Sue said. She looked at her watch. "I got a cab coming. My plane leaves in three hours. Web will follow up with my reports." She twirled like the cheerleader she'd undoubtedly been. "I've never been to Little Rock."

Her assignment was to confirm Bellan's findings. Not that I didn't trust them, but I wanted a woman on the ground there, talking to people who knew Whitney twenty years ago. Pearly Sue had enough Southern charm to crack human safes without spinning the combination.

Turning into my driveway, I spotted the large package on the front porch. I carried it inside. Atlanta Courier Service had delivered it, the mauve slip said, at three-thirty P.M.

I cut the tape. The suit hung in a bag, folded over. Unzipping it, I took out the double-breasted jacket with a pair of vents and the straight-leg slacks, no cuffs and pleated in front. My God, the fabric—so soft it molded to my hand. The label on the back hem said cashmere and silk. The rich charcoal had a tiny, tiny line of pale blue running through it.

The midnight blue satin shirt blended perfectly with the rich suit fabric. A black silk tie completed the ensemble. The shoe-box held a surprise. Sircher had sent round-toed clogs, which caught my breath. Digging into a pocket of the bag, I found a belt, a man's Rolex, and a diamond ring. *What—no tie clip or hanky for the lapel pocket?*

I carried the clothes into my room. I knew immediately they were too large. I scrambled back to the box. In the bottom I found a vest of shoulders and padding that ran down the back along the spine and around the middle. Now I could fill the suit.

Looking at the clock, I figured Sircher would still be in her shop.

"The diLeon is fabulous," I raved. "Perfect."

"They're just on loan, you know, dear girl."

"I was afraid you'd say that. I was rethinking my style."

She quoted, *"To thine own self be true, and it must follow, as the night the day, thou canst not then be false—"*

"Sircher, where'd you go to school?"

"The London School of Economics."

"That hoi polloi place?"

"Kings, queens, and states, maids, matrons, nay, the secrets of the grave this viperous slander enters."

"Okay, Okay. I'm ever in your debt."

She said, "I got a little notion where you might be wanting to go."

"What little notion?"

"It came to me in a dream." Her pause, the drama, iced the marrow in my bones, but I was ready with a comeback when she said, "The Cloisters."

Drat. "If you think I'm going to a church, you sent the wrong damn clothes." *This city of millions is like a goddamn small town in south Georgia.*

"I, too, am a searcher, Miss Dru."

"Very funny, Sircher, but you can guess until the cows come home, I'm not telling."

"Here's a tip for your next research project. Take your tiny thread and follow the bloggers."

"The internet gossips? I wish I had the time."

"It's worth your while. Will you tell me if you are successful in your little quest?"

"Maybe you can tell me, before I know."

"Just remember, the walls have ears."

When Bellan didn't call, I picked out his cell number. The answering voice told me to leave a message or a page. I did both, then went to the shower. I'd practiced again with the putty, this time with a sense that I had to get it perfect or I'd be a dead duck.

Lake called and I told him about Sircher's "little notion."

"Bloggers," he said. "The department is trying to get a geek for minimum wage to sit and monitor the blogs."

"Ought to be a cinch for such a lordly sum," I said. "Even with the blogger hint, I think Sircher got her notion somewhere else."

"You gave her enough hints. You said you wanted to fool men, therefore, men-only places."

"There have to be tons."

"Not when you start cutting out the obvious. There's the Atlanta Men's Bondage Club, but you assured her it wasn't a sex thing. Or the Men's Garden Club of America, Atlanta chapter."

"There is such an animal?"

"Bet your pocket full of posies. You wouldn't be infiltrating the Federated Jewish Men's Club, would you?"

"She gave me a Roman nose."

"The Cloisters is the only club of its kind that I know of in Atlanta, or in all of Georgia, for that matter, that is strictly men only. Sircher would know that."

"*Mea culpa.*"

"On that note, good night, sweet princess."

Before I could think of a comeback, he disconnected.

I tried Bellan's number three more times. Was it time to worry yet?

FORTY-ONE

Now that I was back on Whitney's payroll, I had to answer the SOB's phone calls.

A petulant Whitney asked, "And just when am I going to get a written report of your activities?"

I checked out the people walking on the sidewalk fifteen stories below my office. "When I write it up."

"You haven't much time left on the judge's extension, and I'm getting nervous."

"You're just now getting nervous?"

After more unsatisfactory exchanges, I rang off and looked in on Webdog.

"I need you to find out where Arlo Cameron lives in Los Angeles—his address, phone number, where he likes to dine, etcetera."

"You got it."

I called Bellan again. He didn't answer again.

This is not good.

I tried Dartagnan. No answer.

An hour later, I tried Bellan again, no answer.

I tried Dartagnan again, no answer. My nerves were oozing through my skin.

That afternoon, Lake called.

He'd received the invitation to The Cloisters in the mail.

"We're to be there promptly at seven—not seven-fifteen—and

we're to dress for dinner. No names. We'll be given names."

"Woooo-hoooo."

Lake arrived half an hour before we were to leave. He wore a dark blue silk suit. His shirt was very pale mauve, and his tie was deep maroon with tiny blue stripes. He'd gelled his thick hair slightly and combed it straight back. He looked oh-so-stylish, but it was the man himself who had me dry-swallowing.

As he studied me, the look on his face was priceless. He said, "You've mutated magnificently."

"Honest?"

"How's your eyesight?"

I adjusted the round, rimless glasses. "Magoo, to you."

"You look like a Jewish scholar. If you had on digger clothes, you could be squatting over an archeological pit."

"But will I pass at The Cloisters?"

"Absolutely. The day-old beard looks as if, in your learned state, you'd forgotten to shave. And that shiny suit! Ten years out of date, but what's time to a brain-above-fashion?"

"It's a diLeon. Very retro. Very in. What about my nose?"

"Not too hooked, not too wide. Just right, I'd say."

"I modeled it after yours."

He reached out to grab me playfully, but quickly backed off with his hands up. "Too fragile," he said. "I hope you don't melt."

Me, too.

A tall, befittingly dressed butler opened the door. Wordlessly, and with a graceful wave of a white-gloved hand, he gestured us into a rotunda. The opulent place glowed in the dim golden light. The marble floor looked like white satin. Beneath a massive crystal chandelier, a flowing fountain stood. In the center, on a pedestal, a nude Eros wielded his lethal love weapon.

"Interesting," I muttered. In the fountain, water to their knees, winged girls and boys looked up at the God of Love with naked adoration. The alabaster children looked starkly virginal.

Off this rotunda, I counted four rooms with vaulted openings. From one, piano music and men's voices floated into the rotunda. The butler led us around the fountain and through a door. The mahogany horseshoe bar had a grand piano stuck into the opening of the horseshoe. A handsome pianist played Gershwin. Six men sat in twos at polished wooden tables. The atmosphere was superficially masculine. Missing was the ineffable scent of testosterone that makes a bar a bar. The butler seated us. "I'll tell Mr. White you have arrived."

A waiter came. We ordered martinis—a Blue Sapphire for me, and Grey Goose for Lake. Earlier, we'd flipped a coin to see who got the Sapphire. Couldn't look too cozy with each other. "Place's nice," Lake said.

I almost snickered. "Indeed," I murmured, touching the Waterford vase holding a white fragrant rose. I mouthed, "Wired?" Lake nodded. I asked, "Would it be too gauche to ask who their decorator is?"

"Probably not," Lake said, and looked approving. We'd been practicing my vocals. Luckily, my voice is low-pitched, and I'm a natural mimic.

Sircher had been keen on getting my vocals right, too. She had explained, "Southern men seem to have atrophied larynxes. Draw out your vowels more than you normally do, and forget the r at the end of words. Practice saying 'buddah' for butter. Just remember, when people see a man they expect to *hear* a man. Don't break into a Tiny Tim and you'll be all right."

A man walked into the room quietly. He stood to my left. He was broad-shouldered with a midsection paunch that protruded from his gray linen jacket. His tie, too, was gray, as was his hair and thin mustache. He wore tortoiseshell glasses that magnified his gray eyes.

"Mr. Chapman and Mr. Barton," he said, looking from me to Lake. "Good evening. I am Mr. White."

"Good evening, Mr. White," we answered at the same time.

I am Mr. Chapman.

Mr. White took a seat. "You are our only guests this evening. The others here are regulars." He studied me for an instant as if he were making up his mind about something. Perhaps it was only paranoia on my part. He went on, "We have two guest nights a month. A guest may visit The Cloisters twice within a year. After that, he will be asked to join us—or not. The financial details are worked out, and will be presented to you by your sponsor. Suffice it to say, if you have to ask, you can't afford us."

I looked at Mr. Barton and Mr. White. Mr. White's glance lingered on my face. "We are a men's club. We do not discourage gay guests or members, but we forbid homosexual activities here." He nodded at me, and I back at him, meaning he'd caught me out. Or not. He went on, "Tonight for your introduction, you will follow the routine all members follow before being invited to join us. First you have your pre-prandial aperitifs in this room. When you've finished, you will go into the dining room, across the hall. You will see the small gold plaque at the door. Reservations for members are made a week ahead. Following dinner, you advance to the smoking room for post-prandial brandies, if you so choose. You may remain there as long as you wish, smoke whatever you wish—as long as it's legal. You may wish to depart the club from the smoking room if you feel your evening has been satisfactory. Many find the atmosphere here, the evening meal and the gathering of friends, quite fulfilling in and of itself. But if you want more enjoyment, you are free to go on into the nightclub. The ladies there will guide you through the rest of the evening, but guests cannot choose an exclusive female companion." He pressed his lips into a wry smile and waited a few tics before he said, "Members must be off the premises by four in the morning. Guests must leave by eleven. No money exchanges hands. In a week, you will receive a note with a figure on it. You will pay your sponsor. Any questions at this time?"

"No," I said, taking the lead. "All perfectly clear." *Ah-llll peh-fec-lee cleee-ah.*

Lake nodded his response.

"What do you drink after dinner?" Mr. White asked and looked at me first.

"Benedictine," I drew out.

"That's fine for me, too," Lake said.

"Very nice, then." Mr. White stood and adjusted the knot in his tie. "Bon appétit." At the door, he looked back briefly.

"What a niiiiiice gennelman," I said.

"I like this place," Lake said. We sat back and enjoyed our drinks, then rose, nodded to the two remaining people in the room, and left.

"What do you think?" I whispered as we crossed the foyer to the dining room.

"You're damned good with that voice, but I think Mr. White is suspicious."

"It's the nose. He smells a rat."

"It's not the shape. I think he wondered about the makeup."

"He suspects I'm gay."

"Let's hope that's all he suspects."

FORTY-TWO

Dinner was scrumptious and artfully served in the white and gold room—field greens with a mustard vinaigrette, leek soup, filet mignon, potatoes lyonnaise, asparagus stir-fried with tarragon. For dessert, raspberry torte and strong coffee laced with Bailey's Irish Cream. We'd eaten in silence like the other diners. Perhaps it was the custom—forget the repartee, take pleasure in the food.

I sneaked my torte onto Lake's small plate, and when he'd swallowed the last bite and wiped his mouth, Mr. White appeared to escort us into the smoking room. Since his timing was precise, I was certain there were peepholes in the paintings. Behind Mr. White's back, Lake winked, which was probably seen by someone, too.

Inside the smoking room, I leaned into Lake. "Elvis would love it heah."

"I'm partial to red, too," Lake said.

Mr. White chuckled as he led us across oriental rugs scattered on the parquet floor. At a burgundy sofa, he waved us to sit. "Enjoy the Benedictine," he said, and bowed and walked away. Stems of the divine liquid sat on brass coasters.

The varying shades of red provided the ambience in the long, low-ceilinged room, and despite the reds, it had a soothing quality. Recessed overhead lighting and dim lamps helped. About two dozen men were grouped in twos and threes, with an occasional solo sitting in a chair reading, or just listening to the soft banter. Nothing harsh spoken here and no TVs with ball games blaring to pumping fists.

Crystal and bottles of brandy sat on chests and drink trolleys. On the leather-topped coffee table, next to our brandies, little silver dishes held candies, in case your sweet tooth hadn't been filled. Lake reached for a chocolate mint.

A large man came into the room and poured himself a brandy. I blinked several times to make sure he wasn't Orson Welles. He looked down on us and everyone turned in our direction. Orson raised his brandy glass. "Welcome to The Cloisters, Mr. Barton and Mr. Chapman." The men nodded and held up a glass to our being amongst them. The fake Orson, with an equally fake stentorian voice, said, "I trust you supped well?"

Lake answered, "Wonderful food."

With a nod, I said, "I mus saaay."

Orson said, "Be our guests and don't hesitate to help yourself to whatever pleases you." He placed his glass on the trolley and weaved out of the room. He'd evidently come in for the sole purpose of leading the toast.

I quick-glimpsed everyone, careful that my eyes didn't linger on any one person. Mr. White stood like a sentinel in a far corner. Then he walked to a trolley and prepared a brandy. When he lifted the stem, it must have slipped from his hand because it dropped on the parquet. "A Swarovski," he cried. He waved a hand and called out, "Boy."

A boy who looked to be about fifteen came running from a small door in the opposite corner. He said, "Yes, Father White."

At that very moment, my mouth actually dropped open. Dr. Brommer was sitting by the door, at an antique secretary. The commotion had caused him to look up from whatever he was writing. I looked away quickly.

Noticing my consternation, Lake asked quietly, "Something the matter?"

"Later." La-tah.

We stayed for another half hour and listened to a mildly animated discussion about the upcoming election and what effect it would have on the stock market. Dr. Brommer never looked up again, not that I saw.

"Shall we partake of the entertainment," Lake said at last.

"It's now or nevah."

"Hum a few bars for The King," Lake said, standing.

"It's now or nevah, come hold me tight." It was the two Benedictines.

Mr. White was suddenly at our side. "What shall it be, gentlemen? An early evening, or onward to the theater?"

FORTY-THREE

We followed Mr. White through the back part of the house to a pair of ebony doors. He opened them and ushered us into the annex, the building I had spotted above the original building. My initial impression was *The Blue Angel* and Marlene Dietrich in sooty black-and-white. There were black-draped stages around three walls and catwalks extending into the center of the large, but, incongruously, intimate, room. In the next instant, the movie image ended. This was not a 1930s German cabaret, but an artfully staged sex show. Young beautiful women in white gossamer—no undergarments—danced on their toes on the catwalks. As we moved up a path made by tiny strings of stage lights, Lake leaned into me and whispered that the wisps the young lovelies wore made them more sensual than if they were buck naked. I had to trust the masculine point of view. The music was consciously ethereal—sounds I'd heard during expensive spa massages—sounds from nature: the sea washing ashore, whales singing, breezes through the pines.

I whispered back, "Ballet slippers, no five-inch hooker heels here. No 'heartache tonight, I know.' "

Lake poked me like he would a comrade sharing an off-color joke. "Where're the garters? Got my twenties, they got no garters."

When we were seated, a man dressed in a tuxedo rose and went to a girl who had swooned into a back-bend so far back her long golden hair almost touched her heels. He beckoned, and she slid from the platform into his waiting arms. "Ah, I get it," Lake said. "They're auditioning."

"I got to get out of here," I said, the sticky feeling of decadence weighing on my spirit.

Lake laughed. "See what you got yourself into?"

A woman came to the table wearing a short, shear Roman toga. Very sheer, very short. I could see where her thighs ended. I saw Lake swallow. I ordered a Benedictine. Lake ordered a brandy Alexander. "What?" I whispered. "Mama used to drink those fifty years ago."

Roman Toga served us, and then pulled a chair close to Lake. Hair white-blonde, eyes green, she smiled at Lake, that kind of smile his groupies give him. Lake introduced himself as Mr. Chapman. *Hey, I thought that was me.*

Lake introduced "Mr. Barton," but Toga barely glanced at me.

Shouldn't I feel pissed? I would have been were I not intrigued. As Lake and Toga exchanged barroom talk, I studied the theater. I hadn't seen the second-story balconies before now, nor had I noticed the glass-domed ceiling. I was looking at stars and the moon. Then I saw the back wall, where there was no stage. A Celtic cross, fifteen feet high, stood, with an altar in front of it. My ancestors, as Whitney had pointed out, were Celts, but the altar and the cross gave me the creeps.

I said to Lake and Toga, "If you'll both excuse me, I'll find my way to the john." Don't know about other men, but that's what Lake called it when he was in polite company.

Toga pointed to the right of the altar. "Through the door, down the hall, second on the left." She sounded like a hick from the mountains.

Once I was out of the theater, my instinct was to draw myself in and tiptoe down the red-carpeted hall. The wall sconces were dim and the atmosphere cold, just right for sneaking.

Walk like a man.

I straightened and strode past a door marked FEMMES DRESSING ROOM and came to the men's room. Twenty feet up the corridor I saw that doors went off right and left, like in a hotel. I walked that way and listened at a few. The doors appeared stout, perhaps soundproof. I turned to hurry back the way I'd come.

A faint cry came from behind, like a cat mewing. I looked back and saw a tall red-haired woman hurrying forward. She wore a tailored black pants suit over a black turtleneck sweater. She was slim, going on forty, with auburn hair done up in combs, and her white complexion smoothed by makeup. Her eyes were lined with black kohl and mascara. Maroon blush highlighted her cheekbones. I wondered where she'd come from so suddenly.

Four feet away, she stopped, cocked a hip and spoke from her throat. "Are you lost, handsome?"

Shaking my head no, I murmured like an idiot. "Men's. Passed it."

Her black eyes roved over me, and I damn near panicked. *A woman knows her own.*

She said, "You didn't find anything in the theater that took your fancy?" I gave a defeated sigh, and she moved closer. She reached for my hand, and I let her take my fingers. She didn't need to be feeling the back of my hand, the artificial veins and hair. "So soft," she said, gliding her long fingers over my palm. "No heavy lifting, hmm, sugar?"

"No, ma'yam."

She placed her hands on my jacket. "Lovely, lovely," she said, rolling the lapels between her fingers. She opened the jacket and clapped her palms to my chest.

Don't be alarmed. Relax. Just don't let her hands go around back. She cried, "Ho."

I lifted my chin.

Her vivid mouth was a slit of malice as she tweaked my nipples, then kneaded them with her fingers.

I longed to mash her in the mouth.

She teased, "Don't like being nipped in the bud?" I shook my head. "Too bad. I like men with mammies. Shows their feminine side." Her half-closed eyes fastened on my nose.

Paranoid, you're just paranoid. Trying to smile, and sliding sideways, I said, "Well, yes."

Then she raised a knee and planted it between my legs. It almost took my breath away.

Thank you, Sircher for the cloth dildo.

She ground her knee lightly and got no response from the soft wad in my crouch because my hand was too far from the tiny bulb in my pocket to inflate the thing. She stepped back. "You have other interests?"

I stepped back and pocketed my hands. "I have many inner-ests."

"You're gay."

"My concern."

"Gays belong to the club," she said. "But not normal gays, of course. Nor normal heteros for that matter."

What was normal for this club?

She moved back into me and raised her knee to explore my crotch again. "So many other pleasures."

I smiled like *Now you're talking my language* and pressed the bulb in my pocket.

"Ooooo," she muttered as the dildo slowly filled.

What now? I wondered. *Where's the exit when I slug her in the jaw?*

Then she stepped back. "Temptation, naughty me." She rubbed my arm, the lapel of my jacket. "What's your credo?"

Credo? "Ah-m just a guest."

She looked thoughtful. "Well, I'm not a member, of course, but I'll put in a good word with the membership committee."

"When?" *Weee-yen?*

"That depends."

"On?"

Before I knew it, she leaned into me and grabbed the back of my neck. She pressed her lips to mine. When she bit my lip. I lurched away.

She guffawed and chided, "Pain is not your thing, then?"

I looked offended, which I was.

"We shall find out what is. Come," she beckoned. I fell in step with her long strides to the theater door. Opening it, she said, "Good evening, Mr. Chapman." A streak of light flashed on her face. She looked strangely familiar. My eyes fastened on her chin. She said, "Perhaps we'll meet in therapy." Her laughter soared down the long hall, punctuated by her striding heels.

Lake was sitting alone. I weaved through a crowd of people who hadn't been in the theater twenty minutes ago. A dozen more gossamer ladies were Swan Lake–ing to the sounds of birds on the wing. I saw Mr. Brommer sitting alone at the end of a catwalk. He was looking up, his mouth open. I felt like I'd fallen into a sewer.

"Where's Toga?" I asked Lake.

"She upped and left," he said. "Guests don't get the full magilla."

"I found that out."

I became aware of Mr. White crossing the room, toward us. "Uh oh, I think we're pumpkins."

"Gentlemen," he said, hands entwined over his paunch like a kindly grandfather. "It's time for a different venue, to which our guests are not privy." He looked sad to have to tell us this news.

Lake and I rose. Lake said, "To play, you pay, right, Mr. White?"

Mr. White's smile was jovial when he answered, "Indeed. Tonight was just a tiny sample of our hospitality."

Back in my cottage, stripping off the Roman nose, I listened to the messages on my answering machine. Lake sat nearby. Whitney was at his peeved best.

"Miss Dru. Where are you? I've been trying to reach you? Have you forgotten me? I am your client. How is the investigation into my ex-wife and daughter proceeding? Is it too much to ask for updates when I'm paying for your services. And you have only a short time left?"

"Testy, testy," Lake said, going to the liquor cabinet and taking out the Blue Sapphire. He eyed the crème de menthe.

I said, "You pollute that gin and I'll crack the bottle over your head."

FORTY-FOUR

Six in the morning, and the door bell's ringing? *Who the hell
. . . ?*

Belting my robe, I padded down the hall. I could see through
the stained glass. Lake. He'd left at one o'clock—just five hours
ago—after we'd had a few gins and dissected the evening. I
think we decided that The Cloisters was a high-class whorehouse, but I'm not sure. My brain hadn't cleared the last hurdle
of consciousness. I remember discussing ways of busting the
place and how much fun it would be. We never brought up the
idea of going to bed together, and he'd left. There was still a lot
of rawness in me—probably in Lake, too.

Opening the door, I expected that Lake would look his spiffy
self, but he looked god-awful. "What's . . . ?" I didn't finish.
The news was going to be bad.

"I got a call from Dartagnan," he said, coming into the hall.

"Let me take a deep breath," I said. "I think it might be my
last for a while." I inhaled and held the air in my lungs, thinking
of a grave in the desert.

"Bellan and his PI buddy, Larry, are dead."

"No, oh no." Lake grabbed me as I collapsed against a small
chest. He walked me into the front room and, along with me,
collapsed on the sofa. He held me until I stopped shaking and
raised my head off his shoulder. I managed to say, "What happened?"

"Some Indian kids found them in a gold mine shaft in the

desert. Shot."

"I've been trying—his cell . . ."

"The details are sketchy. Dartagnan talks a lot and says nothing."

I looked up and wiped tears with my fingers. "I liked Bellan."

"I know. From all I heard, he was a good man."

"Is that where they were shot?"

"They were dumped there."

"Who did they see last?"

"The motel people say they saw Bellan drive off the premises Monday morning. Never saw him after that. But their guests have outside entrances, and his room was on the back side of the building."

"So—sometime after I talked to him . . ." My eyes fixed on Lake's face. "They can't do this to him and get away with it."

"Who?"

"The sons-a-bitches who've staged this whole thing."

"Who?"

"I'm going out there."

"No, Dru. You're not."

"Don't tell me I'm not. A man died helping me. His death won't be for nothing." I jumped up and looked down at Lake. "Did you tell Dartagnan about the blood in Arlo's house?"

"A while ago, after he told me about Bellan's death." Lake rose. "I didn't tell him before because I was waiting for another report from Bellan to see if he'd come up with anything else."

"Well?"

"Dartagnan said Arlo's flying in from LA tomorrow."

"How sweet. What's he waiting for? His pals to get cleaning again?"

"If there's blood in that house, they can't clean it all up," Lake said. He took my arm. "Why don't we, for now, let Dartagnan handle things."

"Dartagnan? Investigate Arlo?"

Lake, also known as a devil's advocate, said, "The crime might have nothing to do with Arlo. It may have been something Larry was working on."

"Dream away."

"I want you to take it easy for a while. Give it a day."

"Then what?"

"Hell, I don't know. See what Dartagnan comes up with."

"For all we know Dartagnan killed Bellan and Larry," I said. "So you want the cat to investigate the mice he killed?" I sunk back onto the sofa. "Poor Bellan—him and his open secret—so f-ing theatrical—worth fifteen thou to him." I wiped the tears off my cheeks.

"Think. Any hint who this secret related to?"

"Arlo," I said. "Maybe Dartagnan."

"Why not Eileen?"

"She's Bellan's client."

"He could be keeping it to himself in case she wasn't dead—for the fifteen grand."

"He knew she was dead. Her blood's all over that goddamned house."

He took my wrists. "Stay calm." I wanted to rip my wrists away, but, instead, drew in a whimpering breath. "There are other explanations," he said, and up popped the devil again. "Maybe some drunken guest threw a cocktail glass at another drunken guest. Cut the guy. The gardener came in for a nooner with the maid . . ."

I pulled my wrists away. "Don't go on."

"You see what I'm getting at?"

I pushed back hair hanging in my face. "Yeah, lame excuses."

"What about Kinley? Okay, she's a kid and you love kids and you don't want to think of her dead."

No, I didn't. "She's not," I said. "Eileen recognized the flower man. He spooked her, but she'd already planned not to send Kinley to Atlanta. I think she put Kinley in Tess's safekeeping, then went back to the house."

"But there's no evidence of that."

"Sushi."

"Sushi?"

"Eileen bought sushi that afternoon at Philippe's. She takes Kinley to Tess at the skate park. She'd bought treats at Philippe's for Kinley to take with her. Then Eileen goes home, puts the sushi in the frig, answers the door to the man with the flowers, and bam! When I was at Arlo's house, the kitchen stunk. Arlo said the cartons hadn't been opened, nothing in them eaten."

"Didn't Heidi say she saw Eileen *and Kinley* late Saturday afternoon?"

"I think she lied. She'd lie for Arlo."

"Seems everybody did," Lake said. "But why did Eileen open the door to the flower man, if she feared him?"

"She wanted to confront him, and obviously she didn't think he was a killer."

"So who's the man?"

"Someone from either Atlanta or Palm Springs." *The man who'd followed me in both cities?*

"Why was she killed?" Lake asked.

He was pushing me through hoops, to vocalize my thoughts, see if they made sense to me. "Maybe Arlo suspected she was having an affair—maybe with his good buddy, Dartagnan—or Whitney found out she was having him investigated."

"You've investigated Whitney. Except for lying on his résumé about where he was born and a few other minor things, what have you discovered? A lot of people lie on résumés. Betcha half the PD has."

I was tired of his devil's advocate role. "The Cloisters," I said. "His ties to The Cloisters. His ties to stripping."

"He made money to put himself through college. If Eileen'd cut the drugs, she'd have gotten the girl."

"Stop wearing me down," I said, feeling bleary. "Come over to my side."

"*We* must look at this thing from all sides."

My Lake, the man of many sides. I got up. "I'm going to get dressed now. I need some time."

He rose and caught me around the waist. "Don't go."

"I am."

He looked like he could cry. "My Dru. Will you ever come back to me."

Tears welled in my eyes, my emotions sucking at my bones. I kissed the tip of his nose. "Wish me luck."

FORTY-FIVE

Palm Springs was still as hot as hell. But then, it was still August. Dartagnan wasn't nearly as happy to see me as he'd been weeks ago when he'd waved a cardboard sign with my name misspelled on it. This time he didn't even bother to come to the airport. When I called him before departing for Palm Springs, I sensed that he wanted to tell me to stay in Atlanta, but that wasn't his way. If nothing else, he prided himself on being cavalier, like his namesake, a namesake he'd apparently given himself. One thing I knew for certain: there would be no dinner, nor jovial chit-chat, this evening.

Dartagnan sat back in a swivel chair behind his weathered, desert wood desk. I braced for his accusations. The first question out of his mouth was about my relationship to Bellan Thomas.

Since I had no clue what Bellan had told him, I said, "I was paying him to take up where I left off when I got—hurt."

"He shouldn't of been spraying Luminol in Arlo's house. By the way, Arlo wants to see you later. We got an appointment."

I'd planned on talking to Arlo, but by myself. "You tell Arlo about the Luminol?"

"Not yet," he said. "Don't quite know how. What your man did was illegal. You gotta have a court order."

"I didn't instruct him to spray Luminol."

"I didn't think a smart ol' gal like you'd ask something stupid like that."

"Turns out, though, that Bellan Thomas wasn't so stupid."

"I don't like to say things bad about the dead. But—he *is* the one that's dead."

"How'd it happen?"

He twiddled his thumbs and looked at the ceiling. Ploys. "They were shot in Thomas's motel room. From the blood evidence, they were each sitting in a chair, across from someone sitting on the bed. That someone fired a forty-five caliber slug into Thomas's head while he held his whiskey and water. Larry had an instant to react, jump forward. But not in time. He got his slug in the gut."

"They knew their killer, or killers," I said.

"Just one killer, I think. One gun. The slugs are identical."

"Why did the killer take their bodies to the desert?"

"My guess? Conceal the crime."

"Why?"

Dartagnan sat forward and folded his hands on the desk. "When we know who the killer is, perhaps he, or she, will tell us. Could be, you know, that this doesn't have nothing to do with your case. Maybe Larry was working on something, and your guy was an innocent bystander."

Another f-ing devil's advocate. "What was Larry working on?"

"If I knew, I don't know I'd tell you, but I don't know."

I hoped he could read the scorn on my face, and now was not the time to ask why he'd lied about his background. I needed his help, as reluctant as it was going to be. Another thing, Bellan apparently didn't tell Dartagnan that Eileen had hired him three months ago, otherwise he'd be fishing around that hole. I said, "Let's assume for the moment it's my case that got them killed."

"*You* can."

"Who'd he talk to, besides Larry? And you?"

"You sound accusing."

"Questions needing answers. Did he talk to Philippe or Tess?"

"Why would he?"

"Philippe told me when I got my lunch the day you met me in the skate park that Eileen seemed to recognize a man buying flowers on Saturday afternoon—the day she was last seen. She seemed frightened by this man."

"Yeah? You didn't tell me this."

"The flower girl was vague, and I wanted Bellan to prod her memory."

"I talked to the Phony Frenchman a dozen times since then, he never said anything to me about Eileen being frightened in his shop."

It's hard to believe a man when you know he's lied about his entire past.

Dartagnan fidgeted his fingers. "And why would Bellan Thomas be talking to Tess?"

"I asked him to. Tess is lying about me."

"Tess ain't been in town much since you left."

"Any reason you know of?"

"Maybe it was something I said."

Amusing. "In Bellan's last report, he mentioned an open secret." Dartagnan cocked his head, looking both pleased and quizzical. I said, "Larry told Bellan a secret that isn't so secret."

"Sounds like that buffoon, Larry," he said. "What you don't know is that Larry was The Springs' biggest gossip. If he couldn't top you with the truth, he'd make something up. Don't put no stock in what he says." He got up. "You ready to ride to Arlo's?"

Standing, I said, "Sure."

As we walked outside, he said, "Now you follow my lead. Arlo's one of them funny guys. You know, arty. I can handle him.

He's gonna be pissed when I tell him about the Luminol."

"I'd be, too," I said.

Dartagnan guided the white cruiser onto North Via Las Palmas. The two-story pink stucco with the mission ridge roof and white plantation shutters looked gloomy. A discreet placard with "By Appointment" scribed in gold lettering was planted in the ground next to the security sign.

Before Dartagnan's finger found the bell push, Arlo stood in the doorway. He grabbed Dartagnan's shoulder with one hand, and then knuckled him in the ribs with the other. When the good ol' boy punching was done, he planted a kiss on my cheek.

Pure Hollywood.

"Boy, oh boy, oh boy," he said, shaking his head.

Boy, oh boy, oh boy, indeed.

I glanced around the foyer where Bellan had dropped Luminol in circumspect places. The foyer was lit by the chandelier, but Luminol doesn't effervesce for long. Before I looked away from the crystal fixture, I thought I saw a dull red blemish on a teardrop—blood blow from Eileen's head. This killer went for the head.

We wound through the house toward the French doors and went out onto the covered patio. The palm fans weren't revolving, the white wicker sofas looked faded and forlorn. There were crystal glasses and bottles of booze and ginger ale on the bar. What a difference a couple of weeks made. Cigarette and cigar butts loaded the ash trays. I guess Arlo had stopped showing the house.

Flipping on the fans, Arlo motioned toward the sofas. "I'm having rum and ginger ale. What about you?"

Dartagnan said, "Got a Heiny?"

"Miss Dru?"

"Dru, remember?"

He smiled. I'd forgotten the gap between his two front teeth. I grinned at his engaging smile. "I'll go with the rum, too."

After handing the drinks around, he sat and sighed. He gulped his drink, emptying half his tall glass. "Helluva thing," he said.

"How well did you know Larry Bell?" I asked.

Dartagnan huffed. I was supposed to stay mum.

"Pretty good," Arlo said. "I knew him to be a gent, and that's why I'd recommend him to people who needed his services. Mostly divorce work. Hell, in this town, you can get rich on divorce work alone."

"Larry didn't get rich," Dartagnan said.

"He did all right," Arlo said. "Maybe he had some habits that took up his dough, but if he did, I don't know about them." He downed the rest of his drink and rose to get another.

I avoided Dartagnan's stare and looked at the pool until Arlo sat back down. I asked, "Did you know that Eileen had a detective checking on Whitney?"

I became conscious of how ill at ease he really was. "Yeah," he said. "She told me. That's what the twenty-five Gs were for she took out of the bank."

Dartagnan said, "I'm in the wrong end of the business. That's rich."

"Out here, it ain't," Arlo said.

"You should have told me what the money was for when I was here," I said.

"Eileen was keeping the PI confidential. I went along."

"Did you know who this PI was?" Dartagnan asked.

"I recommended Larry," Arlo said, "but she got someone else, back east."

"Bellan Thomas," I said. "He—"

Arlo finished his second rum and ginger ale. "What was Bellan doing out here anyway?"

"I sent him."

"I don't get it," he said. "He was investigating Whitney—Whitney lives in Atlanta, and he's never been out here."

"Bellan was thorough," I said. "That meant he'd check upon Whitney's ex-wife, his own client. Bellan didn't tell me outright, but I think he'd contacted his buddy Larry here in Palm Springs. Larry knew about Eileen and Kinley, and that I'd been out here investigating their disappearance. I'd talked to several people, any of whom could have gossiped to Larry—including you."

Arlo shot me a gappy-toothed grin. "Barking up that tree, you're wasting your time. I haven't seen Larry Bell in a few months."

"When Eileen and Kinley went missing, didn't it occur to you to hire him?"

"Nope," he said, and then pointed to Dartagnan. "I got him, and he's all I need. He can't find them—they're hiding until they want to be found."

I glanced at Dartagnan, who failed in his attempt to look humble. I asked Arlo, "You still think Eileen took off?"

"Sure."

"And you don't know where?"

"I wish I did."

Dartagnan cleared his throat for attention. "With these two murders, we maybe ought to re-think Eileen and Kinley. Maybe something bad happened to them, and Bellan and Larry got onto it."

Arlo paled, making his caramel skin appear yellow. "I can't think about that."

Dartagnan's eyes shifted upward, to the palm fans overhead. I could read his thought. *There wouldn't be a better time to bring up the Luminol.* "Arlo," Dartagnan said, "I'd like to bring in some lab people and go over the house—"

Arlo raised his chin. "You done that."

"No. We looked around, but we didn't test for fingerprints or blood—"

"Blood? LeRoi, what the fuck!" His head snapped toward me. "Excuse me, ma'am. There's no fucking blood in this house." He appeared to accuse me.

Dartagnan's eyes settled on mine, but imparting this news was up to him. He faced Arlo. "You got to know this, Arlo. This man, Bellan, posed as a prospective buyer for your house. He came in with Luminol. He told Miss Dru that he got positives."

Arlo's eyes bugged. "Positives?"

"Luminol luminesces," I said.

"What's that?"

I didn't believe that a movie director wouldn't know that.

"Turns green when it hits blood," Dartagnan said.

"Aw, Christ sake, show me a house anywhere on the planet that ain't got blood somewhere in it, and I'll show you a brand-new house ain't ever seen humans, which ain't possible because men from Mars don't build the fucking things."

Imaginative.

Arlo got up and headed to the bar. Dartagnan followed, and put his empty bottle on the bar. The two men faced each other. Dartagnan said, "If there's blood, there's typing and DNA testing to be done."

"So what if the blood's Eileen's, or Kinley's? They live here for Christ's sake."

"Arlo, it's got to be done. If not by me, by the state or feds."

Arlo marched to where I stood—his face glowered into mine. "This Bellan—now I'm sorry as anyone the man's dead—but he had no right coming here, testing in my house."

"I know that," I said. "Bellan knew that. What he learned can't be used to get a court order, because what he did was illegal. But he reported to me what he'd done, and Dartagnan had to be told." I looked at the cop.

"So," Arlo said, easing away. "I don't have to do this—this Luminol thing?"

Dartagnan answered, "Not because of what Bellan found. But Arlo, I'm telling you, we didn't do a thorough search when Eileen went missing. Like you, I thought she'd turn up with the kid when the PI, who turns out to be this Bellan, got the material on Whitney."

Dartagnan hadn't meant to blurt the last sentence, and I eye-signaled him that I'd not missed what he'd just said.

Arlo's face was purple. "Keep your fucking mouth shut, Dartagnan."

I raised my hand. "Gentlemen. Once I learned Eileen was having Whitney investigated, it was obvious you people were waiting for the PI's results."

Arlo said angrily, "Don't go reading my mind."

"You won't admit it, and I understand why, but you knew that Eileen wasn't going to return Kinley to Atlanta."

He looked as if he were trying to figure out what I'd said. He worked his mouth over it for a while. "I didn't *know* Eileen was going to skip, but I'm not surprised she didn't send Kinley home." He took a handkerchief from a pocket and wiped his forehead and neck. "When Whitney called that Kinley wasn't on the plane, well, that's when I thought Eileen must have gone into hiding until she could get proof of what Whitney was. And that's just exactly what I told Dartagnan here."

Dartagnan nodded, keeping his eyes on Arlo while avoiding mine.

"So," Arlo concluded, "there's no need to nuke my house. Eileen'll be back once she learns her PI got killed. That should cast some doubt on that bastard Whitney and make you people in Georgia investigate him better."

"I don't think Eileen will be back. I don't think she's going to learn that her investigator is dead," I said.

Dartagnan said, "Arlo, there's a problem about this PI. Legal or not, he found blood in your house. He's told Miss Dru here." He looked at me. "You won't keep it quiet, will you?"

"No."

"Fuck," Arlo muttered. "Okay, so—spray my goddamn house."

Dartagnan seemed relieved. "It won't take long. We'll pick up the clean-up costs—using your maids if you want."

"I ain't worried about no goddamned clean-up costs. Listen, I'm leaving tomorrow, and I ain't coming back. Goddamn, fucking PIs. Got no business coming in here spraying all over the place. Now, you two get out while I'm still not mad!"

Not a bad get-your-ass-to-the-exit line.

When Arlo Cameron slammed the door on my butt, I said to Dartagnan, "I didn't get a chance to ask Arlo about being an extra in his movies."

Dartagnan's lips parted slightly. "What's that got to do with anything?"

I waited until he got the car started and heading down the street. "According to Bellan, Larry Bell said that most of the Indians and half the white people in town are hired as extras when he makes westerns in the desert."

"So?"

"Maybe nothing. You ever been an extra?"

"Maybe. What're you hunting for?"

"Answers."

"Ain't we all. Now, where you want to go?" He turned onto Ramon Road.

"Philippe's," I said. "But you don't have to come with me. Drop me at my car—"

"Where you go, I go."

"Where's Philippe from?" I asked.

Dartagnan frowned. "LA by way of Newark, I think. He says he's originally from Nice in France. Bullcrap."

"I can believe the Newark part. How long's he been here?"

"Don't know exactly. Arlo knew him in LA. He had the same kind of operation on Sunset. Arlo wanted him here, so he's here."

"Arlo set him up?"

"Probably bankrolled him, but don't quote me on that to the Phony Frenchman."

"I'm not without discretion," I said.

"I wonder about that. Discretion don't usually get people killed."

"And you're saying that I do?"

"Nothing like that at all. Just talking through my hat."

Forty-Six

Philippe was behind the counter at Too Busy To Cook? He bid a flamboyant farewell to a pretty young woman who lifted two shopping bags full of goodies and carried them to the door. Dartagnan held the door for her. I glanced over at the floral section. No attendant.

Philippe beamed down at Dartagnan. When he focused on me, he spread his arms wide. *"Mademoiselle."*

"Philippe," Dartagnan said. "How's bidness?"

"It excels." He pointed his finger at his neon sign. "Too busy to cook!"

"Never too busy to make money," Dartagnan drawled. "You remember Miss Dru?"

"I do," Philippe answered with a sweeping bow. "I am honored that you have called upon me once again, *mademoiselle.*"

"Thank you. I'd like to ask a question or two, if I may?"

"Oh, *oui. Je suis à votre service.*"

"I told you that I was on a mission when we met. Do you remember that?"

"*Oui.* I remember, *très bien.*"

"And I guess you found out what that mission was?"

"*Triste.* Your misfortunes in the endeavor to find Mrs. Cameron and her child. But so good that you lived through them."

"I'm still investigating Eileen Cameron's disappearance."

He looked quizzically at Dartagnan.

Dartagnan said through a grimace, "Me and her, we're in this together."

Philippe nodded. I asked, "You remember we talked about other things?"

"*Oui.* We conversed about many things." He smiled. "Sushi."

"Recall, you told me that Eileen saw a man buying flowers from your girl."

"That is correct, *mademoiselle.*"

"You noticed that Eileen seemed frightened?"

"Alarmed, *oui,* she was that."

"I'd like to talk to your flower girl."

"You would have to go to Los Angeles, *mademoiselle,* to talk to Nicole."

"She doesn't work here anymore?"

"A summer job. Back to school she goes."

"What school?"

Big Gallic shrug. "I did not hear."

"What's her last name?"

"Smith? No Schmidt."

"Where did she live in Palm Springs?"

"In an apartment not far from here, but I do not know exactly where." He looked at Dartagnan and spread his hands as if to ask, *Why all this?*

I asked, "Did she have any friends in town that you knew?"

"The young—they do not speak to old men."

Philippe was in his forties and attractive enough to interest young girls, if only for his personality.

Dartagnan asked, "Did a private investigator named Bellan Thomas ask you questions about Eileen and Kinley?"

"Why *non.* He asks about Nicole. I tell him what I tell you. He leaves."

"You know Larry Bell, don't you?" Dartagnan asked.

Philippe grabbed at his chest. "Ah! *La mort! Mon ami!* I cry."

Big tears rolled down his cheeks. *"Merde! Merde."* He picked up the hem of his apron and blew his nose. "My friend. The lonely one." He stopped blowing his nose and shook his head.

Dartagnan asked, "When did you last see Larry?"

"Ah, *mon ami,* Larry. He came in last week." He continued to sniffle. "He is, you know, without the family. He comes in one time a week, maybe two. I give him leftovers, just like I give to you." Dartagnan looked embarrassed; Philippe caught the look. *"Non, mon ami,* not leftover leftovers. I give wonderful food that I cannot bear to throw away. Bread a day old. Caramel rolls, so divine. Chicken salad and pea soup. He enjoyed my food."

"And he didn't have to go out and buy it, and prepare it," Dartagnan said, smiling. "Just like me."

"That is so," Philippe admitted. "I am forced to ask. What happened to Larry, and thees Bellan? They were shot, *non?*"

"Yes," Dartagnan answered. "They were shot."

"They were investigating together?"

I answered his question. "Bellan was working for me. Larry Bell was a PI Bellan knew from Alabama before he moved here."

"I remember," Philippe said. "The South accent, sooooo hard on the ears."

"Did Larry Bell know Eileen Cameron?"

"Surely, *mademoiselle,* this is The Springs."

"Did Larry ever talk about Arlo?"

"Not that I remember. But I think not. In his job, he was discreet."

"Well," Dartagnan said, "if you remember anything that might have anything to do with what happened to the two PIs, you know where to find me."

Philippe sighed and said, *"Certainment."* Then he brightened at Dartagnan. "You must come tomorrow at closing. I make wonderful escargots, and I save a dozen for you."

"I'll be here," Dartagnan said. "And I'll see you at the poker table."

I said, "When you have a minute, if you'd look up Nicole Schmidt's address in your files, or if she gave references, would you please call Dartagnan? I'd appreciate it."

"Of course, I will do that this evening."

We were leaving, and when I turned suddenly, Philippe looked as if he would pass out. "I'm sorry about your friend, Larry," I said.

Grimacing like a buffoon, he said, "And I am sorry for Monsieur Thomas."

We left him wiping his face with his white chef's apron.

My mind was on overload, the kind of overload that comes with exhaustion. The cool whites and tans of the hotel room promised a tranquil nap, and just as I was almost asleep, the telephone binged two staccato bursts. It was the concierge. He said he was sending someone up with flowers.

That uh-oh worm crawled along my spine. Opening the door to someone with flowers was not going to happen. "That's okay," I said. "I'll come down."

In the elevator, I reflected on who could have sent the flowers. Lake, of course. Who else? I lazed against the gold-tone wall and visualized his face—that beautiful face with the dark eyes that delved into my soul and the lips that gave me everything I wanted, and more. And how, when we made love, our need, so urgent and overwhelming, made us forget the sordid world in which we lived. Did I love him? Is there a word that transcends love?

An exquisite vase of deep red, perfect roses nearly overpowered the concierge's desk. He presented me with the card. My breathing ceased as I opened it.

It read: *To Miss Dru. Please accept my apologies for my behavior today. I was out of line. I would ask you to dinner but I am leaving tonight for Los Angeles. Good luck in your quest. Arlo Cameron.*

Arlo. Of course. *Silly me.* I turned for the elevator.

The concierge said, "Here, Miss." He came from behind his desk to hand me a gold box wrapped in blue ribbon. "This is for you, too."

The card with it read: *"The sweetness herein can't compare to you, and the blue ribbon is a poor imitation of your lovely eyes."*

No card. I asked the concierge, "Who brought the candy?"

"Delivery service," he answered.

"Which one?"

"Philippe's."

Flowers from Arlo; candy from Philippe. Dared I hope for balloons from Dartagnan?

In the elevator lobby, a marble-top mahogany table sat under a gilded mirror. Perfect. I placed the flowers on the table, rode up in the elevator, and threw the candy in a closet with firsthand memories of poisons.

Two minutes after I was back in my room, my cell played Mozart. The display read, "Lake." Tears slipped onto my cheeks. Damn. "Yes, Lake."

"How was the plane ride? What's been happening? You haven't answered your phone."

"I've been working."

"On who?"

"Arlo and Philippe." I gave him a thumbnail of the conversations.

"What's Dartagnan saying about Bellan and the PI out there?"

I told him.

"That's some stone killer, to sit there and take them out," Lake said. "You're a good shot. Could you pick off two men from four feet, sitting apart, in three seconds?"

"I've never been an Annie Oakley. But I bet you could."

"I got news."

"About Whitney?"

"I don't know."

"And?"

"You know the Chastain gay who got caught in the sting? Our entrée into The Cloisters?"

"Our sponsor?"

"That guy. Name's Risso. He got out on bond, and hung himself."

My shoulders tightened. "Oh, jeez."

"Yeah."

"You sure it's suicide?"

"Looks like it."

"But . . . ?"

"Easiest way to get away with murder is to strangle a guy with a rope, then hang him up with it. But you've got to know how to do it right with the rope and angles. Even with double rope burn it can be hard to tell. We'll see."

"Where'd it happen?" I asked.

"His house. Risso goes home to his million-dollar shack on Forest Overlook. Kisses the wife, plays with the dogs, feeds the fish, says he's going upstairs to take a nap since it's the first decent rest he's had in a while. Wife goes to the grocery. Three hours later she goes upstairs to check on him. Finds him hanging from a light fixture in the closet."

"What's she saying about his mood?"

"Says he wasn't upset. He was looking forward to getting back to his business."

"What about her as a suspect?"

"She's ten years older than the guy, and weighs ninety pounds. She'd need muscle to strangle a two-hundred-pound man. But we'll find out more about it."

"So our sponsor's dead," I mulled.

"Are you wondering how we're going to pay the piper?" he asked.

"If the piper has anything to do with his death, I don't think we'll have to," I said. "But that means no second invitation to The Cloisters."

"I talked to Risso before he got sprung. He got no bill nor feedback from White and his minions at The Cloisters. But he was signed on to continue his rehab starting next week."

"Has the news about his suicide hit the papers yet?"

"A reporter came nosing. Risso owned a bunch of franchises."

"Are they keeping his sex bust out?"

"Can't."

"So what's your gut telling you?"

"That you need to get back here. Or I need to get out there."

"I'm all right, Lake. I got Dartagnan as a sidekick."

"Then I definitely need to get out there."

FORTY-SEVEN

I showered and changed and walked the few blocks down Palm Canyon Drive to VillageFest. I was starving. At a fancy Nuevo Indian Cuisine stand, I bought two tacos: soft corn wraps filled with eggplant, cheeses, sun-dried tomatoes, and olives. Delicious. I walked down the middle of the street, looking left and right, eating from a paper wrap. Fortunately, I had several big napkins to wipe my arms with.

No Zing with his donuts. No Philippe with his sushi. No Tess with her exquisite weaving. The crowd wasn't as thick as it had been those many weeks ago. The summer tourists were back home, and it wasn't quite time for "the season" crowd to arrive.

I'd almost forgotten about the dark man when I saw him at an Indian jewelry booth. He averted his face and pretended to be intensely interested in a turquoise bracelet. Pitching the white paper in the trash containers, I zipped over to the booth. He'd caught my movement and ran.

"Wait," I shouted.

He looked over his shoulder as he sped away. People scattered. They looked at me like I'd been stalking a recalcitrant lover. But he was gone. I lurched away, back north, the way I'd come. Crossing the street, I ran to the Palkott. When I rounded the acacias, I slowed to a quick walk. The doorman doffed his hat and opened the door. In the lobby, I checked my cell messages. No one I wanted to talk to. I hurried to the side entrance and summoned the parking attendant and headed out to the Rosovo casino.

I knocked on the door marked PRIVATE. The hulk opened it. I think he remembered me. "I'm here to see Mr. or Mrs. Rosovo," I said.

"Who are you?"

"Moriah Dru." What more could I say?

He shut the door with a rude bang. I gave myself odds that he wasn't coming back, but in about a minute he opened the door and wordlessly waved me in.

"Miss Dru." Mrs. Rosovo came from behind her desk. On it, a financial ledger lay open. She had on oversize glasses.

"Thank you for seeing me," I said. "And I apologize for our last encounter."

"No need," the no-nonsense native woman said. "Please have a seat."

She went back to her chair, and I eased into the director's chair where Lake had sat.

"I haven't made inroads in my investigation into the disappearance of Mrs. Cameron or her daughter," I said. She stared without expression. "I went back to Atlanta and worked on other cases, and then an investigator came to my office."

She didn't bat an eye when I told her that Eileen had hired him. I told her that Bellan and I made an agreement, and that he'd come to Palm Springs in search of Eileen—where he was murdered.

"I know of the crime," she said, folding her calm brown hands on the lined pages. "I did not know why he was here working with our Larry."

"You knew Larry?"

"He works, worked, security for us during the season."

"Could Larry's work here be the reason the PIs were killed?"

Her eyes were like an owl's behind the glasses. "If Larry was working on something dangerous, I don't know about it. When he wasn't here working, or playing poker, he was doing divorce work. That was his mainstay. But understand, he did not name his clients."

"Divorce can be deadly," I said, and she agreed without words. "On the other hand, if Larry was helping Bellan find Eileen and her daughter, and if certain people didn't want them found—well—that could be deadly, too."

"I hadn't seen Larry for a couple days, which was unusual," she said. "He played poker here four nights a week. I asked a friend of his if he'd left town. It was this friend who told me that Larry was playing host to an out-of-town investigator."

"Who was the friend?"

"I, too, am discreet."

"I can understand that, but this—this is life and death." I hated that I'd sounded so melodramatic. "When you investigate a person or a situation, you don't have long before it gets out. You ask questions, you follow people. It seems Palm Springs soon learned why Bellan was in town."

"The Springs is a small world."

"So I've been told. Where can I find Tess?"

Her back went up. "Contessa is in the north."

"Where?"

"She's busy with her art."

"It's important that I talk with her."

"She does not want to see you."

"I'm not blaming her for what happened. That's over, but I need to know where to find a man named Ro-all, or something like that."

"Ro-all?" she said. Her mouth stayed open. Her steely nerves had given way.

"Do you know him?"

"That is not a common name."

"And that is not an answer."

She picked up a pencil and hit the eraser on the ledger, twice, three times. "What has this Ro-all to do with you?"

"You know that Lake and I were shot at when we were in the Adobe Flats."

Her head jerked back. "I discussed this with Mr. Lake. You should not have been there."

"But we were."

"It is a sacred place. It represents shame and grief from the days when our land was stolen from us."

"So you're saying that Ro-all fired a shot to warn us to get out of the Lost Coyote Canyon?"

"I don't know that he did, or did not. But you should not have gone there."

"I had to prove to Lake that I had been there the night I *supposedly* wandered off into the desert."

"Did you find your proof?"

"I found proof that Tess was there."

"What is this proof?"

"A single silver earring, with birds on it."

The unwitting glint in her eyes told me that she knew Tess had lost the earring, but she said, "She has many silver earrings."

"Doesn't it bother you that Ro-all and his companions tried to kill us?"

Smiling with her lips, but not her eyes, she said, "I will not be angry with you over your mistaken beliefs. Jimsonweed takes many months to leave the mind after it has left the body."

"My mind is fine. I remember you, and the moon ritual, and the young girl who wasn't Native American."

She stood and came around her desk. She perched one buttock on a corner and crossed her arms, trying to appear relaxed.

"We have many visitors during the moon ritual. You are mistaken in your thoughts. That is all I can say."

"I must speak to Tess."

"That is not possible."

"Bellan Thomas mentioned that people out here knew an *open secret*. Do you know what he meant?"

A smile twisted her mouth, and not pleasantly. "I imagine there are many secrets, whether open or closed."

"That have to do with this case?"

"I am tired of being questioned." She went to the door.

"Did Tess talk to Larry or Bellan about the Cameron disappearances?"

"She had no need to. Now, Miss Dru, *please*. I am sorry for your investigator. I am even more sorry for my friend, Larry. But we are not part of your problem, nor of your investigation. Please focus elsewhere."

"Tell Tess I must see her," I said as I was leaving. "Tell her that I know what happened at Arlo Cameron's house."

Those were my last words, said to a closed door.

FORTY-EIGHT

My plan had been to drive to Los Angeles the next morning, but Webdog told me that Arlo was booked on a morning flight to LA. So I was on my way to LA late in the afternoon. It may have been a fool's errand but I had a hunch. It even smacked of logic. I packed an overnight bag, tipped the valet, and headed west—keeping a watchful eye on my rear.

Mozart played on my cell, and I adjusted my headset. "Mr. Whitney," I said. "I'm in Palm Springs."

"Since when?"

"This morning."

"What's happening there?"

"Things progress."

"What, pray tell, is that supposed to mean?"

"It means I'm getting closer to finding your ex-wife and child. I can't promise—"

"What?"

"That they'll be alive."

"You'd better promise Kinley's alive. You'd better hope you find her alive."

"Is she alive, Mr. Whitney?"

Line dead. End of conversation. Poor Eileen—no hope for her from her ex-loving-husband.

According to MapQuest, Los Angeles was 107 miles from Palm Springs. Most of the drive on I-10.

Arlo lived in Hollywood, off Sunset Boulevard, in a 1930s

building that had been a hotel in the glory days but then slid into decline. In the 1980s, Iranians bought the building, gutted it, and constructed apartments that went for upwards of a million per eighteen hundred square feet.

I got to the Strip. Everyone knows it from the movies and television. It's every bit as tacky-chic as it looks on film. It also looks like it would be deadly after midnight. There's places in Atlanta like that.

Behind the Chinese Theater, Las Hernandos Condominium Homes climbed above the Strip. Arlo owned an apartment on the twelfth floor—the penthouse floor. He'd bought his place for eight million ten years ago. I reminded myself that Webdog insisted he hadn't hacked into Arlo's agent's computer, but he was circumspect about where the knowledge came from. I told myself I didn't need to know.

After scoping out Arlo's Hollywood digs, I drove down the neon Strip. My God, there was a smoking billboard. I braked so short the SUV behind me almost bumped my rental. A movie promo. I hate billboards.

My hotel, The Sunset on Sunset, is a boutique hotel, a renovated 1930s-something six-story, narrow in width, but long in depth. Its architectural style looked Moorish. Webdog boasted he'd found this "chichi place" in the heart of Hollywood. Surprising that a geek would know the meaning of *chichi*.

The Sunset on Sunset's revolving brass doors were one step up off the sidewalk—no lawn, no canopy, but a doorman nonetheless. Alongside the sand-colored building, a ramp led to an underground garage. No one was around, so I nosed the car downward. Concrete catacombs scare the hell out of me. I'd rather walk through a cemetery in New Orleans at midnight. The close-up slots were filled with Mercedes and Lexuses. I had to park hell-and-gone from the elevator. Hurrying across the stark gray concrete, my eyes and ears were tuned to the nuance of footsteps and shadows. I made it to safety in the lobby and considered my pulse rate. It wasn't one particular thing that made my nerves crawl outside my skin, either. So I blamed it on the static in the air.

"Miss," the concierge greeted me with a small salute. "We have valet parking for our guests. It's free."

Feeling stupid, I said, "Thanks, I didn't see your attendant outside. I'm a true believer in valet parking."

"Now you know," he said.

I smiled. "Now I know."

"A suggestion," he said.

"Lay it on me." I'd heard that in a recent film.

He said, "You won't be able to find a place to park around the hot spots. You can walk, or I can have a hotel car drop you off anywhere you want to go. No charge. When you want to return, give us a call. Number's on the desk in your suite. It must be before two o'clock, A.M. 'Course there's always taxis out after that."

I'd seen some of the hot spots. The Charnel House would not see the likes of me tonight. "Thanks," I said. "I just got off the road. I need sleep."

He looked like he needed sleep, too.

The elevator was a small cubicle, like something from a forties film with an operator. My room was on the third floor. The king bed summoned, but I needed a long bath first. Afterward. I fell asleep reading a book called *A History of the Garden of Allah*. I learned that there used to be a mansion at Sunset Boulevard and Crescent Heights that belonged to Alla Nazimova, a silent film star. She turned the grounds into a collection of cottages and bars and restaurants. The rich and famous flocked to Allah, but not before Alla went bankrupt and was reduced to living in a small room in her once-lavish mansion. So many Hollywood stories.

I'd forgotten to draw the drapes, and rays of the bright eastern sun fell upon my face. I rose feeling pretty good from the best sleep I'd had since I followed Lake from the downtown diner to where the third Suburban Girl's body had been tossed.

I pulled into visitor parking at Las Hernandos Condominium Homes and checked my watch for the twentieth time. Nine o'clock—the earliest one could pay a social visit in Atlanta. Probably too early in Hollywood, but if I had to wake up sleeping beauty, I had to. Arlo was taking the ten-fifteen A.M. flight out of Palm Springs. By some dodge, Webdog got the airline agent to confirm that Arlo Cameron was a passenger on the ten o'clock flight rather than the six A.M. I could have dropped a dime that he wouldn't be taking the six.

"Name please," the security guard's voice came through the speakers, coarse and tinny. He sat at a guard station between the outside doors and a wall of glass doors that led into the lobby.

"Moriah Dru," I said. "To see Tess Rosovo."

He looked at a roster, or pretended to. "There is no one on my list of tenants by that name."

"She is visiting Arlo Cameron." I spoke with emphasis. "It's her birthday. I want to surprise her." Silence, maybe head-scratching. I went on, "Tess is a friend of mine from Palm Springs. Actually, her Aunt Rosa is my godmother."

He said, "I don't have any notation on my board about a birthday party, or . . . What's your name?"

"Moriah," I said. "It's not a real birthday party. I plan to surprise her with this little present." I held up a tiny package—a large one might make him think of bombs. "It's a special memento."

"That's real nice, but . . ."

I interrupted, "Mr. Cameron said he'd send word."

"Mr. Cameron is due from Palm Springs at noon."

"Yes, on the ten-fifteen. I guess I'll have to wait until you get in touch with him."

He tilted his head. "You can wait inside."

The lock buzzed on the door, and it released. I placed the little present on the guard's desk and opened my purse to put my car keys inside, making sure that he saw nothing but a wallet and glasses and a few cosmetics occupying the little bag. Snapping the bag shut, I said, "Arlo . . . Mr. Cameron gives me parts in his movies when he shoots in The Springs."

The guard laughed. "I got me a part once. They needed an overweight, out-of-shape walk-on. Got to say a whole sentence."

"Arlo's put half The Springs in the movies."

He looked me over. "Moriah. That's a nice name. You got good hair and nice eyes. Tall, thin—I bet you look good on screen."

"I don't look the same. They darken my face and put dark contacts in my eyes and put me in a teepee with the other squaws."

He shoved a clipboard at me. "Sign in here."

I signed in.

"Apartment twelve-twelve," he said. "Doorbell's on the left." He released the lock on the wall of glass, and a panel slid open.

I gave a little wave. "Thanks, I can't wait to surprise Tessie."

I thought Tessie wasn't going to come to the door after three buzzes, and I got the feeling I was being stared at through a peephole head high. Then the door was flung back. A barefoot Tess stood in the entryway in a yellow sundress that looked like sunshine itself, her pretty face drawn together by hostility. No surprise.

269

"Can I come in?"

She took two steps backward, and I slipped past her. "How did you know I was here?" she said. "My aunt said—"

I held out the present. "This is for you."

She clasped her hands behind her back as if I'd offered a snake. "You didn't come all the way from The Springs to give me something."

I urged the packet on her. "It belongs to you."

She shook her head as if she knew what was in it, and her natural serenity had cut a swath through her hostility. "How did you know to find me here?"

"I found out where Arlo lives."

"Why would you think—?"

"You know the answer to that, Tess."

She looked at her feet and wriggled her toes. "He's—coming . . . on his way . . ."

"I know, and I want to talk to you before he gets here."

"I can't answer your questions."

"You have to. Let's sit someplace and talk." She led me into a hall. I asked, "Is Kinley here?"

She looked back, her face a sheen of perspiration. "No."

"Do you know where she is?" Tess shook her head no. "You're not a good liar, Tess."

She turned and spread her arms. She was frightened, but she looked like if I pushed her too far, she'd freeze up. That wouldn't get me much-needed answers. I said, "I'll only go as far as you let me."

"I do not kidnap children."

"Okay."

I followed her down three steps into a long living room. She sat on a red sofa draped with a striped serape the color of the sunset sinking into the sea. I sat on a chair at her side.

I'd have to initiate conversation, and there was no time for chit-chat. "I don't know that the law would consider a stepsister a kidnapper. It would depend on the circumstances." Her face looked as if it would crack into two ragged pieces. "Arlo's your father. Eileen was your stepmother."

"Who told you?"

"It wasn't Dartagnan," I said. "You've got Arlo's coloring. You have his eyes and his wide mouth, but your features are set in bones that make them beautiful. Beauty is a great disguise."

"My eyes? My mouth? This is how you come up with your conclusions?"

"Bellan Thomas. The name ring a bell?"

She shuddered and put a hand to her stomach. "He was killed with Larry."

"When Bellan last reported to me, your name came up, Bellan mentioned an open secret, without actually telling me what it was. But by that time, I'd guessed the truth. Arlo wouldn't or couldn't marry your mother, so she took you to El Paso, which is about fifteen miles up the road from Arlo's birthplace. She died, and you came back to your mother's people—and your father."

I wondered if it was resignation she swallowed. I asked gravely, "What happened that Sunday when Arlo came home and found Eileen dead in the foyer?"

Her body sagged back. "Arlo didn't have her killed, if that's what you're getting at."

"Convince me." I began opening the little package I brought.

"Arlo loved her."

"He loved a lot of women, including your mother."

"You are pitiless," she said, shaking her head."

"Murder is pitiless. Somebody killed Eileen on Saturday evening, or Sunday before Arlo came home. There's still blood in the house. The police and the FBI are going over the place."

"She lived there," Tess said. "She would bleed there."

"I think you know that the lab people are going to find a lot of blood in that foyer."

Tess rubbed her knuckles on the sofa fabric. "I know nothing." She glanced back and forth before her eyes settled on the hem of her sundress.

I said, "You made a mistake, didn't you, when you took me to the moon ritual? You didn't know that Kinley would be there. You thought she was safely behind the gates of your aunt's house, guarded by Dobermans."

She bit her lower lip and spoke softly. "No one believes you."

"When you noticed me scrutinizing the young girl in the wig, you poisoned me with your ring."

She sat straighter. "I do not poison people."

"Your ring—it scratched me."

She pulled the ring from her finger. "An accident. Here!"

I caught it and examined the onyx and turquoise. No prongs were misaligned. "Isn't the idea for a secret chamber, to keep it secret?" I said, handing the ring back to her. "I'm sure you gave me poisoned tea."

"Ha. You say I did not know the girl would be in the cabin. Why would I poison you before then?"

"To make me very sick. To make me go home. I'd been asking too many questions. Perhaps getting close to the answers."

Her soft mew gave her away. "I never poisoned anyone."

"But poisons are never far away, are they. Your people use poisons in rituals, to get high and to use as aphrodisiacs."

"No more than your people with their pharmacies. Besides, I saved your life that night."

"Yes, and you'll always be in my thoughts—no matter what happens." I tossed the unwrapped box on the sofa next to her. The box top, which I'd partially pulled up, came off.

She looked into the box and drew in a shivering breath. It was the single silver earring.

"What happened that night, Tess?"

She wiped away the wet on her cheeks. She shook her head, defeated. "I—I was in the casino very late after we had called off the search for you until morning. My uncle monitors the televisions himself sometimes. I was in the room with him. He noticed Rowall, a no-account thug that never had any money. Rowall was playing at the crap table, big time, which made my uncle suspicious. So he opened the microphone hidden under the table. Sometimes croupiers wear microphones. We heard Rowall bragging about a woman honeypot. He said a man paid big money to keep—to keep—quiet, so he was going to keep quiet, and keep getting more money. He mumbled about the best way to treat a woman was to keep her tied up and drugged." Tess looked at my shoulder, then above my head, at an arm, everywhere but my eyes. She said, "Rowall laughed, like it was a big joke. I suspected he could be talking about you. My uncle did not think so. He said the man was blowing smoke. Rowall had some creepy friends, mostly white trash. They were with him that night at the casino, and I'd seen them a couple of times hanging out at the Adobe Flats. They smoke dope and drink and take their whores there."

I nodded at her, that I'd seen the evidence. She continued, "Well, I slipped out of the casino, got in my Jeep—and I found you—tied up—drugged. But they were behind me."

"How did I end up at Adobe Flats?"

"When you passed out in the cabin, we called the rez ambulance. The attendants were found tied up in an arroyo."

"Rowall and his friends kidnapped me from the ambulance?"

Tess raised and lowered her shoulders. "It is what we assume."

"Any clue who the man is that paid big money to Rowall?"

"I have no idea."

"Dartagnan?"

She looked out the window and frowned. She shook her head and looked at me. "I don't know."

"Why didn't you tell me this in the beginning?"

"Because, I had to protect—I had reasons."

"You kept Rowall and his buddies busy, giving me time to escape. But how did you escape?"

"I know desert hiding places, and they were drunk and high, and slow."

"Where'd you hide?"

"Not far from Heart's Friend Rock." She said in an apologetic whisper, "It's a cairn. When the monsoon passed I walked home. My uncle has a Jeep like mine. I tried to find you. Then I saw the family who found you at the gold mine. You were going to be helped by them, so I went home."

"And your family made up a story."

"We thought it best to keep ourselves out of it, to protect—"

"Kinley. Where's Rowall and his friends?"

She rubbed her fingers together. "They were found shot dead in the canyon, the day after you and the policeman left for Atlanta. Dartagnan said it was a drug deal gone bad."

"It was Rowall who shot at Lake and I at Adobe Flats."

"The night before they were killed, I talked to Rowall at the casino. He said he was paid to shoot at you, to scare you away. He wouldn't say who paid; he said he got money for not saying."

"And a bullet for knowing. Where is Eileen buried? Where is Heart's Friend Rock?"

Her face flamed, and she jumped up. "You have to leave. Arlo will be home soon. I do not want to talk of this to him. He is very upset. Your Bellan invaded his home without his permission."

I got up. "Kinley has to go back to Atlanta."

"Why, so you can give her back to her pervert father?"

"What has Eileen told you about him?"

"That he is a pervert. He is not like other men."

"Has Kinley said anything?"

"She says he makes her feel funny." She was on her feet, at the steps of the sunken living room.

Sicko. "Has he molested her?"

"Kinley fears him, but she says not," Tess said, running up the steps. She turned. "Eileen promised her she didn't have to go back to Atlanta."

I walked up the steps to face her. "I'm going back to Palm Springs. Please get Kinley ready to travel."

I was the rock, pushing Tess against the hard place. She knew it, and her eyes teared. I wished I could let her keep the little girl. As she stood in the hall, near the door, her bare heels planted firmly on the hardwood, I could see her digging deep, finding strength. She said, "I cannot."

"You must."

"My stepmother, Eileen, put her in my safekeeping. I will not betray her trust. Kinley is a beloved sister. You, too, must trust me. Kinley is never going back to her father." She looked every bit a fearless Indian princess. "Tell that to your judge," she said.

"I found you here. Whitney will find you. She can't stay here."

"I told you Kinley's not here. No one will find her."

"I believe that you've hidden her well. The desert is vast and you have many trusted friends, but you must trust me, too, Tess. I'll protect Kinley. So will the judge. I can tell you this: Bradley Whitney is being investigated by my office and the Atlanta PD."

"Eileen told me her PI said he was onto something that would put Whitney *under* the jail."

"Did she tell you what it was?"

"Didn't the PI tell you?"

"He died," I said. I couldn't keep the bitterness from my

voice, even for a dead man I liked. "Holding out for fifteen thousand dollars."

"Don't you see? If nobody finds this damning evidence, Kinley will have to go back to live in his house. No." She stomped her foot. "Not as long as I breathe."

"If Bellan found something damning, I'll find it, too."

She flung open the door. "Go, then! Find it."

We stood just inside the door. "I'll be in touch. You can tell Arlo I was here, but don't tell him I tricked the guard. He's nice man doing his job, but I did mine better."

"I will not speak of this to Arlo. It makes him crazy."

"I'm sure. Does Kinley know her mother's dead?"

"Nobody knows that."

"Tomorrow, Tess. I take Kinley back to Atlanta with me."

I was getting used to doors closing firmly on my backside.

FORTY-NINE

I drove to Palm Springs a little too fast, too exhilarated. I love being right, as Lake will tell you. I get high on hunches going my way. I still had a long way to go, and I needed a plan that wouldn't get anyone else hurt or killed. These killers were stone-cold motherless bastards, hatched in hell. I didn't know how close Tess was to danger, but I did know her good heart could easily send her to jail. I admired her courage and knew that I would do the same thing—stand my ground and tell the sons-a-bitches to bring it on.

As for sons-a-bitches, Whitney'd rung my cell three times before I got out of sight of the HOLLYWOOD sign on the mountain. I ignored him. I hadn't the stomach to talk to him. I hoped Lake would call, but then again, was glad he didn't. He'd be like Portia, demanding a word-for-word report and an immediate plane ride for Kinley. Kinley was safe with Tess, I thought. If she'd been in that condo with Tess, they were both gone now. Tess would know many ways to Lost Coyote Canyon.

Time flowed like the road ahead, a road wet with mirage. The Mozart concerto played on my cell. I looked at the display. Portia. This was her third call in ten minutes. I let the concerto die because I didn't want to talk to her. There are few people I won't lie to. She and Lake head the list. Not answering her call, you might say, was lying by omission, but come on, that's picking the nit.

Once the cell stopped playing, it flashed in my head—

something was up. Portia wasn't one to tap out a number every five minutes. I grabbed the ear bud and hit dial-back.

"Porsh. You called."

"You heard from Lake?"

"Not since yesterday."

"Yesterday when?"

"Eight-thirtyish, eastern. What . . . ?"

"Lake's commander called."

"Why?" I pulled around a slow-moving car.

"Lake hasn't shown all day. He had an important task force meeting this morning."

My blood pressure dropped fifteen points. I didn't know it could be so cold. Lake never "didn't show," never missed a meeting with Commander Haskell, his rabbi and friend. "You ring his loft? Anybody go there?"

"Answering machine comes on. PD sent officers. No one."

Susanna. "Find his ex-wife. Linda Lake. She lives off Collier Road. Buena Vista. I don't know the number."

"APD knows it."

"Susanna, his daughter . . ." The pickup truck ahead of me was suddenly *there.* My shoulders snapped forward, and I slung my rental car around his truck. His horn blared.

"Moriah." I heard Portia shout through the earpiece. "Pull over."

I straightened. "I'm all right."

"No, you're not. Pull over."

"Get Webdog at my office. Tell him to get me out of here. I'll be at the airport in an hour."

"Finish your work there. The cops will find Lake."

"The Cloisters."

"The what?"

"Tell Commander Haskell. I don't know how much Lake reported about our visit there, but—"

"You and Lake went to The Cloisters. When?"

"Tuesday night. Guest night."

"And?"

"Lake got an entrée for us from a pedophile who was caught in a sting. Commander Haskell will know about it. The pedophile hanged himself. Name's Risso. According to Lake, he was an influential businessman. It'd be in the papers."

"Why am I doing this?"

"Bradley Whitney hangs out there."

"Did you see him?"

I thought about the woman wearing maroon lipstick with the familiar forehead and chin. "I don't know."

"Meaning?"

"I think he may have been in drag."

"Jesus."

"I can't be sure."

"How'd *you* get in? It's men only."

"They have women entertainers."

"You went as entertainment?"

"No. As a man. Porsh, please, get off the line and get Webdog to get me out of Palm Springs."

She clicked off, Portia style.

I called Whitney and got his voice mail. My ESP kicked in. I saw Whitney holding his cell, looking at the display with a supercilious smirk on his face.

The next few hours were, in retrospect, grainy, frozen impressions that kept me from drowning in fear and despair. I arrived at the Palkott and threw my things together. At the airport, I returned the rental and got to check-in. Having downed two straight gins in first class, I didn't notice the bumpy flight. I recall keeping my heart and mind devoid of emotion. I stared out the airliner's porthole and thought of myself as a staunch oak tree. Atlanta Police Academy training has its beneficial attributes for life after PD.

Webdog met me at the Atlanta airport. We drove straight to City Hall East. It was nine-thirty in the evening. Portia waited in Commander Haskell's office. No word from Lake, and they had no idea where Linda and Susanna Lake were. Commander Haskell explained, "The last anyone heard from or saw Lieutenant Lake was at three yesterday when he left here. We know he didn't go to Frankie's; they know him there. Linda Lake and her daughter have been gone for a week. Neighbors say it's unusual that Linda didn't tell them where she was going. She usually has them water the plants and take in the mail."

Portia sat in a straight chair, angled so that she could hold both my hands. I didn't want her to, but I let her.

"We've interviewed the manager at The Cloisters," Haskell said, drawing together his brushy eyebrows. "They have no knowledge of Richard Lake and a companion visiting there Tuesday night." It was evident Lake hadn't told his commander about our operation, and it was evident Haskell wasn't happy about it.

I said, "A man named White gave us phony names. Mr. Barton and Mr. Chapman."

"And you were sponsored by Casper Rossi, a member there?"

"That's what Lake told me, and he doesn't make stuff up."

Haskell almost smiled. "Rossi told vice it was a place for rehabilitation."

"Some rehab," Portia said, squeezing my trembling hands.

"How'd *you* get in?" Haskell asked.

"Disguise. Sircher's Contour Palace."

He couldn't keep from grinning. "I used to arrest Sircher when she gypped the gullible in her palmist days. After that, we had a few run-ins when she tried to establish an AC/DC whorehouse. Changed businesses before the pimps killed her."

"Sircher guessed I was going to The Cloisters," I said. "She must've opened her mouth about it."

Haskell pinched his lower lip between a thumb and forefinger. "Not much Sircher doesn't find out—but she wouldn't open her mouth unless she got paid."

"Blackmail," Portia said.

"It's not because of money they got Lake," I said.

"Who's *they?*" Haskell asked.

"Whitney and his associates at The Cloisters."

He sat back in his big brown leather chair. "Tell me about The Cloisters."

I smelled the stink of desperation seeping from my skin. "We need to find Lake."

"We have every man jack out looking for him. Tell me about The Cloisters."

I did my best to explain the evening. I ended by saying that Dr. Brommer, Whitney's boss at Curriculum Paradigms, Inc., seemed as much a part of the place as the lighting.

"But you didn't see Whitney?" he asked.

"Maybe," I answered. "I—encountered a woman there. One who was not part of the entertainment—at least she wasn't dressed like the dancers. The light was dim, and she was heavily made up. She was my height, like Whitney."

"Even if the woman was Whitney, we have no reason to go busting in there to look for Lieutenant Lake." He addressed Portia. "Would you issue a warrant on what we have?"

She looked at me. "Eat, drink, and be merry? You known damn well I couldn't."

I asked him, "You find Lake's car?"

He shook his head. "It isn't in The Cloisters parking lot. We're watching that place round the clock."

"What about Whitney? What's he saying?"

"Nothing—yet. He wasn't at The Cloisters—at least his car

wasn't, and White said he wasn't."

"He's there. Lake's there."

The lines around Haskell's eyes bunched. He said, "As an ex-cop, you know we make enemies. If somebody harmed Lake, and God forbid that's happened, it could be someone holding a grudge from ten years ago—someone who just got out of prison and just got access to him. We're looking into that, too."

Another devil's advocate. My words of protest stuck in my throat. My heart begged, *Lake. Please be safe.*

"Go on home. Get some rest," Haskell said. "I'll personally call you the minute we hear anything." He looked at Portia. "Maybe I can find a less exacting judge to get us in."

"Hope you do," she said, and squeezed my arm. Her deep empathy brought tears, and I rose and turned away before the commander saw gushers streaking down my face.

FIFTY

From my office window, I watched the dawn come up. *Red sky at morning . . . Moriah take warning.*

Pearly Sue came in at eight. She'd just flown back from Arkansas. I didn't want to talk to her. I wanted to sit in my chair and stare at the telephone, just as I'd lain in my bed and stared at the ceiling with my cell on my belly, until I couldn't stand it, and got up and got dressed and came here—to sit and stare at the telephone.

"Any word," she said, tossing her bags in a chair near my desk.

"No."

"Sorry, Dru. But I know Lieutenant Lake will turn up."

"You psychic?" I should apologize, but I didn't have the energy.

Pearly Sue meant well. Fortunately, she's literal and impervious to sarcasm. "My mama says I'm psychic sometimes," she said. I shook my head. "Maybe Lieutenant Lake went undercover?"

"Maybe."

"He wouldn't tell anybody if he did, would he?"

Me. But then, maybe *not* me. I hadn't been close to Lake since coming back from that dreadful time in the desert. *Close.* We'd lost that closeness. My fault, of course. The happy times I'd spent with Lake seemed wasted. I felt a fraud, a shell of a person, feeble of emotions, selfish and shallow.

Lake, please come back. Please be safe. Please be alive.

"Would he?" Pearly Sue persisted.

"His commander," I said. "I talked to him. Lake isn't undercover."

Pearly Sue's mouth turned down, a real female mime.

I asked, "How was Arkansas?"

She perked up and plopped into a chair. "Real interestin'. I found out Bradley Dewart Whitney was not like anyone I ever knew."

"Tell me," I said, staring at the phone.

"Well, I began at his school. He was in ninth grade in Little Rock. The first time he ever went to school. Can you imagine?"

"No."

"His ninth grade teacher is retired, but everybody knew where Miss Rory lived. This neighborhood is poor, but the people keep it up. You got to admire that when folks haven't got two nickels to buy bubble gum."

"Um-hummm," I said.

"You know, I never knew a lot about Arkansas. They're more like we are than I thought."

What, I wondered, had she thought the people were like: tiny and blue and naked?

"Well," Pearly Sue went on, "Miss Rory lives in this li'l ol' house three blocks from the school. She made me cake and tea. Isn't that nice?"

Pearly Sue's habit of slowly getting to the point was a good way to get answers, but she was driving me plain up the wall. "Very," I said. *Be safe, Lake.*

"We talked a long time about Bradley. She said he was never Brad, or Braddy, but always Bradley. If someone shortened it, he'd look at them with his gray eyes and correct them. They never did it again, Miss Rory said. She said with his ways, he had no boy friends. But he could sure turn on the charm with the girls when he wanted to, she said. Well, you know, Miss Dru, he *is* good-looking."

"Maybe." *In a slimy sort of way.*

"Then Miss Rory says one day he asked to stay after school. He made up something, she didn't remember what. But she thought it was fake, and she didn't know why, but she didn't want him staying. She says by that time she got funny feelings about him. Anyways, he stays and he keeps watching her. He doesn't do nothing, just sits at his desk with his hands folded, looking at her, staring and staring. He just keeps watching until she's about to jump out of her skin. Then he gets up, and says, 'You're a sport, Miss Rory, a real sport.' " Pearly Sue looked at me with her head tilted. "What do you make of that?"

"What did Miss Rory make of that?"

"She was glad when he moved on."

"Taking control," I said.

"What?"

"That's what he was doing, Pearly Sue," I said wearily. "Taking control."

"Well, later he *had* control."

"Who says?"

"His gym teacher, Mr. Tanner. He's still teaching at the school."

I glanced at the telephone. "What's Mr. Tanner got to say?"

"Bradley was good at sports, but there was something about him that Mr. Tanner said was odd. He thought Bradley would be a better ballet dancer than a basketball player."

"He was years younger than the other boys."

"Mr. Tanner said he seemed older than the other boys, more mature. I came right out and ask him if he liked Bradley and he said, 'No, I did not.' But he wouldn't say why not."

"Did Mr. Tanner know what happened to him after high school?"

"He said he didn't, but I knew he was holding back on me. I kept asking more and more, and finally he told me that one time he was searching for a truant boy in a bad neighborhood—drugs and sex and stuff like that—and there was Bradley, walking along like he owned the place."

"And? Did Mr. Tanner see where Bradley went? Who he met?"

"Nope. He said he just passed him by. But he remembered, because it was odd for a snob like Bradley to be down there. He never did drugs, or drink, that Mr. Tanner knew about."

"Did you go to that neighborhood?"

"I surely did. But it was no use. Urban renewal. They tore down all the projects and built a fancy place called Broadhurst Village. It's a place where there are shops, and restaurants, and a hotel, and high-rise condos. Very 'in.' "

"Did you get anything from the Bradley's uncle's neighbors? What's the uncle's name?"

"Uncle Ted. An old man named Mr. Petri lived next door to Uncle Ted when Bradley lived with him. Mr. Petri had his eighty-ninth birthday last week."

"Good for him. Is he reliable?"

"Sharp as you and me."

"Okay, what's Mr. Petri saying about Bradley."

"He said the uncle called the kid Dewey."

"His uncle called him Dewey? For Dewart?"

"I guess."

"I thought he didn't like nicknames?"

"He didn't when he was in school," Pearly Sue said. "Anyway, Mr. Petri said his wife was laid up with arthritis and Dewey would come and do for her until she died. He didn't go to school then, because Uncle Ted said Dewey was smart enough, he didn't need to. Well, Mr. Petri's wife had a little money she put under a mattress. When she died, it wasn't there. Mr. Petri said Dewey stole it. He called the police, but they couldn't

286

prove it. Before all this happened, though, Mr. Petri and Uncle Ted were friends, and Uncle Ted told Mr. Petri that Dewey had one goal in his life: that was to get all his brothers and sisters together again, out of poverty. Then Uncle Ted died, and Dewey goes to the state to become a ward. Mr. Petri didn't hear nothing until years later when the police came asking about a brother of Dewey's."

I asked, "Name of the brother?"

"Mr. Petri couldn't remember. I thought it might be important, too, and I stayed there and drank cider till my kidneys was about to explode trying to help him remember, but all he kept saying was that the police wanted to know about a brother, and where they could find Dewey. Mr. Petri said he was against the police, and wouldn't tell them what little he could. The police let on like it was about a robbery."

My interest was piquing. "Did Mr. Petri tell you what he'd kept from the police?"

"That he knew where Dewey was from originally, because Uncle Ted was bald and the place was in the mountains. Bald Mountain."

I had to laugh. "So you went to Bald Mountain. Who'd you talk to there?"

"The county sheriff and some people in the café. They remembered the family, and the bloody fight. They weren't Whitneys back then. The sheriff said he heard tell some changed their names when they left, but they were born Whiteys. The dad was Earl Whitey."

Whitey? Mr. White?

After a short breather, Pearly Sue went on, "The sheriff said when the retaliation killings happened, the young-uns scattered to the four winds. The only one he knew about was the sister. She moved to Missouri, across the border."

Missouri.

I'd gotten into the story of Bradley's background, and forgotten for a brief time about Lake. When the cell played the concerto, I grabbed at it.

"Yes."

"Dru, it's Haskell."

"Bad news?"

"I don't have any news about Lake, but Linda Lake and her daughter are fine. They're up in Tennessee with relatives."

"Has she heard from Lake?"

"Last she heard he called last Sunday night and told her to take a little vacation with Susanna because he was involved in an unpredictable case."

Lake believed in the man in the stands after all. Lake, please be safe.

"That case is the Whitney case, Commander Haskell."

"Something else," Haskell said. "Remember the man who was blown up in your car?"

My heart shifted against a rib. *Don't let Lake be found in his car, blown up.* "Brody McCracken."

"We got the DNA results. He killed the Roswell and Dunwoody girls."

"The gods of justice acted swiftly."

"I'm as religious as the next man, but I'm not blaming the gods. At first it looked like he blew himself up setting the bomb for you. But the medical examiner found alcohol, cocaine, and potassium chloride in his blood. The latter did him in." I felt another rib stab. Haskell continued, "We found a diary in McCracken's home. He often refers to 'a place of refuge and recovery.' He writes that he failed the courses."

"Failed the courses? The Cloisters."

"His jottings are mostly nonsensical. They could mean anything."

"Have you found out who really owns The Cloisters—the

288

straw man's real name?"

"I don't know any more than you and Lake found out. But we will."

"Look at that membership list."

"Easier to get a list of Augusta National's members."

How was I going to get the APD off its collective ass and get in there? "Look Whitney's child is missing. Why can't we get inside his house, at least?"

"We went in when he reported the child missing. Invited by him. He let us look around. The Cloisters's different."

My spirit felt like a ragged sail on a sinking ship. "He lied about where he's from. He lied about his parentage." I briefed him on Pearly Sue's findings in Arkansas. "He changed his name from Dewey Whitey. Why?"

"It isn't a crime to change your name. It isn't even a crime to lie."

"It is if you're defrauding someone or impeding an investigation. The greeter at The Cloisters is a Mr. White."

"Hardly an uncommon name."

"Taken with the other facts—"

"Dru, I've talked to our lawyers. Without *hard* evidence that links Whitney's life and background with The Cloisters, and with Lake's disappearance, we can't get into that place."

"Risso got Lake into The Cloisters."

"He got you, too, and you're not missing. I'm sorry, Dru."

"He's got Lake. I know it."

"If Whitney's such a genius, he knows better than to mess with a policeman, a detective lieutenant who's investigating his case. So my advice—hang tough. We'll find Lake."

I'll find Lake. Alive.

At the outset of my conversation with Haskell, the office land line rang and Pearly Sue left to answer it. Now, having disconnected from Haskell, I sat back, my mind whirling on what-ifs. I wanted desperately to reverse time, feeling that my internal moorings were about to come loose and the only antidote for my sorry state of mind was action. I eyed the cell. *Play the concerto, damnit!* Then I heard Pearly Sue's voice blare down the hall. "My Lord-a-mighty!" Pearly Sue spoke in exclamation points.

I got up, stepped to her office and stuck my head in the door. She spoke into the phone, "I cain't tell you how grateful we are!" She scribbled on paper while she gulped out *What?*s and *Oh really!*s and *Good!*s. Finally, she sat back and finished the conversation. "I'll mail you a check. Right this minute. Oh, yeah. Monday, first thing."

Slamming the phone and swirling her chair to face me, she yelled, "Bingo! Mr. Petri remembered! He said he worried on it, and then he talked to a woman who was a neighbor before she went into an old folks' home! He went to visit her. They talked and remembered."

"You tell him you'd pay him to remember?"

"Yeah," Pearly Sue said, her eyes shifting across my waist. "He asked. He's poor."

"People will lie for money."

Pearly Sue's slim hands twisted together. "I'm—I'm really sorry if it's against the rules."

"It's not. And sometimes we have to go by our instincts. You got good ones. Now tell me what Mr. Petri remembered."

"Bradley's brother's name was Harry. Harry Whitey. The woman remembered it was the FBI that came to talk to Mr. Petri."

"What did the FBI want Harry Whitey for?"

"Mr. Petri thought that they wanted to talk to him about the armored car robbery."

"Did the FBI tell Mr. Petri this?"

"No, but it was just a week after the robbery that the FBI came. The news was all over the TV. Mr. Petri said the robbers shot the guards and stole the truck. It was abandoned and set on fire."

I thought about this. Were two old people giving free rein to imagination for money? Or were they telling the truth?

Pearly Sue said, "Mr. Petri said that since the police wouldn't do anything to Dewey for stealing his wife's money, he had decided not to cooperate."

Giving her a big smile, I said, "I guess you know what you and Web investigate next?"

"Dope on armored car robberies."

"Got it in one."

FIFTY-ONE

Castleberry Hill looked as desolate as I felt. I hadn't been here since a killer blew himself up in my car. I parked the Bentley on the street in front of Lake's place. There wasn't a soul out. I looked up to the third floor. The high, industrial-paned windows were raised. Green curtains flapped outward. I didn't want to go inside. Not because I might find Lake a victim of homicide or a heart attack—the cops already had been over the place—but the recollections . . . I didn't want to cry that much.

I pulled the bell and looked up with the futile hope that Lake had come home unaware that everybody in the city was looking for him. Some idiot once wrote about hope springing eternal and this idiot believed in it.

Nothing had changed in the hall but the smell. It was hot and stunk more than usual. Black garbage bags sat under the mail table. It was fastidious Lake who usually took them to the Dumpster. Upstairs, I heard a door screech open. Footsteps descended. Then a black face peered around the landing.

"Morning," Lou said. "Haven't seen you in a while."

I wondered if Lake had confided the reason for my absence. Probably not. Lake wasn't the confiding type. "Working a case," I said, climbing the steps.

"Lake said you been in California."

"Lake's missing," I said.

He bowed his head to acknowledge that he knew. "He's okay, Dru. I know it. I can feel it in these bones."

"When did you last see him?"

"I told the police. It was Thursday afternoon."

"What time?"

"Uh, 'bout three. He came home same time I did. We got our mail. I said, 'You're knockin' off early. Holiday? No murders today?' Lieutenant Lake laughed and said, 'Murder never takes a holiday. Neither do I.' "

"Three in the afternoon?" I said. "Lake never gets home before nine or ten at night."

Lou scratched his head. "He didn't say why he was home so early. He seemed, oh, how should I say it, like the Cheshire cat."

"Big smile?"

"No—like the cat that ate the canary. I got cats on the brain. I feed his cats—now you're not around so much."

I was in no mood for self-reproach. "Was it about a case?"

"If it was—he didn't say, but yeah, that's how he looked. Like he was getting ready to pounce on the suspect. You know that look."

I sure did. "The cops take anything away?"

"Not that I saw. I just let them in."

I turned my key in Lake's lock, then looked back at Lou, who stood on the threshold. "I'm going to find him."

He grinned. "I would, too, if I was you. Man loves you like that, you don't let it ride."

"No."

Sensing that he wasn't invited in, he gave me a thumbs-up and turned away. I flipped on the big fans, sending the motors roaring, the blades spinning. I gave a quick look into the bathroom. Neat, nothing out of place. In the kitchen, a donut bag lay in the wastebasket, a quarter of a peach pie the sole occupant of the fridge. Lake and his sweet tooth. Sickening anxiety rolled through my solar plexus.

The oriental screens weren't disturbed. I had a sense of Lake in the place, but no sense that something awful happened here. The big screen of the TV was as black as my spirit. Susanna's room was just as she'd left it, bed piled high with dolls and stuffed animals. Thank the Lord she was safe in Tennessee.

I sat in the old commander's chair. The mail and papers on the desk were scattered. The cops had gone through them. I did, too. Nothing pertinent. Bills, invitations to club openings, tickets to the Policeman's Ball. *The Policeman's Ball.* I couldn't stop the tears then. We always went. Lake could flat dance.

I stepped around the last screen, the one into the bedroom. I stared at the brass bed and didn't bother wiping the tears that bathed my face. Through them, I realized something. The covers were rumpled, but Lake always made the bed neatly when he got up. The rumpled bed meant that Lake had taken a nap. He did that when he was going somewhere in the night. Automatically, I straightened the bedcover, pushing the duvet under the pillows. My hand touched high-quality papers and envelopes. I knew what they were.

Lake damnit, why didn't you tell me Thursday night when you called me. *When I find you—Lake, I'll get you for this.*

The embossed invitation read: *To Mr. Barton: Thursday evening, 9:30* P.M., *casual (but elegant) attire.* There was a letter with the invitation, having a signature of sorts. A single ornate *R.*

Rossi. Our sponsor.

Rossi had written: *"Detective: I'm out of jail. I'm pleading to lesser charges, thanks to my cooperation with you. Hopefully, I can get my life back to normal. Enclosed is a second invitation to the club. Good luck. I hope it can help you more than it did me. Keep your Kevlar on. R."*

"Meet me at The Tavern at Phipps Plaza," I said to Whitney.

"Miss Dru, this is rather short notice."

"It's important."

"You know something?"

"Yes."

"Why can't you tell me over the telephone?"

"I don't want to."

"You're getting on my nerves, but all right, I'll be there in an hour."

Phipps Plaza is a ritzy mall. On Saturdays most malls are noisy, bustling places. Not Phipps. The wealth that shopped at swanky places like Saks, Armani, Versace, Gucci, and Tiffany did it with quiet dignity. I passed Williams-Sonoma and remembered the time I bought Lake a chrome paper-towel holder for his birthday. I think it was the unexpectedness that brought on his giggles. *Christ, these memories.*

My heels clicked more quickly across the marble floor.

The Bar Room and Grill is open-fronted. Chain railing kept the tables from slipping their borders into the mall itself. At midafternoon, the bar and restaurant had few diners and drinkers. Whitney sat at the bar. He picked up his drink, something white and fizzy, and glided toward me wearing pricey casual clothes and tight lips. He waved toward an empty booth. I slid across the leather, and he scooted in opposite me.

"You missed the excitement," he said.

"Oh?"

"Heather Martin, the CNN cutie, just left. She had the men drooling."

"Too bad I missed her," I said, and then joked, "I adore putting blondes to shame."

Why was I in a joking mood? And why had I brazenly begged a compliment?

His gray eyes squinted. "You could easily put her to shame. But on a better day. You look tired, defeated. Are you defeated?"

"No," I said, jutting my chin.

"Want something to drink?"

"Amstel Light, tap."

The waiter set my beer on a cocktail napkin, served another mystery drink to Whitney, and placed a basket of tavern chips between us.

Raising his glass, Whitney said, "To you and to your weary endeavor. Now, where's my daughter?" He set the glass back on the napkin.

"In California."

"Where in California?"

"The desert."

"With Eileen?"

"Eileen's dead."

"Who's got Kinley then?"

"I'm not going to tell you, although I believe you know."

His eyes were cold stones. "I think we'd better have a talk with the judge."

"We will, eventually."

He balled his fist. "Now."

"You don't deserve to have your daughter."

He looked at my throat as if he could gleefully slice it, so I spoke before he could. "Aren't you curious about what happened to Eileen?"

"*If* she's dead, where's her body?"

"Buried in the desert."

"Who killed her? Why?"

"Did you know Eileen hired a PI to investigate you?"

He lifted his eyebrows. "She was having me investigated?"

"She wanted to get Kinley back. Did she have a chance?"

"I told you. Eileen was an unreconstructed drug addict."

"I'd like to talk about conflicting schemas now." He slanted his head; the lids of his eyes lowered, giving him a guarded appearance. I sipped, put my beer down, and said, "Your name was originally Dewey Whitey." His face became a bunker of ice. "You went triple-barrel. Gave yourself Bradley, changed Dewey to Dewart and Whitey to Whitney." His eyes were the slits in the bunker. "Pretentious, don't you think?"

His mouth hardly moved. "So what?"

"We talked to your teachers and neighbors in Little Rock, and people who knew your family up in the hills."

"Again, so what?"

"After your Uncle Ted died, you asked the state juvenile court to change your name. Why?"

He traced the rim of his glass and let his mouth thaw. It seemed more time went by than really did before he said, "Dewey is a white-trash name. Whitey is a name blacks use pejoratively. Imagine a black family with the N-word as a last name."

"You graduated high school when you were fifteen. Came to Atlanta when you were eighteen. Went to college. Worked in strip clubs."

"So Eileen's PI found out about my sorry background—one I've shed."

"Why strip clubs?"

"Why do you want to know?"

"Curiosity."

His bunkered eyes cut across my face. He said, "I was broke. I had no one. I needed money instantly. I was going to the university. Georgia State isn't Harvard, but it costs money. A lot—when you haven't any." He took a sip of his drink, and picked up a chip. Not to eat, but to flip across the table. Every gesture conveyed cold anger.

"You still strip?" I asked.

"Don't be an ass."

I fiddled with the damp napkin under my beer. "Stripping isn't against the law. You needed money."

"You think Portia Devon would take Kinley away from me over that?"

"No."

He emptied his glass and signaled the waiter with a gesture so elegant—even though he was seething—that it was hard to believe this man was born in the backwoods.

I asked, "Where did your money come from?"

If he could have zapped me with an ice wand, he would have. "I invested my leftover lap-dance cash in the stock market."

"Enough to buy you a house that cost millions and a car that cost more than most homes?"

"You know about my car?"

"The one that isn't a Honda?"

"Where are you going with this?"

"What were the names of your brothers and sisters?"

"Don't you know?" he asked, as the fresh drink was put in front of him.

"One was Harry."

He flinched and his lips flattened. But he could recover quickly. "Yes, there was Harry. But first, there was Earl, Junior, who was called Sonny. Harry came next. Then there was Clete, then Barney, then Tami, then Frieda, then Jasper, then Eula, then me, and lastly, the baby, Angel. Angel died in our mother's arms. Her throat had been shot out, right before the bullet pierced our mother's heart."

"You saw it?"

"From the front porch of our shack, yes."

"What was the feud about?"

"Daddy didn't want their hogs dirtying up our water."

"Later, somebody burned the people's house down, with them in it."

"Everybody lived in drafty shacks. Many burned down." He shrugged, and, if anything, his eyes got colder. "It happens."

"Once you went to live with your uncle, did you keep up with your brothers and sisters?"

"As much as a kid can."

"Where'd everybody go?"

He tapped his finger on the table. "Here and there."

"New York? Miami? Across the state line to Missouri?" My reflexes tightened in case he sprang. "Says on your Georgia State résumé that you were born on Long Island, New York."

His eyes slid to his tapping finger. "It was all part of reinventing myself, of doing away with Dewey Whitey—white trash from Podunk, Arkansas."

"Which sister went to New York?"

"Tami."

"She still alive?"

"You know the answer."

"She's in a mental institution. Pretty young for that, isn't she?"

"One of those unfortunates."

"Who went to Miami?"

"Frieda."

"Who moved to Mountain View?"

"Ah, that was Eula, a country girl at heart."

"Did you know that Eula and her husband are dead?"

"I heard."

"Harry wound up in Little Rock, didn't he?" Whitney's eyes were showing too much white. I liked the bunkered look better. I said, "As the second oldest child, he would have been old enough to be on his own when your folks died."

"I don't know where Harry went. He's dead now. Died in New Orleans."

"The FBI wanted to talk to you about Harry and about an armored car robbery. Did you know that?"

"I have no idea what you're talking about."

But he did, and I could see it when his eyes slid to glance at his watch. He glanced back at me, defiance in his smirk.

I said, "I'll enlighten you. You made the mistake a lot of smart people do. You think people around you are blanks, amoeba sucking up air without knowing why. But your Uncle Ted's neighbor in Little Rock wasn't a blank. He had a good memory, and he had a grudge against you for stealing his dying wife's mattress cash."

He gave a quick shake of his head. "I was just a kid. I took her money. I felt bad about it, but I couldn't admit it. It was unthinkable to."

"And Harry?"

"He was ten years older than me. But I don't believe Harry would rob anything." He stared at me for several seconds. "It's obvious where you're heading. Let me save you some verbiage. I did not kill Eileen. Her private investigator couldn't unearth anything to take Kinley away from me, even stealing fifty-five dollars from under a mattress when I was ten years old."

"Do you own The Cloisters?"

His locked jaw gave him away, but he wasn't going to answer directly. "Is my name on record?"

"Manuel Strah," I said. "Straw man."

"Clever."

"What's the purpose of the club?"

He picked up his glass and sipped the clear liquid, his pinkie raised as if to shield his eyes. He placed the empty glass on the napkin. "It's for men who need a place to call their own. I'm not against women's company, but sometimes a man needs a place of refuge." He signaled the waiter for the check.

"Refuge?"

'It's a complicated world. Can we get back to what happened to Eileen and Kinley?"

"Eileen was shot in her doorway. She'd already sent Kinley

away. You're right about one thing. She wasn't going to send Kinley home, but she didn't take off with her."

"Then Arlo has Kinley. That makes him a kidnapper. He'll go to prison."

"Eileen was waiting for news from her PI that would change custody."

Whitney flipped a hand. "Miss Dru, I can compel you to tell me where Kinley is. The judge might be your friend, but she's got to abide by the law."

"Oh, I forgot to mention. The PI Eileen hired is dead." His eyes said so what? I said, "Shot. Murdered. In Palm Springs."

"What was he doing in Palm Springs? I'm here. I've never been in Palm Springs."

I didn't believe that, and I let my doubt show by raising my eyebrows and leaning my head toward my left shoulder.

The waiter brought the check.

"One more thing," I said. "I'm looking for a friend of mine. An Atlanta cop named Richard Lake."

He shook his head. "I'm supposed to know where your fucking friends are? We've been all over the map—with people I barely knew."

"You know who Richard Lake is. He was investigating The Cloisters. He followed the deed trail from here to New York, to Miami, to Mountain View."

When you can't get away from a fact, don't say a word, act like you haven't heard it. Whitney signed the credit card receipt in a cone of silence.

I said, "Two recent homicide victims have a connection to The Cloisters."

He frowned. "And who might these unfortunates be?"

"A man named McCracken and another named Rossi. The funny thing is, they were predators themselves. McCracken killed little girls and Rossi molested boys."

"I have no knowledge of those men or their activities."

"You believe in coincidence?"

"I believe anything that can happen will happen and does happen. Now, Miss Dru," he said, rising, "I must end this mystifying session. I will give you until Monday morning, eight o'clock, to tell me where I can get my daughter, or I will have my lawyer file charges of false imprisonment, abduction, restraining a minor—and whatever else he can think up."

He followed me out into the mall and started to stride away. I seized his arm, something I've rarely done. He jerked to face me. I said, "If you don't let Lake go, or tell me where he is, and *right now,* I'll go to the university and lay out the story of your life. Oh, and that armored car robbery in Arkansas—it happened during the period after you left high school and before you arrived in Atlanta."

He got puffed and venomous like a cobra whose basket had been kicked open. I was glad he didn't have a knife up his sleeve. "I don't have Lieutenant Lake, Miss Dru."

"*Lieutenant Lake.* You know his rank. You also know where he is."

"I don't. I'll prove it. Come to The Cloisters with me."

I thought I'd never get him to say those words.

FIFTY-TWO

I followed Whitney's Mercedes. I'd smirked at seeing it in the underground garage five cars away from my Bentley. I said, "I'll follow your *Honda.*" His snake eyes didn't shift. When he saw my Bentley, he looked like he could strike.

I'd trailed Whitney to Piedmont Road when my cell played Mozart. I got the earpiece in. "Web, what's up?"

"Got some info on the armored car heist."

"Go on."

"Harry Whitey was an employee of the armored car company."

"You didn't bust into their computer file, did you?"

"Nope, talked to an FBI guy in Little Rock who worked the case."

"I like conventional."

"I had to provide bona fides. He wanted the nexus. I told him our kidnapping case led us to Harry Whitey. He apparently checked our shop out with the local feds, because he called me back and gave the load. Harry was a popular guy, gung-ho in the job, and in two years he got to be a money-packer. They do this under the eyes of armed guards. Then Harry took to drinking with the off-duties. The two guards that were killed were his good buddies, everybody said. After the job, everybody's looking for Harry Whitey to give him the bad news. No Harry. Then it's obvious. An inside setup—with everybody's pal as the killer."

When Whitney made the turn onto Cheshire Bridge, through

the darkened window I saw him holding his cell phone to his left ear.

"Then," Webdog went on, "Harry's body turns up in a fire in New Orleans with a few hundreds and a one-way ticket to Rio under it. The cash was banded and marked with an SCC, the name of the company."

"But there were two gunmen."

"That's right. Harry had a pal named Dewey. He kept turning up at the bars, listening to the talk. The Fibbies discovered this pal was his brother and went looking. Never found him."

"He'd changed his name at the time he enrolled in high school. After he graduated, apparently it was necessary to use Dewey again. When he came to Atlanta, he was back to Bradley Whitney."

"I had to give that information up. Hope you're okay with it."

"The Atlanta FBI will be calling soon. Tell them all you know about Whitney and call Commander Haskell with this latest. Tell him I'm following Whitney. We're going to The Cloisters. Whitney says he has something to prove."

"I don't like hearing that."

"If Lake isn't there, he's dead."

"I hope he's there. Are you carrying?"

"Sure am."

The same tall butler dressed in livery let us in. "Good afternoon, Mr. Whitney," he said, ignoring me.

"Good afternoon," Whitney said. The rotunda was gloomy due to the afternoon glance of the sun through the high windows. The winged Eros surrounded by his devotees made me want to throw up. Whitney clasped his hands behind his back like a museum guide, and said, "The Greek Eros, the Roman Cupid, rose out of the Chaos with Gaia and Tartarus.

Some say Aphrodite and Ares are his parents. Not true. But he is associated with Aphrodite, and his most avid followers were duplicates of himself: the Erotes. One wonders why he never grew up."

"One wonders," I said as we moved into the bar. Two men sat together, drinking silently. They looked up, and their mouths froze open from the shock of seeing a woman.

Whitney said, "As you can see, no Richard Lake in here."

In the dining room, the tables were dressed with linens and white flowers. The atmosphere was subdued, as if it knew there would be no more patrons. Something had happened there—to Lake. Prescience made me tense, but often kept me alive. We walked through two administrative offices and arrived at the door of the smoking room. *It's now or nevah* stuck in my mind. When I walked in beside Whitney, eyes averted. The men busied themselves reading, napping, looking at nothing. The Orson Wells look-alike came up and bowed palms-together to Whitney. His puzzled glance bordered on distress. The air was redolent of cigar and tobacco smoke.

"Do I look like I'm from Mars?" I asked him.

"Ahem," the man said.

"Moriah Dru," Whitney said, with an elaborate sweep of his hand. "She's graced our company in hopes of finding her man."

Orson didn't know whether to laugh or leave. Clumsily, he turned and slunk away. Whitney followed, with me at his side. He said, "This is the first time our bastion for the comfort of males has been invaded by a female."

We strode down the hall. I said, "Word on the street is, this is a high-class strip place."

"Women are allowed in the theater for entertainment purposes, and we have women counselors."

"Counselors? Is that a new name for an old profession?"

"We are not a whorehouse."

The theater was as surreal as the night I'd been Mr. Chapman. On the black stages, women in white gossamer swanned. "This is novel," I said to Whitney. "Men choosing ballet over gold poles."

It was Lake who'd called their dance routine ballet. *Where are you Lake? Cry out, if you hear me.*

Whitney said. "Remember I told you this is a place of refuge and reflection."

"The only refugee in here is the head of Curriculum Paradigms, Inc.," I said, pointing to Dr. Brommer, who stared like a zombie at the dancers.

"I forgot to warn you," Whitney said. "No outing the patrons. You've seen Dr. Brommer. Now forget you've seen Dr. Brommer."

"I'm forgetting."

"You don't see Richard Lake, do you?"

"We haven't been everywhere."

I looked for the altar at the back of the theater. No altar, no Celtic cross rising behind it. I reckoned that the theater room wasn't as deep as the night I'd been here and guessed that a floor-to-ceiling wall—one that matched the other three walls—hid the altar. I didn't see any cracks from where I stood—just solid wall. They couldn't have moved that massive cross, unless it was papier-mâché or foam, but I didn't think it was since the room was not as deep as the other night. Then I noticed the catwalks jutted from different positions off the side stages. Everything, it appeared, was moveable.

Turning to Whitney, I said, "Where can I find a—facility?"

His mouth turned up, not a smile exactly. "Exit over there." He pointed toward the exit I'd used as Mr. Chapman. "Go left. Then the first left is a ladies' dressing room. Take care to make sure you're entering the door marked 'Femmes Dressing Room.' I'll wait here for you." *Yeah, he'll run to the first monitor he can to where I'm going.*

Out the door, going left, I saw the hall camera. I came to the dressing room door. I calculated the Celtic cross had to be hiding inside a walled room about ten feet wide, between the auditorium and the dressing room. Alone in the dressing room, where rack after rack held costumes, I looked for peephole cameras and couldn't see any, and, more importantly, I didn't feel like I was being watched. I floated through white gauze. A row of lighted mirrors lined the wall. I touched each mirror panel. Solid, and not two-way. Walking toward the toilet stalls, I entered the one closest to the altar wall and ran my hands over the mahogany panels. I rapped lightly and whispered, "Lake. Lake. Are you there? Can you hear me?" The only thing I heard was my voice catching in my throat.

I left the stall and ran my hands along the wooden wall leading to the mirrors and touched a panel that pushed inward. The panel opened into a skinny hall that curved behind the mirrors. It ended at a door marked LINENS. The door was locked. Why was a linen closet locked? I hurriedly searched my purse for my pick kit. Taking it out, I wondered how long Whitney would give me for a bathroom visit. One, two, and pop, the dinky lock opened. I dropped the slender tool in my purse and palmed my automatic.

The hall continued. It was shoulder wide for me; a fat person would have to slither sideways through it. The walls felt like slabs of slate and got progressively cooler. My gun clicked against something metal. A lever. I pulled down and heard the latch release. The machine that opened the door whined softly, and cold air and the scents of incense and foreboding guided me through the opening. It was seconds before my eyes adjusted to the gloom and shadows. Rooted to the floor, I let my brain process what it could see. A sarcophagus stood in front of the cross. A body lay on it. A wave of terror stopped my breathing. I took two quick steps when suddenly I was yanked backward by an unseen hand.

"Get back from there."

A woman. I slipped the automatic in my slacks pocket and whirled around, breaking her handhold. The redhead was dressed in black as before.

She said, "What the hell are you doing in here?" I moved backward, toward the figure on the vault. "Stop," she called. "Or I'll kill you."

I laid my palms against my thighs, a hand touching my gun.

"Fredrica," a man called.

Whitney's voice, coming from behind the cross. He said, "Back away, Fredrica."

Whitney slinked from the cross to the head of the sarcophagus. He said, "Miss Dru, you have outdone yourself." He lifted a hand. "Unfortunately." I thought he had a gun, but it was a clicker. Two clicks and a sliver of light from the rafters burgeoned and grew. The stage light shined on Lake.

Whitney was at my side, taking my elbow, guiding me toward the ornate altar-crypt, and Lake. I told myself not to panic. *Frenzy will get you killed.* He said, "Remember we talked of religion on the day we met? I was amused when the judge told me your name. I, too, trace my roots to the religion of the Druids."

"The Druids hung people in baskets and burned the basket," I said, grateful for the control in my voice. "What are you doing to Lake?"

"Immolation from the branch of an old oak tree is frowned upon by our enlightened society."

Lake lay so still. *Keep the tension out of your arms and hands.* "Why are you doing this?"

"Lieutenant Lake invaded my privacy, my cloister."

Lake was the color of blue ice. I could almost make out his

facial bones. I reached out. His hands, crossed at his waist, were as cold as death. "Oh no, no, no."

Whitney said, "He's not dead. He lies in a deep sleep."

"Why?" I reached up to rub Lake's cheek; it felt like marble. I looked at Whitney. "Like this?"

"You have my Kinley. I have your Lake. It's time for an exchange."

"You'll never see Kinley again."

"So cocksure, aren't you? Now I have two to swap."

"You could have ten, you'll never get Kinley. You kill us and you'll get the needle."

"Speaking of which," he said, and then turned and beckoned. "Fredrica. Come."

The redhead advanced with a box held between her hands.

I had little time and one chance to pull the automatic from my pocket, one chance at one fluid motion. But first I had to goad him, divert his attention. I said, "After our discussion today, I found out the rest of the story."

"I don't care," he said.

"You should. It's about the armored car robbery. The FBI knew Harry arranged the inside job. They also knew Harry palled around with a man named Dewey. After the robbery, Harry and Dewey disappeared. Then down in New Orleans, they found a body they identified as Harry's. A few hundred-dollar bills from the robbery and a ticket to Rio were under the burned body. A few hundred? A paltry sum to convince the feds that the body they found was one of the robbers. It wasn't, was it? Harry is still alive, isn't he?"

Whitney gave me an oily grin and glanced at Fredrica. I pocketed my right hand and raised my left to point a finger in his face. I said, "Harry's alive and well and living in Palm Springs. He killed Eileen for you because she was having you investigated. When you came to me you knew she was dead, but

Kinley was missing, and you and Harry didn't know where Tess had her hidden. Oh yeah, Harry knew Tess was Arlo's daughter."

"Don't outsmart yourself, Miss Dru."

"But you know something, Dewey, the FBI's still got you on their wanted list. They're still looking for you, *Dewey Whitey.*"

"Don't call me that."

The redhead stood near Whitney. She said, "Bradley, it's okay. This will soon be over." She held a needle up and adjusted the syringe's plunger.

"What's in that?" I said.

"You want to pick your poison?" she said, a cackle in her throat.

"Are you going to personally murder me?" I asked Whitney.

"I am not a murderer. I have never taken a life. My relatives enjoy the undertaking more than I do." He laid the clicker at Lake's feet and casually slid his hand toward his coat pocket.

"Tell me about this place. The purpose." My gun was in my palm, hidden from Fredrica with the needle and from Whitney, who kept his opaque gray eyes on my face as if trying to mesmerize me.

"The Cloisters?" he said. "I thought you'd have figured it out. The members are troubled men. They've been ostracized because of their preferences—their inability to open their souls."

"They're predators, in other words."

"If you wish. They are here to redeem themselves, Miss Dru. Redemption. Don't we all seek redemption?"

"Apparently you haven't found it."

"I certainly have. Time and again."

"You've a yen for little girls, isn't that your problem?"

"I've never harmed a small child."

The woman broke in, "My brother has fought all his life against the evil that invaded him in the hills of our native state. This place is his sanctuary against the temptations in the outer world. This cloister has been his salvation. As it has been many's salvation."

"You've had a few recidivists," I said. "McCracken and Rossi."

"Unhappily," he said.

"So let me get this straight. What happens is, these rich men with a hankering for perverted sex join here to get over their desires by what? Looking at dancing women and drinking fine wines and liquors and having great meals?"

Fredrica tapped the barrel of the syringe. "They come seeking salvation, whenever they feel the ache in their souls . . ."

Don't tense up. "More their loins," I said, finding the trigger with my index finger.

"When they feel the ache, they can retreat here," she said, the shadows flanking her merciless face. "Talk to their counselors."

"An AA for predators," I said and looked at Whitney. "They stand up and say: 'Hi, my name's Dewey. I have a problem. I want to screw little girls.' "

Whitney's hand came out of his pocket. I raised the gun and shot him in the forehead, then swung the gun at the same time Fredrica raised her arm. I saw the needle flash. My bullet went through her wrist. She cried out, dropped the syringe and fell on it.

I ran to Lake and ripped open the soiled dress shirt and listened for a heart beat. None coming from his cold chest. Froth lined his lips, and I wiped it with my fingers. I felt for a pulse. None I could discern. I ran my hand through his hair and down his forehead. No response. *Turn him, get him moving.* I put my arm under his back. I'm strong, but he was dead weight. *Lake, please, please* . . . After slapping his cheeks and getting no reaction, I took his stiff hands in mine. *Warm up.* I tickled his palms, he's ticklish there. Nothing. I wanted to cry. *You can't.*

I was so absorbed in getting life back into him, the thunderous racket didn't penetrate at first. When the altar room became an echo chamber, I raised my head and heard the pandemonium—feet pounding, shouts. But, above the fevered pitch, rode the voice of authority.

Commander Haskell.

A muffled shot like a tinny twenty-two came from the theater. Haskell burst through a door hidden in the auditorium wall. He glanced from me to Whitney—dead on the floor—to Fredrica holding her leg in horror.

Haskell stood over Lake. "My God."

"Ambulance," I said.

"On the way, when I heard the shot . . ." He put his hand on Lake's forehead and said, "What's in him?"

I went to Fredrica. She lifted her grotesque face. I demanded, "What drug?"

She hissed and slumped dead. The needle in the syringe had blood on the tip. Hers.

Four paramedics ran in. One dropped beside Fredrica. Her eyes were wide in death. Three ran to the sarcophagus and opened kits. One clapped a respirator cup over Lake's mouth and nose.

Haskell picked up the syringe and sniffed it. "Cyanide."

"You sure?" the lead paramedic asked.

"I smell almonds."

"Me, too," I said.

"Can't get a beat," a paramedic cried. He moved the stethoscope around Lake's bare chest.

The head paramedic looked at me and Haskell. "I can't smell almonds, but we'd better go with it—and pray." He turned to his crew. "Poison kit!"

"Sodium nitrite and sodium thiosulfate," the leader said, preparing the syringe. They worked furiously, rhythmically, and the needle went in. "Glucose!" the leader cried. His attendant had it ready.

Lake stirred. Moaned.

"Let's go!"

Haskell and I hurried behind the hand-carried gurney through the door into the auditorium where they hoisted Lake onto a wheeled cart, and, while they adjusted his air tube, a detective rushed up. He said, "Man dead." He motioned toward a catwalk, where I'd seen Brommer, and where he was now, slumped. The detective said, "Looks like he was watching a laptop monitor of what went on in that room. He shot himself."

Before Haskell could speak, I said, "Whitney let me go hunting for Lake on purpose."

We followed the rolling gurney. "Why'd he bring you here?" Haskell asked.

"I told him I knew about the robbery."

"Why not kill you somewhere else?"

"He wanted me to see Lake die."

Haskell put an arm on my shoulder, then dropped back to talk to a detective while I ran ahead. At the ambulance, I said, "I'm going with him."

"No room," a paramedic said. I looked inside the jam-packed medical room on wheels. I would have been in their way.

Nodding, I said, "I'll follow."

"Grady," he yelled to the driver, slamming the double doors. Grady Hospital. A long ten minutes from here.

FIFTY-THREE

Commander Haskell was suddenly beside me. "Ride with me."

Ahead of the commander's car, the sirens blared and lights pulsated. He said, "I don't understand Whitney. He was a brilliant man. He had to know he couldn't get away with murdering a cop."

"Brilliant men seem to think they can. Whitney thought his past wouldn't catch up with him, and when it did, things started unraveling too fast. Then all he had left was revenge."

"How'd he get Lake?" His cruiser slid past cars trying to get out of the way.

"By invitation. Cocktails, then dinner. At some point, they put barbiturates, either in his food or wine."

"Lake didn't know about the robbery."

"I think Rossi talked before they killed him. He told his killers who Mr. Barton really was."

"Possible."

We were trailing the ambulance. I could visualize the paramedics' frantic moves to save Lake. I said, "Whitney was suspicious of everyone, had them followed. Me, too, from the minute he hired me. He knew when Bellan Thomas snooped into his past. He knew when Bellan talked to me."

"Whitney was going to lose his daughter."

"He was going to jail for the rest of his life."

"When you told Whitney you knew about the armored car murders, you knew what was in store for you."

"Yes. And Lake."

He sighed, and we didn't speak again until his car rounded the Grady Curve on the downtown connector. "You gambled and won."

I crossed my fingers like I did as a child. "I hope—for Lake."

"It wasn't going to work out for Whitney," Haskell said. "We would have connected the dots. He should have known that."

"He'd gotten away with robbery and murder before."

"He let hubris get to him. Happens to them all."

"Retribution," I said. "It was as much an addiction as his sex thing."

"Retribution," he repeated, with something like awe.

"It got into his soul when he saw his parents gunned down. He had his brother Harry kill the killers. Maybe you could understand that, but he went bonkers with getting revenge, like he had Risso and McCracken killed because they failed his program. Their last temptation did them in."

"Wonder why he didn't kill Lake outright?"

"His harpy sister was poised to. But Whitney kept Lake alive in case he could make a deal. Lake for Kinley."

He shuddered. "Wouldn't happen. I'm glad you found that invitation in Lake's loft. Wish our guys would have."

"Would it have been enough for a search warrant?"

"Probably. Consider yourself reprimanded for not coming to me."

"I didn't want to waste time listening to how your hands were tied." I glanced at him and he at me like we understood each other. He took the hospital exit off the interstate.

I said, "I called Whitney and he readily agreed to meet me this afternoon. He figured I knew where Kinley is and would make a deal."

"Do you know where she is?"

"Yes, and I'll have to tell the judge, and the California

authorities, if Tess refuses to give her up."

"We can sort that out," he said. "Do you trust the law in Palm Springs?"

"No."

"Did you see those two men pass us when they put Lake into the ambulance?"

"No."

"They'll be taking charge of Whitney's body. The feds never traced the money, except for the few hundred under the body in the New Orleans fire. What in hell took Harry and Whitney so long before they started spending it? And how did they launder it?"

"Their patience was due to Whitney's genius. But Harry was no slouch in the diligence department. The laundry trail is probably cold by now, but while they washed their cash, Whitney worked his way through college, and the brother went off to Louisiana, or wherever to do whatever. Remember he's supposed to be dead in a fire."

"Hmmm, well, we don't know for sure that he isn't, but we have DNA now, and the FBI doesn't close armored car robberies until *all* the participants are rounded up, and *all* the money is accounted for."

"But you see, Dewey had a new name, lived in a new town, became an academic, lived a clean life, married, had a child . . ."

"And started a club for penitent deviants. Wonder how many people he's killed in his lifetime?"

"He says none."

"You believe that?"

"He had a brother and a sister willing to kill for him. Dewey was the genius. Their savior. He promised them he'd get them out of poverty. And he did. He planned the robbery, and they were rich for it. So they did what he asked them to."

Haskell took in a great lungful of air. "You know Whitney

didn't have a gun when you shot him."

"I saw—after I shot."

He made a right into the emergency entrance and stopped behind the ambulance.

"I'm keeping your name quiet for as long as I can."

"I'm not sorry I killed him."

He gave a brisk head bob, and we got out of the car. He clutched my shoulder as we walked through the double doors of the emergency room. "Get in there and get Lake well."

I caught up with the gurney as it was pushed into an elevator.

Lake was covered in white to his neck. An oxygen mask hid his lower face. His forehead was wet with sweat.

I said, more to myself than to anyone there, "He's sweating. A good sign."

"Yes, ma'am," a doctor said.

I looked at him. His name tag read W. WILLIAMS.

"How're his vitals?" I asked.

"Weak."

They wheeled him into an operating room. I was led to a grim room with ripped seats and torn magazines to wait. I sat uneasily on the edge of my chair. People came and went. I talked, but don't remember what I said. They asked me for Lake's relatives' names. I told them Lake's parents were dead. Then Portia came in. She sat quietly beside me and held my hand. Dawn showed through the blinds. The waiting room was overflowing with apprehensive people. Cops hovered over me.

Doctor W. Williams suddenly came through the door. Heads jerked up. Word was coming. He walked toward Portia and me. We jumped up. He said, "Let's go talk."

We followed. I held my breath for the seconds it took to get to a tiny private room. *This is where they give you the bad news.*

He faced me, his eyes shining. "Whew. Talk about 'the nick of time.' "

The ten-ton weight on my soul lifted. "He's all right?"

"For now."

Portia said, "What's that mean, for now?"

"We've neutralized the cyanide, but he's not breathing on his own yet."

"He'll live?" she asked.

"Unless there's complications caused by the poisons."

I found my voice. "What complications?"

"Respiratory damage, nerve damage, heart damage. But we won't worry about those now. He's on oxygen. The barbiturates are complicating things. They'll take longer to get out of his system."

"Can we see him?"

"Yes."

As we walked down the wide hall toward the critical care unit, suddenly I noticed that policemen lined the walls. They began to clap, and the noise rose to a crescendo.

A nurse came rushing through the swinging doors and waved her hands. "Shhhhhhhhh."

The clapping stopped, but laughter bubbled through the crowd. The doctor raised his hands and spoke. "We have cause to celebrate, but let's do it quietly." He answered questions readily.

Finally, it sunk in. Lake was going to live. We'd worry about complications later.

After the impromptu conference, the doctor put his arm around my waist and led me through the swinging doors. I turned to wave at Porsh.

Lake lay on a bed, arms to his side, a mask covering most of his face.

"His face?" I said. "It's red."

"It'll go away. Cyanide makes the venal blood pop red when it flows. He'll excrete it in his urine."

I sat on the bed and picked up his hand. "Can you hear me, Lake?"

"He might be able to," the doctor said. "He came out of the coma briefly."

I tickled Lake's palm, and his hand jerked. I struggled to get a handle on my emotions, and the wise doctor left the room.

"I love you, Lake," I whispered. "Hear me? I love you."

His eyelids fluttered. He moaned, and then his eyes fixed into slits. Water trickled from the corners.

I don't know how long I watched the man I loved so much, but nearly lost. Thoughts of love so casually disregarded, and then tossed away in arrogance, only to be realized in peril, filled my heart. Thankfully, no one came in. I laid my head on his chest, and, after a while, fell into a nervous sleep. Next thing I knew an attendant came in and woke me. I waited as doctors came and went. They examined and left, but none looked dour. One said, "Miracle."

Lake was moved to a private room, with two beds, one for me. I didn't think I could sleep, but I did for a while, and then I woke to see that it was dark outside.

Suddenly Lake sat up and tore the mask from his face. I jerked up and reached out. He swung his feet to the side of the bed and leaned forward to stand. He stooped and reached out. I took his hand and pulled him toward me, into my bed. His face fell on my chest.

As expected, bells and whistles went off at the nurse's station, and they came running. A large nurse's aide was astonished. An LPN fussed, "Lordamighty, Mister Lake, the doctor's going to have a heart attack, he sees you without your mask."

"I'm fine," Lake said, lifting his head. "I'm tired. I don't need

319

the mask. I need to be right here." His head flopped back on my breast.

Five minutes later, Williams came in. "Well, my miracle man is throwing off the paraphernalia of the medical profession for the arms of a lovely woman. Best medicine there is." Before he'd finished his pronouncement, Lake was asleep.

"Barbiturates," the doctor said. "They're still running through his body."

The medical trio decamped. My fingers twined Lake's hair, and I listened to the life-affirming snorts and wheezes as he breathed to the rhythm of my heart.

FIFTY-FOUR

The next morning, Doctor Williams checked Lake's vitals. His heart skipped beats, and Williams couldn't explain why. His blood pressure hit low points, and he looked lethargic. He also craved candy. So what was new? An LPN put a glucose bag on an IV pole. Doctor Williams looked at the glucose bag. He said to Lake, "There's something odd about your survival."

"What?" Lake got to a sitting position as if to prove he could survive anything—odd or not.

Williams watched Lake's small struggle. "You had several needle marks in your arms. The barbs were injected, as was the cyanide. A lethal mix was running through your veins. While I'm glad to see you sitting up now, you shouldn't have survived."

Lake swung his feet over the side of the bed. He looked shaky, but Williams didn't caution him. "No way was I going to die and let Dru down. It happened once before. I wasn't going to let it happen again."

The doctor cocked his head, apparently seeking more information. I said, "Lake's referring to a man I was engaged to marry. He was killed in a drive-by."

Lake reached for my hand. "No way in hell was she going through that again." Although I was giddy with tender pride, it was so unlike Lake to be open about his feelings.

Williams fingered the glucose bag. "Did you know that glucose is an antidote for cyanide?" Lake and I looked at one another. The doctor went on, "You remember the story of Rasputin?"

"Is this a 'Once Upon a Time'?" Lake said with a grin.

I said, "I remember a bit about him, thanks to my expensive education at the community college." Lake always got a kick out of my saying that like it was Harvard. "The Russian court got tired of Rasputin's arrogance and poisoned his wine with cyanide. It's said that he drank enough to kill ten men, but kept going all night long. Then they shot him and finally had to drown him in the river."

Williams said, "Wine can be very sweet."

I asked Lake, "What did you eat at The Cloisters?"

"Squab. I don't remember what it tasted like."

"Wine?"

"The whole bottle, myself. A nice fruity white."

"And for dessert?"

"Napoleons and brandy."

Williams held out his hands. "There you are. Sugar laced with sugar. You ate sugar and drank sugar, then they stuck you with barbiturates. Barbs slow digestion. Then they injected the cyanide. Your wine and Napoleons saved your life."

"He was already laced with sugar," I said, winking at him. "I went to your loft. Before your nap, and probably afterward, you ate peach pie and a dozen donut holes."

Lake's lopsided grin ravaged my heart. "I told you, Doc, all that doesn't matter. I wasn't about to die—simple as that."

I thought about Dr. Brommer and his suicide. "Maybe someone gave Lake a shot of glucose while he lay on the altar?"

Lake frowned and rubbed his chin. "I came to, once. Someone was there. I don't know who. It wasn't the woman. It wasn't Whitney. I never saw Whitney."

About that time, we noticed Haskell standing in the doorway.

Doctor Williams greeted the police commander, waved to us,

and went out the door.

Haskell and Lake exchanged the usual chatter: How're you feeling? The press is being obnoxious. The work load is piling up. Then Haskell said, "I heard a little of what you were talking to the doc about—the poisons. We did a fingerprint-backgrounder on Fredrica Lyman. She was a medical technician at the Louisiana State Prison in Angola. I think it's safe to assume she knew how to concoct a lethal injection without subjecting herself to cyanosis while handling the stuff."

"I wondered about that," I said. "I know getting it on your skin is toxic, and breathing it is, too."

"They had an execution chamber going," Haskell said.

I said, "Makes you wonder, doesn't it, if McCracken and Rossi were the only recidivists who had to die?"

"We may find out some day," Haskell said. He looked from Lake to me. "Strange man, strange place. You should have seen the rooms off the corridors. Like shrinks' offices and classrooms. A little dais was set up in front. There were all these case studies, and big charts and graphs, and then there was religious stuff. These guys apparently were taking classes to learn how to get over their addictions. They also had a couple of bedrooms with condoms and dildos—physical therapy, you might say. You can admire his attempt to heal addictions, but his attitude about failure was monstrous."

"Failure was a death sentence," I said.

"Which," Lake added, "McCracken would have gotten if we'd caught him. Whitney hastened his execution by twenty years."

Haskell said, "Imagine cloisters like that all over the US. Some nutcase thinks he's God."

"He won't be the last," Lake said.

The commander agreed, wished Lake well, and said he'd be in to see him tomorrow. He left, and I gently pushed Lake back down onto his back, kissed him until he was losing his lethargy, and said, "Later, baby, rest now." Resting my head on his chest, I listened to his measured breathing and then his snoring, which was crescendo-ing enough to wake the—*not going there.* I'll never gripe about his snoring again.

Lake was raring to go the next morning. He was stuffing his foot in a shoe when the doctor came in and scowled. "What is this?"

Lake looked up. "I peed it all out, like you said, Doc." He finished tying a shoe. "Time to go get the bad guys."

"Up," the doctor ordered, and Lake stood. "Open your shirt."

Williams laid a stethoscope against Lake's bare chest. "The bad guys were killed last I heard. Breathe deeply. Now deeper. Again. Again." He let the stethoscope fall to his waist.

"Two are dead," Lake said. "There's another from the litter, just as nasty. They slithered out of the same womb."

The doctor pried Lake's lower eyelid. He said, "Let your colleagues get him."

"Nope," Lake said, and we exchanged glances. We'd been up since dawn and laid our plans after we discovered that it was going to take a while for Lake to be up to his usual full-bodied lust. "This is personal for me," he said.

By the looks exchanged between Lake and the doctor, I assumed the doctor understood the inference.

Lake went on, "And it's personal for Dru. They poisoned her, too."

Williams cast a quizzical glance at me. I said, "Datura. Next to cyanide, kid's stuff."

Williams examined Lake's throat. "Can I talk you into one more night? Three free meals. No dirty dishes. Clean linens."

"Thanks for your hospitality, Doc, but no." Lake reached for his new jacket. I'd gone to a shop on Marietta Street and bought clothes. The shop was famous for its zoot suits. I picked out the most conservative I could find.

"Well, if you're going to be like that, go on then," Williams said. "We need the bed. Go get your bad guys. And don't come back."

Lake stuck out a hand. The doctor grabbed his arm and hugged him. When Williams looked at me, his eyes were glossy. On his way out, he said to Lake, "And I don't want you caught dead wearing that suit."

When the door closed, I put my arms around Lake's waist and looked into his eyes. How did he manage to look exhausted, vibrant, and sexy all at once? "You know," I said, "saving someone from the grim reaper means you're responsible for that someone for the rest your life."

He put his arms around me and kissed my forehead. "Hmmm. Who said that?"

"Shakespeare. He said everything."

"That's a heavy load," he said, bending to kiss my ear.

Our lips met, and I reveled in his improving vitality. Pulling away, I said, "I'm up for it."

Commander Haskell caught up with us as we were about to board the plane. "Goddamn it, Lake. Have you lost your friggin' mind. You can't go out there like some Wild West cowboy."

"I'm on sick leave," Lake said. "First time in ten years. I'm gong out there to help Dru bring a little girl back home."

Haskell gave up on Lake and looked critically at me. "Tell the FBI what you're holding back."

"I'm not talking to Gila Joe or anyone in PS law enforcement."

"Tell the LA FBI office."

"I might, after . . ."

Lake and I stood like statues, intransigent and determined.

Haskell reached out with both hands and took Lake by his biceps. "If I can't stop you, then—Lieutenant Lake—stay well."

They shook hands. Haskell gave me a squeeze and disappeared down the concourse.

Fifty-Five

Gila Joe and Dartagnan were waiting for us when we deplaned. Gila Joe's native face had that stern, cigar-store-Indian aspect, and Dartagnan hadn't shaved; his hair was greasy and his eyelids drooped.

"Imagine that creep, Whitney," Dartagnan said. "Trying to kill a cop—with the cops on the way."

Lake met with the rental agent and filled out the paperwork. We walked four abreast to our rented four-wheeler. Dartagnan said, "Where to?"

Lake said, "The Palkott."

"Arlo's in town," Dartagnan said. "He wants to talk to you, Miss Dru."

"I know," I said. "He filled my voice mail."

Gila Joe said, "He hasn't cooperated with me."

Lake asked, "What'd you find in his house?"

"Blood. Most in the foyer, even up on the chandelier. Indistinct footprints leading into the kitchen. It's Eileen's type. We're doing DNA now."

"What's Arlo saying?"

"He's cussing everyone, but not much of substance."

I asked, "No clue where Kinley is?" We were standing at the four-wheeler. Lake had unlocked it.

"Not yet," Gila Joe said. "We're putting the pressure on Arlo's family and friends."

Lake said, "If Arlo didn't do the crime, when he's exonerated he'll be famous. Isn't that how Hollywood works?"

Dartagnan laughed. "Most write a book. Arlo'll make a movie."

"Will you be in it?" I asked.

"Play myself, you mean?"

Lake said, "I'd choose a stage name flashier than Dartagnan."

Dartagnan missed a half step, but then he grinned.

Gila Joe looked at me. "When you talk to Arlo, I'd like you to wear a wire."

Lake shook his head. "She'd have to tell him she's wearing. In my state, you can't entrap."

"Here, too," Dartagnan said.

"I'm a fed," Gila Joe said. "I can get a warrant."

"And Arlo can get his lawyer," I said. "Look, I just want to get Kinley back home. Arlo's the key. You've already said he won't cooperate with you. He can't be intimidated." I looked at Dartagnan. "He knows where the bodies are buried, doesn't he?"

Dartagnan feigned a boxing move. "That don't mean he's going to tell," he said. "He's had twenty-five years experience at not telling."

"But that doesn't mean we can't find out for ourselves," I said.

Gila Joe gave a dismissive wave. "You two work with Detective Dartagnan. I'm juggling twenty balls, hoping one's not a terrorist."

We got in the four-wheel rental, turned on Ramon, and headed downtown for the Palkott. Dartagnan was somewhere behind us, of that I could be sure.

At the Palkott, I hung back checking for a tail while Lake went to the desk. We didn't have a reservation.

I caught sight of Arlo. He was in a lobby recess, looking out the window, hands in his pockets. I slipped past him and found Tess sitting on a loveseat in another recess.

She looked up as I came in, sad eyes, but head held high.

"Tess," I said. "You doing okay?"

"Arlo . . ." she said. "He's . . ."

"I saw him," I said, pulling a chair next to her. "Where's Kinley now?"

She didn't bat an eyelash, because she expected the question. "She's safe."

"Where? You know, of course, that her father is dead."

"Now no one will harm her."

"Wrong, Tess. We have no idea what Kinley saw or heard, what she knows, what she can tell. And about whom."

By Tess's rapid eye blinks, I knew I had given her something to think about, but she didn't respond.

Arlo came in, his arms outstretched to give the air a bear hug. "Glad to see you." He dragged an armchair close. "Goddamnedest thing—that freak Whitney."

A movie in the making. "You staying at your house?" I asked.

"No way," he said. "All that invisible blood, and the cops. We're next door. Heidi's invitation."

I looked at Tess. "What about you?"

"Staying on the rez."

"With Kinley?"

Tess looked away. Arlo looked at the ceiling and began banging his fingers together.

"Tess," I said, "has anybody been asking about Kinley? Anyone at all?"

"What do you mean?"

"You're Eileen's stepdaughter. Everyone knows it. Someone looking for her would naturally think you're hiding her."

"Who's the someone, besides you?"

"Whoever killed Eileen." Her brows drew together. She looked at Arlo.

Arlo said, "Anyone thinks Eileen's dead, thinks Kinley's dead."

"Tess, what about it? Anybody asking you questions?"

"No," she said, too quickly.

"Dartagnan, perhaps?"

"No."

"Aren't you two closer than you let on?"

Her eyes flashed to her father before she answered, "We are not lovers, if that's what you're asking."

Arlo leaned forward. "They'd better not be."

"Why?"

"Tessie, she's better than that."

I had to agree. "Who are Dartagnan's good buddies?"

Tess bit the inside of her lip. "He has lots of buddies—all over town."

Arlo sat back. "He plays poker at the casino—with Zing and Philippe. He played with Larry, too, before he was killed."

Lake walked in. He made an air check on his palm, indicating we'd gotten a room. Arlo stood and moved to the window. He stared out for a long moment, and then turned back to look from Lake to me. "Look, you two. I didn't kill Eileen. I'm swearing on all I got." He walked over, sat beside Tess, and took her hand.

Lake drew up a chair next to me.

Arlo rubbed his forehead. "Let's talk." We each leaned closer together. To onlookers, we might be plotting a heist. Arlo's eyes riveted mine. "You got a story to tell?"

"Things come to a head when Kinley confides to her mother that she's unhappy with her father. It strengthens Eileen's determination to get Kinley away from Whitney. First, though, she has to get drug-free."

"She was succeeding," Arlo insisted.

"But she also has to prove that Whitney is unfit. So she hires an investigator. On the surface it looks like Whitney's the perfect father. An academic, no less. But his façade hides a deeply disturbed personality." I explained Whitney's family background—that he was not the son of wealthy parents, that he was from the hills of Arkansas and his parents were killed in a feud over river rights.

"Happens all the time out here," Arlo said with a hand wave. "Riparian shootouts."

"His real name was Whitey—Dewey Whitey."

"I'd change my name, too, if it was that," Arlo said.

I sneaked a glance at Lake, who was amused at Arlo's butting in. When I got to the armored car robbery, Arlo said, "Ho boy. So Eileen's PI learns all this and tells her? I didn't know nothing about that."

"The PI didn't tell her, because she'd disappeared before he could. He didn't tell me, either, because he was holding out for money. Then he was murdered."

"So you think Whitney got the PI?" Arlo said. "And Larry with him?"

"Not personally."

"He couldn't because he wasn't out here—that I know of," Arlo said. "Dartagnan was watching the planes come in from Atlanta."

Tess spoke up. "You're saying he hired someone, aren't you?"

"He knew someone here who would kill for him, yes."

"You got an idea who?" Arlo asked.

"A few more puzzle pieces and proof would help."

"You gonna say who you think it is?"

"Not now."

Apparently he didn't like the way I looked at him. "I'm not your idea, am I?"

"Whitney knew that Eileen was dead, but he didn't know what had happened to Kinley." I looked at Tess. "What he hadn't counted on was Eileen's putting Kinley with someone she trusted."

Arlo wiped his brow again. "Boy, this is unbelievable. I knew Eileen had the private guy, and she was excited about getting some good info. I just didn't know she was in danger. Who could?"

"Then, according to Philippe, she saw a man in his shop who alarmed her."

"Maybe she knew the guy from Atlanta," Arlo said. "Maybe she was just scared. She was pretty jumpy the last couple of days."

"Then Arlo, you came home Sunday morning from LA on the early bird. You always came home on the early bird. You found Eileen lying in the foyer dead."

Arlo held up his hands like he was pushing me away. "I didn't say that."

"I know you did. The cops will get circumstantials at the house."

"Just talk on," Arlo said. Sweat sheened his brow and cheeks.

"You had a situation. You knew Kinley didn't want to go home. You knew Eileen wasn't going to send her home. And you knew that Tess had her."

Tess looked ready to burst into tears.

I held Arlo's eyes with mine. "So you had a brain wave, even if you didn't know who killed Eileen. You and Tess wrapped up the body, cleaned up the mess, and took Eileen into the desert. A few of Tess's people you trusted gave Eileen a native burial." The sudden silence between the four of us hung like a pall. I said, "The idea was to let Whitney and the cops and the court think Eileen had taken off with her daughter. Happens all the time."

"You got some imagination," Arlo said, folding his arms tightly across his chest.

Lake shifted in his chair. "What did you think when you found Eileen dead?"

"Think?" Arlo said belligerently. "Let's say I did find her dead. What would you think? Who did it? Why? Then I'd call Dartagnan."

"Was Dartagnan involved in the cleanup?" Lake asked.

"It would be stupid to ask a cop to do something like that."

"So you didn't call him?"

"I wouldn't have; let's say that."

"But there's a killer out here who knows you covered up for him."

"Or her," Arlo said, and laughed. "A woman can shoot a gun as good as a man can."

"How'd you know she was shot?" Lake asked.

I heard Tess crying softly.

Arlo spread his arms. "Don't go hanging me on a guess."

"I wonder what the killer thought," I said. "Must have been an anxious time, waiting until some hapless mother brings her daughter's friend, Kinley, home, only to discover Kinley's mother's dead body? And then days go by with no news of the murder."

"You could write a script," Arlo said.

Lake spoke up. "Mr. Cameron, we're not asking for you to confess to concealing a death. That's for you and your lawyer. We're sure of what happened. But think about this: the FBI found blood in your house, they've got DNA, and they'll prove that the amount they found was enough to make it likely Eileen was killed. They found it splattered on the walls, on the ceiling, in the keyhole. You probably left footprints in the blood, an overlooked bloody fingerprint in your car. Now they're looking for Kinley. If they don't find her, they'll assume you killed her, too—just at some other location. That's a lot to think about."

Arlo rubbed the sweat on his neck. He looked at the ceiling and then at Tess. He got up from the chair. "You're right. It's a lot to think about."

We all stood. I said, "Tess, Arlo, listen carefully. Let this sink in. The danger didn't die with Whitney. One person besides Whitney knew that Eileen didn't take off with Kinley—Eileen's killer. He's looking for the child. He knows who has her."

Arlo grunted. "In this scenario of yours, did Kinley see what happened to her mother?"

I answered, "In my scenario, the real scenario, Kinley was already with Tess."

"Who would want the kid?" Arlo said.

"This killer is vengeful. Whitney was his brother."

"Eileen never said the dirtbag had a brother."

"There was a lot she didn't know about her ex-husband."

Arlo whirled to stalk away, while Tess hugged her arms like she was freezing.

FIFTY-SIX

We were waiting for the elevator when Dartagnan sauntered up. Earlier, I'd caught sight of him circling through the lobby. The Palm Springs authorities weren't going to let us out of their sight. He asked, "What'd Arlo have to say?"

"I did the talking," I said.

He grinned with his upper lip. "You don't have to convince me." The elevator doors spread open. "Can I come upstairs?"

Lake stood in the way of the door closing. "You got a gun on you?" he asked.

Dartagnan spread his coat. His gun was in a holster under his arm. "Always."

"No, you cannot come to our room."

"Why not?"

"I haven't got a gun on me. It's in my suitcase. Airport security rules."

"You think I'm going to shoot you?"

"Some quick-draw shot two PIs in a hotel room."

Dartagnan made a hand gesture—the quick drawing of a gun. "You got a permit to pack heat in California?"

"Not yet," Lake said. "I'll be down to get one."

Dartagnan and Lake had an eyeball standoff. Dartagnan looked away first. "Okay. I'll give you a temporary permit." His eyes twinkled at me, but not merrily. "Bet you could get off two shots in the shake of a buck's tail."

"I don't carry," I lied. "But I'd like a permit in case I need to." He shrugged.

"We'll be coming along," Lake said.

"Give me an hour to get to the station."

As the elevator rose, I said, " 'Pack heat.' He's been a bit player in too many movies."

The luxurious silk bed cover beckoned. Lake looked at me, and I at him. Simultaneously we checked our watches, then burst into laughter. Our work was not done.

First stop on the way to the cop station, Philippe.

Philippe wasn't behind the computer. A slouch-hatted chef said he was making the rounds of his high-desert shops.

At the station, we waited half an hour for Dartagnan. We were photographed and printed, and finally handed two temporary carrying permits.

I held mine at the knife edge, between two fingers. I grinned at him. "A permit to carry with nothing to carry. You got a spare?"

"Sorry, no," Dartagnan said. "You seek, you'll find."

Lake looked at his piece of plastic. "Two days," he said. "How generous."

"If you don't find what you're lookin' for in two days, it ain't gonna be found. Now, I'm saying this for your own good. Don't do anything stupid. This is not your jurisdiction. And remember, we're in this together."

Lake cocked his head. "I won't forget." We started to leave, then Lake looked back and asked, "Your name really Dartagnan?"

Dartagnan's mouth slipped open. Then he laughed. "Who'd pick an alias like that?"

"Whitney was an alias. His kin took aliases when they left the Arkansas hills."

"What're you getting at?"

"Being out here reminds me that people in the movies take different names."

"I'm not in the movies."

"I heard you were."

"Bit parts."

"What name you use?"

"Sancho Pérez."

Lake touched the identity card to his forehead in a kind of salute. "See you later, Sancho Pérez."

We drove to the FBI office and waited for forty-five minutes for Gila Joe. He took my gun permit by the edge and examined it. "Thumbs and forefinger. Let's see who Mr. Dartagnan LeRoi really is." He slipped it into a small envelope.

We swung back by Too Busy to Cook? but it was closed, so we headed out Ramon for the Mission Palms Casino. No players at the crap or blackjack tables. One roulette wheel spun for a few customers. Obviously, the action hadn't arrived.

In a back corner, up three steps, stood two poker tables. Two men and a dealer sat at one. We perused the buffet. We could have used food, but food lines aren't my thing. Lake lingered at the banana pudding, and we looked at each other and laughed. At the window, we exchanged cash for chips and casually strolled like gawking tourists to the bubbling of the calliopes. I sat at the quarter slots. After two pulls, twenty bucks in coins crashed into the tray. Lake kept pumping his arm and losing.

At last, Zing rushed in and passed us without a glimpse. Ten minutes later, Philippe swooped in. He had on a black beret, the first time I'd seen him without his tall hat.

The heavies had arrived at the poker table. We got up and made our way to the tables. Philippe spied me at the same time my eyes met his. He smiled big and waved toward the empty seat next to him. "Play!" he cried.

"I don't," I said, and gestured toward Lake. "He does."

"Join us," Philippe invited. Zing and the other men at the table seemed less than pleased at the invitation.

The dealer looked up at Lake. "You in?"

"Sure," Lake said.

"You are taking the place of our Dartagnan," Philippe said, picking up two cards.

"If he comes in, I'll get up," Lake said.

"He never misses. He is never late, too," Philippe said. He looked up at me. "Sit, *mademoiselle*. Between Monsieur Lake and myself."

I fetched a chair that sat near the rail for watchers.

They played the hand. Lake scooped the winnings and stacked the chips. I watched for an hour as silent men played seriously. I could see most of the casino. No Dartagnan. No Tess. No Rosovos, but I had the slithery feeling someone watched from a television screen, having remembered Tess saying that bugs were hidden all over the place.

Lake couldn't lose. Three men left. As three new players took their places and lined up their chips, Philippe leaned close to Lake. "You are the beautiful *mademoiselle*'s paramour?"

Lake laughed. "Ask her."

Bending to his ear, I said, "He's my partner. In crime."

Philippe's eyebrows went up. "You are still looking for Madame Cameron?"

"Still," I said.

"Ah, the dogged ones."

"Also we're looking for her daughter."

"She is no doubt with her mama. I hear her papa is dead. Shot in a place of ill repute."

"True," Lake said.

The dealer called, "Everyone in?"

I rose and ventured away, toward the fifty-dollar slots. A voice came from behind, very softly. "Try your luck?"

Rosa Rosovo.

I grinned. "Not with the fifties. Quarters."

She waved me to the bar. "Last night, a man got a twenty-five-thousand-dollar payout."

"How much did it cost him?"

She laughed. "Over time, about twenty-five-thousand-dollars. I'd like to buy you a drink."

"Thanks. Amstel Light."

We sat on cushioned bar stools. Her poison was some kind of brown whiskey with water. "To you," she said, lifting her glass.

"And you," I said, toasting. "And to Tess."

"Yes. To a good heart."

"A good heart, indeed. But she hasn't told me the truth."

"She does not lie without cause."

"I know the cause."

"Yes," she acknowledged matter-of-factly.

I heard someone behind me and asked Mrs. Rosovo, "Where can I buy a gun?"

A half turn of the bar stool, and I faced Philippe, who air-kissed me. He asked Mrs. Rosovo, "Where is Mademoiselle Tess?"

Rosa Rosovo floated her eyes over mine. "She is at a showing up near Bakersfield."

"When did she depart?"

"I helped pack her art this morning."

Philippe gripped my arm. "She is the dog, *celle-ci*. Determined to find our missing madam. And she wishes a gun, *mon dieu!*"

Rosa Rosovo looked at me, and I gave a quick nod. She said to Philippe, "Miss Dru here would like to purchase a gun."

Philippe sized me up. "You can shoot good?"

"Not good," I said. "A snake bit me in the desert, and I'm not going there again without a gun."

"Bonne idée," Philippe said. *"J'ai beaucoup.* I will lend you one of mine."

"I'll buy it."

"Non," he said. "A leetle loan."

"Settled then," Mrs. Rosovo said.

Philippe said, "I wish to know sometheeng. Who would get the little girl if"—he dramatically clutched his chest near his heart—*"qui peut penser une telle chose?"*

"She would be an orphan," I said, seeing Adele Carter's face as she sat in a wicker rocker on her porch that stifling afternoon so very long ago.

Philippe said to Mrs. Rosovo. "You have the gift of the desert, *entendu.* Can you help this dogged one find what she seeks?"

"Our people have searched," Mrs. Rosovo said. "The spirits have not touched me, so they have nothing to tell me. That is all I can say." She got up from the stool. "I must go now. Good luck, Miss Dru."

"Give Tess my best," I said.

Philippe took her place on the stool and ordered a pinot grigio. "Where do you begin again?" he asked after the wine arrived and he'd made all the motions of a wine connoisseur.

"I'd like to talk to Dartagnan. I thought he'd be here tonight."

"Ah, that is *le mystere.*"

"He's a cop. Maybe he's out doing cop things?"

Philippe laughed. "Cop things *jamais!* He does what he wants. He is a—how you say—pariah?"

I yearned to grab his throat and stifle the phony accent and, most likely, the bad French. "Pariah?"

"A cop like no other."

"I think you got something there, Philippe." I looked off in the distance. "I wonder if being a pariah in Louisiana is what made him leave? You know anything about his past?"

He scratched his forehead and pulled the beret lower. *"Non.* I talk on and on about what I did years ago, how I learn the cooking and the baking and who was my mentor and how I grow up, but him—he never talks about his past." He upended his wine glass, placed it on the bar, and signaled the bartender by scribbling on his palm.

"He told me about growing up in a bayou. That's not far from New Orleans, is it?"

"*Moi,* I would not know."

"Never been there? All that good food?" Lake was suddenly next to me. I asked, "Win or lose?"

"He took all my money," Philippe said. "I will raise my prices tomorrow. For now, sleep." He rose.

I told Lake I'd be right back and walked to the front of the casino with Philippe. Along the way, he gestured with his hands and talked nonsense to a few patrons, making them laugh. Outside he said, "You must let me prepare for you and the handsome policeman a nice dinner—*juste pour deux*—in your hotel room. Romantic, *non?*"

"You got some good vino?"

"Excellent, the best. And for you, *et pour votre amour,* I donate two bottles of the best in my cellars—for the future of a happy pair and success in your quest."

I laughed. "Sounds divine. What's on the menu?"

"Ah, *boeuf* of tenderloin, baby vegetables, and marrows. What is your pleasure for dessert?"

"Napoleons."

"My especiality."

"Just don't send over any anise cheesecake."

He raised his face. "Anise cheesecake?"

"The last time I ate your cooking—cooking made especially for me—I got deathly ill."

One hand went to his heart, the other to his forehead. He nearly swooned. "*Mon dieu. Mon dieu.* Impossible."

I laughed. "I'm kidding, Philippe. It was datura."

He righted himself and looked at me with a doe-eyed stare. "Oh, the *mademoiselle*. Has her fun at poor Philippe."

"We'll take you up on that dinner. I'll let you know in the morning."

"*Que sera parfait.*"

He toddled off toward his car. I watched as he drove away.

We showered together. It was something we'd done many times before, but this time was different. We washed the weariness off and the lies that had dried and clung to our skins like stale sweat. Refreshed, we lay in bed and continued to explore each other, as if we'd never touched before. An hour later, Lake fell into exhausted sleep. I went outside on the balcony and focused on majestic black mountains that rose almost straight above me, serene now that my atavistic moorings were tightly wrapped.

FIFTY-SEVEN

The next morning, I rang Dartagnan's cell number and got his answering machine. Twice. Three times. Four times. We rolled by the police station. No Dartagnan. Lake got us in to see Dartagnan's superior, who said that Detective LeRoi's work had taken him to the desert for a few days.

"The Whitney case?" Lake asked.

"Look," Superior said, "LeRoi's got other cases, too. You know how detectives work, being one yourself."

When Lake smirks like that, you really shouldn't say anything more. But when we turned to leave, Superior fired a parting round: "Remember you're in our jurisdiction under Corlee's direction."

We drove by Dartagnan's condo complex. The blinds were drawn tight. I didn't have to be shown in by the manager to know that the interior was empty and smelled of pine sol and bleach. There was no physical evidence of the man ever having lived there.

"Wait until he hears this," Gila Joe Corlee said. He was talking about Dartagnan's superior. "He's going to have a shit fit. His star guy's not so starry."

I love it when cops stick it to each other. We women can't do it, not got the mental equipment.

Dartagnan's print results had come through.

Twelve years ago, his fingerprints had been submitted to the

FBI when he hired on as a Palm Springs policeman. They were a match for the fingerprints of a man who'd been arrested in New Orleans on a bank robbery charge. No conviction. The name he'd been booked under was Sancho Pérez.

"Sancho Pérez," I said. "Dartagnan has a sense of humor. Anything else?"

"That's all I got for you," Gila Joe said. "We'll get the shovel digging deeper."

Lake said, "Wonder why the PSPD didn't pick up on those prints?"

"Who knows?" Gila Joe said. "He wasn't convicted of the New Orleans crime. He was a popular guy. Worked for Arlo when he first got here. Security. Then Arlo got him on the force."

It being lunchtime, Gila Joe ordered sandwiches from Philippe, who personally delivered them and stayed fifteen minutes to speak half-English, half-bad-French.

When he left, Gila Joe shook his head. "You wouldn't know it, but he's a helluva pilot."

"I'll pass on his vectoring," Lake said.

We ate while Gila Joe brought us *au courant* on the results of the blood evidence in Arlo's house. The DNA was Eileen's. There were unknown hair and fibers and a footprint. When we parted ways, Gila Joe reminded us, in his firm but mannerly way, that they'd be keeping track of our activities. "Just don't make us look too bad," he said with a wide grin.

We left, not having told him about Tess and Kinley. Something about him, a closed book that only opens for his own benefit.

In the four-wheeler, I called Webdog, and told him to check with the New Orleans cops, get details on the Sancho Pérez arrest. I gave him Gila Joe Corlee's name if they questioned his credentials.

At Heidi's house, Lake pushed the sandstone bell button. I

expected Arlo to come through the door ready for battle, but a Native American woman timidly drew the door open. Heidi and Arlo were not home. She didn't know where they were. No, she didn't think they had gone back to Los Angeles. No, Tess was not in the house, either. Goodbye.

Later, Arlo called our hotel.

A half hour after that, he, Lake, and I sat in the nearly empty bar of the Palkott under the casually watchful eyes and listening ears of the bartender. "He's diggin' the dirt," Arlo laughed.

"For ermine and pearls?" I asked.

Arlo tilted his head like a sad jester. "My lady was no tramp."

Lake brought him back to the land of the living. "Heidi didn't see Eileen or Kinley that Saturday, did she?"

Arlo blew out. "She says she did."

"You asked her to say she did, didn't you?"

"She's not that good of a friend."

"But she's your neighbor, and she's an opportunist," Lake said.

"What's that supposed to mean?"

"She's there in case Eileen isn't. Nothing lasts forever in never-never land."

Arlo looked pained. He said, "Heidi thought she saw Eileen's car parked by the smoke tree, and somebody get out."

"When did she see this?" I asked.

"I don't know. She told you she doesn't look at clocks. She's always way early for parties, or way late. She's a little scatty."

"Try and remember what she said about seeing Eileen and Kinley," I urged.

"She said she saw the car as she went by. The back of a white car. She doesn't know cars, but Eileen's Lexus was white."

"Was?" I asked.

Arlo was angry suddenly. "Don't try to trip me up, Miss Dru."

Lake asked, "Did you know that Dartagnan had an arrest record in New Orleans under the name Sancho Pérez?"

He hadn't expected the question. He rolled his eyes. "You people. Know everything—or make it up. Yeah, but maybe no. Maybe I did. It's been so long. No, I don't think so."

"Robbery," Lake said. "Didn't go to trial. Pérez had a partner. He was killed. The charges were dropped, and Pérez came west—as Dartagnan."

"Didn't know all that," Arlo said. "But so what? He didn't do nothing out here."

"That you know of. Before the cops, he worked for you, right?"

"Security on the sets. Watching stuff didn't get stolen. You wouldn't believe how people like to break into trailers and steal costumes and props and all that crap. Dartagnan did a good job. He'd find out who was planning the op, and go get him. I told him he should be a cop. And so he became a cop. Look, my people checked his background. He didn't get convicted."

"No, he didn't," I said. "How did you meet Eileen?"

He snapped, "What's it matter?"

"Atlanta's a long way from Palm Springs," I said.

"Her turd of a husband sent her out here to think things out," Arlo said. "I don't mind speaking ill of this dead guy because the facts speak for themselves."

"Why Palm Springs?" Lake asked.

"Visit his friend," Arlo said. "Dartagnan introduced us one afternoon at tennis."

Lake said, "And you became lovers?"

"Whoa," Arlo said, holding up his hands. "Eileen wasn't that kind. She went back to Atlanta. She wanted to make a go of her marriage with that slimeball, but two months later she was back here, and she looked me up. Well, she came to the tennis courts and I was there. I'm always there or on the golf course. We hit it off. She told me she'd left him. She was worried about Kinley, but she couldn't take being married to him any longer."

"Did she think he was a pervert?" Lake asked.

"She said he was getting weirder, but she couldn't prove nothing."

"Where is Kinley now?"

"I don't know. I don't want to know."

"Dartagnan know?"

Arlo shook his head. "Only if he followed Tess."

"Would he?"

"Sure. If he wanted to know. He was a good cop." Then he squinted and looked off into wherever his brain was taking him. Then his eyes found mine. "But Tess—you don't mess with Tess. She's got my blood, too."

We were to dine on Philippe's cuisine. But first we had business, and pleasure.

I returned Portia's call. She reported that police and the FBI questioned Robert White. He'd been cooperative. He was Whitney's uncle. He'd lived in Atlanta for several years—from the time Whitney established SAA.

"What's SAA?" I asked Portia.

"Sex Addicts Anonymous. They started in a rented house by the university campus. They called the place The Cloisters. The clandestine program was based on AA, where rich men shared their problems in the hopes of finding a cure. All the therapists, doctors, clients, social workers were all cut from the same bolt of cloth—all were criminal sexual deviants."

"Did White say what his deviation was?"

"Adolescent boys. He liked them to call him Father White."

"I heard one," I said. "I nearly vomited."

"White says he didn't know what went on in that altar room."

"I wouldn't expect him to put himself on death row. He say

where Harry is?"

"California is all."

"Under our very noses."

"Keep in touch," Portia said. "And love Lake."

It was my pleasure to love Lake. Afterward, Lake fell asleep, and I took a shower. Sometimes I sing when the hot water beats down. Tonight, my brain stuck on a tuneful phrase: *Make something happen, Make someone happen . . .*

Lake had two Blue Sapphire martinis ready when I got out of the shower. Wrapped in a plush white towel, I snuggled next to him on the bed. We agreed to give the case a rest. We'd make a cocoon—regroup, refresh—for tomorrow we would make something happen.

I clicked on television, the news. Nothing new on the Whitney case. Arlo waved at the reporters as he boarded his flight to LA, Heidi in the background.

Martinis finished, we turned to each other. The longing to smother him with kisses reared like a beast. I rushed at him. "Hey!" he cried. "I'm only one man." When the torment eased, I didn't want his flawless body to leave mine; I needed to savor the passion, to immortalize our communion of body and soul so that it would be everlasting.

He gently rolled away. "Philippe," he said. "Due in ten."

Philippe arrived in ten.

The hotel allowed him to bring his food up on a cart. It was draped in white. White linen, white candles, shining chrome, brass cutlery, and domes.

Philippe flashed through his sommelier duties. "First, we open the cabernet sauvignon to let her breathe."

"That's an Estate cabernet," I said.

"Indeed. Nineteen-ninety-six. You do not think I would bring you anything but the Californian?"

"Indeed not," I said. "When in California, drink Californian."

"Napa Valley's very finest, *vraiment*," Philippe said, fussing over domes. The rich aromas seeping from them made my mouth water.

Lake, too, enjoyed the show. He turned to me and winked. He twined his fingers in mine.

I couldn't get over the two bottles of wine. They had to be seven, eight hundred dollars a bottle. Lake and I bought good wines, but this cab was way out of our league.

"You're very generous," Lake said. "I'd have to rob an armored car to afford it."

"Eh, I think not," said Philippe. "I have prepared a marvelous *boeuf* of tenderloin. It must have a good companion. This cab is perfect—tightly wound and compact." He flipped his fingers. "She is chewy with currant and blackberry, with hints of espresso and mocha. *Et, voilà, ce qui une finish!*"

Lake laughed. "I've always wondered. What does 'finish' mean?"

"Ah, what it is you can taste after swallowing. The longer the taste lingers on the palate, the better the finish. *Voyez?*"

Truly divine, the wine lingered and went down rose-petal smooth. "I don't know if two bottles will be enough," Lake said.

"We send for more, *voilà!*" Philippe said as he dressed the plates, first with a brown sauce, then perfect rounds of rare tenderloin, framed by marrows and baby vegetables.

"I must ask the *mademoiselle*. Do you still desire a pistol?"

"I do," I answered.

"When are you in the desert?" he asked.

I looked at Lake. "I believe we will go tomorrow late in the day, before we go to the desert casino for our last evening here."

Lake grinned. "She wants one last look at her prison, Adobe Flats."

"I will be visiting one of my restaurants near there in the afternoon, and I will provide you with a gun to point at the snakes. Very bad, there, very bad. Come to my Joshua Tree restaurant and fetch your firearm."

"Sounds good," I said.

Philippe served while he talked compulsively. "A simple gravy, that is best. Never, *non* never, cover the meat, unless it is bad meat. Then why eat it? I straddle my pan between two burners and pour in red wine, not this good cab, but a good red wine, some beef broth and *un peu de* butter. Reduce and there, purr-fect!"

I nodded vigorously, letting the buttery beef wallow in my mouth and wondering if Philippe was going to stay through dinner.

He seemed to have read my mind. "I will just open this bottle, *et je vous* let you alone with *votre appétit et votre diner.* It is good, *n'est-ce pas?*"

"Excellent," Lake and I said together.

"Underneath the trolley is the ice block and the mousse. *Bon appetite.*"

With that flourish, the man was gone. We leaned together and laughed. We raised our wine in celebration. "To us!" we said. "To us!"

We made love again, despite our protruding bellies and light heads.

Lake fell asleep quickly, as he'd been doing since the poisoning. I brushed his hair with my hand. He stirred, and I let my fingers run across his forehead. He was sweating lightly. I worried. He was my baby. I must keep him safe. The pain came again, a sharp needle in my breast. I'd almost lost him. Tears welled and it hurt like hell. He stirred and turned toward me, one of his legs pinning mine. I gently extricated myself and went to the balcony to look at the purple mountains below the silver gibbous moon.

Tomorrow.

"Dru?" I heard his voice. I turned. He was sitting. I came in and sat on the bed, up close and face-to-face with him. "Yes, my love."

He ran a hand down my cheek. "Am I your love? Do you love me?"

"Yes, I do."

He lifted my chin and smiled. "Care for some wine talk?"

"Only if it's mushy and will embarrass you in the morning."

"It's wine talk. I won't remember."

"Then, yes. Talk to me in *vino veritas.*"

He looked sober and serious. He said, "I've loved you from the moment I saw you. I knew why you couldn't commit to loving me, and I understood. I loved Linda when I married her; I knew you loved your fiancé. It takes time when you lose someone you love, by either divorce or death. Am I making sense?"

"Um-hum."

"I thought in time—the sex was good, wasn't it?"

"Very good."

"First comes sex, then love, I think."

"Ummmm."

"I'm not doing good."

"You're doing very good."

"I didn't do good when you were nearly killed. I'm so very, very sorry."

"Neither of us did good with that," I said, touching his cheek. "I thought everybody considered me a crazy woman, imagining things."

He wound his arms around me. "I knew you weren't. But you had to recover on your own. It's your strength that makes you who you are. My mealy-mouthing wouldn't have convinced you that you were whole again. You had to force the truth to the surface to be sure of yourself."

351

I was treading on fluffy clouds, my chest filled with his words. "You mean you were *mean* to me on purpose."

"Something like that."

The clock said three before we were too exhausted to heap love on top of love.

My eyes popped open. Lake sat beside me, a tray of goodies at the bottom of the bed. Coffee. Juice. Sweet rolls. "For sleeping beauty," Lake said, handing me coffee. He kissed my toes. "Sorry, I can't be more original."

"You've never kissed my toes before. I call that original."

"Your cell phone has been a symphony all morning," he said.

"Oh, God. Who?"

"I haven't taken to answering your phones or opening your mail. Give me a week."

Lake handed me the cell and went to shower.

Fifteen voice mails. Portia, Portia, Webdog, Web, Portia, Arlo, Corlee, Web, Portia. "Criminy."

Something told me I didn't want to talk to Portia, or Gila Joe, or Arlo. I punched up Webdog's last message: "If you ever get this, call. It's important."

When I called, Webdog asked, "Where you been?"

"Sleeping," I said. "I have to sometimes. My inner self makes me."

"Judge Devon's crazy to get hold of you," he said.

"She's left messages. I'll call her."

"I don't know if you want to," he said.

"Why?"

"She's going to tell you to come home, *now*."

"Why?"

"They took the DNA of Whitney's sister and compared it with the guy who died in the fire in New Orleans. They exhumed him. No match."

"So now we know for certain that Harry Whitey's alive and doing us all mischief."

"Yes, well . . . Judge Devon said the FBI is taking over the case. It's theirs and theirs only."

"Harry robbed a bank truck. So, okay, but we're in this to get Kinley home."

"Judge Devon says you have no client now that Whitney's dead, and the state is terminating you—for your own good."

"Shit."

"Ditto."

"Web, you haven't heard from me, okay?"

"One hundred percent okay. But—please, stay safe."

Lake was coming out of the bathroom, rubbing himself with a towel, looking vulnerable, and yet staring at my nakedness with a hunger that took my breath away. I said to Web, "I will. I have to."

Lake sat beside me and draped the towel over my nakedness. "Do we have to go rushing off somewhere?" he asked.

"That was Webdog. Whitney's sister's DNA didn't match the New Orleans body. It's not Harry."

"Who didn't know that. But it's good to confirm. So where's Harry?"

"Where's Dartagnan?"

Lake shrugged and took away the towel.

Afterward, I told him what I thought we needed to make happen.

"Whether we like him or not, we need to get Corlee in on this, too," he said.

Since the FBI was taking full control, Gila Joe would see to it that we were on the next plane to Atlanta. I said, "Let's give it one more go ourselves."

"I trust your instincts."

"Thank you."

"So let's go have us a picnic."

FIFTY-EIGHT

On our ride into the desert that afternoon, we talked about what we knew and what we'd set up. But would our killer show, like the black-bottomed high-tops riding in from the west behind us?

"You sure we weren't followed?" I asked Lake.

"This killer's good."

"He knows the desert. He knows where we're going."

"Yeah and he knows what we're up to."

"Yeah," I said, drawing in a deep breath. "He knows it's him or us."

We rode, keeping to our own thoughts, until Lake said, "What produces a man like Bradley Dewart Whitney, and his repulsive siblings? Nature or nurture?"

We'd come to Lost Coyote Canyon. The four-wheeler jostled on the tuff bed. I said, "Nature gave little Dewey his brains. But nurture gave him his desires. His family was incestuous, which is all right if you live in the hills all your life and follow the ways that everyone accepts, or at least doesn't complain about."

"So when his folks got themselves killed, and he had to move to Little Rock, he began to see his leanings weren't in line with society's way of thinking."

"Or the law's. So since Dewey was a genius, he knew he had to hide what he was. Compartmentalize. He set goals, probably wrote them down."

"Which were?"

"Of utmost importance was to acquire money."

"Armored cars have lots of money. Lots of risk, but lots of reward."

"Also he needed a place to hide once he'd gotten the millions."

"Nobody's looking for bank robbers in college classrooms."

"That was the practical part of Whitey."

The four-wheeler jostled across the desert floor, climbing up the canyon. The walls hid the western sun. I rolled down my window. The high-tops had assembled and marched across the sky, gathering darkness. We passed the gold mine. I mentally made the sign of the cross. Three men, on Harry's payroll—one named Rowall—had lost their lives there.

"Do you believe Whitney never killed anyone himself?"

"Whitney didn't have to kill when he had Harry around. Or his sister."

"I don't think I admire Whitney as much as you do."

I draped my hand across the back of the driver's seat, touching Lake's neck. "It's not admiration, my darling. He was a curious madman, one who talked of redemption."

"All the while exacting retribution."

"He died because of it," I said, rubbing the muscles of his back.

We were passing Ripple Rock. I felt the phantom tug of heavy, rushing water, the bumping and swooshing on the way down . . .

"Are you sorry you killed him?" he asked quietly.

It was the first time Lake had asked me that, but I'd known he would, in time. Now was the right time. I considered the man I loved, his strong arms outstretched on the wheel of a jouncing four-wheeler, listening for an honest answer.

"I'll never regret firing that bullet into his brain. It was for all the innocents who are the prey of madmen."

Lake reached for my hand and kissed it.

The tuff road ended at the top of the canyon. Desert dirt grabbed the tires, and we passed the rock cairn and the junipers that led into the palm oasis and to Heart's Friend Rock. As it had been with Tess those many days ago, it felt good to get out and stretch the muscles after the grinding drive through the canyon.

We leaned against the rocks surrounding the hot spring. I said, "I remember that day here with Tess. We drank dreadful creosote tea from small clay cups that were twenty subtle shades of blue and green. Stick birds were etched into them. Tess said they were religious symbols, and that she couldn't explain them. Bad luck, she said. I thought then that I didn't want any bad luck. We ate guacamole by the hot—"

Something moved in the thornscrub. A small animal, but it made me cry out.

Lake said quickly, "What?"

We hurried toward the brush, and something caught my notice. I knelt and picked up a piece of leather, a piece I recognized. Grinning, I rose and handed Lake the leather scrap from Tess's jacket and explained how I'd torn the piece the night of the moon ritual. "It came out of my pocket here." I looked over the landscape. "This is where I crawled that night after the Jeep burned. I looked out through this very scrub, and saw Tess and the three men. That night, I didn't recognize it as the palm oasis where Tess and I ate. God only knows how long I wandered in that storm."

I pushed through the brush and trudged through the sandy dirt.

Lake spoke behind me. "Too much time, and rain, for there to be evidence of the burning Jeep."

But something was protruding from the sand, and I hurried to it. Lake came up behind me and pulled the piece of chrome and glass from the sand. "A tail light fragment." He turned it over. "Jeep." He looked at me, his eyes earnest. "I told you, I've always been a believer."

I let out a loud, "Yes."

Lake said, "Exoneration looks good on you."

I took his hand, and we walked through the oasis to the geode artwork. I placed my foot where it had sunk into the desert dirt and put my weight on it. No sinking this time.

Lake's stared at me. "What are you doing?"

I told him, "A subset of the Mission Hills Indians used to dig graves and line them with brush. They'd lay the deceased in the grave. For three days they'd burn the body. Then for three days they'd let it cool. They celebrated the spirit of the dead by singing and dancing."

"Is this a grave?"

"I think it's Eileen's. Heart's Friend Rock."

"They burnt her body for three days?"

"That's the old ritual. I believe they buried her in her sable coat. A symbolic gesture."

Lake knelt and put his hand on a stone, then drew it back. "I can't dig here now."

"It's consecrated, even if not by our standards."

He rose and brushed his hands together. Then, with a tenderness that comes from deep devotion, he held me until the winds swept over us. I made the sign of the cross, and we left Heart's Friend Rock.

We got to the four-wheeler, boarded, and headed for the Adobe Flats.

I dialed Portia's cell.

She came on the line like a spitfire, and I crossed my fingers that she wasn't reminded of the Bentley.

"Portia," I said, "I know who has Kinley. When we get the killer, we'll bring her home."

"If you had returned my phone calls, you'd have learned

something very significant," she said. *Goodbye Bentley.*

"What?"

"Kinley is already home."

"What?"

Lake jumped at the sound of my voice. He braked as if he might need to render aid.

Portia said, "Tess flew from LA to Birmingham and drove to Atlanta with her."

I laughed, and threw the cell to Lake. "I'm hearing things. Ask her?"

He listened, his smile growing as big as the canyon.

He gave the phone back to me.

"Where is she now?" I asked Portia.

"With me. So is Tess. Quite a young woman." I could practically see Portia's dark eyes gleaming with delight. "But Tess can't have Kinley."

"I know. So does Tess."

"She's trying to make her case."

"Give Adele Carter another chance," I said.

I listened to dead air for several seconds. "You're serious," Portia said.

"As a crutch. Porsh, she's blood kin, and deep down, she cares."

"Get on back here and convince me."

FIFTY-NINE

Helicopters fly over the desert constantly. There's the Marine Corps base at Twenty-Nine Palms and a lot of tourist services. But the lone helicopter chopping the air this evening was unusual because a storm was fast approaching. "He's nuts," I said.

"Looks like he's accepted our invitation," Lake said.

We sat on the mud-brick stoop and watched the helicopter disappear to the north. The black clouds swirled and descended, creating angry skies like in one of Goya's landscapes where villagers go to a funeral to laugh at Death.

I said, "Heidi saw a white car that afternoon. She thought it was Eileen's, but it wasn't. Eileen's car was in the garage, and the white car Heidi saw was that of Eileen's killer."

"He took a chance. It could have been recognized."

"A Camry isn't a Lexus, but at a distance, and to someone who doesn't know cars, they can be mistaken. Besides, he's everywhere in The Springs."

Suddenly a spray of water hit my face. We fled into the dark flats. Inside the dark hall, I felt a presence and said, "The ghosts will always be here."

"This is a perfect place for them."

"Where else could they go?"

We went into a first-floor room that had a window facing west and a small chest leaning beneath it. Shards of lightning lit beer cans, bottles, food litter. We checked out three other small rooms on the first floor, then went back into the first room.

Lake said, "This is as good a place as any."

I stood next to Lake, holding his hand, hearing thunder gods hurl lightning bolts through the shadows.

The time came when Lake said, "Did you hear that?"

I strained my ears but couldn't tell if it was rotors or wind whipping the air. Lake reached for the gun in his waist holster. I bent down for the Glock in its ankle holster. I wrapped both hands around the automatic and held it shoulder-height. Lake liked to point both hands toward the ground. We walked to the door. He stood on one side of the frame. I, on the other.

The fast-moving storm was abating, but thunder still moaned and caroused overhead. Our invitee wouldn't need excessive stealth if he had an attack in mind. Maybe he just wanted to talk. The man could talk.

I heard silence. The silence of acute awareness, of anticipation that something vital was about to happen, and knowing that Lake and I would have to do a perfectly timed *pas de deux* if the killer had more in mind than a verbal dance. The intensity was as palpable as my very life.

All of a sudden, a man stumbled through the doorway.

What the . . . ?

He crashed to the ground, face down, soaking wet, his hands tied behind his back, his feet in walking shackles. He cried out. "Run. Get out."

Dartagnan. *I thought him dead already.*

His right foot rubbed the dirt floor, trying for a foothold to raise himself, but his shoe couldn't get a grip. He cursed hoarsely and rocked back on his stomach, trying to flip his body over. This happened in seconds. Lake and I looked at each other. Neither of us had expected this. Lake gave a quick, negative shake of his head, meaning, *don't move.* I felt the same presence he did. It stood just outside the door, out of sight, waiting for someone—me, us—to run to Dartagnan's aid.

A voice said, "Throw down the guns, detective, or I will shoot him now."

"Gun," Lake called out. "*One* gun."

I jerked my shirt out of my jeans and pushed the barrel of my gun into the hollow of my left hip bone, gun butt above the waistband.

The unseen presence snapped on a bright lantern and said, "Throw your gun between Dartagnan's legs." The lantern spot-lit the expected zone.

Lake bent his knees and flipped his Beretta onto Dartagnan's butt, close to his tied hands.

"Hands in the air, detective. Kick the gun between his legs. Now."

Lake brushed the gun from Dartagnan's backside; it slid between his legs.

"I want to see four hands high in the air."

I raised mine, maneuvering to Lake's right.

"Walk toward Dartagnan's head."

We took small, cautious steps as an oblique bolt of lightning lit the room. Dartagnan lay between the killer and us. Dartag-nan kicked the floor and cried out, "No, no, don't let him—"

"Shut up." A leg flew out and smashed into Dartagnan's foot.

I flexed my hips and torso, feeling the gun rise a fraction higher.

"Now turn and face the light. No stunts. I am quick."

"Like with Bellan and Larry?" Lake asked.

"You get the picture," the voice said.

The lantern blinding my eyes kept me from seeing the man's face, but we knew who our adversary was. He may have come to talk, but I made out the large automatic he waved from Lake to me. "I have come as you have summoned—to give you a pistol."

"Philippe," I said. "You've lost your accent. You sound more like Harry."

"You are a funny one. You forgot to pick up the gun I left you at Joshua Tree."

Lightning flickered in the room. The storm was leaving a little memory of itself. I said, "We were just leaving for Joshua Tree. We weren't expecting you this early."

He held the lantern lower and looked into my eyes, which were no longer blinded. He said, "You lured me. But I turned *les tables.*"

Lake spoke up. "What the hell do you think you're going to do to us?"

"What do you think?" he said, thrusting the big handgun at Lake.

"You won't get away with it. Your cover's blown, and the feds are on your ass."

"I have no fear. I will merely change into another character."

I asked, "Why didn't you kill Dartagnan, bury him, and let people think the PIs' killer left town?"

"I was going to, but then, the *mademoiselle,* she changes my plan." Harry had played the part of a phony French chef for so long, he couldn't drop the act. Either that, or he liked to hide behind it.

"How?" I asked.

"New Orleans."

"You mean I accidentally struck a chord?" I laughed hard enough to make the gun creep upward, but I didn't want the thing going off.

"You are more calculating than that," Harry said. "You were telling me what you had learned. You came to the casino to goad me."

"Here I thought I was being coy. You know, killing Eileen for Dewey was your undoing."

Harry chuckled. "Even dead, Dewey wouldn't want to be called Dewey. But you are wrong. I did not kill her for Bradley. I killed her for myself."

"Why? She didn't like your sushi?" I grunted in an effort to flex my stomach muscles harder.

Harry said, "You laugh, but I tell you I hated her. Bradley sent her to The Springs to heal their bad marriage. Bah! Of all the places on the fucking planet, he sends her to visit a *friend* of his. Me. His brother, who no one knows about."

"Once Dewey started making mistakes, it was over for all of you."

"I take care of me."

"Did Eileen accuse you of being Bradley's kin?"

His neck jerked. "The sly one told me I'd look like Bradley if my eyes were gray."

"But they are, aren't they?" I said. "Without contacts. Your family has distinctive features. Isn't the high forehead why you wear a hat all the time?"

"It is my persona. Everybody sees a cartoon in me. Not a man. But Eileen, she pulls my hat off. It is over for her."

Dartagnan reared up. "Son-of-a-bitch!"

Harry shifted his gaze to Dartagnan, but he kept the gun barrel on Lake's heart. When he lowered the lantern to check Dartagnan's bindings, I saw that Harry—with his wet hair flung back from his forehead—was indeed a whimsical imitation of his younger brother. But there was nothing funny about our circumstances. We'd planned on having the upper hand with two guns when he thought we would only have one. And no Dartagnan. If Lake and I were killed in this haunted place, it was our own ego that killed us.

Shake it off. I will not let this comic strip character kill us.

Lake asked, "Was it coincidence that Eileen wasn't sending Kinley back to Atlanta when you decided to kill her?"

Dartagnan let out a string of curses, and Harry slammed his shoe into Dartagnan's side. I leaned right, lifting my left shoulder to loosen and raise my shirt. Harry said, "I didn't know what the silly woman was going to do. Bradley asked me to keep an eye on her while Kinley was out here."

"There was no man buying flowers in your shop," I said.

Dartagnan yelled, "Fucking stone killer."

Harry appeared to enjoy kicking Dartagnan. "You will know soon enough, dupe."

My left hip pressed into Lake's side, and, inch by inch, I rotated forward. Dartagnan continued to curse while Harry kicked him twice, three times, in the hip, giving me a chance to lower my left arm. Harry spoke while he swung his attention back to us. "I watched Arlo and Tess take the body to the desert. Good riddance to the wife, hello to the bimbo."

"Then you called Whitney and told him what you'd done?"

"He went up like the flames. *Voilà.* Such a pussy. It was that club. The fucking Cloisters. It made his head soft." Subtly, he took tiny steps toward Dartagnan's head, like a cat sneaking up on a titmouse. "He went mad when I told him Kinley was missing."

I inched my arm down while I said, "You needed to find and kill Kinley to make the authorities here think they'd gone into hiding, to disappear for the rest of their lives."

"Bastard," Dartagnan called out.

Harry swung the gun at Dartagnan's head. "No, *mon ami,* I am not that."

I thought Harry was going to fire. I said, "It was a race who would find her first, Bradley or you."

Lake said, "Brotherly love."

Dartagnan cried out again. "Bastard."

Harry's foot came down on Dartagnan's back.

Dartagnan croaked out more curses while Harry tiptoed around Dartagnan's head to get us in profile. The gun came close to my face, and he sang out, "Hands high, *mademoiselle!*"

My arms shot higher.

"Our time together is up," he said. "See, what I am going to do is make it look like you two went looking for our friend here. Dartagnan was everybody's idea of a bad guy, *n'est-ce pas?*"

Keeping my eyes straight ahead, off him, I said, "I believed Dartagnan killed Eileen and the PIs."

"Yet you taunted me about the food I cooked."

"I was joking. You would never poison your own food. Tess's ring poisoned me."

"And you, detective? Did you joke about robbing an armored car to pay for expensive wine?"

"No joke."

"How could you be sure it was me?"

I looked at him, engaging his eyes. "Once I knew about Harry, I took a good look at you. You look more like Bradley than Dartagnan. To nail it, I saw the back end of your white car at the casino, the one in which you had delivered sushi to Eileen. You shot her and put it in the refrigerator."

"Bah." He stepped sideways, preparing to get behind us. It was quiet for strained moments. Had Harry finally finished talking?

And was Lake ready? Was I?

Instinct will let you know when to spring. The tension becomes unbearable.

We weren't quite there yet.

Harry could have shot us dead in three seconds, but, no, he hadn't finished talking. "It was an excellent last meal I prepared for you, wasn't it? The condemned should always have a last meal."

"Eileen never had a chance to eat her sushi."

He sniffed, but the gun didn't waver.

"And Larry and Bellan—did they get a chance to finish their last supper?"

"I would not prepare a supper for them."

Dartagnan moaned.

The gun wavered when Harry looked at Dartagnan.

I felt Lake's right elbow bend and lower. I reached higher, for the ceiling, shirt just covering the Glock's butt.

"So what we have in this room," Harry said, waving the gun with the bravado of a movie villain. "We have three people in a gunfight. Two against one. But Dartagnan, he is cunning, too. He gets the detective in the back before *la mademoiselle* can react. He gets *mademoiselle* in the shoulder, but she lives to get into a shoot-it-out with the gun that lays by his body now. Alas, all are killed."

Lake asked, "Is the gun you're holding the one that killed the PIs?"

"And it will be the gun Dartagnan kills you with." He began his move behind Lake. "Please step forward, *mademoiselle*." I stayed still, knowing it would make him angry. He shouted, "Do it now."

I leaned forward, but didn't move my feet.

"You will be heroes, getting the bad guy. Dead heroes."

Dartagnan suddenly flopped like a fish out of water, catching Harry's attention, his gun hand sinking floorward. "Stop, *mon ami*."

That's when Lake pulled the Glock from my waistband and shot Harry in his left ear.

ABOUT THE AUTHOR

Retired journalist for the *Atlanta-Journal Constitution,* **Gerrie Ferris Finger** won the 2009 St. Martin's Press/Malice Domestic Best First Traditional Mystery Novel for ***The End Game. The Last Temptation*** is the second in the Moriah Dru/ Richard Lake series. She lives on the coast of Georgia with her husband, Alan, and standard poodle, Bogey.

www.gerrieferrisfinger.com
www.gerrieferrisfinger.blogspot.com